The Public Policy Exception to the Enforcement of Arbitral Awards

Gizem Halis Kasap

The Public Policy Exception to the Enforcement of Arbitral Awards

A Comparative Study of United States and Turkish Law and Practice

PETER LANG

Bibliographic Information published by the Deutsche Nationalbibliothek
The Deutsche Nationalbibliothek lists this publication in the Deutsche Nationalbibliografie; detailed bibliographic data is available online at http://dnb.d-nb.de.

Library of Congress Cataloging-in-Publication Data
A CIP catalog record for this book has been applied for at the Library of Congress.

ISBN 978-3-631-86824-9 (Print)
E-ISBN 978-3-631-86825-6 (E-PDF)
E-ISBN 978-3-631-87836-1 (EPUB)
DOI 10.3726/b19684

Peter Lang – Berlin · Bern · Bruxelles · New York · Oxford · Warszawa · Wien

This publication has been peer reviewed.

www.peterlang.com

To Dr.Ayça Akkayan-Yıldırım, who rises by lifting others

Preface

The book titled, “The Public Policy Exception to the Enforcement of Arbitral Awards: A Comparative Study of U.S. and Turkish Law and Practice” is focused on the public policy exception as applied in the United States and Turkey under the New York Convention on Arbitral Awards. In addition, this book aims to identify the reasons behind the approach toward international arbitration in each jurisdiction and the role that public policy plays in this regard.

The book is divided into five chapters. The first chapter is designed as an primer on arbitration and lays out the goal of the book. The first chapter offers an overview of the historical background of arbitration laws and practice in both the United States and in Turkey, alongside the essential aspects of the enforcement of arbitral awards in each case. In so doing, it seeks to detail the social and political context in which arbitration has developed in each jurisdiction. The second chapter explores the concept of the public policy exception to the enforcement of arbitral awards under the New York Convention and lays the foundation for the analysis presented in subsequent chapters.

The focus of Chapter 3 is an examination of public policy as an exception and as a mindest in the United States. This chapter not only examines public policy in the context of international arbitration under the New York Convention as applied in the United States but also investigates the relationship between statutory and common law to the extent it pertains to public policy. Chapter 4, in turn, discusses the public policy exception as legislated and applied in Turkey in light of U.S. practice. The book ends with a review of the key findings and analysis and provides some suggestions that can act as focal points for reform and further research.

Abbreviations and Acronyms

ADR	Alternative dispute resolutions
AI	Artificial intelligence
BOT	Build-operate-transfer
BP	British Petroleum
CCP	Code of Civil Procedure
COMPAS	Correctional Offender Management Profiling for Alternative Sanctions
EI	Emotional intelligence
FAA	Federal Arbitration Act
GDPR	General Data Protection Regulation
HKIAC	Hong Kong International Arbitration Centre
IBA	International Bar Association
ICA	International Cotton Association
ICC	International Chamber of Commerce
ICCA	International Council for Commercial Arbitration
ICSID	International Centre for Settlement of Investment Disputes
ILA	International Law Association
IPPA	International Private Law and Procedural Law
ISI	Import-substitution industrialization
ISTA	Istanbul Arbitration Association
ISTAC	Istanbul Arbitration Center
LCIA	London Court of International Arbitration
METEX	Osuuskunta METEX Andelslag V.S.
NLP	Natural language processing
PM	Prime Minister
RUAA	Revised Uniform Arbitration Act
SCC	Stockholm Chamber of Commerce
SIAC	Singapore International Arbitration Centre
TEK	Turkish Electricity Authority
TIAL	Turkish International Arbitration Act
TOKI	Housing Development Administration of Turkey
TPF	Third-party funding
UAA	Uniform Arbitration Act
UYAP	National Judiciary Informatics System
VAT	Value-added tax

Acknowledgments

I owe many people my sincerest gratitude for their assistance and support over the course of writing this book and my academic and personal development. In the first place, I would like to offer thanks to the *taxpayers of the Republic of Turkey* whose hard-earned taxes contributed to the public funds that were used for financial support toward this book and Turkey's Ministry of National Education, which supported my academic endeavors. I am immensely grateful to *Professor Richard C. Schneider*, whose patience and invaluable guidance saw this study through. Along with him, I wish to thank *Professor Chris Meazell* and *Professor Steve Nickles* for generously offering their time and goodwill throughout the review of the manuscript of this book.

I would like to take this opportunity to acknowledge and thank *Professor Dr. Zekeriya Kurşat* for trusting in my capabilities and helping me to better understand the issues dealt with in arbitration and litigation practice. I cannot begin to express my thanks to my mentor *Dr. Ayça Akkayan-Yıldırım*, who envisaged this incredible path for me; her guidance has allowed me to navigate through it. Her encouragement helped me through critical times in both my professional and personal life. She empowered me to pursue what seemed a far-fetched goal and assured me when I wavered. She provided her advice at every turn while giving me the freedom to make my own decisions and mistakes. For your incredible mentoring and for molding me into a better person, I am eternally grateful.

My deepest gratitude is reserved for my husband and best friend, *Atilla Kasap*, who shared this entire experience with me. The camaraderie shared between us made the regular times happier and the trying times easier to endure. This thesis would never have been possible without the love, support, and patience from *my parents*, *Sevim&Hüseyin Halis*, and *my sister*, *Sinem Halis Atılan*. My parents have worked tirelessly and at great sacrifice to ensure that they could invest everything possible in allowing me to reach this moment. They have been unfaltering in their encouragement. Thank you for making to feel like a gifted daughter and being the most supportive family, one could ever hope for.

Through marriage, I have gained an outstanding second set of family members, *my parents- and siblings-in-law*, who have whole-heartedly welcomed me into their life. Moreover, we have been fortunate to have been welcomed into a local family, *the Kinnisons*, who provided social support and extended their hospitality throughout this study. Together with the Kinnisons, I also extend gratitude to *Mary Beth Vann* and *Wendy Kok* for making us feel welcome during our time in the United States.

I would like to extend my sincere thanks to particular friends and colleagues. I owe a debt of gratitude to *Tuncay Dursun* and *Atilla Uzun* for kindly providing me with all the materials I requested that assisted me in forming this book and his encouragement along the way. To *Bartu Ünlü*, *Mine Akarsu*, *Banu Akşahin*, and *Atakan Keskin*, I am most thankful for their profound belief in my abilities and constant support.

Finally, I would like to offer my special thanks to *Dr. Simon Watmough* for his invaluable insights into my study and professional pursuits and *Kelia Hubbard*, *Blair Bocook*, *Tara Grischow*, *Greta Smith* and *Rayna Minnigan Harris* for caring and supporting me wholeheartedly.

Table

Figure

Contents

Introduction

Arbitration is the hallmark of international commerce. It is at the core of alternative dispute resolutions ("ADR"). The well-known expression, "I'll see you in court," is increasingly fading for any kind of dispute as arbitration becomes the prevalent mode of recourse in international commerce.

The best way to define arbitration is by explaining what it is not. Arbitration is neither mediation, nor negotiation, nor conciliation, nor settlement. What makes arbitration distinctive is that it is a dispute resolution mechanism featuring a final and binding adjudication.[1] Although it is private or quasi-private, and less formal than a court trial, it is nevertheless adjudication. Therefore, arbitration, unlike settlement, does not attempt to resolve the dispute through a voluntary agreement. Once the parties agree to arbitrate, they surrender their right to go to court to resolve their disputes, and the agreement becomes the law between the parties.[2] This relinquishment gives exclusive jurisdiction and autonomy to the arbitrators to decide upon the dispute.[3]

Arbitration is not necessarily to be favored over litigation, except in cases of dispute between merchants engaged in cross-border trade.[4] Whether arbitration

---

1 See *e.g.* Glaser, Weil, Fink, Jacobs & Shapiro, LLP v. Goff, 194 Cal. App. 4th 423, 438 (2011); Schaefer v. Allstate Ins. Co., 63 Ohio St. 3d 708, 718 (1992) (stating that in order for an ADR method to be deemed as arbitration, it should yield a final and binding award); Minkowitz v. Israeli, 433 N.J. Super. 111, 151 (Super. Ct. App. Div. 2013) (emphasizing that when arbitration is agreed upon, the parties should not return to the court other than to confirm the final arbitration award).

2 *E.g.* Scherk v. Alberto-Culver Co., 417 U.S. 506, 511–12 (1974); M/S Bremen v. Zapata Off-Shore Co., 407 U.S. 1, 12 (1972).

3 Thomas E. Carbonneau & William E. Butler, International Litigation and Arbitration 572 (2nd ed. 2013).

4 In cross-border commerce, arbitration appears as a vital dispute mechanism because it provides greater ease for parties to enforce the award thanks to the international treaties. Further, it provides a neutral, non-national venue, thereby eliminating the concern of having a dispute adjudicated by a court in another country that may show preference to perceived interests of the forum. *See* Margaret Wang, *Are Alternative Dispute Resolution Methods Superior to Litigation in Resolving Disputes in International Commerce?*, 16 Arb. Int'l. 189, 211 (2000); Stephen L. Brodsky, *Cross-Border Arbitration: A Beneficial Alternative to Resolving International Commercial Disputes*, A.B.A. (July 03, 2019), https://www.americanbar.org/groups/litigation/committees/commercial-business/articles/2019/spring2019-cross-border-arbitration-international-commercial-disputes/.

is the best ADR depends on the specific legal issue at hand. That is to say, the view that arbitration is a better option than litigation depends on a subjective perception. For instance, the strengths and weaknesses of international commercial arbitration would most probably differ from those of adhesive arbitration, *e.g.*, arbitration agreements with employees or consumers.[5] Hence, many of the elements in the following discussion could appear both as advantages and disadvantages.

i. Freedom of contract: The parties can tailor the arbitral proceeding by means of their contracts as to their wishes. This is especially critical in international commercial arbitration because of the shortage in applicable trans-border legislation.[6] The parties may decide between ad hoc or administered arbitration, on how arbitrators will be selected, where the arbitration will be held, the language of arbitration and more besides. It is worth noting that less is perhaps more when exercising the freedom of contract. That is so since "over-drafting" opens the arbitration to interpretations, which—besides other drawbacks—may cause delay and increase the costs of proceedings.[7]
ii. Expense: It is often said that arbitration is less costly than litigation.[8] Yet, the administrative charges and the expenses associated with recruiting arbitrators are typically higher than court filing fees.[9] Hence, there is no

5 *See* Ljiljana Biukovic, *International Commercial Arbitration in Cyberspace: Recent Developments*, 22 NW. J. INT'L L. & BUS. 319, 331 (2002) ("[I]nternational commercial arbitration is expensive and is not a particularly speedy procedure. It is cheaper and quicker than litigation, but for individuals and for disputes involving small amounts, it is not as affordable as ADR.")

6 Thomas E. Carbonneau, *The Exercise of Contract Freedom in the Making of Arbitration Agreements*, 36 VAND. J. TRANSNAT'L L. 1189, 1191 (2003). *See also* S.I. Strong, *Limits of Procedural Choice of Law*, 39 BROOKLYN J. INT'L L. 1027, 1082 (2014) (discussing the problem that international commercial litigation faces).

7 John M. Townsend, *Drafting Arbitration Clauses: Avoiding the Seven Deadly Sins*, 58 DISP. RESOL. J. 28, 30 (2003). *See* Oliver Dillenz, *Drafting International Commercial Arbitration Clauses*, 21 SUFFOLK TRANSNAT'L L. REV. 221, 223 (1998) (noting that drafting an arbitration clause requires as much attention as drafting a statute).

8 *E.g.* Harry T. Edwards, *Advantages of Arbitration Over Litigation: Reflections of a Judge*, *in* ARBITRATION1982 CONDUCT OF THE HEARING PROCEEDINGS OF THE THIRTY-FIFTH ANNUAL MEETING NATIONAL ACADEMY OF ARBITRATORS 16, 23 (James L. Stern et al. eds., 1983); Ljiljana Biukovic, *supra* note 5, at 331.

9 *See e.g.* Sebastian Perry, *The cost of Yukos*, GLOBAL ARB. REV. (Aug. 15, 2014), http://globalarbitrationreview.com/article/1033686/the-cost-of-yukos. (stating that fees and costs added up to USD 124 Million in the final instance); TONY COLE & PIETRO

one-size-fits-all approach.[10] More cost-effective arbitration can be achieved through a well-written arbitration clause and efficient arbitral practices during proceedings.

iii. Privacy and Confidentiality: Parties who do not want to "air their dirty linen in public" value the privacy and confidentiality that arbitration offers. The public is not entitled to attend the hearing and has no access to the documents filed in the proceedings.[11] Transcripts are also not part of the public record, and arbitration awards generally remain unpublished.[12] While arbitration offers these benefits to parties seeking them, privacy can make referring to past awards challenging when attempting to persuade the tribunal in the dispute or in conducting effective scholarly research.

iv. Expertise: "Shopping around" to find the most competent judge to hear a case is not possible in litigation. In arbitration, however, parties are free to appoint an arbitrator with extensive experience in a relevant industry or sector or substantive legal knowledge about the subject matter because of freedom of contract.[13]

Ortolani, Understanding International Arbitration 21–22 (2019); Henry S. Noyes, *If You (Re)Build It, They Will Come: Contracts To Remake The Rules Of Litigation In Arbitration's Image*, 30 Harv. J.L. & Pub. Pol'y 579, 586–87 (2007).

10 *See e.g.* Jennifer Kirby, *Efficiency in International Arbitration: Whose Duty Is It?*, 32 J. Int'l Arb. 689, 690–91 (2015) (drawing an analogy between some dry cleaners' signs in the United States which state "Fast. Good. Cheap. Pick two" and arbitration in terms of efficiency); Henry S. Noyes, *supra* note 9, at 587. ("The high cost of arbitration can be a significant deterrent that precludes consumers, employees, and those with fewer resources from pursuing claims in arbitration.")

11 *See* Cole & Ortolani *supra* note 9 at 21 (distinguishing between privacy and confidentiality, saying that privacy refers to the provision that only parties may attend arbitral proceedings whereas confidentiality refers to disclosure of the information regarding arbitration to third parties).

12 *E.g.* Ali Shipping Corporation v. Shipyard Trogir [1997] APP.L.R. 12/19 (Eng.); Cole & Ortolani, *supra* note 9, at 22. *See* Laurie Kratky Dore, *Public Courts Versus Private Justice: It's Time To Let Some Sun Shine In On Alternative Dispute Resolution*, 81 Chi.-Kent L. Rev. 463, 466 (2006).

13 Cole & Ortolani, *supra* note 9, at 20. *See e.g.* Fernando Dias Simões, *Powered by expertise: Selecting arbitrators in energy disputes*, 8 J World Energy L. & Bus 501, 502 (2015); Sergio Puig, *Social Capital in the Arbitration Market*, 25 Eur J Int Law 387, 397 (2014).

v. Neutrality: The arbitrator is considered "neutral" when his or her nationality differs from that of either of the parties.[14] Especially in the context of cross-border disputes, arbitration can, therefore, offer a straightforward way to avoid any perception of bias that might arise in the proceedings.
vi. Enforcement: Without enforceability, an award is merely paper. Arbitral awards are much easier to enforce in foreign jurisdictions than judgments from foreign courts due to the Convention on the Recognition and Enforcement of Arbitral Awards ("the New York Convention"),[15] which has been ratified by 169 countries to date.[16] Arbitration ensures that the award will be enforced, provided that the losing parties' assets are situated in the court's jurisdiction.[17]
vii. Finality: The principle of finality aims to prevent courts from engaging in merit review and parties from appealing on the merits.[18] In a way, arbitration is a compromise, in so far as the parties forsake their rights to have the arbitration award reviewed in the interests of finality and avoiding delays.[19] Considering the concerns of parties who wish to appeal the award, some arbitration administrations offer an optional appellate tribunal.[20]

---

14 *See* Gary B. Born, International Arbitration: Cases and Materials 99 (2011); M. Scott Dohaney, *The Independence and Neutrality of Arbitrators*, 9 J. Int'l Arb. 31, 32 (1992).

15 The Convention on the Recognition and Enforcement of Arbitral Awards 21 U.S.T. 2617, 330 U.N.T.S. 3 9 codified in 9 U.S.C.A. §§ 201–208 [1970] [hereinafter the New York Convention]

16 *Status: Convention on the Recognition and Enforcement of Foreign Arbitral Awards*, UNCITRAL, http://www.uncitral.org/uncitral/en/uncitral_texts/arbitration/NYConvention_status.html (last visited Feb. 27, 2022). [hereinafter the New York Convention Status]

17 Cole & Ortolani, *supra* note 9, at 19–20; Born, *supra* note 14, at 100.

18 Rowan Platt, *The Appeal of Appeal Mechanisms in International Arbitration: Fairness over Finality?*, 30 J. Int'l Arb 531, 531–32 (2013).

19 *See 2015 International Arbitration Survey: Improvements and Innovations in International Arbitration*, Queen Mary University of London 8 (2015), available at http://www.arbitration.qmul.ac.uk/docs/164761.pdf [hereinafter *2015 International Arbitration Survey*] (indicating that neither in commercial nor investment treaty arbitration, the majority of respondents favor an appeal on the merits). Cole & Ortolani, *supra* note 9, at 19.

20 *E.g. Appellate Arbitration Procedure*, CPR, https://www.cpradr.org/resource-center/rules/arbitration/appellate-arbitration-procedure (last visited Feb. 27, 2022).

Concluded in 1958, the New York Convention has as one of its primary goals to encourage international commerce by creating an effective and neutral arbitration process that can function across borders and ensure the reliability of international contracts. With the sheer number of its signatories, the New York Convention has proved to be an immense success in comparison to its predecessors. Over its 60 years of existence, the Convention has provided a setting in which cross-border commercial transactions can thrive, by allowing recognition of arbitral awards in a reliable manner and one that ensures the rule of law.

As we approach the end of the first quarter of the twenty-first century, national courts are becoming more reluctant to refuse enforcement of foreign arbitral awards under the public policy exception. This is especially true in those countries in which the pro-enforcement stance has been faithfully observed. Though it is often raised, the public policy exception is usually unsuccessful not only in actions to refuse to recognize or enforce foreign arbitral awards but also in setting aside actions. This raises the question of why the public policy exception as applied in the United States and Turkey is still a crucial concept to the extent that it has become the subject of this book.

Global lawyering is not about knowing every nation's laws, but rather knowing how to handle an issue that includes components from different legal systems. Lawyers and scholars in the field of legal research must develop solutions that work best for clients. Hence, the necessities of this era demand lawyers have both substantive knowledge of the law and a broadened horizon in cross-border settings to resolve legal issues.

The case of the Gulf of Mexico oil spill provides an excellent example of how such a perspective would operate in practice. In 2010, the disaster—recognized as the worst oil spill in U.S. history—saw 11 workers killed and severe environmental damage inflicted on the environment.[21] British Petroleum (BP), headquartered in England, had leased an oil-drilling rig, Deepwater Horizon.[22] The spill was the result of faulty cement in the well,[23] prompting a flood of litigation against BP, both civil and criminal, when the rig failed, and oil gushed into the environment.[24] Tragic as this incident was, the question of greater moment for

---

21 NAT'L COMM'N ON THE BP DEEPWATER HORIZON OIL SPILL AND OFFSHORE DRILLING, DEEP WATER: THE GULF OIL DISASTER AND THE FUTURE OF OFFSHORE DRILLING 17 (2011).

22 *Id.* at 92.

23 *Id.* at 99.

24 In re Oil Spill by the Oil Rig "Deepwater Horizon" in the Gulf of Mex., 77 F. Supp. 3d 500, 525 (E.D. La. 2015).

the discussion here is why the aggravated parties sought to have an English company subjected to U.S. jurisdiction and U.S. legal standards.[25] The advantages of the adversarial system in the United States, the chance for the award of punitive damages, and jury trial meant, in all likelihood, considerably more damages recovered compared to an ordinary lawsuit in England. In this example, a global lawyer is one who considers the possible jurisdictions—namely, the United States and the United Kingdom—and chooses the best one for his or her plaintiff.

Comparative law is dissimilar to contracts or torts that are established upon cases, acts, treaties and other primary sources of law. Comparative law is, instead, an approach to correlate different legal systems.[26] It concerns itself not with substantive law per se but in how legal principles differ comparatively across systems. It is a two-pronged notion. On the micro-level, a global lawyer practices comparative law to find solutions to material client problems. On the macro-level, comparative law aims to enrich the understanding of the law and to find optimum ways for different laws in the same field—in our case, international commercial arbitration—to be integrated and to coexist. [27] The purpose of this book is to address both objectives of comparative law.

Here the legal context in which a comparison is sought is the public policy exception in international arbitration. The relevant countries are the United States and Turkey. The United States has a preeminent position in international commerce, and this affects the position of U.S. courts in worldwide arbitration.[28] As a result, any policy followed by U.S. courts—good or bad—will most probably flow through to other countries' jurisprudence. Turkey, on the other hand, is a developing country, and international arbitration is a relatively fledgling practice. As the book discusses later, the public policy concept is central to the research at hand because it has long been employed as a tool to achieve particular goals in Turkey.[29]

Each profession has its tools—for mathematicians, it is numbers; for architects, it could be a drafting table, compass, scale, and the like. The primary

25 Carbonneau & Butler *supra* note 3, at 8.

26 *See* Alan Watson, Legal Transplants: An Approach to Comparative Law 7 (2nd ed. 1993).

27 See Igor Stramignoni, *The King's One Too Many Eyes: Language, Thought, and Comparative Law*, 2 Utah L. Rev. 739, 747 (2002).

28 Mark A. Buchanan, *Public Policy and International Commercial Arbitration*, 6 Am. Bus. L.J. 511, 519 (1988).

29 Ali Ulusoy & Fuat Oğuz, *The Privatization of Electricity Distribution in Turkey: A Legal and Economic Analysis*, 35 Energy Pol'y 5021, 5022 (2007).

tool that legal professionals have at their disposal is words and their absolute meaning in a particular legal context. The precise definition of terms is therefore of paramount importance as this will have a determinative bearing on the specific meaning, notion, and legal consequences of these words.

There are several concepts in law, the application of which may differ from time to time and from one jurisdiction to another. Estoppel doctrine is a case in point. Estoppel is prominent and of long standing in common law countries. In civil law countries, this doctrine exists under a different name; namely, the doctrine of good faith or *culpa in contrahendo*.[30] Both principles, however, function similarly[31] and have emerged as bedrock approaches to establishing significant protections over time. Nonetheless, the reflexive reach for this solution may discourage legal professionals from considering other rationales when an issue occurs. To that extent, the doctrine of good faith has become something of a skeleton key that opens every door, at least in civil law jurisdictions.[32] And it is why this doctrine has been criticized for being vague and arduous to define in legal terminology.[33]

As good faith is to contract law, so public policy is to arbitration. This may not be so obvious on first reading, however. Arbitration is mostly related to commercial activities between private parties, so much so that public interests in arbitration are supposed to be a matter of minor discussion. Contrary to expectations, however, the concept of public policy is crucial. So much so, that it has become a subject of much recent research, including this book.

Joining the dots between public policy and arbitration asks us to assume a historical perspective. In the eighteenth century, with the appearance of modern sovereign states, a uniform judicial system was considered to be a fundamental

---

30 In common law, i.e,. Anglo–Saxon legal systems, civil law means all law that is not criminal law. In this context, however, the civil law connotes a type of legal system originating in ancient Rome that has spread to many nations in Europe, Latin American and Africa. A good example for U.S. readers might be the legal system in the State of Louisiana. *See* Adnan Guriz, *Sources of Turkish Law*, in INTRODUCTION TO TURKISH LAW 1 (Don Wallace, Jr. & Tuğrul Ansay eds., 5th ed. 2004).

31 *E.g.* David V. Snyder, *Comparative Law in Action: Promissory Estoppel, the Civil Law, and the Mixed Jurisdiction*, 15 ARIZ. J. INT'L & COMP. L. 695, 704 (1998) (stating that promissory estoppel is analogous to *culpa in contrahendo*).

32 *See* Ejan Mackaay, *Good Faith in Civil Law Systems. A Legal-Economic Analysis*, 18 REVISTA CHILENA DE DERECHO PRIVADO 149 (2012) (describing how the good faith doctrine is used in different civil law jurisdictions).

33 *Id.* at 170–71. Snyder, *supra* note 31, at 747.

dimension of autonomous statehood. Hence, ADRs, as opposed to litigation, were seen as a violation of sovereignty.[34] Back then, public policy was employed as an argument against arbitration, not merely as an exception in certain cases, but in principle. Such a public policy stance was referred to readily by judges, primarily as a justification to vacate arbitral awards. In this context, public policy represents a mindset rather than an exception, and this is the first facet of our "public policy" analysis.

The progression that arbitration has made since this time can be seen as the outcome of an evolving historical negotiation. In this negotiation, arbitration and sovereign states have been the parties, and "public policy" has been the matter subject to the negotiation. The requirements of global trade have given arbitration leverage. The twentieth century saw the need for arbitration to reach its climax. Today, with the leverage arbitration has, sovereign states have accepted arbitration as an ADR, all the while overseeing and supporting it within their sovereignty. In this context, the emphasis has flipped, and public policy has evolved to become an exception to arbitration, rather than a being a rule/mindset *against arbitration as a whole*. For example, Art. V(2)(b) of the New York Convention recognizes a public policy exception as a ground for refusing the recognition or enforcement of a foreign arbitral award. This represents the second and subsequent facet of "public policy" analysis in this book.

Most people tend to assume a linear progression of human evolution, one species following another in historical time. However, this is not the case. As Yuval Noah Harari notes in his book, several human species have coexisted at various times in history.[35] Yet, only Homo sapiens remain today.[36] Like human species, the concept of public policy has not evolved in a linear fashion—it has borrowed some parameters and tests and dropped others at various times, depending on the period or the jurisdiction in which it has been applied. Unlike Homo sapiens, however, many distinct ideas of public policy coexist today across the various legal systems. Public policy is, in a word, fuzzy—although it is a long-established concept and is discussed broadly, it still lacks a uniform definition.

The definition of public policy, to the extent that a definition can be offered at all, depends on the legal context in which a definition is sought. Moreover, within the same legal context, definitions can vary among countries because of differing backgrounds and legal traditions. At this point in the book, the attempt

---

34 See Section *infra* 1.1.2

35 Yuval Noah Harari, Sapiens: A Brief History of Humankind 7–8 (2015).

36 *Id.* at 8.

is not to define public policy and make it distinct from other concepts, but simply to emphasize the gap in the field that demands legal scholars come at the topic from a resolutely comparative perspective. Although some previous scholarships that have addressed the application of public policy exception in international arbitration, no study has provided a systematic and more in-depth analysis of the application of public policy exception as applied in the United States and Turkey. This book uses a comparative study approach to attempt to fill this lacuna.

This book has two primary aims. First, it offers extensive guidance indicating the possible risks of non-enforcement with respect to public policy in the United States and Turkey. Such a need arises because some enforcing courts have continued to deny enforcement under the guise of public policy and thwarted the effectiveness of international commercial arbitration, especially in those countries where arbitration encounters firm resistance. Acting with ulterior motives, some national courts have taken a more interventionist stance in enforcing arbitral awards. For this reason, controversy surrounds the scope that public policy ought to be accorded based on the Convention. Thus, not only legal scholars but also practitioners, international commercial actors, and other stakeholders can benefit from the guidance that this book sets forth.

The second aim of the book is to understand the reasons behind the approach toward international arbitration in each jurisdiction and the role that public policy plays therein. It pursues this objective by identifying the current disposition toward arbitration and its interplay with the public policy (exception). In so doing, it seeks to provide an in-depth analysis of the law and of practice as it pertains to the public policy (exception) in each jurisdiction, thereby casting a critical eye over the entire field.

1 Tracing the Roots of Arbitration in the United States and Turkey Through The Lens of Public Policy

Abstract: The first chapter presents an overview of the historical background of the practice and the laws concerning arbitration in both the United States and in Turkey as well as approaches to the enforcement of arbitral awards in each jurisdiction. The chapter starts with a survey of the basics of arbitration, outlining its key characteristics and how it functions. Next, it details the notion of public policy both as an exception to the enforcement of arbitral awards and as a mindset toward arbitration. The first chapter thus seeks to show that the social and political context in which arbitration has developed has influenced how arbitration practice has been perceived in each jurisdiction. For this purpose, the chapter uses the degree of state intervention in commerce and the legislative backgrounds of arbitration in each jurisdiction—both in terms of chronology and content—as criteria. Finally, this chapter foregrounds the importance of judicial position on arbitration and emphasizes its importance and implications for international arbitration—and arbitration in general.

Keywords: arbitration history, mindsets, state intervention, legislative history

1.1 Evolution of Arbitration in the United States and Public Policy

1.1.1 Arbitration in Early Stages

Arbitration in the United States has evolved in two distinct phases: the period before the 1925 FAA—in other words, common law arbitration—and the period after. Yet, legal scholars remain divided as to whether the opposition to arbitration in early American courts arose from pure envy of the arbitration process or some other kind of judicial hostility. No matter the answer, the history of the evolution of American arbitration tracks closely that of international commercial arbitration, which had its origins in North America and Europe.[37]

---

37 *E.g.* Thomas E. Carbonneau, *Judicial Approbation in Building the Civilization of Arbitration*, 113 Penn State Rev. 1343, 1343 (2009) [hereinafter Carbonneau, *Judicial Approbation*]; Thomas E. Carbonneau, *Arbitral Law-Making*, 25 Mich. J. Int'l L. 1183, 1195 (2004)[Carbonneau, *Arbitral Law-Making*].

In *Scherk*, the U.S. Supreme Court stated that the FAA was enacted to overrule the judiciary's longstanding, antagonistic stance vis-à-vis arbitration[38] by referring to Congressional intent in crafting the legislation.[39] Other Supreme Court cases have also cited *Scherk*, upholding the notion that the FAA's purpose was to reverse "the longstanding judicial hostility to arbitration agreements," which was originally part of English common law.[40]

The report that the House of Representatives published suggests that the judiciary was, in fact, hostile toward arbitration, [41] a conclusion supported by a number of U.S. Supreme Court cases. This section seeks to sketch the origins of that hostility and assess its impact on the use of arbitration.

1.1.2 Old Judicial Hostility Toward Arbitrations

The well-known case of *Tobey v. County of Bristol* provides a window into the classic hostility of the American judiciary toward arbitration. [42] Here, Justice Story rationalized his judgment that an arbitration agreement cannot be specifically enforced in court.[43] The Court held that arbitration agreements were

---

38 *Scherk*, 417 U.S. at 510.

39 *Id.* at 510 n.4. *See also* H. R. Rep. No. 96, 68th Cong., 1st Sess., 1–2 (1924) ("[T]he need for the law arises from an anachronism of our American law. Some centuries ago, because of the jealousy of the English courts for their own jurisdiction, they refused to enforce specific agreements to arbitrate upon the ground that the courts were thereby ousted from their jurisdiction … The courts have felt that the precedent was too strongly fixed to be overturned without legislative enactment, although they have frequently criticized the rule and recognized its illogical nature and the injustice which results from it. This bill declares simply that such agreements for arbitration shall be enforced and provides a procedure in the Federal courts for their enforcement.")

40 Gilmer v. Interstate/Johnson Lane Corp., 500 U.S. 20, 24 (1991). *See* AT&T Mobility LLC v. Concepcion, 563 U.S. 333, 339 (2011); EEOC v. Waffle House, Inc., 534 U.S. 279, 289 (2002); Circuit City Stores v. Adams, 532 U.S. 105, 118 (2001); Green Tree Fin. Corp.-Ala. v. Randolph, 531 U.S. 79, 89 (2000); Allied-Bruce Terminix Cos. v. Dobson, 513 U.S. 265, 272 (1995); Shearson/Am. Express v. McMahon, 482 U.S. 220, 225 (1987). *But see* Stavros Brekoulakis, *The Historical Treatment of Arbitration under English Law and the Development of the Policy Favouring Arbitration*, 39 Oxford J. Legal Stud. 124 (2019) ("[T]he attitude of English courts in the eighteenth and 19th centuries never reflected a broader ideological opposition to arbitration, as was the case in certain periods of time in other jurisdictions, such as in … the United States …")

41 H. R. Rep. No. 96 *supra* note 39.

42 Tobey v. County of Bristol, 23 F. Cas. 1313 (C.C.D. Mass. 1845)

43 *Id.* at 1321.

against the policy of the common law, and were "revocable" only provided an award had not yet been made.[44] There were many other examples of judicial hostility of this sort, and, like in *Tobey*,[45] the seeds of the trend can be traced back to English common law.[46] Altogether, certain key points underpin a definition of the old judicial suspicion:

i. An agreement to arbitrate before the dispute arises was revocable at will because arbitration agreements were against public policy to the extent that they

---

44 That is to say, arbitration agreements are, in fact, severable from the underlying contract and not legally binding despite the universal principle of *pacta sunt servanda. Id.* (reasoning that the courts were not there to force parties "to submit their rights and interests to arbitration, or to enforce agreements for such a purpose."). Here, Justice Story discredited arbitration, which also represent the position of arbitration in the eyes of the jurists, because "arbitrators, at the common law, possess no authority whatsoever, even to administer an oath,... to compel the attendance of witnesses[,]... or insist upon a discovery of facts from the parties under oath... " *But see* Brekoulakis, *supra* note 40 at 125("[T]he suggestion that English courts were generally hostile to arbitration is exaggerated, if not inaccurate... [T]he historical attitude of English courts toward arbitration can be more accurately described as one of cautious trust... ")

45 *Tobey* is one example indicating the impact of English common law arbitration upon American common law. Justice Story cited only English cases as the authorities, including Vynior's Case 77 Eng. Rep. 597 (K.B. 1609) (Eng.) (applying the revocability doctrine to the submission to arbitration), Kill v. Hollister, 95 Eng. Rep. 532 (K.B. 1746) (Eng.) (reasoning that arbitration agreements were revocable because they "oust[ed] courts of their jurisdiction") and Wellington v. Mackintosh, 2 Atk. 569 (1743) (Eng.). *See* Tobey, 23 F. Cas. at 1320–21.

46 Under the English doctrine, English courts were reluctant to recognize an agreement to arbitrate as a legally binding obligation. The legitimaticy of this hinged on the notion that the arbitrator was an agent appointed by the party so that the arbitration was revocable at the will of the party holding the position of a principal. Although the agency theory left its place to the acceptance of the contractual nature of the arbitration clause, the next level to refuse to enforce the arbitration clause was based on the idea that "[a mere] agreement of the parties cannot oust [the] court of its jurisdiction." *Kill*, 95 Eng. Rep. at 532. *E.g.* Linda R. Hirshman, *The Second Arbitration Trilogy: The Federalization of Arbitration Law*, 71 Va. L. Rev. 1305, 1309 (1985). *See also* Niall Mackay Roberts, *Definitional Avoidance: Arbitration's Common-Law Meaning and the Federal Arbitration Act Note*, 49 UC Davis L. Rev. 1570, 1576 (2015) (indicating that English common law on arbitration has a considerable amount of bearing on U.S. arbitration); Herbert Pope, *The English Common Law in the United States*, 24 Harv. L. Rev. 6, 30 (1910) (discussing the adoption of the common law of England).

ousted the courts of their jurisdiction.[47] Notwithstanding this, arbitration agreements were valid to the degree that they did not, in fact, oust the courts from their jurisdiction.[48]

ii. Even though an agreement to arbitrate was deemed binding, the court did not order specific performance to compel the reluctant party to arbitrate.[49]

iii. If the arbitral tribunal had already rendered an award, then courts would enforce it. The courts nonetheless were more prone to reverse the awards on the grounds of minor procedural problems.[50]

To bring to an end, at an early stage, the courts had a judicial control over the awards in the name of not "clos[ing] against him [a reluctant party] the doors of the common courts of justice, provided by the government to protect rights and to redress wrongs."[51] Hence, in this first facet of our "public policy" analysis,

---

47 The English revocability doctrine was adopted by most U.S. courts. Although the justification was quite different, it yielded the same outcome. The U.S. courts found that a mere agreement to arbitrate could not oust the courts of their jurisdiction to render the arbitration agreements unenforceable on the ground that it violated the right of access to the courts. Arbitration agreements were also revocable at the discretion of either party prior to commencing the arbitral proceeding. *See* Hirshman, *supra* note 46, at 1310–11. *See also* Doyle v. Cont'l Ins. Co., 94 U.S. 535, 537 (1876); Home Ins. Co. of N.Y. v. Morse, 87 U.S. 445, 451 (1874); Hurst v. Litchfield, 39 N.Y. 377, 379 (N.Y. 1868); Prince Steam-Shipping Co. v. Lehman, 39 F. 704, 704 (S.D.N.Y. 1889).

48 *E.g.* Hamilton v. Home Ins. Co., 137 U.S. 370, 385 (1890); Hamilton v. Liverpool, London & Globe Ins. Co., 136 U.S. 242, 255 (1890).

49 Supposing that there was a real, not conditional, agreement, Justice Story assessed whether a specific enforcement (in this case, the appointment of arbitrators) could be enforced by a court of equity. In answering, Justice Story found that it was still unenforceable because "so far as the authorities go, they are altogether the other way." *Tobey*, 23 F. Cas. at 1320. *See also id.* at 1319 (reasoning that there was no agreement because "an agreement to refer without saying more, how, and when, and to whom the submission is to be, can hardly be deemed anything more than an inchoate and imperfect agreement, the first step, only, in a negotiation,... if the arbitrators are not subsequently agreed upon. It is rather of the nature of a conditional consent to refer, provided the parties can agree upon the arbitrators."); *id.* at 1320–21 (stating that the courts enforce arbitral awards if the award is fairly and lawfully made, however, do not enforce the reluctant party to arbitrate because it is against the public policy); Oregon & W. Mortg. Sav. Bank v. American Mortg. Co., 35 F. 22, 23 (C.C.D. Or. 1888). *See* also 1 GARY BORN, INTERNATIONAL COMMERCIAL ARBITRATION: COMMENTARY AND MATERIALS 156 (2001). [hereinafter BORN, COMMERCIAL ARBITRATION]

50 *See e.g.* Mansfield v. Doughty, 3 Mass. 398 (1807); Maybin v. Coulon, 4 U.S. 298 (1804).

51 *Tobey*, 23 F. Cas. at 1320–21.

public policy was a concept referred to readily by judges (as in *Tobey*)—one that was used as a justification not to enforce an arbitration agreement or arbitral award and represented a mindset rather than an exception.

1.1.3 The Relationship Between Judicial Hostility and The Use of Arbitration

One might conclude prima facie from the aforementioned hostility that arbitration was, as a practical matter, rare in the colonial period. [52] Certainly, there are few court records to substantiate the claim that it was common, let alone extensively practiced. [53] Nevertheless, other resources provide ample evidence indicating that arbitration was, in fact, widespread in the early colonial period and later.

Arbitration was, in fact, a novel and effective method for resolving business disputes within or between the colonies for its time and was used widely in the United States.[54] The lack of public court records on arbitration is understandable because the communal understanding was to live in peace and amity, and therefore, resolutions to the disputes were more consensual as opposed to adversarial.[55] Among the colonists, the regular practice was to fall back on litigation as

52 It must be noted that while some scholars accepted the existence of judicial hostility without any reservation, others recognized the existence of pro-arbitration colonial practice. *Compare* James Oldham & Su Jin Kim, *Arbitration in America: The Early History*, 31 L. Hist. Rev. 241 (2013) *with* Steven Burton, *New Judicial Hostility to Arbitration: Federal Preemption, Contract Unconscionability, and Agreements to Arbitrate*, 2006 J. Dispute Resol. 469 (2007).

53 Bruce Benson, *An Exploration of the Impact of Modern Arbitration Statutes on the Development of Arbitration in the United States*, 11 J. L. Econ. Organ. 479, 481 (1995).

54 L. Donegan, *ADR in Colonial America: A Covenant for Survival*, Arb. J., June 1993, at 14,15; Julius Cohen & Kenneth Dayton, *The New Federal Arbitration Law*, 12 Va. L. Rev. 265, 266 (1926).

55 Donegan, *supra* note 54 at 15 n.7. (stating that the colonists, of course, experienced conflicts and disputes, but the role of the courts was limited); Bruce H. Mann, *The Formalization of Informal Law: Arbitration Before the American Revolution,* 59 N.Y.U. L. Rev. 443 (1984) (illustrating the Connecticut example to prove the idea that in the mid-seventeenth century, arbitration was a voluntary process in a small society, just as in Connecticut).

a last resort in the event of a dispute,[56] and a common prejudice toward lawyers was another reason not to go to court.[57]

In the seventeenth century, Dutch colonization in America employed alternative dispute resolutions, and this legal practice later provided a basis for acknowledging the English tradition of arbitration in New York.[58] In the same commercial vein, the use of arbitration in colonial America can be seen in Connecticut.[59] Arbitration was also adopted in Pennsylvania and New Jersey, which was also related to the commercial practices of the colonies.[60]

Arbitration remained in use throughout the eighteenth and nineteenth centuries in a commercial sense, especially in New York. To illustrate, in the mid-eighteenth century, commercial arbitration was so favored by merchants that in 1768, the New York Chamber of Commerce established the first private tribunal in the United States for the extra-judicial settlement of disputes between merchants.[61] The courts, however, were more involved this time because the effect

---

56 *Id.* at 15. (stating that by the 1680s, the colonists enjoyed this limited independence from England and developed dispute resolution methods to stay outside of English common law); *See also* Mann *supra* note 55, at 456.

57 Donegan, *supra* note 54 at 17; Michael McManus & Brianna Silverstein, *Brief History of Alternative Dispute Resolution in the United States*, CADMUS J., Oct. 2016 at 101 ("Pilgrim colonists, convinced that lawyers threatened Christian harmony, scrupulously avoided lawyers and courts, preferring to use their own mediation process to deal with community conflicts.")

58 Eben Moglen, *Commercial Arbitration in the Eighteenth Century: Searching for the Transformation of American Law*, 93 YALE LAW J. 135, 135–36 (1983); Benson, *supra* note 53, at 481.

59 Mann, *supra* note 55, at 454–56 (stating that in the seventeenth century, arbitration practice in Connecticut was informal, but as the communities grew and changed, arbitration started being formal. During the eighteenth century, arbitration was more often made the subject of legislation, and as a result, litigation.)

60 F. Peter Phillips, *Ancient and Comely Order: The Use and Disuse of Arbitration By New York Quakers,* 2016 J. DISP. RESOL. 81, 107 (2016) (explaining that arbitration mostly adopted by the Quakers, and although it was religious arbitration, it was parallel with the commercial use of it). Given that the Quaker merchants frequently engaged in international trade, arbitration must have had an optimal setting to develop. *See* THOMAS K. MCCRAW, CREATING MODERN CAPITALISM: HOW ENTREPRENEURS, COMPANIES, AND COUNTRIES TRIUMPHED IN THREE INDUSTRIAL REVOLUTIONS 301 (2003).

61 FRANCES KELLOR, ARBITRATION AND THE LEGAL PROFESSION: A REPORT PREPARED FOR THE SURVEY OF THE LEGAL PROFESSION 7 (1952)

of formalization of informal arbitration resulted in more adversarial and formal arbitral proceedings.[62]

In discussing these matters, it emerges that "[…] there was no time during this period when arbitration was not known and used by a significant number of people,"[63] notwithstanding the existence of the antagonism to arbitration in the common law practice of the colonial courts.

1.1.4 The Undeniable Effect of the FAA and the U.S. Supreme Court Upon International Commercial Arbitration

1.1.4.1 Historical Background and the Policy Behind the FAA

Although Chapter 1 of the FAA governs federal arbitration, federal courts have taken the federal policy favoring arbitration into consideration when they resolve international arbitration cases as well. The reasoning underlying this approach is that the United States adopted the New York Convention through the FAA, and thus the "FAA principles guide the analysis."[64] To understand the FAA principles, we will examine Congress's motive in enacting the FAA and whether it serves this purpose today.

In enacting the FAA, Congress was essentially facing up to the reality of commercial necessity. New York merchants and lawyers were mainly the proponents of the legislation, because of the congestion in the courts and delays in the distribution of justice.[65] It was the result of the growing momentum against the procedural drawbacks of judicial litigation and their negative impact on the business world.

The New York Arbitration Law of 1920 catalyzed the enactment of the FAA.[66] One might ask why New York business people would seek legislation at the

---

62 *See e.g.* Maybin, 4 U.S. at 298; Watson v. Ins. Co. of N. Am., 4 U.S. 283 (1803).

63 William Catron Jones, *Three Centuries of Commercial Arbitration in New York: A Brief Survey*, 1956 Wash. Univ. L. Q. 193, 213 (1956).

64 Mitsubishi Motors Corp. v. Soler Chrysler-Plymouth, 473 U.S. 614, 626 (1985). *See also* Doe v. Princess Cruise Lines, Ltd., 657 F.3d 1204, 1213, n.9 (11th Cir. 2011) (referring both the FAA and the New York Convention).

65 The New York State Bar Association and New York Chamber of Commerce were representing the visible portion of the iceberg. This movement was also supported by the American Bar Association and New Jersey Bar Association. *See generally* Imre Szalai, Outsourcing Justice: The Rise Of Modern Arbitration Laws In America 104–5, 155 (2013).

66 New York Arbitration Law, 1920. N.Y. Sess. Laws 1920, c. 275 (current version at N.Y. C.P.L.R. Law §§ 7501–7515 (Consol., Lexis Advance through 2020 released Chapters

federal level that would simply mirror the New York law on arbitration. On reflection, the reason is apparent enough: *Swift v. Tyson* had ruled that the federal courts were not obliged to respect the applicability or governing character of state law. [67] Federal courts applied federal law, whereas state courts applied state law.[68] In effect, commercial interests, especially in New York, lobbied the U.S. Congress for legislation that would parallel state law for federal arbitration.

As it stood at the beginning of the 20th century, the FAA was intended to make arbitration more available and effective for the parties engaged in commercial and maritime transactions.[69] The FAA, a law written with the interests of a narrow commercial elite very much in mind, was clearly no "sequel to the Magna Carta."[70] To inaugurate the new era in arbitration, Art. 2 of the Act set forth that arbitration agreements are "valid, irrevocable, and enforceable."[71] By means of Art.2, arbitral clauses became equal to traditional contracts.[72] In effect, the parties could enter into an agreement to submit future disputes to arbitration. This

---

1–22)); Angelina M. Petti, *Judicial Enforcement of Arbitration Agreements: The Stay-Dismissal Dichotomy of FAA Section 3*, 34 Hofstra L. Rev. 565, 573 (2005); Cohen & Dayton, *supra* note 54, at 275.

67 Swift v. Tyson, 41 U.S. 1, 18 (1842) *overruled by* Erie R.R. v. Tompkins, 304 U.S. 64 (1938) (holding that federal courts sitting in diversity had to follow "federal common law"); Thomas E. Carbonneau, The Law and Practice of Arbitration 279 (5th ed. 2014) [hereinafter Carbonneau, The Law and Practice].

68 *Id.*

69 Prima Paint Corp. v. Flood & Conklin Mfg. Co., 388 U.S. 395, 404 n. 12 (1967); Sebastien Besson, *The Utility of State Laws Regulating International Commercial Arbitration and Their Compatibility with the FAA*, 11 Am. Rev. Int'l Arb. 211, 212 (2000).

70 Thomas E. Carbonneau, *The Revolution in Law Through Arbitration*, 56 Clev. St. L. Rev. 233, 244 (2008) [hereinafter Carbonneau, *The Revolution in Law*] (stating that the FAA only represented the privileged few of New York City's commercial class, rather than being inclusive of everyone like Magna Carta)

71 9 U.S.C.A. § 2 (establishing both arbitral and submission clauses are legally valid forms of contracts)

72 Robert Lawrence Co. v. Devonshire Fabrics, Inc., 271 F.2d 402, 409–11 (2nd Cir. 1959); Kulukundis Shipping Co. v. Amtorg Trading Corp., 126 F.2d 978, 982–83 (2nd Cir. 1942). It must be noted that today arbitration agreements are no longer merely on an equal footing with other contracts; they are "super contracts" under the FAA s.2 because of the Supreme Court's policy of overly favoring arbitration. *E.g.* Richard Frankel, *The Arbitration Clause As Super Contract*, 91 Wash. U.L. Rev. 531, 534 (2014); Jodi Wilson, *How the Supreme Court Thwarted the Purpose of the Federal Arbitration Act*, 63 Case W. Res. L. Rev. 91, 97 (2012).

provision permitted parties to submit their disputes to arbitration as a lawful exercise of freedom of contract.[73]

Until the FAA was enacted, the traditional approach to arbitration was to accept it as a defective form of adjudication, even though it was common practice among the autonomous industries, *e.g.*, New York Chamber of Commerce, New York Stock Exchange.[74] From then until the present, the FAA has reached a superior level that it preempts state law on arbitration, including New York.[75] The legislators did not propose that the FAA would have the present-day impact upon the U.S. civil system that it has had in terms of its size and potency.[76] The U.S. Supreme Court, however, has interpreted the FAA to such a generous extent that it has established an all-encompassing deference to arbitration, first for international matters and after for domestic matters.[77]

1.1.4.2 The Relationship Between the FAA, the U.S. Supreme Court, and International Commercial Arbitration

The U.S. Supreme Court has been central to the diffusion of arbitration within the United States, a judicial stance that runs contrary to the traditional judicial hostility to the form seen in many Asian, Middle Eastern, and South American jurisdictions.[78] Indeed, the FAA has been "an edifice of [the Supreme Court's] own creation." [79] The U.S. Supreme Court has embraced a pro-arbitration stance in its elaboration of U.S. laws on international commercial arbitration or international private law in general.

The U.S. Supreme Court has remained particularly cognizant of the fact that international transactions present particular challenges in managing conflict, and that arbitration is an ideal way to address these. Hence, the Court has cultivated a sound and thorough policy of respecting the principle of freedom

---

73 *E.g.* Am. Sugar Ref. Co. v. Anaconda, 138 F.2d 765, 766–67 (5th Cir. 1943) (holding that "[t]he act was passed not to oust the jurisdiction of the courts but to provide for maintaining their jurisdiction while at the same time recognizing arbitration agreements as affirmative defenses and providing a forum for their specific enforcement."). *See also* Genesco, Inc. v. United Shoe Workers, 341 F.2d 482, 484 (2nd Cir. 1965) (quoting above language from *Am. Sugar*)

74 Benson, *supra* note 53 at 485.

75 Besson, *supra* note 69 at 224.

76 Carbonneau, *The Revolution in Law supra* note 70 at 244.

77 Carbonneau, The Law and Practice, *supra* note 67 614.

78 1 Born, Commercial Arbitration, *supra* note 49, at 156.

79 *Allied-Bruce*, 513 U.S. at 283.

of contract.[80] In this regard, the Court has deemed international transactions privileged and has refused to recognize any conflict even between arbitration agreements and U.S. domestic regulatory claims.[81] That is to say, international merchants are sovereign and are at liberty to include arbitration agreements in contracts in the first place, and what the provisions of contract will be in that context.

The ratification of the New York Convention in 1970 was a defining moment for U.S. international private law. Since 1970, the U.S. Supreme Court has accumulated decisions forming the principles of international commercial arbitration. Nonetheless, the number of cases evaluating or applying to the New York Convention is limited. In fact, most cases leading and forming a part of decisional law have been related to the FAA.[82] Today, the only clear point of consensus in U.S. law on arbitration is at the federal level, where rulings on domestic and international arbitration case law are united.[83]

1.1.4.3 Landmark Rulings on International Private Law and the Merging Of International And Domestic Case Law

This part of the discussion will not delve into the details of U.S. international commercial arbitration case law, which later chapters will outline in more detail. Suffice it here to lay out the gist of the U.S. policy of favoring arbitration.

From 1972 to 1985, a trilogy of cases decided by the U.S. Supreme Court established the hegemony of arbitration for resolving international commercial disputes.[84] In *Bremen*, the German and American parties vested a non-U.S. court

---

80 *See e.g.* Volt Info. Scis., Inc. v. Bd. of Trustees of Leland Stanford Junior Univ., 489 U.S. 468, 479 (1989)

81 *See e.g. Mitsubishi*, 473 U.S at 627; *Scherk*, 417 U.S. at 506.

82 *E.g.* Stolt-Nielsen S. A. v. AnimalFeeds Int'l Corp., 559 U.S. 662 (2010); Vimar Seguros Y Reaseguros v. M/V Sky Reefer, 515 U.S. 528 (1995); *Mitsubishi*, 473 U.S at 614; *Scherk*, 417 U.S. at 506; *Bremen*, 407 U.S. at 1.

83 *E.g. AT&T Mobility*, 563 U.S. at 351; *McMahon*, 482 U.S. at 220; Carbonneau, The Law and Practice, *supra* note 67 at 614; Pamela K. Bookman, *The Arbitration-Litigation Paradox*, 72 Vand. L. Rev. 1119, 1140–41 (2019).

84 *See generally* Pedro J. Martinez-Fraga, *Wilko v. Swan, Scherk v. Alberto-Culver, and Mitsubishi v. Soler: Crafting a Level Playing Field, in* The American Influences on International Commercial Arbitration: Doctrinal Developments and Discovery Methods 15 (2009); Russell A. Miller & Rebecca M. Bratspies, Progress in International Law 518 (2008).

with exclusive jurisdiction.[85] The Court held that the forum-selection clause in an international contract was valid.[86] Although this case was not directly connected to arbitration, it is the first pillar of the trilogy because the U.S. Supreme Court respected the international parties' exclusive choice of forum clause or, in general, the principle of *pacta sunt servanda.* Arbitration clauses designate both the forum and the form of adjudication.[87] In *Bremen,* the U.S. Supreme Court deferred to the international parties' exclusive choice of forum clause, and that laid the basis for deferring to the contracted form of adjudication—namely, arbitration.

In the second and third cases—*Scherk* [88] and *Mitsubishi*[89]—the issue was whether the arbitrators or the domestic courts had jurisdiction to rule on regulatory claims. In *Scherk*, the issue was related to the Securities Exchange Act,[90] whereas in *Mitsubishi*, it was about antitrust law—namely, the Sherman Act.[91] As is evident from the nature of the regulatory claims, it could have been straightforward to rule that the issues were non-arbitrable because the motive behind the non-arbitrability of regulatory claims is generally that if the arbitrator does not effectively enforce public law rules, then the public at large will suffer.[92] In both cases, the Court has taken liberties with the facts to promote the policy and choose the necessities of trans-border commerce over domestic regulatory laws and held that there is no statutory FAA prohibition against the arbitration of statutory claims.[93]

It is ordinary that states differentiate between their international and domestic law and establish different standards for the cases in terms of arbitration.[94] Most

---

85 *Bremen*, 407 U.S. at 2 (the arbitration agreement stating that "any dispute arising must be treated before the London Court of Justice.")

86 *Id.* at 15 (stating that unless "enforcement would be unreasonable and unjust, or that the clause was invalid for... fraud or overreaching").

87 Carbonneau, The Law and Practice, *supra* note 67 at 614.

88 *Scherk*, 417 U.S. at 506.

89 *Mitsubishi*, 473 U.S at 614.

90 *Scherk*, 417 U.S. at 514.

91 *Mitsubishi*, 473 U.S at 636–37.

92 *E.g.* Mahmood Bagheri, International Contracts And National Economic Regulation: Dispute Resolution Through International Commercial Arbitration 134 (2000).

93 *Mitsubishi*, 473 U.S at 632–34; *Scherk*, 417 U.S. at 519–21.

94 *See e.g. Mitsubishi*, 473 U.S at 629; Georges R. Delaume, *Arbitration with Governments: "Domestic" v. "International" Awards*, 17 Int. Lawyer 687, 690–91 (1983); William W. Park, *Amending the Federal Arbitration Act*, 13 Am. Rev. Int'l Arb. 75 (2002).

of the time, the scope of arbitrability is wider regarding international disputes than domestic ones. In the case of the United States, however, we can see a unitary law on arbitration, which covers most disputes that are non-arbitrable in the eyes of other countries.

To illustrate, subject-matter non-arbitrability begins with *Mitsubishi* and continues to *McMahon* and *Rodriguez de Quijas v. Shearson/American Express, Inc.*,[95] which embeds the international doctrine of universal subject-matter arbitrability into U.S. domestic law. In *Mitsubishi*, the Court stated that a different result would be forthcoming on the domestic side in terms of the arbitrability of the regulatory claims.[96] In doing so, the Court acknowledged the difference between domestic and international arbitration, while disregarding it in *McMahon* and *Rodriguez.*

In both *McMahon* and *Rodriguez*, the Court differentiated between the procedural and substantive provisions of U.S. securities law, holding that arbitration was merely the procedural portion of the dispute; therefore, it did not have any bearing on the substantive portion of the case law.[97] Overall, the Court established that the presumption of arbitrability existed under the FAA unless "Congress intended to make an exception" to the FAA.[98]

The federal policy favoring arbitration has been so absolute that the Supreme Court has adamantly denied any exception to the policy, thinking that one exception hurts the efficiency of the policy.[99] It is not hyperbole to state that the FAA covers virtually all types of non-criminal disputes, applied to both state and federal courts, including statutory disputes, disputes arising from adhesive contracts such as consumer contracts, and employment arbitration.[100]

1.1.5 Current Law on Arbitration

In terms of domestic law, the FAA governs the arbitration process in maritime transactions and contracts "evidencing a transaction involving commerce" at the federal level.[101] If state law governs arbitration, it falls under the scope of

95 Rodriguez de Quijas v. Shearson/American Express, Inc., 490 U.S. 477 (1989)

96 *Mitsubishi*, 473 U.S at 629.

97 *Rodriguez,* 490 U.S. at 481–82; *McMahon*, 482 U.S. at 229–30.

98 *Id.* at 227.

99 Carbonneau, The Law and Practice, *supra* note 67 at 641.

100 Imre Stephen Szalai, *Exploring the Federal Arbitration Act through the Lens of History Symposium*, 2016 J. Disp. Resol. 115, 117 (2016). *See* Frankel, *supra* note 72 at 534; Wilson, *supra* note 72 at 97.

101 9 U.S.C.A. § 1.

arbitration statutes that are grounded on the Uniform Arbitration Act (UAA) or the Revised Uniform Arbitration Act (RUAA).[102] A state law on arbitration governs the process—to fill the gaps in the FAA mostly—so long as it is not in conflict with the FAA. [103] As a result, it can be suggested that the FAA is applicable to both state and federal courts because, in the event of a conflict, the FAA preempts state laws.[104]

In terms of international law, multilateral conventions set out the recognition and enforcement of foreign arbitral awards. Nonetheless, Chapter 1 of the FAA also applies to international arbitration to the extent that it does not contradict international conventions.[105] Incorporation of both the New York and Panama Conventions has been achieved through Chapters 2[106] and 3,[107] respectively, of the FAA. For purposes of discussion through this paper, we mainly discuss the New York Convention considering that a similar outcome[108] emanates from both conventions. The Washington Convention on the Settlement of Investment Disputes between States and Nationals of Other States (ICSID) was also ratified by the United States on October 14, 1966.[109]

---

102 *Understanding US Arbitration Law, Practice Note Overview* WestLaw, https://www.westlaw.com/4-500-4468?transitionType=Default&contextData=(sc.Default)&VR=3.0&RS=cblt1.0 (last visited Feb. 27, 2022).

103 Southland Corp. v. Keating, 465 U.S. 1, 12 (1984) (referring the Congress's intent of promoting and favoring arbitration); *Understanding US Arbitration Law, supra* note 102.

104 Besson, *supra* note 69 at 225 (stating that preemption is especially true in international commercial arbitration where "speak[ing] with one voice" is of greater importance).

105 9 U.S.C.A. § 208.

106 *Id.* §§ 201–208.

107 *Id.* §§ 301–307. The Inter-American Convention on International Commercial Arbitration, commonly referred to as the Panama Convention, is the controlling treaty for U.S. parties arbitrating in or with parties from most Central or South American countries. The provisions of the Panama Convention are akin to those in the New York Convention. *See* Helena Tavares Erickson et al., *Looking Back, and Ahead: The Panama Convention After 30 Years*, Alternatives to High Cost Litig. Dec. 2005, at 184, 184.

108 *E.g.* Productos Mercantiles E. Industriales, S.A. v. Faberge USA, 23 F.3d 41, 45 (2nd Cir. 1994) (citing *Bergesen v. Joseph Muller Corp.*, 710 F.2d 928 (1983) which applies the New York Convention to the similar issue)

109 22 U.S.C. § 1650a.

1.2 The Evolution of Arbitration in Turkey and Public Policy

1.2.1 Ottoman Arbitration

The important point about the Ottoman Empire's approach to Sharia law, within the ambit of this book, is whether arbitration was promoted by Sharia and, if so, what the subject matter of arbitration was.

Under Sharia law, disputes between married partners may be submitted to arbitration.[110] Also, the Prophet Muhammad had, in his lifetime, the power to arbitrate disputes between Muslims and non-Muslims.[111] Matters under Allah's scopes of judgment—theft, sexual crimes, and rebellion—are not arbitrable.[112] Such disputes could only be settled by those with the title of the caliph or *qadis* appointed by caliphs to pass judgment. This, in fact, comports with modern law, in which criminal matters cannot be referred to arbitration.[113] Nonetheless, Sharia promotes authoritarianism. In other words, under Sharia, the centralized government of the Ottoman Empire and caliphs were responsible for the allocation of justice, and therefore, caliphs or *qadis*, as opposed to private people or tribunals, filled the gaps in the justice system.[114] These institutions guarded their jurisdiction against arbitration fiercely.

There are also other arguments to explain why arbitration was not favored in the Ottoman Empire:

1. *Fiqh*, Islamic jurisprudence, encouraged Muslim scholars not to give affirmative fatwas about arbitration.

---

110 THE QURAN 4:35 "And if you fear dissension between the two, send an arbitrator from his people and an arbitrator from her people. If they both desire reconciliation, Allah will cause it between them. Indeed, Allah is ever Knowing and Acquainted [with all things]."

111 THE QURAN 5:42–43 "[They are] avid listeners to falsehood, devourers of [what is] unlawful. So if they come to you, [O Muhammad], judge between them or turn away from them. And if you turn away from them—never will they harm you at all. And if you judge, judge between them with justice. Indeed, Allah loves those who act justly."

112 MUHARREM BALCI, IHTILAFLARIN ÇÖZÜM YOLLARI VE TAHKIM [Methods of Dispute Resolution and Arbitration] 76 (1999) (Turk.).

113 *E.g.* Szalai, *supra* note 100; Karim Youssef, *The Death of Inarbitrability, in* ARBITRABILITY: INTERNATIONAL AND COMPARATIVE PERSPECTIVES 47, 59 (Loukas A. Mistelis & Stavros L. Brekoulakis eds., 2009).

114 BALCI, *supra* note 112, at 82.

2. Arbitral awards were also required to be in accordance with both the arbitrator's and the *qadis*' Islamic sect to be confirmed.[115]
3. The notion of arbitration-friendliness created a concern that *qadis*—as opposed to arbitrators—would cease to be in demand.[116]

The frame demonstrated above held good for the Ottoman Empire until the Tanzimat Edict of 1839, and the Imperial Reform Edict of 1856. Even though the Ottoman Empire had not embraced the concept of arbitration before, the Tanzimat reforms laid the foundation for Western codification movements.[117] As a result of this trend, arbitration gained a foothold in the "Commercial Act" (*Kanunname-i Ticaret*) as early as 1850.[118] This Act was adapted from the French Commercial Code, and its provisions on arbitration applied to corporate disputes arising from shareholder relationships in corporate settings. The Regulations on Commercial Procedure (*Ticaret Usulu Muhakemesine Ait Nizamname*) of 1861 followed, setting forth court-ordered arbitration for disputes arising from commercial relations.[119] Yet, the awards were subject to confirmation,

115 *See* George Khoukaz, *Sharia Law and International Commercial Arbitration: The Need for an Intra-Islamic Arbitral Institution*, 2017 J. Disp. Resol. 181, 188 (2017)

116 Balci, *supra* note 112, at 81.

117 The reforms attempted to integrate non-Muslims to the society by granting additional civil liberties as well as equality that aims to put non-Muslims on equal footing with Muslims. The Empire had been dominated by the pursuit of protecting its territory, and these reforms, in fact, were a reaction to the 19th century naturalization movements. *See* Dawood I. Ahmed & Moamen Gouda, *Measuring Constitutional Islamization: The Islamic Constitutions Index*, 38 Hastings Int'l & Comp. L. Rev. 1, 21 (2015). This was the beginning of the Western-based laws in the Ottomans/Turks life. This was followed by moves to codify law, with French statutes emerging as exemplars, France being the role model recognized by the Ottoman government in its drive for reform and modernization. *E.g.* Aydın Yetkin, *Development Process of the Rule of Law in the Ottoman Empire*, 6 J. Int'l Soc. Res. 380, 400 (2013). *See also* Fatma Muge Gocek, East Encounters West: France and the Ottoman Empire in the Eighteenth Century 86 (1987) ("France had... maintained long satisfactory diplomatic relations with the Ottoman Empire; there had not been any direct military clashes between France and the Ottoman Empire. In addition, the French had good trade relations with the Ottomans. The Ottoman attitude toward France was therefore favorable and receptive.")

118 *Id.* at 87–88; Murat Çizakça, A Comparative Evolution of Business Partnerships: The Islamic World and Europe, With Specific Reference to the Ottoman Archives 56 (1996)

119 Balci, *supra* note 112 at 88.

modification, or vacation by competent courts.[120] Afterward, the Ottoman Civil Code Act ("the Mecelle") dated 1869 to 1877 Art. 1790 et seq. recognized arbitration.[121] It remained in force until 1927 when the Code of Civil Procedure of 1927 replaced it.[122]

The contemporary era in Turkish arbitration began in 1927 when the Code of Civil Procedure was adapted from the corresponding code of the Swiss Canton of Neuchatel.[123] The Code of Civil Procedure, however, regulated only domestic arbitration.[124] Turkey introduced international arbitration in the 1980s, gradually expanding its remit it after a long-lasting battle between the legislative and executive branches and the judicial branch. It is noteworthy that when international arbitration was introduced to the Turkish legal system, domestic arbitration was dormant, although it had only been set out in the Code of Civil Procedure dated 1927. Thus, arbitration was available in theory but had not yet been in demand in the practice of Turkish law.

1.2.2 Turkey at a Crossroad: After the 1980s

When we think about the critical figures that have shaped Turkey's fate, Prime Minister and later President Turgut Özal probably ranks one of the tops in history. His strategies in the spheres of politics and the opening of the economy to international investment and trade have seen Turkey undergo transformations since the 1980s. Özal's neoliberal development model saw the practice of international commercial arbitration introduced to the Turkish judiciary in very concrete terms. In retrospect, Özal's neoliberal revolution was akin to that of Ronald

---

120 *Id. See* Mark Wakim, *Public Policy Concerns regarding Enforcement of Foreign International Arbitral Awards in the Middle East*, 21 NY Int'l L Rev 1, 34(2008) ("The Ottoman Turks, influenced by the civil law tradition, attempted to codify Hanafi fiqh. Those provisions confirmed the conciliatory nature of arbitration. Because judges could set aside arbitral awards, the Ottoman legal provisions gave less force to arbitral awards than court judgments. However, Ottoman laws did note that arbitral decisions would be binding on the parties just as a contract would be binding under Shari`a.")

121 Balci, *supra* note 112 at 89.

122 As discussed above, the Civil Procedure Code of the Swiss Canton of Neuchatel was adopted in 1927. The legislation was named the "Code of Civil Procedure." *See* Act No.: 1086, Hukuk Usulü Muhakemeleri Kanunu [Code of Civil Procedure] Official Gazette: 18 June 1927, No.: 622–624, enacted: 2–4 July 1927 (Turk.) [hereinafter the Original CCP].

123 *Id.*

124 *Id.* Articles 516–536.

Reagan in the United States or Margaret Thatcher in Britain, to such an extent that they constituted a triumvirate in terms of parallel economic growth plans in the Middle East, North America, and the United Kingdom, respectively.[125]

Özal was an ambitious, center-right politician who—to be frank—often initiated market-oriented reforms impulsively (*i.e.*, through decrees as opposed to legislation). Turkey, as a result, adopted a model that emphasized concessions, build-operate-transfer agreements (BOTs), and privatization of state enterprises in the 1980s, although the required legal infrastructure was not established until the 1990s.

Concession agreements or BOT's are long-term, high-value contracts, and require expert technology as well as significant amounts of labor. Multinational enterprises (MNEs), in general, have cared diligently to protect their investments by submitting disputes to arbitration as opposed to host countries' domestic courts.[126] It is also crucial for foreign investors to elect for arbitration because any political turmoil in the host nation may adversely affect them.[127]

At the time, the ubiquitous influence of neoliberal economic policies was felt by most MNEs and foreign investors, and investing in developing countries such as Turkey gained momentum. Considering the reasons mentioned above, foreign investors have brought up the necessity of arbitration as a dispute resolution method before Turkish executives. To illustrate, when U.S. Secretary of Commerce William Daley visited Turkey in 1998, he declared that "Turkey is the place where we want to do business, and the U.S. government is eager to help out investors in the Turkish energy sector."[128] He also urged Turkey "to allow *international arbitration* in disputes involving American investments."[129]

This period was the first time that (international) arbitration was available as an ADR for concession agreements in Turkey—albeit through a decree—and

---

125 Ziya Öniş, *Turgut Özal and His Economic Legacy: Turkish Neo-Liberalism in Critical Perspective*, 40 Middle Eastern Studies 113, 120 (2004); William Hale, Turkish Foreign Policy 1774–2000 164 (2002); Marvine Howe, *Man In The News: Turgut Özal; Turkish Ally of Capitalism*, N.Y. Times, Nov. 9, 1983, at A11.

126 *E.g.* Carbonneau, *Arbitral Law-Making supra* note 37 at 1194; Howard M. Holtzmann, *Arbitration: An Indispensible Aid to Multinational Enterprise,* 10 J. Int'l L. & Econ. 337, 337 (1975).

127 *See id.*

128 Hürriyet Daily News, *Daley to Support Turkish Energy Projects* (Jan. 24, 1998), http://web.hurriyetdailynews.com/daley-us-to-support-turkish-energy-projects.aspx?pageID=438&n=daley-u.s.-to-support-turkish-energy-projects-1998-01-24

129 *Id.* (emphasis added)

a discussion about whether or not to employ arbitration continued with protracted court decisions and legislative actions.

To address the issue chronologically, we start with the Act dated 1910, which set forth the rules governing public service concession agreements.[130] Although this Act is still in force, its frequency of application was limited until the 1980s. A long-standing cultural legacy of the period of humiliation during the Ottoman Empire—when European powers used the extraterritorial jurisdiction acquired under the capitulations[131] to bypass Ottoman law and undermine the Empire—goes a long way to explaining why concessions were not a preferred form.[132] Its successor, the Turkish Republic, adopted statism as its official economic strategy under the motto of "full national liberation."[133]

---

130 Act No.: 576, Menafii Umumiyeye Müteallik İmtiyazat Hakkında Kanun [Act on Concessions Relating to Public Service] Official Gazette: 24 June 1910, No: 576, Enacted 10 June 1910 (Turk.).

131 The term "capitulations" as used by the Ottomans refers to privileges, grants, or concessions for foreigners. Feroz Ahmad, *Ottoman Perceptions of The Capitulations: 1800–1914*, 11 J. Islamic Stud. 1, 1(2000). Although traditionally, the capitulations were unilaterally granted subject to revocation at the Sultan's will, they later transformed to a bilateral nature where the other party sought not a privilege but a right. *Id.* at 1–4. Nonetheless, starting from the end of the seventeenth century, the Western powers used the capitulations against the Ottoman Empire which were originally intended to stimulate trade with the West. Maurits H. Van Den Boogert, Capitulations and the Ottoman Legal System: Qadis, Consuls and Beratlis in the eighteenth Century 7 (2005). Hence, the capitulations were regarded as a nuisance, violating Ottoman sovereignty. In the last years of the Ottoman Empire, abrogation the capitulations became the most important goal of Ottoman policy. Norman Bentwich, *The Abrogation of the Turkish Capitulations,* 5 J. Comp. Legislation & Int'l L. no.4, 1923, at 182, 183.

132 Serdar Bezen, *Recent Developments in International Commercial Arbitration* in Turkey, 67 Chartered Inst. of Arb. J., no. 2, May 2001, at 165.

133 The Republican People's Party (CHP) was the major political establishment during the single-party period. It was founded by Atatürk under the principles of republicanism, nationalism, statism, populism, laicism and reformism, which are represented by the party's logo, the Six Arrows. *See* Cemil Koçak, *Parliament Membership during the Single-Party System in Turkey (1925–1945)*, European J. Turkish Stud. vol. 3, 2005, available at https://journals.openedition.org/ejts/497?lang=tr Statism is one of the six principles on which the CHP was founded. See *id.*

The first example of rules governing the BOTs came into force in 1984, under Act No. 3096.[134] This Act cleared the way for the private sector (and, therefore, foreign investors) to venture into electrical energy in Turkey. Act No. 3465, enacted four years later, was akin to Act No. 3096, except it set forth the rules governing concessions of highways.[135]

There are several points worth highlighting. Neither of the enactments cited the BOT model or set forth general rules on concessions. They instead specified the areas—electrical energy and highways—in which the private sector might participate and the means of participation. Through these enactments, the legislator wanted to render the BOTs subject to private law.[136] The legislator's reasoning was that the BOT model was not a variation of concession agreements, so much so that it might be governed by private law as opposed to administrative law,[137] and thus attempted to bypass the Constitution as well as formulate a foundation for international arbitration.

Although the enactments mentioned above seemed sufficient for concessions and BOTs to operate in Turkey legally, a problem arose with respect to Art. 155 of the Turkish Constitution and its application by the Turkish administrative courts.[138] The public service concession contracts were under the

---

134 Act No.: 3096, Türkiye Elektrik Kurumu Dışındaki Kuruluşların Elektrik Üretimi, İletimi, Dağıtımı ve Ticareti ile Görevlendirilmesi Hakkında Kanun [Act on Granting Authorization of Generation, Transmission, Distribution, and Trade of Electricity to Enterprises other than the Turkish Electricity Institution] Official Gazette, 19 Dec. 1984, No.: 18610, Enacted 4 Dec. 1984 (Turk.).

135 Act No.: 3465, Karayolları Genel Müdürlüğü Dışındaki Kuruluşlarla Erişme Kontrollü Karayolu (Otoyol) Yapımı, Bakımı ve İşletilmesi ile Görevlendirilmesi Hakkında Kanun [Act on Granting Authorization of Construction, Maintenance, and Operation of Highways to Enterprises other than the General Directorate of Highways] Official Gazette, 2 June 1988 No.: 19830, Enacted 28 May 1988 (Turk.).

136 Bezen, *supra* note 132, at 161.

137 Under Turkish law, administrative/public law governs matters between the government and private parties whereas private law governs only matters between private parties—such as contracts or torts. Although the BOTs are private in nature, arbitration was not allowed because administrative law was established upon the idea that if a public agency is involved, the public interest may be at stake, and therefore administrative law should be there to protect the public. *See id*. This is also the principle of statism, one of the principles governing the CHP and the left-wing parties in Turkey in general. See *infra* Section 4.3.2.2.2

138 Similar to French law, the contracts of administrative nature were not arbitrable at the time. *See* Thomas H. Webster & Michael Buhler, Handbook of ICC Arbitration: Commentary, Precedents, Materials 143 (2014).Turkish administrative law

Turkish Council of State's jurisdiction as well as that of the Turkish Constitutional Court.[139] The Council of State and the Turkish Constitutional Court had delivered their decisions under the excuse of "public policy," "public interest," and/or "public service" for an extended period, with the Turkish Council of State having "oversight" of the concession agreements under Art. 155 of the Constitution.[140] The Article not only granted the Council of State the power of review of concession agreements before closure but also to modify or revoke some of the provisions unilaterally. Moreover, the Council of State had exclusive jurisdiction over disputes arising from the concessions. In fact, this represents something of a violation of the separation of powers, as the Council of State was vested with both executive and judicial power.[141]

---

has been adopted mostly from French administrative law. The French Conseil d'Etat was an inspiring model for the Turkish Council of State so much so that the Turkish Council of State referred to a considerable number of Conseil d'Etat's rulings and French scholars' doctrines. *E.g.* the General Assembly of the Turkish Council of State Case No: 1973/12 Decision No:1975/8 dated 28.2.1975 (Lexpera Hukuk Bilgi Sistemi) [Lexpera Legal Information System] (Turk.); the Board of Administrative Affairs of the Turkish Council of State 1998/85, Decision No: 1998/81, dated 11.06.1998 (Lexpera Hukuk Bilgi Sistemi) [Lexpera Legal Information System] (Turk.) (referring four different Conseil d'Etat Cases). *See also* Gocek *supra* note 117 and accompanying text; Esin Örücü, *Conseil d'Etat: The French Layer of Turkish Administrative Law*, 49 Int. Comp. Law Q. 679, 683 fn.14 (2000).

139 Former Art. 155 of the Constitution set out that "The Council of State is the last instance for reviewing decisions and judgments given by administrative courts and which are not referred by law to other administrative courts. It shall also be the first and last instance for dealing with specific cases stipulated by law. The Council of State shall hear administrative cases, *give its opinions* on draft legislation submitted by the PM and the Council of Ministers and *the conditions and contracts under which concessions are granted within two months*, examine draft regulations, settle administrative disputes and discharge other duties as stipulated by law. …" [emphasis added]. Art. 155 of Act No: 2709, The Constitution of the Republic of Turkey, Official Gazette: 9 Nov. 1982, No: 17863, Enacted: 7 Nov. 1982, *amended by* Act No. 4446, Türkiye Cumhuriyeti Anayasasının Bazı Maddelerinde Değişiklik Yapılmasına Ilişkin Kanun [Law on the Amendment of Some Articles of the Constitution of the Republic of Turkey] Official Gazette: 14 Aug. 1999, No: 23786, Enacted: 13 Aug. 1999 (Turk.). *See* Yusuf Çalışkan, The Development of International Investment Law: Lessons from the OECD MAI Negotiations and Their Application to a Possible Multilateral Agreement on Investment 312 (2008).

140 See *id.*

141 Although French administrative law had a similar system, the Turkish interpretation of the system was not limited to the provisions in the contract relating to public interest.

Overall, the tension between the legislative body and the judiciary meant the process of adopting international arbitration was arduous. That difficulty was itself a product of the differing political outlooks of the judiciary and the legislature. As a result, and in tandem with the Council of State's extreme hostility toward international arbitration, neither BOTs nor arbitration itself found a friendly reception in Turkey.

Viewed objectively, the mistake of post-1983 legislatures and executives in Turkey was to attempt to bypass the Constitution instead of amending the challenging provisions in the first place.[142] The leading state of mind of the courts was that arbitration was a "modern form of capitulation,"[143] and it was not welcomed because capitulations were postulated to be the underlying reason the Ottoman Empire's collapse. Left-wing parties (*i.e.*, secular–Western Turks) blamed the right-wing (conservative) parties for introducing international arbitration, which was a recipe for disaster that would lead Turkey to share the same fate as the Ottoman Empire.[144] The judicial branch was erroneous, as much as the executives and legislators, when they created a "public policy/interest/service" basis to refuse each attempt of privatization even though it was not related to these notions, *e.g.*, arbitration.

As then left-wing PM Bulent Ecevit rightly pointed out, when supporting the constitutional amendments allowing international arbitration, "Some groups in Turkey believe that modernism and revolution require us to argue against novelties... I recall that when Hilton Hotels were established in Turkey for the first time, some group argued that capitulations were coming back. They were against

The fundamental reason to refuse arbitration was not that it was harmful to the public interest/policy/services, but that the Council of State was skeptical of arbitration. *See* Ulusoy & Oguz *supra* note 29, at 5026.

142 *Cf.* Kemal Gözler, Idare Hukuku II [Administrative Law] 209 (2003) (Turk.) (stating that there was no need to amend the Constitution because there was no provision in the Constitution preventing arbitration for concession agreements. Hence, the exception to Art. 155 could have been made through the law); Mahmut Tevfik Birsel, *Türkiye'de Yabancı Hakem Kararlarının Tenfizinin Anayasal ve Küresel Boyutları [Constitutional and Global Dimensions of Enforcement of Foreign Arbitral Awards in Turkey]*, 7 Dokuz Eylul Universitesi Hukuk Fakultesi Dergisi 1, 24 (2005) (Turk.).

143 Bezen, *supra* note 132, at 165. *See also supra* note 131 and accompanying text.

144 Türkiye Barolar Birliği [the Union of Turkish Bar Associations] Idari Sözleşmeler ve Uluslararasi Tahkim [Administrative Contracts and International Arbitration] 56 (1999) (Turk.).

the color TVs, private broadcasting... The Left has been against every novelty in the name of purported modernism and revolution, believing that this the basis of leftism."[145]

The issue was finally resolved when Articles 47, 125 and 155 of the Constitution were amended. Three related pieces of legislation followed the amendment to reassure foreign investors that concessions would be governed by private law, and therefore, international arbitration might be implemented in the contract.

1.2.3 The Current Law on Arbitration

To start with the most significant document of Turkey, international arbitration finds its rationalization under Article 125(1) of the Turkish Constitution.[146] It might seem peculiar for the reader that a constitutional document would establish such a secondary matter, given that they are supposed to be short documents, stating the fundamental values governing the organization of the states. The discussion above, however, has clarified the main reason, which is that international arbitration was not welcomed in Turkey before, and the way to make it possible was to amend the Constitution.

Art. 90(5) is the second significant article of the Constitution on the matter of arbitration. It declares that the provisions of international treaties shall prevail in the event of a conflict between international treaties and domestic laws due to differences in provisions on the same matter.[147] Moreover, the unconstitutionality of international treaties cannot be alleged before the Constitutional Court.[148] Hence, if there is a conflict between Turkish codes and international treaties on the matter of arbitration, the courts shall take the treaties into consideration and give them determinative force.

---

145 *Ecevit Sol'ladi [Ecevit Overtook on the Left]* SABAH (Aug. 5, 1999), http://arsiv.sabah.com.tr/1999/08/05/p01.html (Turk.).

146 Art. 125(1) of Act No: 2709, The Constitution of the Republic of Turkey, *amended by* Act No.: 5170, Türkiye Cumhuriyeti Anayasasının Bazı Maddelerinin Değiştirilmesi Hakkında Kanun [Law Amending Some Articles of the Constitution of the Republic of Turkey] Official Gazette: 22 May. 2004, No: 25469, Enacted: 7 May. 2004 (Turk.) ("In concession, conditions and contracts concerning public services and national or international arbitration may be suggested to settle the disputes arising from them. Only those disputes involving an element of foreignness may be submitted to international arbitration.").

147 *Id.* Art. 90(5).

148 *Id.*

After the Constitution, the second important type of legislation is international treaties. Turkey ratified various major international conventions on arbitration, such as the Washington Convention on the Settlement of Investment Disputes between States and Nationals of Other States (ICSID) in 1987[149] and the New York Convention in 1991.[150] It is not surprising that the ratification of these major conventions happened in the late 1980s and the beginning of the 1990s, considering the historical background of Turkish arbitration.

Statutes governing arbitration can be divided into two parts as domestic and international law. In terms of domestic law, the Code of Civil Procedure[151] was re-enacted, and the articles[152] of the new Code of Civil Procedure ("the New CCP") governing arbitration are largely based on the UNCITRAL Model Law on International Commercial Arbitration ("UNCITRAL Model Law") and Switzerland's Federal Code on Private International Law.[153] Thus, the most significant revisions of the New CCP in terms of arbitration are to bring the domestic arbitration procedure closer to international standards.

International arbitration in Turkey is governed by the Turkish International Arbitration Act ("TIAL").[154] The TIAL's incentive came from being a strong participant in global finance and its dedication to foster extraterritorial

149 Act No: 3460, Devletler ve Diğer Devletlerin Vatandaşları Arasındaki Yatırım Uyuşmazlıklarının C⊠özümlenmesi Hakkında Sözleşmenin Onaylanmasının Uygun Bulunduğuna Dair Kanun [Law on the Ratification of the ICSID Convention], Official Gazette: 2 June 1988, No.: 20011, Enacted: 6 Dec. 1988 (Turk.).

150 Act No: 3731, Yabancı Hakem Kararlarının Tanınması ve Icrası Hakkındaki New York Sözleşmesinin Onaylanmasının Uygun Bulunduğuna Dair Kanun [Law on the Ratification of the New York Convention], Official Gazette: 21 May 1991, No.: 20011, Enacted: 8 May 1991 (Turk.).

151 Act No.: 6100, Hukuk Muhakemeleri Kanunu [Code of Civil Procedure] Official Gazette: 12 Jan. 2011, No.: 27836, Enacted 4 Feb. 2011 (Turk.). [hereinafter New CCP]

152 Articles 407–444 of Act No. 6100, New CCP.

153 Turkiye Buyuk Millet Meclisi [Grand Nat'l Assemb. of Turk], Hukuk Muhakemeleri Kanunu Tasarısı ve Adalet Komisyonu Raporu [Draft Act No. 6100 and its Preamble] 4 (2008) (Turk.), available at http://www.kgm.adalet.gov.tr/Tasariasamalari/Kanunlasan/2011Yili/kanmetni/6100ss.pdf. *See also* U.N. Comm'n on Int'l Trade Law (UNCITRAL), Report of the United Nations Commission on International Trade Law on the Work of Its Eighteenth Session, Annex I, U.N. Doc. A/40/17 (June 21, 1985) [hereinafter UNCITRAL Model Law]

154 Act No.: 4686, Milletlerarası Tahkim Kanunu [Turkish International Arbitration Law], Official Gazette: 21 Jun. 2001 No.: 24453, Enacted 5 July 2001 (Turk.) [hereinafter TIAL].

investments.[155] Before the TIAL entered into effect, there was no distinction between applicable domestic and international arbitration laws. Thus, the modern law of the arbitration, the TIAL, was adopted on July 5, 2001. Likewise, the TIAL is based on Chapter 12 of Switzerland's Federal Code on Private International Law and UNCITRAL Model Law.[156]

There might be a chance that the New York Convention and TIAL will not apply when the dispute is beyond the scope of application. In that case, the International Private Law and Procedural Law Act governs the recognition and enforcement of foreign arbitral awards.[157] For example, should there is an arbitral award made in Taiwan, the law of the seat of arbitration will be Taiwanese law so that it does not fall within the scope of the TIAL. Assuming that the award-winning party sought enforcement in Turkey, Turkish courts would be unable to apply to the New York Convention to the award as Taiwan is not a signatory to the Convention. Hence, the International Private Law and Procedural Law Act No. 5718 ("IPPA") would govern the enforceability of the Taiwanese arbitral award.

This legislation denotes that Turkey allows the pro-arbitration grounds for the practitioners and the judges to utilize. This legislation, indeed, gives the judges flexibility to create precedents favoring arbitration. The more courts lessen their lingering suspicion toward arbitration, the more Turkish laws on arbitration could flourish.

---

155 Turkiye Buyuk Millet Meclisi [Grand Nat'l Assemb. of Turk], Milletlerarası Tahkim Kanunu Tasarisi[Draft Act No.4686 and its Preamble] 1 (2001), available at http://www2.tbmm.gov.tr/d21/1/1-0874.pdf

156 *See id.* at 1.

157 Act No.: 5718, Milletlerarası Özel Hukuk ve Usul Hukuku Hakkında Kanun [The Turkish International Private and Procedural Law], Official Gazette: 27 Nov. 2007, No.: 26728, Enacted 12 Dec. 2007 [hereinafter the IPPA]. *See also* The General Assembly of the Turkish Court of Cassation, Case No: 2011/13-568, Decision No: 2012/47, dated 8.2.2012 (Kazancı İçtihat Bilgi Bankası) [Kazanci Case Law Database] (Turk.) (stating that although its scope of application has become narrower, the IPPA applies when there is an award made in a non-signatory country).

1.3 Comparison and Contrast: Whether Different Foundations of Arbitration Laws May Affect Judicial Application

The discussion has indicated that—as far as the development of arbitration is concerned—social and political history and the nature of relations between the branches of government matters a great deal. An outgrowth of the expansion of British mercantile imperialism in the sixteenth and seventeenth centuries, the American colonies were essentially business ventures engaged in trans-Atlantic commercial trade. It is not surprising that arbitration blossomed in North America in that context, as it did in Europe and other developed trading regions.[158] At first, arbitration was a set of informal practices that arose from the exigencies of the mercantile business class, but later it became the subject of state interest, being formalized and legislated in the process.

When it comes to the Turkish case, the seven-century-long evolution of commerce—and, arguably, law and politics—in the Ottoman Empire bears strongly on the history of arbitration. Although by the late eighteenth century, no major religious community in the Ottoman Empire had dominance in trade or commerce, with the economic modernization in the West and its control over the Middle East, Jews and Christians started to dominate the commerce in the Ottoman Empire, and Muslims participation in trade and finance has decreased.[159] Because the Ottoman Empire allowed them to conduct business under their own laws, non-Muslims took advantage of the legal institutions and mechanisms of the modern economy, *e.g.*, dispute resolutions methods, whereas the Muslim Ottomans continued their established practices under Islamic law.[160] As a result, when the Empire fell, the legislation on arbitration was limited, as discussed before.

It is partly true that—as an Islamic society—trade and commercial activity was less expansive than in other civilizations, dampened somewhat by the prohibition on usury and a cultural partiality against the merchant classes.[161] Also,

---

158 Thomas K. McCraw, *supra* note 60, at 301; Carbonneau, *Arbitral Law-Making supra* note 37 at 1195.

159 Timur Kuran, *The Economic Ascent of the Middle East's Religious Minorities: The Role of Islamic Legal Pluralism*, 33 J. Legal Stud. 475, 475-76 (2004).

160 *Id.* at 476–77.

161 *See e.g.* Suraiya Faroqhi, Osmanlı'da kentler ve kentliler: kent mekânında ticaret zanaat ve gıda üretimi [Towns and Townsmen of Anatolia: Trade, Crafts and Food Production in an Urban Setting] 76 (Neyyir Kalaycıoğlu trans., 2000) (Turk.) (mentioning that merchants were called as "cheat," "swindler" and "hoaxer"). *Contra* Kuran, *supra*

the Ottoman tradition saw a strong role for state intervention in commerce, at the expense of private parties, in the interests of the authority and stability of the state.[162] Within the Muslim community, being a public officer was more respectable than being a merchant.[163]

The legislative background of arbitration also differs in terms of both chronology and content. The FAA was enacted in 1925, not long after the Ottoman Empire had collapsed, and the Republic of Turkey was still finding its feet. While the FAA is not based on the UNCITRAL Model Law, the Turkish law on arbitration is, and its enactment came as late as 2001. One can argue that Turkish legislation is much more modern compared to the FAA, and therefore it yields results in favor of arbitration. This argument brings us, however, to the last but the most important branch of this discussion, which is the judiciary's position on arbitration.

Quidquid iudicii placuit, habet legis vigorem—in other words, "whatever pleases the judiciary, has the force of law."[164] When the FAA was enacted, the purpose was to eradicate the "old [judicial] hostility toward arbitration."[165] After almost a century of application by the federal courts and the U.S. Supreme Court, we can state that the FAA has out-served its usefulness. Due to the federal policy favoring arbitration, any dispute of a civil or commercial nature between private persons or entities can be arbitrable, including consumer and employment arbitration. At this point, the question arises as to whether it is benign for the future of arbitration or not. The author argues that although it supports cross-border

---

note 159 at 482. ("In fact, from the early days of Islam, Muslims routinely gave and took interest, sometimes openly and without apology.")

162 *See* MEHMET GENÇ, OSMANLI IMPARATORLUGUNDA DEVLET VE EKONOMI [STATE AND ECONOMY IN THE OTTOMAN EMPIRE] 13 (2000) (Turk.)

163 *E.g.* ZAFER TOPRAK, MILLI IKTISAT—MILLI BURJUVAZI [NATIONAL ECONOMICS–NATIONAL BOURGEOISIE] 99–100 (1995) (Turk.); MUSTAFA AKDAĞ, TÜRK HALKININ DIRLIK VE DÜZENLIK KAVGASI & "CELALILER İSYANLARI [TURKISH PEOPLE'S FIGHT FOR PEACE AND HARMONY: THE CELALI REBELLIONS] 48 (1974) (Turk.). *Contra* Kuran, *supra* note 159 at 482. (stating that this perception was prevalent only after the nineteenth century). This could be explained by the fact that only Muslims could enter public service in the Ottoman Empire. Gülnihal Bozkurt, *Türk Hukuk Tarihinde Azınlıklar [Minorities in History of Turkish Law]*, 64 ANKARA UNIVERSITESI HUKUK FAKULTESI DERGISI [AUHFD] 49, 51 (1993) (Turk.).

164 AARON X. FELLMETH & MAURICE HORWITZ, GUIDE TO LATIN IN INTERNATIONAL LAW 241 (2011).

165 *Southland*, 465 U.S. at 14.

commerce, it is inevitable that consumers and employees will confront the reality that arbitration is an "ill-advised action."[166] Therefore, there should be a difference between commercial and adhesive arbitration.

As we have seen—and will see through the remainder of the book—the Turkish judiciary has struggled to accept arbitration as an alternative form of adjudication. To summarize, the whole point of the discussion on the historical aspects of arbitration is to demonstrate that judges in Turkey have partially distrusted arbitration while their American counterparts created an entire arbitration system seemingly out of little more than a founding statute.[167] In terms of the three branches, the author argues that the judicial position on arbitration is the most significant one for the advance of arbitration as an ADR in Turkey.

166 *E.g.* Knepp v. Credit Acceptance Corp. (In re Knepp), 229 B.R. 821, 828 (Bankr. N.D. Ala. 1999) (making an analogy between the plant kudzu and arbitration by stating that "when introduced as a method to control soil erosion, kudzu was hailed as an asset to agriculture, but it has become a creeping monster. Arbitration was innocuous when limited to negotiated commercial contracts, but it developed sinister characteristics when it became ubiquitous."); Thomas E. Carbonneau, *Arbitration and the U.S. Supreme Court: A Plea for Statutory Reform*, 5 Ohio St. J. Disp. Resol. 231, 275 (1990).

167 *Allied-Bruce*, 513 U.S. at 283.

2 Past and Future Coverage Under the Umbrella of Public Policy

Abstract: The second chapter investigates the enigma of public policy as an exception to the enforcement of arbitral awards under the New York Convention. This chapter is thus primarily concerned with the public policy exception, which is the second facet of public policy applied in this book. The second chapter begins with the natural starting point—namely, the terminology and definition of public policy. It emphasizes that the existence of myriad definitions of public policy does not constitute a pathological situation that needs to be resolved. After identifying the burden of proof requirements for a public policy exception under the New York Convention, the second chapter discusses what the applicable law should be when evaluating the public policy ground and whether the courts should consider public policy when deciding not to enforce an award, and if so, whose public policy should apply. Another important topic that the second chapter seeks to shed light on is the division between domestic, international, and transnational public policy standards and how these compare one to another. After analyzing the scope offered by each standard, the chapter will answer which of the public policy standards should apply to arbitral awards when the courts of the Contracting States encounter a dispute requiring the consideration of public policy. One aim of the second chapter is to identify, in broad strokes, substantive or procedural reasons that enforcement of an award might be contrary to public policy. This chapter, however, does not seek to catalog the substantive and procedural public policy violations—which are vast in number. Instead, an attempt is made here to pinpoint the grounds that have remained ambiguous in terms of whether the public policy exception can encompass them.

Keywords: definition, burden of proof, substantive public policy, procedural public policy

2.1 Terminology: Public Policy or Public Order (*Ordre Public*)?

Public policy defense has often been invoked as if it were a blanket term in international arbitration. Legal practitioners, the judiciary, and commentators have all shared the job of elaborating the concept of public policy, keeping the term itself loose enough to allow for quite extensive coverage. Seemingly taking a leaf from Rihanna's invitation to listeners near and far—"you can stand under my umbrella"—public policy offers a wide range of justifications to welcome protection under its broad canopy.

Notwithstanding this, there is no doubt that the application of the public policy defense is significantly narrower than it has been in the past. Modern practice suggests that the public policy defense presents no significant obstacle in the way of enforcement of arbitral awards. Thus, we arrive at the question of why public policy defense remains an important issue worthy of discussion, and which challenging aspects of it have yet to be resolved.

The author has observed various reactions when sharing the title of her book with different people. Those who practice law in civil law states have suggested replacing "public policy" with the term "public order" (or *ordre public* in the French). Some who have not studied arbitration were surprised to learn that "public policy" is a legal concept, while others were aware but still prefer the term "public order." The question arises, then, as to what the proper terminology should be, and whether these terms entirely coincide (this book prefers the term "public policy.")

In a basic sense, public order in civil law is analogous to public policy in common law. The distinct developments of these terms have their genesis in the conflicts of law doctrines where public policy or public order supersede an otherwise valid choice-of-law agreement.[168] As the study discussed earlier, public policy has its origins in English common law.[169] It was later adopted in the U.S. legal order. Public order, however, is a product of French law, which is deemed the pioneer of conflict of law for the civil law states.[170] Thus, it is not surprising that whereas common law countries have embraced the wording "public policy," civil law countries have embraced the wording "public order."[171]

---

168 Simona Grossi, Rethinking the Harmonization of Jurisdictional Rules, 86 TUL. L. REV. 623, 649 (2012).

169 *See supra* Section 1.1.2.

170 *E.g.* Kent Murphy, *The Traditional View of Public Policy and Ordre Public in Private International Law*, 11 GA. J. INT. COMP. L. 591, 596 (2015); Ernest G. Lorenzen, The French Rules of the Conflict of Laws, 36 YALE L. J. 731, 731 (1927).

171 Nonetheless, although the United States is a mostly a common law country, certain states whose legal system is based on civil law or a mix of common and civil law espouse the term "public order." *See e.g.*, LA. CIV. CODE ANN. Art.2030 ("A contract is absolutely null when it violates a rule of *public order....* ") (emphasis added); 31 L.P.R.A. § 3372 ("The contracting parties may make the agreement... provided they are not in contravention of law, morals, or *public order.*") (emphasis added).

Both public policy and public order serve similar purposes within the context of Art.V(2)(b),[172] although some commentators have pointed out that the concepts do not fully correspond to each other.[173] This criticism might be valid in other contexts. For international arbitration, however, this book argues that theoretical discussion as to what the proper term should be is useless overall since the result would be arbitrary. As we stated earlier, public policy has been the concern mostly of jurisprudence rather than legal practice. Supposing that the statutes and courts used the term "public policy" or "public order," the issue would still arise as to how the respective jurisdiction understands the concept and applies it. Hence, public policy and public order can be used interchangeably in international arbitration.

Another fact to support this argument is that the New York Convention used the term "public policy" in the English version and "public order" in the French version. Moreover, English and French versions have been deemed equally authentic under Art. XVI sub.1 of the Convention. Given that, not the term itself but how the courts interpret it is crucial.

2.2 Definition of Public Policy

In 2002, the International Law Association Committee ("ILA") presented its Final ILA Report on Public Policy as a Bar to Enforcement of International Arbitral Awards, which was the result of a six-year study.[174] The Committee stated: "The New York Convention's goal was to provide uniform procedures for enforcing foreign arbitral awards while minimizing the effect of discrepancies between the laws of different countries. Fifty years on, public policy remains the

---

172 *E.g.* Albert Jan van den Berg, The New York Arbitration Convention of 1958–Towards a Uniform Judicial Interpretation 369 (1981); Audley Sheppard, *Interim ILA Report on Public Policy as a Bar to Enforcement of International Arbitral Awards*, 19 Arbitr. Int. 217, 224 n.36 (2003) (stating that the two terms have the same meaning) [hereinafter *ILA's Interim Report*]; Pierre Mayer & Audley Sheppard, *Final ILA Report on Public Policy as a Bar to Enforcement of International Arbitral Awards*, 19 Arbitr. Int. 249, 249 (2003) [hereinafter *ILA's Final Report*] (providing that "*[p]ublic policy*' and '*ordre public*' are now 'considered to be synonymous.")

173 *E.g.* Murphy, *supra* note 170, at 595–96 (mentioning that public order is a result of positive legislative action); 2 Gerald Fitzmaurice, The Law and Procedure of the International Court of Justice 704 (1986) (stating that equating "public policy" with "*ordre public*" would be criticized by many English lawyers).

174 Mayer & Sheppard, *supra* note 172, at 249.

most significant aspect of the Convention in respect of which such discrepancies might still exist."[175] As the discrepancies have not disappeared despite the lapse of 70 years and numerous court decisions, the unsettled features of public policy have still prevented the concept from being consistent.

Although there is no uniform definition of public policy, the correlation is clear: the judiciary (and the legal order more generally) in pro-arbitration countries have narrowly defined what is meant by public policy. Thus, national courts in these jurisdictions seldom fail to enforce arbitral awards on this basis. By contrast, courts in countries that are less friendly to arbitration have been prone to interpret public policy more broadly, leading to more frequent refusal of enforcement on public policy grounds.

If one were to attempt to provide insight on the definition of public policy in light of its previous application and commentators' observations, one would discover that public policy is a dynamic concept, one that appears to have many of the adaptive qualities of a living organism.[176] It gradually changes and develops in response to the altering needs of society over time. This alteration may have social, cultural, moral, religious, or economic aspects.[177] These values are so essential for the concerned states that it underpins the states' interests and sovereignty, and a deviation from these fundamental values becomes intolerable.[178]

It is of importance for the national courts to strive to elaborate and narrowly construe the notion of public policy. For example, in *Parsons & Whittemore Overseas Co. v. Societe Generale de L'Industrie du Papier (RAKTA),* when the

---

175 *Id.* at 254–55.

176 Pierre Lalive, *Transnational (or Truly International) Public Policy and International Arbitration, in* COMPARATIVE ARBITRATION PRACTICE AND PUBLIC POLICY IN ARBITRATION 258, 295 (Pieter Sanders ed., 2005).

177 E.g., Christopher S. Gibson, *Arbitration, Civilization and Public Policy: Seeking Counterpoise between Arbitral Autonomy and the Public Policy Defense in View of Foreign Mandatory Public Law,* 113 PENN STATE LAW REV. 1227,1230 (2008).

178 *See e.g.* Ciments Français v. OAO Holding Company Siberian Cement, Highest Arbitrazh Court, Russian Federation, No. VAS-17458/11, 27 August 2012 (establishing that the award conflicted with a previous judgment of the courts that the forum violates public policy); Oberlandesgericht [OLG] Düsseldorf Germany, VI Sch (Kart) 1/02, 21 July 2004 (noting that in order for the public policy exception to apply, violation of the fundamental principles of the legal, economic and/or social order of the state should be evident and sufficiently significant that the decision is unacceptable); Maḥkamat al Isti'nāf [Court of Appeal], session of 23 May 2001, case no. 25/116 (Egypt) (deeming that a rule for the maximum rate of interest in civil disputes concerns public policy).

public policy defense was raised, the Second Circuit held that "enforcement of foreign arbitral awards may be denied… only where enforcement would violate the forum state's most basic notions of morality and justice"[179], and it has become a landmark case that presented the threshold requirements for the U.S. public policy. Other courts have made similar definitions.[180] Nevertheless, the courts have been loath to base their holdings on a precise guideline for the use of the public policy exception.[181]

The time factor is also worth considering because the values and principles of the states and communities change and develop over time. While the earliest use of public policy was to reject morally unacceptable agreements, *e.g.*, the right to hold slaves as property, [182] today the unacceptability of these has become universal, and discussion is mostly off the table. In the middle ages, if a stranger provided money to a person to fund his claims, it was seen as a violation of public policy.[183] Centuries later, third-party funding has become one of the pillars of investment arbitration and commercial arbitration.[184] These have exemplified the fact that the definition of public policy is closely connected with a particular time and jurisdiction. Under today's circumstances, the commercial, as well as the political stance of the engaged state to promote commerce and foreign

179 Parsons & Whittemore Overseas Co. v. Societe Generale De L'Industrie Du Papier (RAKTA), 508 F.2d 969, 974 (2nd Cir. 1974).

180 *See e.g.* Traxys Europe S.A. v. Balaji Coke Industry Pvt Ltd., [2012] FCA 276 (Austl.) (stating that an award that runs afoul of the fundamental questions of morality and justice in the jurisdiction would be contrary to public policy); Hebei Import & Export Corp. v. Polytek Engineering Co. Ltd., [1999] 2 H.K.C 205 (H.K.). (prioritizing the New York Convention and stating that an award would be contrary to public policy if it is so fundamentally offensive to the enforcing jurisdiction's notions of justice despite being a signatory to the Convention); Renusagar v. General Electric (1994) AIR SC 860 (India) (noting that a foreign award would be contrary to public policy if it contradicts with the fundamental policy of Indian law, the interests of India, or justice or morality).

181 E.g. Richard A. Cole, *The Public Policy Exception to the New York Convention on the Recognition and Enforcement of Arbitral Awards*, 1 Ohio St. J. on Disp. Res. 365, 382 (1986).

182 Knight, *Public Policy in English Law*, 38 L.Q. Rev. 207, 209–210 (1922).

183 Re Trepca Mines (No. 2) [1962] 3 All E.R. 351 (Eng.) (explaining the risk that champertous maintainer can manipulate the case for his own good, to suppress evidence, or cause frivolous claims)

184 See generally *infra* Section 2.6.2.7

investment, attract attention as two of the most important factors encouraging international arbitration.

The New York Convention does not provide a specific definition of public policy, leaving the meaning to the discretion of the Contracting States. Could this be deemed as a deficit of the Convention that gives rise to the existence of the discrepancies despite long-term practice? Unquestionably, the drafters of the Convention were smart enough to formulate a proper definition. Thus, the absence of a definition per se was indeed a smart move that renders the Convention appealing to States. The Convention could not have reached its present success without a public policy exception at all, or with a narrow and exhaustive list of exceptions of public policy.[185]

The author believes that acceptance of the lack of definition might be considered as a factor enhancing the arbitral proceedings, rather than being stuck in the prejudicial impacts originating from the absence of a definition or the undetermined nature of the concept. Saving these remarks for later, we can conclude here noting that, "what constitutes a violation of public policy is largely a question of fact and is to be decided on an ad hoc basis."[186] This preserves the specificity of the concept.

2.3 The Burden of Proof Under the Public Policy Exception

The New York Convention exemplified an ideal to create a compelling regime for recognition and enforcement of foreign awards. To construct this regime, the drafters of the New York Convention enumerated the defenses exhaustively and laid the burden of proof on the party opposing the enforcement. In a way, they developed an assumption that a foreign arbitral award is enforceable unless one of the grounds listed in Art. V is met.[187]

That being said, there is a subtle difference between the wording of Art.V(1) and V(2). Art.V(1) stipulates that "Recognition and enforcement of the award may be refused..., *only if that party furnishes* to the competent [emphasis added]." In Art.V(2), however, "Recognition and enforcement of an arbitral award may

---

185 *E.g.* Helena Hsi-Chia Chen, Predictability of 'Public Policy' in Article V of the New York Convention under Mainland China's Judicial Practice 16 (2017)

186 Van den Berg, *supra* note 172, at 376. *See* Leon Trakman, *Domestic Courts Declining to Recognize and Enforce Foreign Arbitral Awards: A Comparative Reflection*, 6 Chinese J. Comp. L., 174, 188 (2018).

187 *See e.g.* Fotochrome, Inc. v. Copal Co., 517 F.2d 512, 518 (2nd Cir. 1975); *Parsons & Whittemore*, 508 F.2d at 973.

also be *refused if the competent authority... finds that*." Reading both articles provides certain data about the allocation of the burden of proof. The first remark in Art.V(1) requires the opposing party to raise the grounds for refusal whereas, under Art.V(2), an enforcing court may also ex officio or sua sponte consider the grounds for refusal, namely non-arbitrability and public policy. This stance of the New York Convention mirrors the importance of the public policy grounds for the Contracting States.

With this caveat in mind, a question arises as to whether the burden of proof has become lighter than required under Art.V(1) for the opposing party, since public policy is so significant for the court of the forum that it will observe this ground in any event. In today's practice, the answer is negative. Considering the pro-enforcement bias under the Convention, the courts put the same heavy burden of proof on the opposing party.[188] Thus, it would be rare to see the opposing party not assert the public policy ground, and yet have the court still deny the recognition of the award, holding that it is contrary to public policy.[189]

2.4 Whose Public Policy? Locating the Applicable Law

2.4.1 The Public Policy of *That* Country

In international arbitration, more than one forum—and thereby more than one legal regime—can be applicable regarding the issue of public policy. It is possible for the law of the place of arbitration (*lex loci arbitri*) to apply in cases where a party seeks to vacate an award or the law of the place of performance of the contract or the law of the enforcing court (*lex fori*). Art. V(2)(b) clearly states that "the public policy of that country," *i.e.*, the public policy of the forum of enforcement, is applicable when determining public policy. Given the language of the Convention, the answer is manifest. However, it is noteworthy that this was not the exact case in *Victrix S.S. Co. v. Salen Dry Cargo AB*[190] and *Skandia America Reinsurance Corp. v. Seguros La Republica.*[191]

---

188 *E.g.* Stone v. E.F. Hutton & Co., Inc., 898 F.2d 1542, 1543 (11th Cir. 1990)

189 *See* ANTON G. MAURER, PUBLIC POLICY EXCEPTION UNDER THE NEW YORK CONVENTION: HISTORY, INTERPRETATION, AND APPLICATION 71 (rev. ed. 2013) (stating that facts that may support the defenses under the Art. V(1) cannot be used to raise the public policy exception where the opposing party did not raise enumerated defenses under Art. V(1)).

190 Victrix S.S. Co. v. Salen Dry Cargo AB, 825 F.2d 709 (2nd Cir. 1987).

191 Skandia Am. Reinsurance Corp. v. Seguros Law Republica, No. 96-CIV-2289 SS, 1996 WL 622559 (S.D.N.Y. Sept. 20, 1996).

In Victrix, the parties concluded a charter agreement, including an arbitration clause requiring the arbitration proceeding to be held in London. [192] Shortly after, the debtor filed for bankruptcy in Stockholm.[193] Upon the debtor's default, the creditor sought and obtained a favorable award in London[194] and moved to New York to have the award confirmed under the New York Convention.[195] The District Court, however, refused to enforce the London award and decided to defer to the Swedish bankruptcy court's decision on the issue of whether to enforce the London award.[196] In affirming the District Court's decision, the Second Circuit held that enforcing the London award "would conflict with the public policy of ensuring equitable and orderly distribution of local assets of a foreign bankrupt."[197]

In this case, neither the District Court nor the Second Circuit explicitly addressed Art. V(2)(b) of the New York Convention. Still, the courts determined that enforcing the London award, which would cause a payment from the debtor's estate, would conflict with U.S. public policy, giving effect to a foreign state's (Swedish) public policy (bankruptcy proceedings for the equitable distribution of the estate's assets).[198]

In *Skandia*, the insurance contract between the parties contained an arbitration clause, which stipulated that any dispute under the contract would be submitted to arbitration in NY and under NY Law. [199] When the dispute arose concerning payments, the claimant sought and obtained an arbitral award against the defendant, which was a Mexican company.[200] When confirming the award, the District Court found that the award was contrary neither to U.S. public policy nor international comity.[201]

Notwithstanding the fact that the New York Convention was the applicable legislation in both cases, the U.S. courts took not only U.S. public policy but also foreign public policy or international comity into account, respectively. Given *Victrix* and *Skandia*, the question arises as to whether it could be presumed that

192 *Victrix,* 825 F.2d at 711.
193 *Id.*
194 *Id.*
195 *Id.* at 711–12.
196 *Id.* at 711.
197 *Id.* at 714.
198 *Id.*
199 *Skandia,* No. 96-CIV-2289 at 1039.
200 *Id.* at 1040.
201 *Id.* at 1041.

the courts should also consider other states' public policies when deciding to confirm or not enforce an award based on the violation of public policy. The primary problem that arises out of this context is to identify what the applicable law should be when evaluating the public policy ground.

It is noteworthy that not only U.S. courts but also English ones have considered and given effect to the public policy of foreign states.[202] In other words, they have considered the public policy of the non-enforcing forum when asked to consider the public policy of the enforcing one. In so doing, these judiciaries may be giving a subtle message by means of this practice of deviating from the dictate of Art. V(2)(b). On the one hand, countries that are developed and arbitration-friendly—such as the United States and England—take one step back to move two steps forward. It is one step back because the higher the number of the applicable public policies, the greater the risk of non-enforceability.[203] On the other hand, it may be two steps forward because it may create a unified, foreseeable public policy concept at the end.

The hidden message might well lie in the recent trend toward the globalization of the concept of public policy, and the principle of comity.[204] Here, two different camps can be identified: (1) those who argue that the enforcing court should consider not only the public policy of *lex fori* (the law of the enforcing court) but also *lex loci arbitri* (the law of the place of arbitration) or the law of

---

202 *See e.g.* Soleimany v. Soleimany [1999] QB 785 (CA) (Eng.) (refusing to enforce the award on the basis of public policy because the underlying agreement was illegal under Iranian export controls); Westacre Investment, Inc. v. Jugoimport-SP-DR Holdings, [2000] Q.B. 288 (Eng.) (considering the Swiss law together with the English law when deciding upon the public policy defense).

203 *E.g. Renusagar*, AIR SC 860, *translated in* 20 Y.B. COMM. ARB. 681, 692 (1995). In this case, the plaintiff objected to enforcement by raising the public policy defense under the s.7(1)(b)(ii) of the Indian Foreign Awards Act, which is the implementing act of the New York Convention in India. *Id.* In the hope of finding a loophole, the plaintiff claimed that although Art.V(2)(b) requires the violation of public policy of that country, s.7(1)(b)(ii) merely requires "the award will be contrary to public policy." *Id.* at 693–95. Thus, the plaintiff alleged that the court ought to take an into account not only the public policy of India (*lex fori*) but also "public policy of the courts whose law governs the contract or of the country of place of arbitration."*Id.* at 692. In doing so, the plaintiff aimed to enlarge the number of public policy exceptions that would applicable to the dispute. Rightly, the Court held that this interpretation was at odds with the objectives brought by the New York Convention and rejected the claim. *Id.* at 695.

204 See e.g. Gibson, *supra* note 177, at 1259; *ILA's Final Report*, *supra* note 172, at 252.

the place with the closest connection to the underlying contract,[205] and; (2) those who argue that the enforcing court should examine only the public policy of *lex fori* as indicated in the language of the New York Convention.[206]

The book believes that the most persuasive argument is presented by the latter for the following reasons. First, given the language and drafting history of the New York Convention, the literal interpretation should be given more weight to provide a narrow scope of application. The New York Convention does not aim to create a uniform public policy concept. The New York Convention was framed in realistic rather than idealistic terms, and that is what makes it remarkably successful. Second, it can be argued that a strict reading of the language of the Convention would mean awards are delocalized and thus carry no national identity.[207] As a result of this, any given legal system (*lex fori, lex loc arbitri,* or the governing law) may claim its own jurisdiction and make its own determination as to the dispute in question. In principle, Swedish public policy should be a matter for Swedish courts—as one might have expected in *Victrix*, for example—and not for U.S. Courts. Nonetheless, the enforcing court may give effect to the public policy of other countries as a part of the public policy of *lex fori* when determining enforcement of the award for the purposes of comity. This, in fact, was the case in *Victrix,* where effect was given to Swedish public policy.

2.4.2 Federally Governed States

One may further ponder the situation of federally governed states, such as the U.S. and Germany. Here the question arises as to whether the public policy of a single state preempts federal public policy or, indeed, vice versa. In *Laminoirs-Trefileries-Cableries de Lens, S. A. v. Southwire Co.*, a United States Federal District Court sitting in the State of Georgia partly refused the enforcement of an

---

205 Gibson, *supra* note 177, at 1244 n.66 (stating that the mandatory laws of the jurisdiction where the contract is performed are not given adequate weight so much so that the enforcing courts should supervise these matters as well as the public policy of *lex fori*). *See generally* John J. Chung, *In Re Qimonda Ag: The Conflict Between Comity and The Public Policy Exception in Chapter 15 of the Bankruptcy Code*, 32 B.U. Int'l L.J. 89 (2014).

206 *See e.g ILA's Final Report, supra* note 172, at 252–53 (stating that considering other laws is a matter for the tribunal, not for the enforcing court).

207 See *e.g.*, Emmanuel Gaillard, *The Representations of International Arbitration*, 1 J. Int'l Dispute Sett. 271, 279–80 (2010); Margaret L. Moses, The Principles and Practice of International Commercial Arbitration 64 (2008).

arbitral award rendered under French law on the basis of the violation of public policy under the New York Convention. [208] The arbitral award provided that the award debtor, a Georgia corporation, should pay the award to the French creditor party and an additional 5 per cent interest if the payment was delayed.[209] The Court held that the additional 5 per cent interest had the purpose of penalizing rather than compensating under Georgia law; thus, it was deemed not enforceable.[210]

The decision is legitimate since penalty interest provisions are void and unenforceable in the United States. The most striking part of this decision is, however, that the court upheld the other French interest rates in the award not because they did not violate the public policy of the State of Georgia, but rather that of the United States.[211] Some commentators have stated that the public policy exception in Art. V(2)(b) should be interpreted exclusively with reference to federal law—not state law—in the United States.[212]

As a last remark, in international commercial arbitration, where the parties are at arm's length, the courts should not be there to "babysit" but to enforce the award that is left to the arbitrators to enter in the first place.[213] In today's practice, the highest number of national courts apply the public policy of *lex fori*, and this practice should not be abandoned. On the contrary, possible drawbacks on the enforceability of the award may be more likely.

---

208 Laminoirs-Trefileries-Cableries de Lens, S. A. v. Southwire Co., 484 F. Supp. 1063, 1069 (N.D. Ga. 1980).

209 *Id.*

210 *Id.*

211 *Id.* at 1068.

212 E.g. Robert A.J. Barry, *Application of the Public Policy Exception to the Enforcement of Foreign Arbitral Awards under the New York Convention: A Modest Proposal*, 51 TEMPLE L.Q. 832, 838 (1978) (noting that the Convention is ratified by the United States, and the implementing legislation enacted by Congress, and thus it presents federal questions to be determined by federal, and not state, law.)

213 *But see* Gibson, *supra* note 177, at 1266 (stating that the place with the closest connection to the underlying contract should be considered in order to globalize application of public policy in the name of globalization).

2.5 Public Policy Standards: Domestic, International and Transnational Public Policy

The meaning of public policy will likely vary in diverse contexts. For example, a contract may be deemed void because it violates public policy, or an employer's discharge may be contrary to public policy within the context of employment-at-will. Here, of particular interest are arbitral awards because this study primarily centers on the application of public policy in the context of the recognition and enforceability of foreign arbitral awards under Art. V(2)(b) of the New York Convention. Within this context, commentators and courts analyze public policy as a concept consisting of three different dimensions: domestic, international, and transnational.

2.5.1 The Dichotomy Between Domestic and International Public Policy

The dichotomy between the domestic and international public policy is a crucial element for plenty of states today when courts face the issue of determining whether the public policy exception is applicable in the relative dispute. [214] The violation of domestic public policy becomes a current issue when a party departs from moral standards or the mandatory rules that are established by the state for application in domestic disputes within their jurisdiction.[215] Both domestic public policy and international public policy see the public policy exception through the lens of the enforcing court's own law or, in other words, the law of the forum. Whereas domestic public policy applies to purely domestic matters, international public policy becomes a matter of discussion when a foreign element is involved in the dispute.[216] That is to say, domestic public policy brings a national standard for the enforcement of national awards while international public policy (public policy in conflict of laws) establishes the national standard for enforcement of international awards.[217] At this point, the courts of

214 *See e.g.* Denis Coakley Ltd. v. Sté Michel Reverdy, [Cour d'appel of Reims] 23 July 1981, *translated in* 9 Y.B. COMM. ARB.400, 400 (1984) (deciding that "... public policy governing the enforcement of foreign arbitral awards is not domestic public policy, but the public policy of international law of the State where the decision is invoked.")

215 VAN DEN BERG *supra* note 172, at 361; Javier Garcia de Enterria, *The Role of Public Policy in International Commercial Arbitration*, 21 LAW POLICY INT. BUS. 389, 396 (1989).

216 Albert Jan van den Berg, *Why Are Some Awards Not Enforceable?, in* NEW HORIZONS IN INTERNATIONAL COMMERCIAL ARBITRATION AND BEYOND 291, 309 (2005).

217 CHEN, *supra* note 185, at 18–19.

the Contracting States are forced to balance the interests between the necessities of the international commerce and their national public policy, *e.g.*, mandatory laws, fundamental values.[218]

The cases of *Wilko v. Swan*[219] and *Scherk*[220] together offer an excellent example to illustrate the distinction between domestic and international public policy. In *Wilko*, the U.S. Supreme Court held that where the dispute was an entirely domestic matter, the arbitration clause in the parties' margin agreements was invalid under the Securities Act of 1933.[221] In *Scherk*, however, the arbitration clause in an international margin agreement was not deemed invalid, although it was contrary to the domestic securities law in the same way.[222] Although the Court did not refer to the categorization of the domestic or international public policy, it stated that "[s]uch a contract involves considerations and policies significantly different from those found controlling in *Wilko*."[223]

In *Scherk*, the agreement between the parties and the arbitration proceedings were international in several respects. The parties were American and German, and the contract negotiated in several places—the United States, England, and Germany.[224] Moreover, the arbitration clause provided that the proceedings would be held in Paris under ICC rules.[225] The Court considered the arbitration clause as a special forum-selection clause and emphasized that it was "an almost indispensable precondition to achievement of the orderliness and predictability essential to any international business transaction."[226] The Court further pointed out that refusing the arbitration agreement would open the door to "unseemly and mutually destructive jockeying by the parties to secure tactical litigation advantages."[227] An international arbitral award that is considered contrary to a domestic public policy could, quite the reverse, be enforceable according to the international public policy standard of that country. This was the case in *Scherk*,

218 *See* George Schwarzenberger, International Law and Order 28–29 (1971).
219 Wilko v. Swan, 346 U.S. 427 (1953), *overruled by Rodriguez*, 490 U.S. at 477.
220 *Scherk*, 417 U.S. at 506.
221 *Wilko*, 346 U.S. at 434.
222 *Scherk*, 417 U.S. at 516.
223 *Id.* at 515.
224 *Id.* at 508.
225 *Id.*
226 *Id.* at 516.
227 *Id.* at 517.

and the motive behind the international public policy in question was to promote efficient international commerce.[228]

The legislation of some countries' explicitly treats domestic and international public policy differently. For example, Art. 1502(5) of the French Code of Civil Procedure states that a foreign arbitral award may be refused in those cases where the recognition or enforcement of the arbitral award is contrary to international public policy.[229] Other legislation, in contrast, will simply assert the concept of public policy, without differentiating between domestic or international; here, courts tend to interpret the legislation in a way that applies varying standards for domestic and international cases. The Singapore Court of Appeal, for example, adopted this classification, stating that "public policy in the conflict of laws operates with less vigor than public policy in the domestic law."[230] This practice indicates that although the legislation does not explicitly provide any variations, the judiciary is still capable of doing so.[231]

Although it is expected that international public policy has a narrower scope than the domestic public policy, this scope is still mostly at the discretion of the courts, and how much they compromise from their domestic public policy.

2.5.2 Transnational Public Policy

The notion of transnational public policy was introduced by the renowned scholar Pierre Lalive at the ICCA Congress in 1986.[232] Now, it has become a *sine qua non* of international arbitration literature with the intent of creating better standards for the public policy concept. Lalive suggested that the fundamental

---

228 *Id.* at 516. *See also Bremen*, 407 U.S. at 9 (stating that "[w]e cannot have trade and commerce in world markets and international waters exclusively on our terms, governed by our laws, and resolved in our courts.")

229 Décret n°2011-48 du 13 janvier 2011–Art. 1520, Code de procédure civile, *translated in* The French Code Of Civil Procedure in English (2019); Intrafor Cofor v. Gagnant, [1985] 299 Rev Arb, 212/n98 (Fr.) (stating that "international public policy" and "domestic public policy" are two different concepts).

230 Liao Eng Kiat v. Burswood Nominees Ltd. [2004] SGCA 45 (Sing.) *as discussed in* George A. Bermann, *Interpretation and Application of the New York Convention by National Courts*, *in* General Reports of the XIXth Congress of the International Academy of Comparative Law 29, 63, n.256 (Martin Schauer & Bea Verschraegen ed., 2017).

231 *Parsons & Whittemore*, 508 F.2d at 974 (stating that "supranational emphasis" is required rather than the observance of "national political interests.")

232 Lalive, *supra* note 176, at 259.

rules of the law of nations or international trade law be accepted as "transnational public policy" to create a centralized public policy doctrine.[233] Both the Interim and Final ILA Reports have defined transnational public policy as "fundamental rules of natural law,[234] principles of universal justice, jus cogens in public international law, and the general principles of morality accepted by what are referred to as 'civilised nations.'"[235] Thus, transnational public policy is independent of the rules and values of a specific country; it preferably indicates a universal consensus on a set of norms[236], *e.g.*, condemning "piracy, terrorism, genocide, slavery, smuggling, drug trafficking,"[237] prohibition of bribery and fraud or establishing due process.

Transnational public policy is expected to have a narrower scope than international public policy since it requires a certain level of consensus developed over time.[238] As the standards of transnational public policy offer a narrower scope for the non-enforcement of awards, the application by the national courts can be considered as the ultimate point since it maximizes the numbers of enforceable

233 *Id.* at 261.

234 *E.g.* Good faith and prohibition of abuse of rights, *pacta sunt servanda*, the prohibition against uncompensated expropriation, and the prohibition against discrimination. *ILA's Final Report*, *supra* note 199 at 256.

235 *ILA's Final Report*, *supra* note 172, at 259; ILA's Interim Report *supra* note 172, at 218. *But see* Pierre Mayer, *Effect of International Public Policy in International Arbitration*, *in* PERVASIVE PROBLEMS IN INTERNATIONAL ARBITRATION, INTERNATIONAL ARBITRATION 61, 62 (Loukas A. Mistelis et al. eds., 2006) (criticizing the confusion that international public policy in the sense of public international law is sometimes considered to be transnational public policy).

236 Lalive, *supra* note 176, at 311 (noting that transnational public policy has both negative and positive functions. The former concerns avoiding applying foreign law when it is contrary to public policy. The latter has a producing function, positively affecting the arbitrators where there is a matter with fundamental and universal notions of contractual morality). See also Audley Sheppard, *Public Policy and the Enforcement of Arbitral Awards: Should there be a Global Standard?*, 1 TRANSNAT'L DISP. MGMT. 1 (2004)

237 *ILA's Final Report*, *supra* note 172, at 361.

238 ABDULHAY SAYED, CORRUPTION IN INTERNATIONAL TRADE AND COMMERCIAL ARBITRATION 287–88 (2004). ("[W]hen one talks of transnational public policy or universal values, one is at some point bound to refer to values, which are perceived as (1) essential; (2) supported by a large adherence or what in a usual language is called large consensus, let alone a universal one; and (3) therefore requiring immediate application, regardless of any contrary agreement.").

arbitral awards. That is to say, this assumption would mean less application of the public policy exception.

It is difficult to concur with the arguments favoring the application of transnational public policy by national courts for certain reasons. First, charity begins at home. Before searching for universally agreed concepts, a national court should primarily apply its own rules to protect national values. For example, if we assume that the standards of transnational public policy are applied, a jurisdiction governed by Sharia law would have to enforce interest awards since there is no universal consensus on the prohibition requiring non-enforceability. Second, transnational public policy is partly a redundant concept since universally condemned behaviors are already outlawed under national laws and international treaties.[239] Moreover, countries are always capable of adopting universally agreed principles as part of their international public policy if they wish to underscore their international commitments.[240]

Becoming aware of this reality and the reluctance of the national courts to apply the standard, the ILA Report also acknowledged that the actual application of transnational public policy among the Contracting States is limited, although it advocated setting the public policy standard as high as that.[241]

This brings us to the question of what is left of Lalive's initiative. As we mentioned above, transnational public policy is not attributable to a component of any given legal system, nor are the arbitrators an organ of any State.[242] Hence, transnational public policy operates as a device for arbitrators, rather than any national court, which has a duty to observe the concerned State's public policy.[243] Here, transnational public policy should be considered as a part of *lex mercatoria*.[244] If States wish to adopt these rules individually or unify by means of treaties, they are free to do so, which was the case, for example, when the United Nations Convention on Contracts for the International Sale of Goods (CISG) [245]

---

239 Santiago Alvarez González, Liber amicorum Bernardo Cremades 708 (M.A. Fernández Ballesteros & D. Arias eds. 2011).

240 Gaillard, Fouchard, Goldman on International Commercial Arbitration 997 (Emmanuel Gaillard & John Savage eds., 1999).

241 *ILA's Final Report*, *supra* note 172, at 361.

242 Mayer, *supra* note 235, at 64–65.

243 *Id.* at 67.

244 *Id.* at 64; Moritz Renner, *Towards a Hierarchy of Norms in Transnational Law?*, 26 J. Int'l Arbitration 533, 541 (2009).

245 United Nations Convention on Contracts for the International Sale of Goods, Apr. 11, 1980, 1489 U.N.T.S. 3.

was established to unify international sales of goods. Suffice it to say, domestic and international public policies and transnational public policy represent two different universes, the former being for courts and the latter for arbitrators.[246] In this regard, transnational public policy is a necessary tool for arbitrators when the arbitrator refuses to enforce a contract or to apply a given rule, which is at odds with the values deemed to be universally essential.[247]

2.5.3 Public Policy Standard Under the New York Convention

Where the courts of the Contracting States encounter a dispute requiring the consideration of public policy, the question arises which one of the abovementioned types of public policy should apply to the arbitral awards. As it is surmised from the articulation, Art. V(2)(b) of the Convention addresses public policy without differentiating between domestic, international, and transnational public policy. The Convention gives freedom to the Contracting States to outline their public policy.

Theoretically speaking, the enforcing courts are entitled to apply any of the three abovementioned standards, even one as restrictive as the domestic public policy standard. The application of domestic public policy standards, however, mostly obstructs international commerce because, for example, they will generally make the arbitral award subject to every mandatory rule of the Contracting State under the disguise of public policy.The scales have been tipped heavily in favor of international public policy within most Contracting States because of its narrower scope and because pro-enforcement bias is the cornerstone upon which the Convention rests. Today, an overwhelming number of courts and

246 *See* Lalive, *supra* note 176, at 290–91.

247 Mayer, *supra* note 235, at 67.

248 *See Renusagar*, 1994 AIR 860 (highlighting the public policy of the enforcement forum rather than a transnational public policy). *But see* Allsop Automatic Inc. v. Tecnoski snc, Corte d'Apello di Milano, 4 December 1992 (It.), *translated in* 22 Y.B. Com. Arb. 725. (defining public policy as "a body of universal principles shared by nations of the same civilization, aiming at the protection of fundamental human rights, often embodied in international declarations or conventions" in parallel with the definition of transnational public policy.)

249 *See* Bundesgericht [BGer] [Federal Supreme Court] Mar. 8, 2006, 4 P. 278/2005 (Switz.), X. S.p.A. v. Y. S.r.l. *as discussed in* Charles Poncet, T*he Decision of the Swiss Supreme Court ("Federal Tribunal") of March 8, 2006,* 24 ASA Bulletin, 550, 555 (2006).

commentators favor international public policy.[251] That being said, although the courts are expected to narrowly construct the public policy exception under the rubric of international public policy, differences remain because of the very nature of the public policy exception. Here, we are speaking of the lack of a precise definition of the public policy exception itself and the reliance, therefore, on subjective criteria established within the relevant jurisdiction.

2.6 Substantive Public Policy and Procedural Public Policy

2.6.1 Substantive Public Policy

Enforcement of an award might be contrary to public policy due to certain substantive or procedural reasons. The basis on which this happens regarding classification speaks for itself: substantive public policy deals with the merits of an award, whereas procedural public policy concerns the manner in which the dispute was adjudicated.

To catalog the numerous substantive public policy violations that could potentially be applicable in all jurisdictions would be so arduous that one imagines no one would even contemplate doing so. One such list, albeit one of narrow scope, does, however, arise plainly in international law. To wit, it is almost universally agreed that some issues are so central to the public policy of states that no derogation is possible. Examples here include terrorism, piracy, human and drug trafficking, torture, kidnapping, genocide, and slavery.[252] Nevertheless, these acts are today so universally denounced that it is virtually self-evident they contravene public policy.

What is more, these matters seldom arise in international commercial arbitration precisely because it oriented toward cross-border business. Violations of the principles of *pacta sunt servanda,* good faith, and the prohibition of abuse of rights[253] are also contrary to substantive public policy of the forum in general,

---

250 Kenneth-Michael Curtin, *Redefining Public Policy in International Arbitration of Mandatory National Laws*, 64 Def. Counsel J. 271, 281 (1997).

251 *See, e.g., Traxys Europe*, [2012] FCA 276; K.M. v. UAB A. Sabonio Žalgirio krepšinio centras, 3K-3-411/2011 (Lith.); Petrotesting Colombia S.A. & Southeast Investment Corporation v. Ross Energy S.A., Corte Suprema de Justicia [C.S.J.] [Supreme Court], julio 27, 2011, 11001-0203-000-2007-01956-00 (Colom.)

252 *E.g.* HTM LLC v. Fomento de Catalizadores–FOCA S.A.S., Corte Suprema de Justicia, SC8453-2016, Junio 24, 2016 (Colom.); 3 Born, Commercial Arbitration, *supra* note 49, at 3672 n. 1401.

253 The abuse of right doctrine has been recognized by civil law countries such as Turkey or federal states where civil law applies, *e.g.*, Louisiana. In terms of common law

but again this is largely self-evident.[254] While the status of these exceptions is clear enough, many others remain ambiguous in so far as there is debate over whether they can legitimately shelter under the public policy exception. Our concern here is to identify them.

2.6.1.1 Erroneous Application of Substantive Law Is Not a Ground

Before delving into a discussion of the more controversial grounds, it is noteworthy that the misapplication of substantive law does not result in non-enforcement on the grounds of violation of substantive public policy. Thus, the word "substantive" in both cases should not mislead the reader.

It is true enough that substantive public policy gives certain latitude to enforcing courts when they confirm or refuse the enforcement. This is so since the courts must review the award on the merits, albeit to a limited extent, to see if it runs afoul of the state's public policy. Nonetheless, the enforcing court's freedom does not furnish an ability to analyze the application of the law where the losing party argues that the arbitrators are in error in applying the law, [255] and thus making an incorrect substantive

---

systems, it is similar to the doctrine of unconscionability. In U.S. practice, the Supreme Court has held that contracts of adhesion which include mandatory arbitration clauses are enforceable, and state laws are preempted by the FAA where state law prohibits the enforcement of forced arbitration clauses in adhesive contracts due to unconscionability. *See e.g. AT&T Mobility*, 563 U.S. at 340-41; 14 Penn Plaza, LLC v. Pyett, 556 U.S. 247 (2009). Although this book is mainly concerned with international commercial arbitration, it is worth indicating the extent that favorability toward arbitration in federal policy has reached in the United States.

254 *Id.*

255 Although it is related, the erroneous application of law is different than manifest disregard of law, which is a common-law ground for vacatur. 2 DOMKE ON COM. ARB. § 39:16 ("Manifest disregard of the law is different than error in interpreting the law. Manifest disregard of the law, warranting the setting aside of an arbitration award, must go beyond a mere error in the law or failure on the part of the arbitrators to understand or apply the law; it must so affect the rights of a party that it may be said to deprive the party of a fair hearing. The manifest disregard of the law must involve a well-defined, explicit, and clearly applicable law.") In the international context, the "manifest disregard of law" is not enough to apply the public policy exception under the Convention in the United States. *See e.g. Karaha Bodas*, 364 F.3d at 306 (stating the public policy is a narrow exception that "[e]rroneous legal reasoning or misapplication of law is generally not a violation of public policy within the meaning of the New York Convention."); Europcar Italia, S.P.A. v. Maiellano Tours, 156 F.3d 310, 315–16 (2nd

decision.[256]

There is, of course, nothing untoward in the losing party seeking a review of the application of the substantive governing law from the appellate court in the context of litigation. In arbitral proceedings, however, the enforcing court should prioritize the core interests and fundamental values of the society when testing for the public policy exception rather than acting like an appellate court and engaging in the merits. The reasoning behind this is plain enough—the parties leave the dispute at the discretion of the arbitrators, not the courts. The parties would thus obtain what they bargained for, notwithstanding the occasional misapplication of substantive law.

2.6.1.2 Mandatory Laws, Subject-Matter Arbitrability, and the Second-Look Doctrine

The arbitrability concept simply addresses the question of what is—and what is not—arbitrable. The scope of non-arbitrable matters hinges on the relevant jurisdiction. For example, whereas in U.S. practice, disputes arising from employment and consumer contracts are arbitrable, the Turkish Court of Cassation has held that arbitration clauses in employment and consumer contracts are not enforceable in principle because of the power imbalances between the parties.[257]

Cir. 1998) (holding that even the disregard manifest of law is not enough to apply the public policy exception under the Convention).

256 *E.g.* Ssangyong Engineering v. National Highways Authority of India (2019) 3 ARBLR 152(SC) ("It is trite that mere errors of law or even fact are not sufficient to warrant setting aside an arbitral award"); *Quarella SpA v. Scelta Marble Australia Pty Ltd*, [2012] SGHC 166 (holding that arbitrators did not fail to apply the choice-of-law provisions, and even had they done so, the error of law would not be a ground for vacatur); Electrolux Home Prods. v. United Auto. Aero. & Agric. Implement Workers of Am., 416 F.3d 848 (8th Cir. 2005).

257 *Compare* AT&T Mobility, 563 U.S. at 356–57 (allowing enforcement of class action waivers in consumer arbitration agreements) *and 14 Penn Plaza*, 556 U.S. at 247 (finding that a clause in a collective bargaining agreement requiring arbitration of statutory claims is enforceable) *with* 9th Civil Chamber of Turkish Court of Cassation, Case No.: 2013/1773 Decision No.: 2013/6664, dated 25.02.2013 (Kazancı İçtihat Bilgi Bankası) [Kazanci Case Law Database] (Turk.) (finding pre-dispute arbitration agreements binding employees to be unenforceable) *and* 13th Civil Chamber of Turkish Court of Cassation, Case No.: 2008/6195 Decision No.: 2008/12026, dated 20.10.2008 (Kazancı İçtihat Bilgi Bankası) [Kazanci Case Law Database] (Turk.) (finding that arbitration clauses in tour package contracts are invalided because consumer disputes concern public policy and cannot be freely submit to arbitration).

Our purpose here is, therefore, to elaborate the intersection between arbitrability and public policy concepts within the ambit of international commercial arbitration. In this regard, the author will be examining the applicability of mandatory laws and the so-called "second-look" doctrine, which is the place where the arbitrability and public policy concepts come into play.

Mandatory laws are designated by the State to apply to certain matters, regardless of the law that the parties agree to govern their relationship on that matter, with the intent of protecting its overriding public interest.[258] For example, securities regulation, currency control, and competition law may be regulated mandatorily in the enforcing state's national law, whereas the relevant State also considers the sanctions imposed by the United Nations.[259]

Traditionally, some delicate public law matters, as exemplified above, are deemed non-arbitrable owing to their intrusion on the public interest. That is so since arbitration is a confidential and private process that may result in the public interest being inexcusably disregarded.[260] National courts were seen as the exclusive protectors that had a duty and responsibility to safeguard these national interests.[261] As an illustration, when discussing the arbitrability of private federal antitrust claims, the Second Circuit held that "the Sherman Act is designated to promote national interests"[262] so much so that "a claim under the antitrust laws is not merely a private matter" that could be submitted to arbitration.[263]

---

258 Andrew Barraclough & Jeff Waincymer, *Mandatory Rules of Law in International Commercial Arbitration,* 6 Melb. J. Int'l L. 205, 205 (2005); Pierre Mayer, *Mandatory Rules of Law in International Arbitration*, 2 Arb. Int'l 274, 274–75 (1986).

259 *See e.g.* COSID Inc v. Steel Authority of India Ltd (1985) XI Y.C.A. 502 (HC India) (refusing to recognize the award on the basis that it would violate an Indian export ban).

260 *See e.g.*, Walter Mattli & Thomas Dietz, *Mapping and Assessing the Rise of International Commercial Arbitration in the Globalization Era: An Introduction, in* International Arbitration and Global Governance: Contending Theories and Evidence 1, 14 (Walter Mattli & Thomas Dietz eds., 2014); George A. Bermann, *Mandatory rules of law in international arbitration, in* Conflict of Laws in International Arbitration 325, 326 (2010).

261 *E.g.*, Dirk Otto & Omaia Elwan, *Article V(2), in* Recognition and Enforcement of Foreign Arbitral Awards: A Global Commentary on the New York Convention 346, 347 (Herbert Kronke et al. eds, 2010)

262 American Safety Equipment Corp. v. J.P. Maguire & Co. 391 F.2d 821, 827 (2nd Cir. 1968)

263 *Id.*

As international arbitration has become more widespread and an ordinary means of adjudicating disputes, the extent to which mandatory rules of law should hinder arbitrability has become a matter of discussion. As underlined earlier, the United States has a prominent position in international commerce, and the U.S. Supreme Court's decisions on the relevant matters open the gate for the courts of other nations.[264] This was proven again when international antitrust claims were deemed arbitrable by the U.S. Supreme Court in the name of international commerce.[265]

The liberal approach toward arbitrability started with *Scherk*, in which the U.S. Supreme Court held that the disputes under the Securities Act of 1933 were arbitrable.[266] This decision was handed down in the two decades following *Wilko*[267] and broke substantially with it.[268] The arbitrability of statutory rights has continued to expand with the landmark U.S. Supreme Court decision *Mitsubishi*.[269] In *Mitsubishi*, there was a supplier agreement between the Japanese and Puerto Rican parties, which included arbitration and choice of Swiss law clauses.[270] When the dispute arose, the Japanese party sued the Puerto Rican party in the U.S. District Court to obtain an order to compel arbitration in Japan.[271] The

264 Buchanan, *supra* note 28, at 519.

265 *Mitsubishi*, 473 U.S at 616.

266 *Scherk*, 417 U.S. at 514.

267 *Wilko*, 346 U.S. at 427(voiding the arbitration agreement contained in a margin contract between the regular customer and the brokerage house governed by the Securities Act of 1933).

268 Unlike *Wilko*, *Scherk* included an international matter and equal bargaining power. *See* Alberto-Culver Co. v. Scherk, 484 F.2d 611, 617 (7th Cir. 1973), *rev'd*, 417 U.S. 506 (Stevens, J., dissenting) (stating that "[I]n transactions which are sufficiently large and complex that the parties typically contemplate the possibility of future controversy, the method of resolving foreseeable disputes is itself a proper subject of bargaining. In the international market, the inability to agree on a neutral forum quite clearly may have an impact on the price of the transaction, or even the acceptability of a prospective purchaser.")

269 *Mitsubishi*, 473 U.S at 628. (emphasizing that "[b]y agreeing to arbitrate a statutory claim, a party does not forgo the substantive rights afforded by the statute; it only submits to their resolution in an arbitral, rather than a judicial, forum."); *See also McMahon*, 482 U.S. at 220 (holding the Securities Exchange Act and RICO claims arbitrable, even in purely domestic contexts); *Rodriguez*, 490 U.S. at 477 (holding that Securities Act claims are arbitrable); *Gilmer*, 500 U.S. at 20 (holding that claims that arise under the Age Discrimination in Employment Act are arbitrable).

270 *Mitsubishi*, 473 U.S at 638, n.19.

271 *Id.* at 619–20.

Puerto Rican party, however, counterclaimed that there were Sherman Act violations.[272] Upon that, the Japanese party asked the court to compel arbitration of antitrust claims.[273]

Here, we should take a brief moment to explain why a matter at the outset of the arbitral process has become a matter of discussion where we discuss enforcement of arbitral awards. Under Art. II(1) of the New York Convention, courts of Contracting States have a duty to enforce arbitration agreements where the agreement "concern[s] a subject matter capable of settlement by arbitration," *i.e.*, are arbitrable. Stipulating a similar provision for the enforcement phase of arbitral awards, the courts of Contracting States may refuse to enforce the award if the subject matter is non-arbitrable under the laws of *lex fori,* according to Art.V(2)(a) of the New York Convention. Thus, Art. II(1) and Art.V(2)(a) go hand in hand.

In *Mitsubishi*, the U.S. Supreme Court, reversing the court of appeals, held that antitrust claims are arbitrable, and thus agreement to arbitrate is enforceable.[274] This decision, however, came with a caveat—the second-look doctrine.[275] After holding that antitrust matters are arbitrable, the U.S. Supreme Court reserved its right to protect U.S. regulatory interests at the enforcement stage through the public policy exception under Art.V(2)(b). In so doing, the Court did not find the arbitration agreement unenforceable due to the subject matter for now but cautioned the parties to consider beforehand U.S. antitrust regulations in the arbitration process.[276]

Following Supreme Court's leadership in *Mitsubishi*, the mandatory rules of law that had been deemed non-arbitrable have now become arbitrable in most

272 *Id.* at 620–21.

273 *Id.* at 625.

274 *Id.* at 638. (holding that antitrust claims arising out of international commercial disputes are arbitrable).

275 *See id.* n.19; Yves Derains, *Specific Issues Arising in the Enforcement of EC Antitrust Rules by Arbitration Courts*, 2001 EUR. COMPETITION. L. ANN. 323, 323 (2001) (comparing the EU and U.S. antitrust laws); Luca G. Radicati Di Brozolo, *Antitrust: A Paradigm of the Relations Between Mandatory Rules and Arbitration–A Fresh Look at the "Second Look"*, 7 INT'L ARB. L. REV. 23, 23 (2004).

276 *Mitsubishi*, 473 U.S at 638. ("... having permitted the arbitration to go forward, the national courts of the United States will have the opportunity at the award-enforcement stage to *ensure* that the legitimate interest in the enforcement of the antitrust laws has been addressed.") [emphasis added]

cases.[277] The wider the scope of arbitrability has become, the more the public policy defense has drawn attention as a potential counterbalancing mechanism to arbitrability.[278] Bursting out of the cage provided by the non-arbitrability defense at the outset of the arbitral proceeding, matters regarding mandatory laws are increasingly running head first into the stone wall of public policy defense at the stage of enforcement. That is to say, public policy and non-arbitrability have become two concepts that overlap.[279] So much so that a considerable number of commentators have developed the idea that the non-arbitrability defense in Art. V(2)(a) is no longer needed, in so far as the public policy defense in Art. V(2)(b) has already covered its scope and goals.[280]

Given the above results, several issues are arising out of the second-look doctrine. Suffice here to raise the issue of whether the second-look doctrine is opening the doors for merits reviews under the disguise of public policy exception,[281] or the second-look doctrine should be perceived as a development broadening the scope of arbitrable matters and encouraging arbitration. In the U.S. practice, the second-look doctrine has been invoked to challenge arbitral awards on the grounds for violation of public policy only in a few cases.

In Baxter International v. Abbott Laboratories, the Court of Appeals for the Seventh Circuit refused to give the issue of whether the tribunal had correctly applied the U.S. antitrust law a "second look." The Court emphasized that the standard for review is whether "the tribunal took cognizance of the antitrust claims and actually decided them"[282] and whether it showed deference to the arbitral award.[283] *Baxter* is an important case that demonstrates once again how

277 E.g. Attorney General of New Zealand v. Mobil Oil New Zealand Ltd. [1989] 2 NZLR 668, *as discussed in* Karim Youssef, *supra* note 113, at 57.

278 Catherine A. Rogers, *The Arrival of the "Have-Nots" in International Arbitration*, 8 NEV. L.J. 341, 366 (2007).

279 VAN DEN BERG, *supra* note 172, at 360.

280 *E.g. id.* at 368; Bernard Hanotiau, *The Law Applicable to Arbitrability*, *in* IMPROVING THE EFFICIENCY OF ARBITRATION AGREEMENTS AND AWARDS: 40 YEARS OF APPLICATION OF THE NEW YORK CONVENTION 146, 158 (1998).

281 Youssef, *supra* note 113, at 66.

282 Baxter Int'l, Inc. v. Abbott Labs., 315 F.3d 829, 831 (7th Cir. 2003) *as discussed in* Jennifer Vincent, *Oh, What a Tangled Web We Weave: The Implications of Conflicting Domestic on Arbitrability and Award Enforcement*, 38 HASTINGS INT'L & COMP. L. REV. 141, 156–57 (2015) (commenting that the Seventh Circuit erred because in Mitsubishi, the U.S. Supreme Court did not establish a standard for review of whether the tribunal addressed the antitrust issue).

283 Vincent, *supra* note 282, at 157.

reluctant U.S. courts have been to refuse to enforce arbitration agreements and arbitral awards due to the federal policy that favors arbitration.

In contrast to U.S. practice, European courts have not been at all shy in applying the second-look doctrine.[284] In *Eco Swiss China Time Ltd. v. Benetton International NV*, the European Court of Justice held that any award that gives effect to contracts infringing European competition laws should be held contrary to the international public policy of the European Community.[285] Some commentators even have stated that arbitrators may more tend to adjudicate the dispute favoring the European law due to their concerns about the enforceability of the award when they have faced with conflicting laws issues.[286]

Despite the different position of U.S. and EU courts, the author argues that the second-look doctrine is no hostage to fortune, but rather a means to prize open the door to the ready arbitration of a greater range of matters. It has to be said that international commerce has benefited enormously from the fact that the number of arbitrable matters has been expanding over time. Why? Because arbitration allows parties to avoid the idiosyncratic application of national laws in a way that litigation cannot. Although the public policy exception still exists as a safety valve, [287] it does not necessarily mean that all awards concerning the statutory rights are violative of public policy.

---

284 *See e.g.*, Hof's-Gravenhage 24 maart 2005, NJF 2005, 239 (Marketing Displays International Inc. (MDI)/VR) (Neth.), *translated in* 31 Y.B. COMM. ARB. 808 (2006) (refusing to enforce a foreign award on public policy grounds for violation of EU competition law). *See also* Assimakis Komninos, *Dutch Court Refuses to Enforce US Arbitral Awards on Public Policy Grounds for Violation of EU Competition Law*, 19 INT'L DISPUTE RESOL. 5, 7 (2006) ("The judgment of the Court of Appeal of the Hague is a disappointing development for international arbitration in Europe."). Radicati Di Brozolo, *supra* note 275, at 182 ("The judgment... is in contrast with mainstream thinking and case law, according to which... court control over awards should be limited to exceptional circumstances, where there is a manifest disregard of a fundamental principle, or where the contract entered into by the parties amounted to fraud. Where competition law comes into play, such a manifest and flagrant violation would occur, for instance, in the presence of a hardcore price-fixing or market-partitioning cartel.")

285 Eco Swiss China Time Ltd. v. Benetton International, NV [1999] 2 All ER (Comm) (Eng.).

286 Niccolo Landi &Catherine A. Rogers, *Arbitration of Antitrust Claims in the United States and Europe* 13–14 (Bocconi Legal Studies Research, Paper No. 07-01, 2007), available at https://ssrn.com/abstract=962334.

287 Bundesgericht [BGer] [Federal Supreme Court] Mar. 8, 2006, 4 P. 278/2005, X. S.p.A. v. Y. S.r.l (Switz), *translated in* 24 ASA BULLETIN 554 (2006) (stating that the public

From *Mitsubishi*—where the second-look doctrine was born—to today, a more-than-thirty-year application of case law shows clearly that the second-look doctrine has so far proven an idle threat.[288]

2.6.1.3 Punitive Damages

Punitive damages aim to punish certain conduct rather than to compensate. They also have the function of deterrence. The roots of this practice roots are in common law, particularly that of England.[289] However, it is in the United States, where the long-endorsed practice of punitive damages has proven most common. In civil law jurisdictions, however, awarding punitive damages in private actions is prohibited on the grounds that punitive damages are penalizing in nature, which is an exercise of criminal law rather than private law.[290] That leads us to the question of whether an arbitral award of punitive damages is enforceable when it violates the enforcing states' mandatory rules, *e.g.*, the prohibition of punitive damages.

Variation in the way punitive damages are awarded reflects the different approaches to the interpretation of Art. V(2)(b) of the Convention among jurisdictions.[291] As discussed earlier, it is a remedy that is mostly available in common law countries. Nonetheless, the availability of punitive damages in breach of contract cases is recognized only in the United States and Canada.[292] Indeed, in most

---

policy excpetion is a safety valve helping to preserve fundamental rules—which, ideally, every state should ensure are respected).

288 E.g. Margaret L. Moses, *Arbitration Law: Who's in Charge?*, 40 SETON HALL L. REV. 147, 179 (2010); Susan L. Karamanian, The Road to the Tribunal and Beyond: International Commercial Arbitration and United States Courts, 34 GEO. WASH. INT'L L. REV. 17, 52 (2002) (stating that the second-look doctrine is one that "courts have yet to engage in"); Travis Newport, Tortious Interference with International Contracts, 9 CURRENTS INT'L TRADE L.J. 80, 84 (2000) (noting that the Supreme Court's second-look doctrine has not been exemplified so far).

289 *See* Rookes v. Barnard [1964] AC 1129 (Eng.) (distinguishing punitive damages from compensation and emphasizing the function of deterrence in the former).

290 *E.g.* SYMEON C. SYMEONIDES, CHOICE OF LAW 84 (2016); Madeleine Tolani, *U.S. Punitive Damages Before German Courts: A Comparative Analysis with Respect to the Ordre Public*, 17 ANNUAL SURVEY OF INT'L & COMP. LAW 185, 186 (2011).

291 *See* GIRSBERGER & VOSER, *supra* note 291, at 447.

292 Markus A. Petsche, *Punitive Damages in International Commercial Arbitration: Much Ado about Nothing?*, 29 ARBITR. INT. 89, 95 (2013). *But see* Solène Rowan, *Reflections on the Introduction of Punitive Damages for Breach of Contract*, 30 OXF. J. LEG. STUD. 495, 498 (2010) (mentioning the recent trends and decisions under English law and

common law states, punitive damages are a relief typically awarded only in tort actions.[293]

In conjunction with the fact that international arbitration mostly arises from contracts claims and not torts—and the fact that punitive damages are not generally available in civil law countries—an intriguing question arises: Is the award of punitive damages enforceable in states where punitive damages are not enforced or where the scope of enforcement is limited?

Despite the effort devoted to the search for an answer, no consensus has yet emerged. While some courts have held that punitive damages offend the public policy of the forum in question,[294] some have not,[295] the author believes that the standard of public policy defense under the New York Convention should

---

the growing view in academic circles that indicate that punitive damages may be awarded in breach of contract cases in the future). *See also* Andrew Tettenborn, *Punitive Damages—A View from England Symposium: Remedies Discussion Forum*, 41 San Diego Law Rev. 1551, 1561–65 (2004). It is noteworthy that in the United States and Canada, punitive damages are not completely unrelated to tort claims. E.g. Restatement (Second) on Contract § 355 (1981) ("Punitive damages are not recoverable for a breach of contract unless the conduct constituting the breach is also a tort for which punitive damages are recoverable.")

293 *See e.g.*, Ruxley Electronics and Construction Ltd v. Forsyth [1996] AC 344 (HL) 365 (Eng.) ("[T]he 'purpose of the law of contract is not to punish wrongdoing but to satisfy the expectations of the party entitled to performance.... "); *Rookes*, [1964] AC 1129; Addis v. Gramophone Co Ltd [1909] UKHL 1 (Eng.) (establishing that punitive damages are rarely available in breach of contract actions because contractual damages should only compensate and not punish); O'Gilvie v. United States, 519 U.S. 79 (1996); Honda Motor Co. v. Oberg, 512 U.S. 415 (1994).

294 *See e.g.* Saikō Saibansho [Sup.. Ct.] July 11, 1997, 51 no 6 Minshu 2573 (Japan), *translated in* Takashi B. Yamamoto, *Japanese Court Jurisdiction Over International Cases*, 30 Comp. L. Y.B Int'l Bus. 1, 17 (2008) (holding that a foreign judgment ordering punitive damages is contrary to public policy because of its penalizing nature); Corte d'Appello di Venezia, 15 ottobre 2001, n. 1359, Giur. it. 2002, II (It.), *translated in* Lucia Ostoni, *Italian Rejection of Punitive Damages in a U.S. Judgement*, 24 J. L. & Com. 245 (2005) (refusing the U.S. award including punitive damages on the basis that punitive damages are penalizing in nature, and thus similar to criminal punishment). *See also* J.Y. Gotanda, *Charting Developments Concerning Punitive Damages: Is the Tide Changing?*, 45 Columbia J. Trans'l L., 515 (2007) (noting that there is greater receptivity to the award of punitive damages).

295 *E.g.* Dandong Shuguang Axel Corp. v. Brilliance Mach. Co., No. C 00-4480 SC, 2001 WL 637446, at *1 (N.D. Cal. June 1, 2001)(holding that the enforcement of an award ordering punitive damages did not offend U.S. public policy).

be international rather than domestic public policy when evaluating awards including punitive damages. Hence, even though awards of punitive damages are contrary to the domestic policy of the enforcing state, they possibly do not violate the accepted international fundamentals of morality and justice of that country. To conclude otherwise would be an affront, not least because doing so would suggest that justice cannot be served in common law countries that allow punitive damages—even more so in the United States, where the practice is widespread.

Luckily, the recent trends indicate increasing receptivity to punitive damages, which may give arbitrating parties a certain foreseeability in terms of whether the award will likely be enforceable. In *Miller Import Corp. v. Alabastres Alfredo*, for example, the Spanish Supreme Court recognized the U.S. judgment awarding punitive damages, although the Spanish statute is silent on the issue.[296] Although this case is not directly related to arbitral awards, it bodes well for the enforceability of arbitral awards since the arbitral awards are more readily enforceable than the foreign judgments thanks to the New York Convention. Spain is not alone. The current era is witnessing a shift from the old practice of refusing punitive damages to a new-found receptivity to—and enforceability of—such damages in arbitral awards.[297]

2.6.1.4 Penalties and Liquidated Damages

Penalties and liquidated damages are similar concepts that have been approached differently by common and civil law systems. Under common law, liquidated damages aim to pre-estimate the loss in cases of nonperformance or breach of contract.[298] It is a practical tool in cases where the damage is hard to estimate,

---

296 S.T.S., Nov. 13, 2001 (Exequátur, No. 2039/1999) (Spain), *translated in* Scott R. Jablonski, *Translation and Comment: Enforcing U.S. Punitive Damages Awards in Foreign Courts–A Recent Case in the Supreme Court of Spain*, 24 J.L. & Com. 225, 231–43 (2005).

297 *See e.g.* Matthew Parker, *Changing Tides: The Introduction of Punitive Damages into The French Legal System*, 41 Ga. J. Int'l & Comp. L. 389, 424 (2013) (discussing that Article 1371 of the Draft Civil Code of Procedure of France provides for the possibility of judges awarding punitive damages); Volker Behr, *Punitive Damages in American and German Law–Tendencies Towards Approximation of Apparently Irreconcilable Concepts*, 78 Chi. Kent L. Rev. 105, 130 (2003) (stating that German courts frequently award damages that are more punitive than compensatory in cases including infringement of the right to personality and intellectual property rights).

298 *See* Restatement (Second) on Contract § 356.

but where the amount stipulated in the liquidated damages is sufficiently proportionate to compensate. However, if liquidated damages are disproportionate and aim to deter rather than to compensate, they can be deemed as a penalty and consequently unenforceable on the grounds that they contravene public policy.[299] Under civil law systems, parties are free to agree on liquidated damages as well as penalty clauses.[300] That is to say, the penalty clauses may be freely agreed upon by the parties without associating any damages. Penalty clauses, indeed, aim to penalize and, by doing so, encourage the party to perform properly. Similar to the common law understanding, the judge may reduce liquidated damages as well as penalty clauses if extremely excessive.[301] Overall, if the award of penalties

---

299 *Id.* One may question why punitive damages are allowable in the United States but not penalty clauses, as they appear to be similar concepts. To start with, although U.S. courts allow punitive damages in tort actions, punitive damages for breach of contract are not allowed in most U.S. jurisdictions if the breach neither constitutes—nor is accompanied by—a tortious conduct. Charles R. Calleros, *Punitive Damages, Liquidated Damages, and Clauses Penales in Contract Actions: A Comparative Analysis of the American Common Law and the French Code Civil*, 32 BROOKLYN J. INT' L. 67, 69 (2006). This is due to the historical dichotomy between torts and contracts based on early English common law. Historically, the English courts prevented the conditional bond where "a debtor would, for a fee, make a bond to pay a certain sum of money to the creditor, which would be discharged if the debtor timely completed some other performance, such as constructing a bridge, which was the true object of the transaction." *Id.* at 75. Essentially, the old English courts found that framing the liquidated damages in this penalizing manner provided certain unfair advantages for the creditor and violated principles of equity. *Id.* at 109. Unlike common law, penalty clauses in civil law systems are enforceable (although the court may reduce a contractual penalty if extremely excessive). *E.g.* BÜRGERLICHES GESETZBUCH [BGB] [CIVIL CODE], § 343 *translation at* https://www.gesetze-im-internet.de/englisch_bgb/englisch_bgb.html#p1244 (Ger.) As the term suggests, they are deemed to be penalizing rather than compensatory, but regardless, most civil law systems honor freedom of contract and the autonomy of the parties. Although it is not the subject of this book, it is today fair to question the policy justifications for the general rule against punitive damages in contract actions in the United States. It is a paradox that U.S. courts enforce adhesive arbitration agreements concerning consumers and employees but find the penalty clauses freely negotiated by sophisticated parties unenforceable.

300 Ayça Akkayan-Yıldırım, *Cezai Şartin İşlevi Türk ve Amerikan Hukukları Açısından Karşılaştırmalı Bir Değerlendirme, [A Comparative Study on Functions of Penalty Clause under Turkish and American Laws]*, 61 ISTANBUL HUKUK MECMUASI [IUHFM] 357, 405–6 (2003) (Turk.)

301 *Id.*

or liquidated damages are found excessive by the enforcing court, the courts may deny the enforcement under the public policy exception.

In current practice, the enforcing courts are more open to awards of penalty clauses and liquidated damages. For example, in *Pencil Hill Limited v. U.S. Citta di Palermo S.p.A.*, the English High Court upheld an arbitral award directing a penalty clause in the contract between the parties,[302] although under English law such clauses are unenforceable.[303] In this decision, notably, the court gave greater weight to enforcing the international arbitration award than applying its own public policy.[304] To justify this, the Court further stated that the arbitral tribunal had already reduced the excessive payment, and under the governing law—which was Swiss law—the penalty clause would be upheld so long as it were "neither exorbitant nor unconscionable."[305]

This is a pro-arbitration case, an excellent example of a court applying an international public policy standard instead of a domestic one to find an award enforceable. Nonetheless, there is a caveat here. The Court further reviewed the application of the (Swiss) law governing the contract by the arbitral tribunal.[306] This suggests that English courts may potentially find an international arbitral award unenforceable under the Convention if the penalty clause is egregious or punitive enough, or has not been considered by the arbitral tribunal.

Similarly, in *Chelsea Football Club Ltd v. Mutu*, the U.S. Court confirmed the foreign arbitral award based on penalties decided under English law.[307] The reasoning of the court is worth discussing in further detail. Although the award directing penalty clauses are unenforceable under U.S. law, the Court confirmed the award on the grounds that the arbitration award was related to the actual damages and "independently and properly decided pursuant to English law."[308]

Both in *Pencil Hill* and *Mutu*, the courts' assessment of whether the award directing penalties is compatible with the applicable law (Swiss and English law, respectively) is at odds with the purpose of the New York Convention since both

302 Limited v. US Citta Di Palermo S.p.A, [2016] EWHC (QB) 71 (Eng.), *as discussed in* 42 Y.B. Comm. Arb. 535, 535 (2017)

303 Cavendish Square Holding BV v. Talal El Makdessi [2015] UKSC 67 (applying the test of "[w]hether the sum or remedy stipulated as a consequence of a breach of contract is exorbitant or unconscionable…")

304 *Pencil Hill supra* note 302 at 535.

305 *Id.*at 537.

306 *Id.*

307 Chelsea Football Club Ltd v. Mutu, 849 F.Supp.2d 1341 (S.D. Fla. 2012).

308 *Id.* at 1345.

cases re-opened the issues on the merits. The application of the New York Convention requires the enforcing court to decide whether the award is contrary to the public policy of *lex fori* (English and U.S. public policy, respectively). Although both decisions found that the awards were not contrary to the UK and U.S. public policy of *lex fori*, respectively, they still further considered whether the law governing the dispute was applied to the case correctly by the arbitral tribunal.

In comparison, the appropriate application of Art V(2)(b) can be seen in *A. v. R.*[309] In this case, the contract between a Danish company and a Hong Kong company included a liquated damages clause as well as an arbitration clause.[310] Danish law governed the contract.[311] When the Hong Kong High Court asked to enforce the award directing liquidated damages, the respondent invoked the public policy exception under Art. V(2)(b) on the grounds that the liquidated clause is excessive and penalizing, and thus void under the Hong Kong and Danish law.[312] In its decision, the Hong Kong High Court did not consider whether the law governing the contract (Danish law) applied correctly to the dispute. Instead, the Court examined the clause regarding the public policy of *lex fori* (Hong Kong law) and found it enforceable.[313] As the winning party noted, the penalty clause argument may have been raised in the arbitral proceeding or before the Danish Court, as both constituted a proper forum to do so.[314] Thus, unlike *Pencil Hill* and *Mutu*, the enforcing court in *A. v. R.* did not re-open matters "which have been (or ought to have been) determined in an arbitration."[315]

In short, the public policy exception to awards that include penalty clauses or liquidated damages of a penalizing nature is narrower than before.[316] The courts, nonetheless, should not re-evaluate the merits under the applicable law governing the dispute. In order not to re-open disputes on merit, the public policy

---

309 A. v. R. [2009] 3 H.K.L.R.D. 389 (H.C.)
310 *Id.* at para. 6–7.
311 *Id.* at para. 7.
312 *Id.* at para. 40.
313 *Id.* at para. 66–72.
314 *Id.* at para.65
315 *Id.* at para. 24.
316 3 Born, Commercial Arbitration, *supra* note 49, at 3678; *The Supreme Arbitrazh Court Clarifies Russian Public Policy*, Lexology (May 24, 2013), https://www.lexology.com/library/detail.aspx?g=bf8077ed-8ab0-4fed-9f9d-4b18cf643309 (stating that enforcing awards of liquidated damages and penalties does not violate Russian public policy provided that the amount of such damages is not unduly high)

of *lex fori* should be the only concern for the enforcing courts given the dictate of Art.V(2)(b).

2.6.1.5 Interest

Recognition and enforcement of interest awards have been treated variously in different jurisdictions. The most distinct position is held by Islamic law countries where the Sharia law applies. The teachings of the Qur'an expressly prohibit the payment of interest,[317] in other words, *riba*.[318] That being said, the scope of the prohibition against interest is debated among Muslim scholars.[319] Nonetheless, where the prohibition of interest applies, interest awards would not be enforceable on the grounds of public policy.[320] As an intermediate form, some Islamic countries have moved from Sharia to Western-based legal systems. In these countries, interest payments are allowed.[321]

---

317 *E.g.*, Ingo Karsten, *Islam and Financial Intermediation*, 29 STAFF PAP. INT. MONET. FUND 108, 111 (1982) (stating three main reasons: First, to eliminate the tendency for wealth to gather in the hands of a few; second, Islam does not allow gain from financial activity unless the beneficiary of the interest is also subject to a risk of potential lost, and; third, Islam promotes accumulation of wealth through hard work rather than easy-money-making ways such as interest)

318 NABIL A. SALEH, UNLAWFUL GAIN AND LEGITIMATE PROFIT IN ISLAMIC LAW 16 (2nd ed. 1992) (defining *riba* as "[u]nlawful gain derived from the quantitative inequality of the counter-values in any transaction purporting to affect the exchange of two or more species which belong to the same genus and are governed by the same efficient cause.")

319 *Compare* G. Gregory Letterman, LETTERMAN'S LAW OF PRIVATE INTERNATIONAL BUSINESS 43, 48 (1990) (stating that usury is strictly prohibited rather than all kinds of interests) *with* S.H. AMINN, ISLAMIC BANKING AND FINANCE: THE EXPERIENCE OF IRAN 15,25 (1986) (stating that the Qur'an does not allow a liberal interpretation insomuch as that all form of interest is forbidden)

320 *E.g.* REYADH MOHAMED SEYADI, THE EFFECT OF THE 1958 NEW YORK CONVENTION ON FOREIGN ARBITRAL AWARDS IN THE ARAB GULF STATES 200 (2017); Samir Saleh, *The Recognition and Enforcement of Foreign Arbitral Awards in the States of the Arab Middle East*, *in* CONTEMPORARY PROBLEMS IN INTERNATIONAL ARBITRATION 340, 348–49 (Julian D. M. Lew ed., 1987).

321 *See e.g.*, Iraqi Civil Code No. 40 of 1951, Art. 171 (Iraq); Law No. 131 of 1948 (Civil Code), *al Waqā'i' al Miṣrīyah*, vol. 108 bis (a), 29 July 1948, arts. 226–32 (Egypt); Maḥkamat al Naqḍ [Court of Cassation], case no. 810/71, 25 January 2008 (Egypt), *reported in* 1 INT'L J. ARAB ARB. 148, 149 (2009) (finding that interest awarded beyond the legal limitation is not enforceable, but can be separated from the rest of the arbitral award, so that remainder is enforceable).

In Western-based legal systems, interest is legal, but the award of interest may still be subject to a public policy exception. In theory, the award of interest is part of the compensation. It aims to restore the claimant to the position that he or she would have been in if the wrong had not been committed. Nonetheless, high-interest rates will most probably result in excessive amounts in the commercial setting provided that long periods of time have passed after the dispute arises. In this context, escalated interest rates have been treated as though they penalize the breaching party such that there is a conflict with public policy—also known as usury.

In *Buyer (Austria) v. Seller (Serbia and Montenegro)*, the Austrian Supreme Court upheld the District Court's decision to enforce merely the principal amount of the award, denying the enforcement of an interest rate of 73 per cent per year.[322] The Supreme Court reasoned that interest should neither facilitate the unjust enrichment of the creditor nor be intended as a deterrent.[323] As we stated earlier, in *Laminoirs*, the U.S. Court found that 5 per cent excess interest violated U.S. public policy against contractual penalties.[324] It worth bearing in mind that both courts still enforced the awards, only denying the enforcement of the amount they deemed to be excessive.

In conclusion, current practice indicates that if interest is illegal under the *lex fori, e.g.*, Sharia law, then the award will not be enforceable in its entirety, or the award will be enforceable but without the part awarding interest. If interest is allowed under the *lex fori*, then the interest award will be enforceable, but the enforcing court may reduce the interest on the grounds that it is penalizing or partially enforce it if the interest exceeds the legal limitation under the *lex fori*.

2.6.1.6 *Insolvencies and Bankruptcy*

Arbitration and the national bankruptcy courts may "present a conflict of near-polar extremes: bankruptcy policy exerts an inexorable pull towards centralization while arbitration policy advocates a decentralized approach towards dispute resolution."[325] Furthermore, resolving issues through arbitration processes may trigger transparency problems in insolvency

---

322 Oberster Gerichtshof [OGH] [Supreme Court], Jan. 26, 2005, 30 Y.B. COMM. ARB 421 (2005) (Austria).

323 *Id.*

324 *Laminoirs,* 484 F. Supp. at 1063.

325 Societe Nationale Algerienne Pour La Recherche, etc. v. Distrigas Corp., 80 B.R. 606, 610 (D. Mass. 1987).

proceedings.[326] Because arbitration is a private and confidential process, it can conflict with insolvency proceedings for the reason that an unsecured creditor will most likely want to know if another creditor has a privileged claim and the priority ranking of such a claim.

Given these and similar concerns, the question arises here as to what kind of role the public policy exception plays in reconciling arbitration and bankruptcy proceedings. In *United World v. Krasny Yakor*, for example, the Russian Court refused to enforce an ICC award against Krasny Yakor—a state-owned entity—holding that enforcement would lead the losing party to declare bankruptcy so much so that the effects of bankruptcy would harm the social and economic stability of Russia.[327] Nonetheless, this kind of broad application of a public policy exception is, indeed, exceptional.

In most of the cases, the issue actually arises from the mandatory bankruptcy laws of *lex fori*. That is to say, bankruptcy laws can form a part of the public policy in cases that the losing party had filed for bankruptcy in the same jurisdiction where the enforcement is sought. For example, most jurisdictions require mandatory stay when the debtor files for bankruptcy.[328] Here, the jurisdiction where the enforcement is sought may refuse to enforce the award on public policy grounds where a failure to stay the proceedings is considered violative of the principle of equal treatment of the creditors so much so that it constitutes a part of public policy.[329]

In *In Re Fotochrome, Inc.*, for example, the Japanese creditor corporation and the U.S.-incorporated debtor company proceeded to arbitration in Japan.[330] While the arbitration was pending, the U.S.-incorporated company filed for bankruptcy.[331] In affirming the District Court's decision,[332] the Second Circuit

326 Jonathan Sutcliffe & James Rogers, *Effect of Party Insolvency on Arbitration Proceedings: Pause for Thought in Testing Times*, 76 ARB. 277, 279 (2010).

327 [United World Ltd., v. Krasny Yakor] Fed. Com. Ct. of Volga-Vyatka Cir., Case No. A43-10716/02-27-10isp (2003) (Russ.) *as discussed in* Funke Adekoya, *The Public Policy Defense to Enforcement of Arbitral Awards: Rising Star or Setting Sun?*, 2 BCDR INT'L ARB. REV. 203, 215 (2015).

328 Gabrielle Nater-Bass & Olivier Mosimann, *The Award and Courts–Effects of Foreign Bankruptcy on International Arbitration in* 2011 AUSTRIAN Y.B. ON INT'L ARB. 163, 177 (Nikolaus Pitkowitz et al. eds, 2011).

329 *Id.*

330 *Fotochrome*, 517 F.2d at 512.

331 *Id.* at 514–15.

332 In re Fotochrome Inc., 377 F. Supp. 26, 27 (E.D.N.Y. 1974) *affd sub. nom.* Fotochrome, Inc. v. Copal Co., 517 F.2d 512 (2nd Cir. 1975).

observed that the bankruptcy court's order to stay all proceedings had no effect on the arbitral tribunal presiding in Japan. Thus, a foreign award against the bankrupt defendant could be recognized so that the creditor would be able to use the award as evidence in U.S. bankruptcy proceedings.[333] Unlike the U.S. Court, the French *Cour de cassation*, when refusing to recognize and enforce a foreign award, held that "with respect to bankruptcy matters, the stay of proceedings is a rule of both national and international public policy."[334]

Similar to the U.S. courts, German courts have also enforced the foreign award against the insolvent German party where the enforcement is sought in Germany. In *H v. F in liquidation*, for example, the German Court held that the violation of German bankruptcy law when registering a non-final or insufficiently final claim in the insolvency register was not a serious defect, and thus was not contrary to international public policy.[335] In *Buyer v. Seller*, the German Court made a distinction between the recognition and enforcement of an award and attaching the assets, holding that the enforcement of an arbitral award against the insolvent party not be violative of German public policy because enforceability of a foreign arbitral award was not an executory measure that was prohibited under the German Bankruptcy Act.[336]

In *Indosuez International Finance B.V. v. OAO AB Inkombank*, the Russian lower court refused the recognition and enforcement of the London award against the debtor who was in liquidation in Russia on the basis of a violation of public policy. [337] The appellate court overturned the lower court by holding that a public policy exception is possible "only in those isolated cases when the application of the foreign law could produce a result that is impermissible from the

333 *Fotochrome*, 517 F.2d at 518–19.

334 Cour de cassation [Cass.] [supreme court for judicial matters] 1e civ., May 6, 2009, n°08-10.281, JCP Ed. Gen. 2009, n°20, May 13, 2009, act. 135 (Fr.), *as discussed in* Dany Khayat, *Bankruptcy and Arbitration Laws in France, in* Mayer Brown, International Arbitration Perspectives on Insolvency 15, 16 (2010).

335 Rechtsprechung der Oberlandesgerichte in Zivilsachen [OLGZ] [Higher Regional Court in Civil Matters] Jan. 4, 2012, No. 9 Sch 2/09 (Ger.); Bundesgerichtshof [BGH] [Federal Court of Justice] Dec. 20, 2012, III ZB 8/12 (Ger.), *as reported in* 38 Y.B. Comm. Arb. 379, 381 (2013).

336 Oberlandesgericht [OLG], Sep.2 1999, 8 Sch 01/99, *reported in* 29 Y.B. Comm. Arb. 697, 697–99 (2004).

337 [Federal Arbitrazh Court], KG-A40/8723-05-P, 22 September 2005, *reported in* 33 Y.B. Comm. Arb. 678, 678 (2008).

perspective of Russian legal consciousness" so that enforcement of the award did not violate the Russian public policy.[338]

The above examples indicate that, although it is rare, when mandatory bankruptcy laws are deemed part of the public policy, they can lead the non-enforcement of the award. Other than the situations above, the award creditor may attempt to have the award enforced in a third country where the assets of the insolvent company are located.

In *Brostrom Tankers*, the issue was whether enforcement of a foreign arbitration award ordering payment of a certain sum of money violated public policy.[339] In this case, the plaintiff and defendant were a Swedish and a Spanish company, respectively.[340] The Swedish company sought to enforce the award in Ireland because the plaintiff believed that there was an intercompany debt owed to the Spanish company by an Irish company.[341] The subtle point in this case is that the Spanish bankruptcy court had ordered the suspension of payment in effect that the Spanish defendant could pay only 10 per cent of all debts to its creditors.[342] Emphasizing a pro-arbitration bias, the Irish Court considered Art. V(2) of the Convention explicitly referred to "the public policy of that (*enforcing court's*) country" [emphasis added] and decided that Spanish bankruptcy law had no bearing on Irish public policy.[343] Similarly, in the *supra* Second Circuit case, *Victrix,* the defendant was subject to Swiss bankruptcy proceedings.[344] Unlike the Irish Court, the U.S. Court refused to enforce the London arbitration award against the bankrupt Swedish defendant, holding that enforcement would result in a payment from the debtor's estate, and this would conflict with a U.S. public policy giving effect to Swedish public policy.[345]

Although both *Fotochrome* and *Victrix* were decided by the Second Circuit, in *Fotochrome,* there was a U.S. bankruptcy proceeding.[346] In Victrix, *however,*

---

338 *Id.* at 682.

339 Brostrom Tankers AB (Sweden) v. Factorias Vulcano SA (Spain), [2004] IEHC 198 2003 44 SP (Ir.), *reported in* 30 Y.B. Comm. Arb. 591 (2005).

340 *Id.*

341 *Id.*

342 *Id.* at 592.

343 *Id.* at 598 (holding that "[t]here is no aspect of Irish public policy which could justify a refusal of an enforcement order even assuming that all of the foreign legal questions are decided in favour of the defendant.")

344 *Victrix,* 825 F.2d at 709.

345 Id. at 714.

346 *In re Fotochrome*, 377 F. Supp. at 27. *affd sub. nom. Fotochrome*, 517 F.2d at 512.

there was a foreign bankruptcy proceeding,[347] and the Second Circuit observed the strong U.S. pledge to universalism when foreign bankruptcy proceedings involve.[348]

To draw a conclusion from these cases, some courts have observed the mandatory rules of their insolvency laws and decided whether the award violated the public policy. The majority of courts, however, have found no violation of public policy when they recognize and enforce the award if the creditor uses the award as proof of a claimed debt to participate in the proceeds of the liquidation.

2.6.2 Procedural Public Policy

2.6.2.1 The Gist: Violation of Fundamental Procedural Rules

Arbitration has often been praised for being less time consuming than litigation since it has far fewer rules. This, however, does not mean that arbitration offers a less fair adjudication. In this regard, the procedural public policy exception becomes a matter of discussion where the arbitral procedure suffers from serious irregularities such as fraud or bribery, violation of the right to be heard, or a lack of impartiality.[349]

To secure procedural fairness, Art. V(1)(b) provides the non-recognition of arbitral awards where the losing party "was not given proper notice of the appointment of the arbitrator or of the arbitration proceedings or was otherwise unable to present his case." In the same vein, Art. V(1)(d) ensures that the arbitral proceeding is conducted in accordance with the parties' agreement or the law of the situs. Art. V(1)(b) and Art. V(1)(d) are related to, but distinguishable from, Art. V(2)(b).[350] First, the procedural public policy exception requires a gross violation, and second, courts must consider ex officio the violation of procedural public policy, even when not raised by parties.

As stated earlier, the public policy exception under Art. V(2)(b) operates as a blanket provision. The losing parties tend to raise the defense of procedural unfairness both under Art. V(1)(b) or Art. V(1)(d) and Art. V(2)(b). [351] This is

347 *Victrix*, 825 F.2d at 711.

348 Jay L. Westbrook, *Theory and Pragmatism in Global Insolvencies: Choice of Law and Choice of Forum*, 65 Am. Bankr. L.J. 457, 482 (1991).

349 3 Born, Commercial Arbitration, *supra* note 49, at 3684; New York Convention Guide, *Article V(2)(b)*, http://newyorkconvention1958.org/index.php?lvl=cmspage&pageid=10&menu=626&opac_view=-1 (last visited Feb. 27, 2022)

350 *See* 3 Born, Commercial Arbitration, *supra* note 49, at 3493.

351 Inae Yang, *Procedural Public Policy Cases in International Commercial Arbitration*, 69 Disp. Resolution J. 61, 65 (2014).

true even though the breach does not amount to a violation of procedural public policy, but merely that the losing party believes that invoking the public policy exception will be more striking in the eyes of an enforcing court, so strengthening the defense.[352] Thus, a question arises as to what the standard is for an enforcing court when deciding whether there is a violation of procedural public policy. For example, should a U.S. court evaluate an international arbitral award under the due process standards established by the Fifth and Fourteenth Amendments of the U.S. Constitution?

As we stated earlier, *lex fori* is the applicable law when deciding whether there is a public policy exception under Art.V(2)(b). Because the public policy ground for non-enforcement should be construed narrowly, the courts have tended to uphold the arbitral awards even though they do not provide all the requirements of procedural fairness under the relevant *lex fori*. Hence, for example, in the United States, when the arbitral procedure has not provided all the due process requirements, the courts have found that the award is still enforceable so long as the parties have had "the opportunity to be heard at a meaningful time and in a meaningful manner."[353]

Procedural irregularities, which may cause the non-enforcement of an award under procedural public policy, are neither exclusive nor universally agreed. Where the award was obtained by means of bribery or fraud, it is universally established that it amounts to a violation of procedural public policy. However, it is not easy to say the same thing where the award fails to provide sufficient reasoning. After briefly stating the basic concepts, our purpose here is to discuss matters which have not been settled yet.

---

352 Felix Dasser, *International Arbitration and Setting Aside Proceedings in Switzerland: A Statistical Analysis*, 25 ASA Bul. 444, 456 (2007); Van den Berg, *supra* note 172, at 300.

353 *E.g.* 3 Born, Commercial Arbitration, *supra* note 49, at 3683. It should be noted that the courts apply this standard when determining whether due process defense applies under Art. V(1)(b). However this could be also applicable to the Art.V(2)(b). *See* Generica Ltd. v. Pharm. Basics, Inc., No. 95 C 5935, 1996 WL 535321, at *3 (N.D. Ill. Sept. 18, 1996), *aff'd*, 125 F.3d 1123 (7th Cir. 1997) (stating that losing parties' defense of Article V(2)(b) is duplicative of the due process defense under Article V(1)(b). Thus the Court would treat the two defenses as one).

2.6.2.2 *Prohibition of Corruption and Fraudulent Conduct*

It is almost universally agreed that corruption is prohibited, so much so that it is classified now as part of transnational public policy.[354] Corruption is mostly a matter of discussion when the contract involves an arbitration clause procured by public officials through a bribe. Because one of the most commonly known types of bribery involves public officials, the majority of the disputes involving bribery in arbitration fall within the scope of investment arbitration, where the parties are foreign investors and host states. That is to say, if the alleged bribery is based on a contract, not an investment treaty, then the New York Convention applies, otherwise it is governed by ICSID.[355]

Refusal to enforce the awards on the grounds of public policy is generally the case where the "commission payments" made to a public official to conclude a contract at issue.[356] It is noteworthy that enforcing courts tend to uphold the award, notwithstanding bribery, where the alleged bribery has been considered and handled in the award by the arbitral tribunal. Thus, the exception of public policy is construed narrowly.[357]

Although the prohibition against fraudulent conduct is not as widely recognized as the prohibition of corruption, there is an emerging consensus in this direction.[358] Within the context of arbitration, fraud can be defined as a knowing misrepresentation in the underlying contract or falsity intended to induce the tribunal or the adverse party to act in a manner that materially and detrimentally

---

354 Bernardo M. Cremades & David J. A. Cairns, *Trans-national Public Policy in International Arbitral Decisionmaking: The Cases of Bribery, Money Laundering and Fraud, in* ARBITRATION: MONEY LAUNDERING, CORRUPTION AND FRAUD, DOSSIERS OF THE ICC INSTITUTE OF WORLD BUSINESS LAW 65,67 (Kristine Karsten & Andrew Berkeley eds., 2003) (stating that the main reason behind this universal acceptance could be traced back to the Foreign Corrupt Practices Act—and then with the lobbying efforts of the United States—to the OECD Convention on Combating Bribery of Foreign Public Officials in International Business Transactions).

355 *E.g.* World Duty Free Co. Ltd v. Kenya (Respondent) (ICSID Case No. ARB/00/7); Metal-Tech v. Republic of Uzbekistan (ICSID Case No. ARB/10/3)

356 Lemenda Trading Co. v. African Middle East Petroleum Co., [1988] QB 448 (High Court, England); Cour d'appel [CA] [regional court of appeal] (1Ch. C), civ., Sep. 30, 1993 *as discussed in* Otto & Elwan *supra* note 289 at 375.

357 Cremades & Cairns, *supra* note 354, at 79.

358 Carolyn B. Lamm, et al., *Fraud and Corruption in International Arbitration in* LIBER AMICORUM: BERNARDO CREMADES 699, 715 (Miguel Angel Fernandez-Ballester & David Arias eds. 2010); Cremades & Cairns, *supra* note 354, at 65,76.

affects the tribunal's decision regarding the adverse party.[359] In this regard, if the alleged fraud regarding the underlying contract is alleged during the arbitral proceeding, the enforcing court will most probably not review the merits.[360] When the alleged fraud—*e.g.*, perjury, fabricated documents—takes place in the arbitral proceeding to obtain a favorable award and cannot be invoked during the proceeding, it is more likely that the alleged fraud can be considered by the enforcing court and result in non-enforcement.[361]

2.6.2.3 The Right to Be Heard

As one of the most essential rights—the right to be heard—empowers each party to present their cases fully. In other words, the parties cannot be deprived of their days in an arbitral hearing. The right to be heard encompasses "the right to be summoned to a hearing in due time,"[362] the opportunity to respond to the adverse party's statements, submit evidence, and view the case file.[363] However, if the parties have sufficient opportunity to present their cases but have failed to do so, then they will be stopped from invoking it as a defense.[364]

Because the violation of the right to be heard is explicitly protected under Art.V(1)(b) and because the public policy exception under Art.V(2)(b) ought to be interpreted narrowly, national courts tend to hold that not every violation of the right to be heard constitutes a violation of public policy.[365] In one case, the

---

359 Yang, *supra* note 351, at 61; Carolyn B. Lamm, et al., *supra* note 358 at 699.

360 *E.g.*, Karaha Bodas Co. LLC v. Perusahaan Pertambangan Minyak Dan Gas Bumi Negara, [2007] 4 H.K.L.R.D. 1002 (H.K.); *Europcar Italia*, 156 F.3d at 315.

361 *E.g.*, Karppinen v. Karl Kiefer Mach. Co., 187 F.2d 32, 35 (2nd Cir. 1951); Westacre Investments Inc. v. Judoimport-SDPR Holdings Co. [1999] 3 All ER 864 (Eng.); Born, *supra* note 14, at 1109.

362 *E.g.* Bayerusches Oberstes Landesgericht [BayObLG] [Bavarian Higher Regional Court], 4Z Sch 50/99, Mar. 16, 2000 (Ger.), *translated in* 27 Y.B. Comm. Arb. 445, 446 (2002).

363 Bundesgericht [BGer] [Federal Supreme Court] Mar. 2, 2017 4A_405/2016 (Switz.).

364 *E.g.* Tribunal fédéral [TF] [Federal Tribunal] Feb. 26, 2015 4A_374/2014 (Switz.), *reported in* 41 Y.B. Comm. Arb. 567, 571 (2016) (stating that the defendants were not estopped from raising the public policy defense because they had had no opportunity to raise it in the arbitral proceeding); Tribunal fédéral [TF] [Federal Tribunal] Oct. 18, 2004 4P. 104/2004 (Switz.), *reported in* 23 ASA Bul. 164, 169–70 (2005).

365 *E.g.* Stuttgart Oberstes Landesgericht [OLG Stuttgart] [Stuttgart Higher Regional Court] July 30, 2010, 1 Sch 3/10, SchiedsVZ 2011 49 (Ger.) (finding that the right to be heard and public policy are not violated when the tribunal does not notify the parties of its intended views); Daniel Girsberger & Nathalie Voser, International

Dutch Court did not enforce the award on the grounds of public policy, where the arbitrator failed to submit the adverse party's documents to the appellant.[366] Nonetheless, the overwhelming number of cases examined by the author reveals that the public policy exception has been invoked under Art.V(1)(b) almost all the time, yet has seldom been successful.[367]

2.6.2.4 *Lack of Impartiality*

In the event that the tribunal or one of the members of the tribunal favors one of the parties or is prejudiced as to the subject matter of the dispute, then the award may not be enforced under the New York Convention. The lack of impartiality is generally invoked under Art.V(1)(b), Art.V(1)(d) and/or Art.V(2)(b) although the public policy exception in this regard is more general compared to other grounds.[368] In either case, the appearance of bias does not suffice, and thus actual bias should be proven.

For example, in line with this heightened standard, in *FDIC v. IIG Capital LLC*, the Eleventh Circuit found that the arbitrator's failure to disclose prior relationships with the defendant's counsel was a not a bar for enforceability on the ground that "mere appearance of bias or partiality is not enough" for non-enforcement.[369]

ARBITRATION: COMPARATIVE AND SWISS PERSPECTIVES 431,454 (3rd ed., 2016); Stefan Michael Kröll, *Commentary on the German Arbitration Law (10th Book of the German Code of Civil Procedure), in* ARBITRATION IN GERMANY: THE MODEL LAW IN PRACTICE 443, 469 (2nd ed., 2015).

366 (Hof) Amsterdam 16 juli 1992 NJ 1994, 181 HKB (G.W.L. Kersten & Co. B.V. / Société Commerciale Raoul-Duval et Cie (Neth.), *translated in* 19 Y.B. COMM. ARB. 708, 708–09 (1994).

367 The research was conducted through analysis of the cases on the LexisNexis, WestLaw and KluwerArbitration databases by using the keywords "right to be heard," "public policy," "New York Convention," and/or "unable to present his case."

368 3 BORN, COMMERCIAL ARBITRATION, *supra* note 49, at 3586-87.

369 *E.g.*, F.D.I.C. v. IIG Capital LLC, 525 F. App'x 904, 905 (11th Cir. 2013) (*quoting* Univ. Commons-Urbana v. Universal Constructors, Inc., 304 F.3d 1331, 1340 (11th Cir. 2002)). *See* Nikolay Viktorovich Maximov v. Open Joint Stock Company "Novolipetsky Metallurgichesky Kombinat," [2017] EWHC 1911 (Eng.), *reported* in 42 Y.B. COMM. ARB., 558, 561–63 (2017).

Causation is also necessary to successfully invoke the public policy exception. In this regard, it is necessary to prove that a reasonable suspicion of partiality exists, and the partiality affected the arbitrator when entering an award.[370]

2.6.2.5 Lack of Reasons

It has been often said there is a split between civil law and common law jurisdictions as to whether an award should necessarily include reasoning despite the fact that civil court decisions generally have much less reasoning then common law court decisions.[371] Broadly speaking, civil law systems are more prone to require an arbitral award to have a reasoning, whereas common law systems are not. This is based on an old common law practice in which arbitrators delivered their decisions in a separate confidential form to the parties in order to exclude the courts from reviewing the merits.[372]

The New York Convention does not specify that the lack of reasoning as a ground for non-enforcement. In these cases, the parties are prone to invoke Art.(V)(2) as well as Art.(1)(b) and Art.(1)(d) where the award is unreasoned.[373] On the other hand, Art. 31 of the UNCITRAL Model Law requires that the award should contain reasoning, unless the parties agree otherwise, but does not specifically set forth the absence of reasoning as a ground for non-enforcement.

At this point, the national laws and case law become important to demonstrate how receptive the jurisdictions are to an award that does not include a reasoning, which can suggest an idea when determining whether an unreasoned award violated Art.(V)(2). The national laws vary as to whether an award should contain reasoning. For example, although Belgium adopted UNCITRAL, the Belgian legislator set forth the lack of reasoning of the award as a ground to set

---

370 *E.g.*, A & Ors v. B & Anor [2011] EWHC 2345 (Comm) (Eng.) (finding that the mere fact merely because the arbitrator acted as counsel for one of the firms involved in the arbitration does not suffice to establish bias).

371 S. I. Strong, *Writing Reasoned Decisions and Opinions: A Guide for Novice, Experienced, and Foreign Judges*, 2015 J. Disp. Resol. 93, 101 (2015); Yang, *supra* note 351, at 72.

372 Tame Shipping Ltd v. Easy Nav. Ltd [2004] EWHC (Comm.) 1862 (Eng.)

373 *See e.g.* Corte Cost., Cass., 8 febbraio 1982, n.722, Foro it., 1982, I, 2285 (It.) *as discussed in* Aldo Frignani, *Interpretation and Application of the New York Convention in Italy, in* Recognition and Enforcement of Foreign Arbitral Awards: The Interpretation and Application of the New York Convention by National Courts 561, 567 (George A. Bermann ed., 2017)

it aside, a move not originally stipulated in UNCITRAL.[374] Some national laws, on the other hand, are more liberal. Art. 45 of the English Arbitration Act 1996 explicitly sets forth that where the parties exclude reasoning, this agreement is also considered "to exclude the court's jurisdiction" in the matter.

As with legislation, case law is also variable. In cases where the national courts deem themselves as appellate courts, they interpret the public policy exception more extensively. The Georgian Court, for example, held that an award absent from reasoning is violative of procedural public policy.[375] The Greek Supreme Court, however, found that "the lack of reasons in the arbitral award is not in itself contrary to" public policy.[376] That being said, it is important to distinguish the situation where the parties agreed on the award would have a reasoning in their contract. In these situations, the Canadian appellate court found the award in violation of public policy, not because of a lack of reasons, but because the award did not reflect what the parties bargained for.[377]

Although we commenced our discussion by stating that there is a split between common law and civil law, with the far-reaching power of international commercial arbitration, it has been recently noticeable that civil jurisdictions have become more welcoming to unreasoned awards. Recruiting the above examples, high courts of civil law countries, *e.g.*, Greece, have decided that unreasoned awards are not violative of public policy. Similarly, Brazil[378] and Switzerland,[379] civil law countries both recognize an unreasoned award under the

---

374 Maud Piers & Dirk de Meulemeester, *The New Arbitration Law–Belgium Adopted the UNCITRAL Model Law*, 9 Asian Int'l Arb. J. 147, 179–80 (2013); Olivier van der Haegen, *Belgium in the Spotlight*, Kluwer Arb. Blog (Apr. 30, 2014), http://arbitrationblog.kluwerarbitration.com/2014/04/30/belgium-in-the-spotlight/

375 Nata Ghibradze, *Georgia–Positive Changes in the Caucasus Region?!*, Kluwer Arb. Blog (Dec. 1, 2015), http://arbitrationblog.kluwerarbitration.com/2015/12/01/georgia-positive-changes-in-the-caucasus-region/

376 Areios Pagos [A.P.] [Supreme Court] 1665/2009 (Greece), *reported in* 36 Y.B. Comm. Arb., 284, 284–86 (2011.)

377 *See* Smart Systems Technologies Inc. v. Domotique Secant Inc., [2008] QCCA 444 (Can.), *reported in* 33 Y.B. Comm. Arb. 464, 464 (2008); Schreter v. Gasmac Inc., [1992] 7 O.R. (3d) 608, *as discussed in* Yang, *supra* note 351, at 65.

378 S.T.J. No. 5.692/US, Relator: Ministro Ari Pargendler 20.08.2014, Superior Tribunal de Justiça Jurisprudência [S.T.J.J.], 01.09.2014, 1 (Braz.), *as discussed in* Baker & McKenzie, Baker and McKenzie International Arbitration Yearbook 2014–2015 54 (2015).

379 Bundesgericht [BGer] [Federal Supreme Court] Feb. 7, 2017 4A_478/2016 (Switz.), *reported in* 30 ASA Bull. 591 (2012).

New York Convention. Thus, this recent trend is a positive step and in harmony with the narrowly construed Art.V(2)(b) of the New York Convention.

2.6.2.6 Robot Justice: Artificial Intelligence (AI) and Arbitration

Is there any chance in the future that we will witness the extinction of arbitrators because AI devices will replace them to acquire a more predictable award, or is this just a myth because AI cannot be anthropomorphized since they are not capable of replacing emotions such as feeling empathy?[380]

Although AI seems to be a breakthrough technology in the twenty-first century and aimed toward improving human lives, this does not mean that it does not portend risks. AI differentiates from other inventions in terms of autonomy, foreseeability, and causation, and this is where AI systems become complicated.[381] Even though engineers can adapt internal concepts, they could not predict AI system's response to the problems they face.[382] When we look at some instances, Google's new AI-used app, which recognized faces, has recently tagged black people as gorillas.[383] Further, another called Correctional Offender Management Profiling for Alternative Sanctions (COMPAS), which is being employed by U.S. courts to assess the risk criminals will likely re-commit crime after release, is alleged to be biased against people of color.[384]

---

380 Dyalá Jiménez-Figueres et al., *Report on the VIII Congress on International Commercial Arbitration–ICC Costa Rica 2017*, *in* Revista Brasileira de Arbitragem 182, 186 (João Bosco Lee & Daniel de Andrade Levy eds., 2017)

381 Matthew U. Scherer, *Regulating Artificial Intelligence Systems: Risks, Challenges, Competencies, and Strategies*, 29 Harv. J.L. & Tech 353, 362–73 (2015)

382 *See e.g.*, Taha Yasseri, *Forget killer robots–Wikipedia Bot Study Warns Even 'Good' AI can be 'Scarily Unpredictable'*, DailyMail (Aug. 25 2017), http://www.dailymail.co.uk/sciencetech/article-4823684/Even-good-robots-scarily-unpredictable.html#ixzz56oo1I6hd; Jonathan Tapson, *Google's Go Victory Shows AI Thinking Can be Unpredictable, and That's a Concern,* The Conversation (Mar. 18, 2016), https://theconversation.com/googles-go-victory-shows-ai-thinking-can-be-unpredictable-and-thats-a-concern-56209

383 Sean Keach, *Google Fixed 'Racist' Photos App by Banning Gorillas from Auto-tagging Feature, After Black Developer Was Incorrectly Marked as an Ape*, The Sun (Jan. 15, 2018), https://www.thesun.co.uk/tech/5341606/google-photos-racist-gorillas/

384 Julia Angwin et al.. *Machine Bias*, ProPublica (May 23, 2016), https://www.propublica.org/article/machine-bias-risk-assessments-in-criminal-sentencing (comparing white and black persons both committing crimes. For example, a white criminal in the report had convicted of armed robbery before and was also found guilty of theft due to stealing tools which were worth of $80. Accordingly a black person who had a

These recent examples demonstrate the risk inherent in AI systems and how they are different from the technologies being used in an arbitral proceeding such as hearings by video conference or transferring bulk information via Dropbox or Google Drive. With the advent of AI, the question arises as to whether possible procedural irregularities may amount to a violation of public policy when AI systems are employed in arbitral proceedings.

For purposes of our discussion, we can make a classification of two different situations in which AI systems are employed in an arbitral proceeding. First, although there is a human arbitrator as a decision-making body, arbitrators or arbitration institutions may use autonomous AI systems as an aid, *e.g.*, to understand the case before them.

In this regard, predictive justice is one of the hotly debated areas which cast doubt upon the due process in arbitral proceedings. Predictive analytics is a method that uses machine learning and data mining to analyze the facts of the cases, law, and the reasoning which was retrieved from the past decisions to offer a possible resolution.[385] The method helps arbitrators to understand the case before them and realize the subtle details. Nonetheless, these methods have been criticized for not being enough for now so much so that it could hinder justice.[386] Thus, the heavy use of predictive analytics in the process of decision-making by arbitrators may be invoked as a violation of public policy on the ground that the procedural irregularities caused by the AI system have a substantial bearing on the award. Nonetheless, proving causation seems quite challenging in this case.

Another situation could be a matter where parties in an arbitral proceeding are forced to use AI systems, *e.g.*, to reach the documents. In this scenario, if the system is inaccessible or unfeasible for one of the parties provided that the parties are not agreed on the use of the system or the use of the system is unusual in an arbitral proceeding, then the party may invoke the public policy exception

---

petty crime in her record usurped the equivalent bicycle and scooter, but COMPAS rated black person riskier than her white counterpart, rating 8 and 3 respectively. Overall, according to the report, although 44.9 per cent of Afro-American defendants were labeled higher-risk, they did not commit a crime again after releasing. This figure for white defendants remained 23.5 per cent whereas 47.7 per cent of those labeled lower risk reoffended after releasing.)

385 *E.g.* Case Crunch, http://www.case-crunch.com (last visited Feb. 27, 2022); eBrevia, https://ebrevia.com/ (last visited Feb. 27, 2022).

386 *E. g.* Gauthier Vannieuwenhuyse, *Arbitration and New Technologies: Mutual Benefits*, 35 J. Int'l Arb. 119, 126 (2018).

on the grounds for violation of the right to be heard.[387] This scenario would be easier for proving causation compared to the first scenario.

Moving back to our two-fold classification, secondly, an autonomous AI system may be a decision-maker itself instead of an arbitrator. However, will arbitration laws allow this? An overwhelming number of laws existing today have been written based on a presumption that the arbitrators are human beings.[388] But this is merely a presumption, not a requirement established by law. These laws are not suggesting any data regarding whether an AI system can substitute for an arbitrator, nor do they forbid it. Hence, it can be said there is a loophole that the arbitration practice could benefit from.

Some regulations are more explicit regarding the machine arbitrator. For example, the EU General Data Protection Regulation (GDPR), which entered into force in May 2018, allows machine decision-makers and provides certain rights to the user. For example, it has been commented that under the Art. 13 and 14 of the GDPR, machine arbitrators are not allowed if the algorithms of the machine arbitrators cannot be explained to the users later.[389] On the other hand, some national laws explicitly require arbitrators to be human.[390] In this case, it is most likely that the award will be easily challenged under the public policy exception.

Even though we assume that arbitration laws allow using machine arbitrators, there are still certain concerns that need to be addressed. The main criticism against the machine arbitrators is that they lack emotional intelligence.[391] Great importance has been attributed to the role of emotional intelligence (EI) in an

---

387 *See* THOMAS SCHULTZ, INFORMATION TECHNOLOGY AND ARBITRATION: A PRACTITIONER'S GUIDE 122 (2006).

388 *See e.g.* UNCITRAL Model Law *supra* note 153 Art.11-15 (when referring arbitrators using his or him); English Arbitration Act 1996 c. 23 Art.24–29 (Eng.), http://www.legislation.gov.uk/ukpga/1996/23/data.pdf (referring arbitrators using his or him).

389 Bryce Goodman & Seth Flaxman, *European Union Regulations on Algorithmic Decision-Making and A "Right to Explanation*, 38 AI MAG. 50, 56 (2017).

390 Mohamed S. Abdel Wahab & Ethan Katsh, *Revolutionizing Technologies and the Use of Technology in International Arbitration: Innovation, Legitimacy, Prospects and Challenges, in* ARBITRATION IN THE DIGITAL AGE: THE BRAVE NEW WORLD OF ARBITRATION 27, 48 (Maud Piers&Christian Aschauer et al.,2018) (stating that French and Egypt arbitration laws require arbitrators to be a human); José María de la Jara et al., Machine Arbitrator: Are We Ready?, KLUWER ARB. BLOG (May 4, 2017) (stating that the arbitration laws of Peru, Brazil and Colombia requires arbitrators to be a human).

391 *E.g., id.*; Paul Cohen & Sophie Nappert, *The March of The Robots*, GLOBAL ARB. REVIEW (Feb. 15, 2017), https://globalarbitrationreview.com/article/1080951/the-march-of-the-robots

arbitral proceeding since EI allows arbitrators to understand the parties' hopes, struggles, and expectations from the given legal relationship.[392] The effect of EI and machine arbitrators on the arbitration process is ripe for discussion. However, our purpose here is to indicate that in a proceeding purely arbitrated by a machine, the absence of emotions could be the best ground to argue that the award is not enforceable because it violates the right to be heard and may be argued under the public policy exception.

Before concluding, it is also worth flagging the extent to which it is possible for enforcing courts to decide whether an award is against the public policy because of the procedural irregularities arising from the AI technologies. In order to answer the causation-based questions, it is no doubt that the courts will need technical experts more than ever, which means that "computer scientists first, jurists second."[393]

In conclusion, every new concept can be placed under the umbrella of public policy exception because of fear of the unknown. Future decisions will most probably show us that AI will share the same fate. It has already been observed that the international arbitration community may not be keen to adopt new technological innovations for fear that the change in procedure may lead to non-enforcement of the award.[394] This, however, does not mean that the majority of courts would find that AI per se is against public policy. Nonetheless, the author believes that it is no doubt that the losing parties will invoke it. In this regard, the countries that could not keep up with legal or technological innovations or refuse to enforce an award merely because AI systems were adopted in the arbitral proceeding will see their positions deteriorate against the evolving nature of the international commercial arbitration market.[395]

---

392 José María de la Jara et al., *supra* note 390, at 28. *See also* Harry F. Harlow, *The Nature of Love*, 13 Am. Psychologist 673 (1958) (The psychologist Harlow separated infant monkeys from their mothers shortly after birth and later gave a choice between a wire-mesh metal mother equipped with a milk bottle, and a soft cloth-covered mother with no milk. The baby monkeys chose the cloth mother with no milk, or in other words, the contact comfort over food, thereby indicating the priority of mammals' emotional needs).

393 Paul Cohen & Sophie Nappert, *Case Study: The Practitioner's Perspective*, *in* The Brave New World of Arbitration: The Role of Technology and the Internet in International Arbitration–The Practitioner's Perspective 126, 147 (2018).

394 José María de la Jara et al., *supra* note 390; Cohen & Nappert, *supra* note 391.

395 Jiménez-Figueres et al., *supra* note 380, at 186.

2.6.2.7 One Rising Trend: Third-Party Funding

The 2015 Queen Mary International Arbitration Survey reported that 71 per cent of respondents thought that third-party funding (TPF) in international arbitration is an area that requires regulation.[396] It is not surprising that 68 per cent of the respondents also indicated that the worst characteristic of the arbitration is its cost.[397] There is an increasing growth in TPF in recent years in the context of international commercial arbitration because of the large amounts at stake and the effective enforcement system assured by the New York Convention.

TPF is such an untraceable concept that suggests a limited amount of data. Yet, a slew of regulations, conferences, symposiums, and the like indicates how it is expanding. TPF in the context of international commercial arbitration was regulated for the first time under the IBA Guidelines on Conflicts of Interest in International Arbitration in 2014.[398] Although this guideline is not legally binding, it has often been referred to by arbitrators, arbitral institutions, and courts in terms of ethical concerns such as impartiality and conflict of interest.

To begin, TPF is a relationship where a third-party funder agrees to pay a certain or a whole amount of the claimant/respondent's legal fees and expenses in return for a favorable percentage of the merits of the successful case, or a multiple of the monies invested, or a combination of both.[399] By logical extension, the greater the risk, the more the funder's fee increases. The advantages and disadvantages of TPF are two sides of the same coin. On the one hand, TPF enables to access to justice where the claimant is unable to finance his meritorious claim, or reluctant to do so considering the financial risks. On the other hand, TPF may lead to frivolous claims[400] and specific concerns about transparency in the arbitration proceeding.

---

396 2015 International Arbitration Survey, *supra* note 19, at 37,47.

397 *Id.* at 7,37.

398 Guidelines on Conflicts of Interest in International Arbitration, Art.6(b) (Int'l Bar Assoc, 2014) [hereinafter IBA Guidelines].

399 Lisa Bench Nieuwveld & Victoria Shannon, Third-Party Funding in International Arbitration 1 (2nd ed., 2017); Françoise Lefèvre, et al., *Legality of Third-party Funding Mechanisms Under Belgian Law*, 2017 Belgian Rev. of Arb 35, 26 (2017).

400 *See e.g.* S&T Oil Equipment and Machinery Ltd. v. Romania, ICSID Case No. ARB/07/13, Order of Discontinuance of the Proceeding (July 16, 2010), https://www.italaw.com/sites/default/files/case-documents/ita0743.pdf. In this case, S&T Oil Equipment was bankrupt, yet its claim was funded. The case resumed after two years thanks to

The relationship between TPF and public policy can be examined both under substantive and procedural public policy. On the substantive side, the issue is whether the doctrine of champerty and maintenance would be a ground to find TPF contrary to public policy.[401] On the other hand, most controversial and trending concerns are on the procedural side, which is potential conflicts of interests and impartiality of the arbitrators. This book chooses its procedural side over the substantial side when categorizing it although it will examine both sides.

Although the rules against maintenance and champerty extend to arbitration, the traditional common law doctrine of champerty and maintenance have mostly faded away in England,[402] the United States,[403] and Australia,[404] Canada.[405] Nonetheless, in these jurisdictions, TPF may be found contrary to public policy where the element of impropriety exists, such as third-party funder's excessive control or disproportionate profit of the third-party funder.[406] Although the abovementioned states have not yet regulated TPF in arbitration in

---

monetary support from the funder. When the funder exited the agreement, S&T Oil Equipment had to discontinue the case, leaving Romania stuck with the legal costs.

401 The doctrine of champerty and maintenance was originally drawn from common law concept, and is mostly unknown in civil law jurisdictions. It aims to discourage frivolous lawsuits and prevent corruption of civil justice. Litigation funding used to be deemed as serious as a crime and a tort in certain jurisdictions. Such funding agreements were not enforceable on the grounds that they are contrary to the nation's public policy. *See* Gian Marco Solas, *Alternative Litigation Funding and the Italian Perspective*, 2 Eur. Rev. Private L. 253, 253 (2016) (mentioning that the concept has not emerged in Italy yet); Marco de Morpurgo, *A Comparative Legal and Economic Approach to Third-Party Litigation Funding*, 9 Cardozo J. Int'l & Comp. L. 360 (2011) (stating that Germany, Austria, and Switzerland are the countries where the TPF is developing).

402 *See e.g.* Arkin v. Borchard Lines Ltd and others [2005] EWCA Civ 655(Eng.) (recognizing the validity of the funding arrangements); Giles v. Thompson [1993] UKHL 2 (Eng.)(stating that funding arrangements are valid and enforceable).

403 *E.g.*, Didier Matray & Sigrid van Rompaey, *An Introduction to Third-Party Funding*, 2017 Belgian Rev. of Arb 175, 183 (2017) (noting that the doctrine of maintenance and champerty is still in force in some states).

404 *E.g.*, Campbell's Cash and Carry Pty Ltd v. Fostif Pty Ltd [2006] 229 ALR 58 (Aust.).

405 *See* Nieuwveld & Shannon, *supra* note 399, at 207.

406 *See generally Campbells Cash* [2006] HCA (applying the prohibition of maintenance and champerty as public policy grounds when deciding whether funding arrangements are unenforceable).

a legally binding way, they have now mostly accepted that funding agreements are not contrary to public policy in principle.[407]

There are more specific national laws that directly allow TPF in arbitration. For instance, Singapore passed an amendment to the Civil Law Act on January 10, 2017, introducing and legalizing TPF in international commercial arbitration.[408] Similarly, on June 14, 2017, Hong Kong has approved the Arbitration and Mediation Legislation (Third-Party Funding) (Amendment) Bill 2016, which allows TPF in arbitration and mediation and establishes both monetary and ethical standards.[409] Regulations at the national level are still limited, yet it is encouraging.

Asian states have also started to set trends when certain international arbitration rules have been amended to regulate TPF. For example, the Singapore International Arbitration Centre (SIAC) published a Practice Note "On arbitrator conduct in cases involving external funding" on March 31, 2017, which applies to all cases conducted under the SIAC Rules and administered by the SIAC.

In conclusion, there are differing stands to the TPF in arbitration. In most of the countries, TPF itself has not yet been regulated. Some of the countries in these groups are not accustomed to the doctrine of champerty and maintenance, although the rest have accepted or used it. The number of countries directly regulating TPF in arbitration is limited. Thus, when searching for funding, the claimant should be aware of the place of arbitration and possible enforcement places as to what the country's position in terms of acknowledging TPF in arbitration. Otherwise, it might lead to the award becoming unenforceable.

Assuming that TPF in arbitration is allowed in certain jurisdictions, there are several ethical concerns surrounding TPF, which may become a reason for the unenforceability of the award on the grounds of procedural public policy. The requirement of an impartial tribunal is one of the chief principles in international arbitration. If this requirement is violated, the award may not be enforced since it is contrary to public policy in almost every jurisdiction. It is possible to make certain assumptions where the tribunal's impartiality may be questioned. For example, in arbitration A1, one of the parties is funded by funder F, and X sits

---

407 See e.g. Tenke Fungurume Mining SA v. Katanga Contracting Services SAS [2021] EWHC 3301 (Comm) (Eng.) (upholding an award of third-party funding costs rendered by a London-seated ICC arbitral tribunal)

408 Civil Law (Third-Party Funding) Regulations 2017 (No. S 68) (Sing.)

409 Arbitration and Mediation Legislation (Third-Party Funding) (Amendment) Ordinance, No. 6 (2017) A137 O.H.K. (H.K.)

as a presiding arbitrator. In arbitration A2, however, one of the parties is again funded by F, where X acts as a counsel of the funded party this time. Considering this example, there are certain challenges that need an answer—namely, whether disclosure is necessary, what the scope of disclosure is, to whom and when such disclosure should occur, and what the possible results of non-disclosure are.

Arbitral rules require arbitrators to be independent and make relevant disclosure of conflicts of interest in cases of doubt. But in the case of TPF, the arbitrator may not be aware that one of the parties is funded by a third-party. On the other hand, the funded party may not disclose because of confidentiality clauses that preclude such disclosure, which is a prevalent practice.[410] The voluntary[411] or accidental[412] disclosure might be the case, although it is not typical. There are promising attempts to regulate TPF, although mandatory regulations are scarce. For example, Art. 44 of the 2018 HKIAC Administered Arbitration Rules requires the funded party to give notice to all other parties, the arbitral tribunal, and HKIAC, where a funding agreement is made.[413]

What is the solution? It is evident that "the use of third-party funding in major arbitration cases is a development that is here to stay."[414] Hence, failure to disclose may cause conflicts of interests and impact the impartiality of the tribunal and award, and thus, it may fatally lead to annulment or non-recognition of the award. There is no hard data today where the award is annulled or not enforced on the grounds of procedural public policy due to conflict of interests resulting from TPF in international arbitration. However, this does not mean that this will never be the case.

The international arbitrational rules and national laws should address this expanding practice of international commercial arbitration before it becomes pathological. Currently, the IBA Guidelines require disclosure of a TPF if a previous relationship exists between the arbitrator and the funder. HKIAC rules

---

410 Maxi Scherer et al., *Third-Party Funding in International Arbitration in Europe: 1–Funders' Perspectives*, 2 Int'l Bus. L. J. 207, 218 (2012) (stating that there is a belief that disclosure may harm the result and influence the tribunal).

411 Oxus Gold v. Republic of Uzbekistan, UNCITRAL, Final Award (Dec. 17, 2015).

412 X v. Y and Z, 2 Le Cahiers de l'Arbitrage 399 (ICC Arb., 2013).

413 2018 HKIAC Administered Arbitration Rules, Art.44, https://www.hkiac.org/sites/default/files/ck_filebrowser/PDF/arbitration/2018_hkiac_rules.pdf

414 Jean E. Kalicki, *Third-Party Funding in Arbitration: Innovations and Limits in Self-Regulation (Part 2 of 2)*, Kluwer Arb. Blog (Mar. 14, 2012), http://kluwerarbitrationblog.com/blog/2012/03/14/third- party-funding-in-arbitration-innovations-and-limits-in-self-regulation-part-2-of-2.

take a step further and requires the disclosure of a TPF to the arbitral tribunal and all other parties, regardless of the pre-existing relationship between the funder and an arbitrator.

The author argues that the disclosure of the TPF relationship regardless of the pre-existing relationship between the parties is the desired solution as it will prevent not only conflicts of interest problems but also protect the legitimacy of arbitration given that "third-party funders are less interested in justice and more interested in portfolio gains."[415] The former function would prevent the application of the public policy exception, whereas the latter would preclude any questioning about the integrity of arbitration, thereby preventing any revival of public policy as a mindset *against* arbitration

415 Gary J. Shaw, *Third-party funding in investment arbitration: how nondisclosure can cause harm for the sake of profit*, 33 Arb. Int'l. 109, 120 (2017).

3 The Public Policy Exception Under the U.S. Law on Arbitration

Abstract: The third chapter is committed to addressing the public policy exception as legislated and applied in the United States. It first reviews statutory law on arbitration. The starting point is the FAA as it applies to all contracts involving interstate commerce and creates "a body of federal substantive law" establishing enforceability of arbitral awards in both state and federal courts. Particular emphasis will be directed toward international awards that are made in the United States and the laws applicable to such awards, as these laws have a direct bearing on the public policy exception. Subsequently, the effect of federalism on international awards will be studied with the aim of elucidating the interplay between state public policy and the FAA. The third chapter will further examine the common law public policy ground by looking at its roots and the circumstances that prepared the way for it to arise. Public policy in the context of international arbitration under the New York Convention as applied in the United States is another core concept that the third chapter covers. The third chapter subsequently examines the case law that deals with challenges to enforcement of foreign arbitral awards based on substantive and procedural public policy. Finally, the third chapter investigates the interface between arbitration and two as yet underexplored fields—namely, AI and third-party funding—as far as the public policy exception is concerned. Given that AI is set to become an important component in international arbitration in the next few years—and that there has been a considerable rise in the use of third-party funding for arbitration—the potential impacts of AI and third-party funding on the public policy exception as applied in the United States will be explored.

Keywords: FAA arbitration, common law arbitration, U.S. arbitration, Federal Arbitration Act

3.1 The Taxonomy of Bodies of Law: Why Does it Matter?

Arbitral awards are formed by virtue of a private agreement between the parties, but require the assistance of national courts to be enforced. In fact, some commentators note that the law of arbitration has been perceived subordinate to and anchored in national courts and their respective laws.[416] They further argue that

---

416 Stavros L. Brekoulakis, *International Arbitration Scholarship and The Concept of*

the material scope of arbitration in a given country directly reflects its stance toward arbitration when it comes to the enforcement. Here, the term international arbitration is a "misnomer" because "every arbitration is a national arbitration … subject to a specific system of national law."[417] Given the importance of national law, this chapter aims to understand U.S. laws on arbitration, focusing closely on the public policy exception. In so doing, the author seeks to reveal whether—and if so, how—the public policy exception has been judicially codified and applied by U.S. courts.

As indicated before, the United States is a leading proponent of modern arbitration law and has remained so in part by championing the growth of international arbitration worldwide. That being said, the legal framework governing international arbitration in the United States remains murky and difficult to grasp for those unfamiliar with it, such as foreign lawyers, scholars, and even U.S. judges and practitioners.[418] This is due to the significant number of laws and precedents potentially applicable to international arbitration cases.[419] For purposes of this book, the author could enumerate at least three different bodies of law governing the enforcement of an international arbitral award as follows:

i. the Federal Arbitration Act (FAA),
ii. the common law on arbitration, and, finally,
iii. the New York Convention itself.[420]

When discussing the reach of the public policy exception in the United States, an initial question arises as to whether these bodies of law have set out this exception differently as a ground for refusing the enforcement of or vacating an arbitral award, and if so, how. To that end, in this section, the author examine how the public policy ground has been interpreted under each body of law. Given that our main concern is the Convention, the author will also consider the interplay

---

Arbitration Law, 36 FORDHAM INT'L L.J. 745, 771–72 (2013).

417 *Id.* at 772 (*citing* Francis A. Mann, *The UNCITRAL Model Law-Lex Facit Arbitrum*, ARB. INT'L, July 1986, at 241, 245).

418 George A. Bermann et al., *Restating the U.S. Law of International Commercial Arbitration*, 113 PENN ST. L. REV. 1333, 1334 (2009).

419 E.g., Jian Zhou, *Judicial Intervention in International Arbitration: A Comparative Study of the Scope of the New York Convention in U.S. And Chinese Courts*, 15 PAC. RIM L. & POL'Y J. 403, 414 (2006); Besson, supra note 69, at 212.

420 E.g., Lea H. Kuck & Amanda R. Kalantirsky, *Vacating an International Arbitration Award Rendered in the United States: Does the New York Convention, the Federal Arbitration Act or State Law Apply?*, 3 Y.B. ARB. & MEDIATION 1 (2011).

between it and the statutory and common law. The author then focus on the Convention itself, discussing the public policy standard and the possible challenges to an award on such a ground. Finally, the author considers the use of third-party funding or Artificial Intelligence (AI) systems in international arbitration and the possible implications in terms of any public policy challenge.

3.2 Statutory Law on The Public Policy Exception

3.2.1 The Federal Arbitration Act and the Public Policy Exception

Enacted in 1925, the FAA was one of the first modern arbitration statutes.[421] Since the FAA pre-dates the Model Law and the Convention, it is based on neither. In 1985, sixty years after the FAA was enacted, the Model Law was created, and legislators were encouraged to adopt it as part of domestic legislation.[422] The Model Law offered a structure for governing arbitration in a national setting, whereas the Convention provided a parallel regime for enforcing arbitral awards internationally. For example, Article 36(1) of the Model Law adopts the same grounds provided in Article V of the Convention, including the public policy exception. More specifically, the violation of public policy has been asserted as a ground for setting aside—the American counterpart to "vacating"—an award under the Model Law, which is also a ground for refusing enforcement under the Convention.

Diverging from the Convention and the Model Law, Section 10 of FAA Chapter 1 enumerates four different grounds for vacating an arbitral award: (i) where the award "was procured by corruption, fraud, or undue means;" (ii) where there was "evident partiality or corruption" by the arbitrators; (iii) where the arbitrators were guilty of misconduct in the hearing process prejudicing a party; or (iv) where the arbitrators "exceeded their powers."[423] It would appear at first sight obvious that the FAA did not serve as a strong model for Model Law or the Convention, as FAA Chapter 1, and therefore its Section 10, is not akin to the Model Law or the Convention. Nor, as a close reading of the text will show, does Section 10 make reference to a public policy ground for vacating the award.

421 Thomas E. Carbonneau, *The Reception of Arbitration in United States Law*, 40 ME. L. REV. 263, 268 (1988).

422 The New York Convention Status, *supra* note 16.

423 9 U.S.C.A. § 10.

One may argue that Section 10 of the FAA Chapter 1 has no substantial place in this book as the book originally concerns the public policy exception under the Convention. This argument, however, is not well taken. First of all, throughout its application, all four grounds provided in Section 10 are subsumed in the public policy exception. For example, arbitrator bias is a ground for vacatur under Section 10 but also justifies the refusal of an enforcement wherein the award is deemed contrary to public policy from the Convention's standpoint.[424] To that extent, Section 10 grounds and the case law application of them are, in fact, quite relevant for drawing an analogy and for seeing how U.S. courts have considered these challenges—thus providing a clue as to when the enforcement of an award is likely to be challenged before U.S. courts on public policy grounds under the Convention.[425]

Further, the application of Section 10 grounds is a great source of guidance because U.S. courts, as opposed to the courts in civil law countries, do not severely distinguish between ordinary public policy and international public policy (*ordre public international*).[426] Therefore, this allows us to draw a bigger picture and infer standards on the application of the public policy exception in the United States.

FAA grounds are also of importance because they may become applicable to a foreign award rendered by a tribunal seated in the United States.[427] As such, U.S.

424 See *infra* Section 3.2.2.2

425 *See* RZS Holdings AVV v. PDVSA Petroleos S.A., 598 F. Supp. 2d 762 (E.D. Va. 2009) (where the Court considered FAA § 10 grounds and the public policy exception under Panama Convention which is analogous to the New York Convention); Yasmine Lahlou *et al.*, *Substantive Barriers to Recognition and Enforcement of Foreign Awards under Article V(2) of New York and Panama Conventions*, *in* ENFORCEMENT OF FOREIGN ARBITRAL AWARDS AND JUDGMENTS IN NEW YORK 153, 166 (Andreas A. Frischknecht et al. eds., 2018); Alan Scott Rau, *The New York Convention in American Courts*, 7 AM. REV. INT'L ARB. 213, 236 (1996) ("[A]s a general matter I think it is reasonably safe to assume that in operation the standards of the Convention and the FAA will be identical.")

426 RESTATEMENT (THIRD) U.S. LAW OF INT'L COMM. ARB. § 4–16 (AM. LAW INST., Proposed Final Draft No. 4, 2019) ("Courts in the United States do not expressly differentiate between ordinary public policy and international public policy (ordre public international) in the fashion that civil-law courts commonly do.")

427 A determination of which law governing arbitration should be applied is made depending upon the question of whether the award is a "domestic" award, a "non-domestic" award, or a "foreign" award. CBF Industria de Gusa v. AMCI Holdings, Inc., 850 F.3d 58 (2nd Cir. 2017). Domestic awards refer to awards that "do not bear a reasonable relationship with one or more foreign States." RESTATEMENT (THIRD) U.S.

courts have applied FAA. Section 10 to the enforcement of non-domestic awards, but not universally.[428] Therefore, the following assessment will contribute to the overall evaluation of the application of the public policy exception in U.S. courts.

3.2.2 FAA Section 10 Grounds for Vacatur and the Public Policy Exception Within the Meaning of Article V(2)(b)

3.2.2.1 FAA Section 10(a)(1): Where the Award "Was Procured by Corruption, Fraud, or Undue Means"

This ground is analogous to Article V(1)(b) of the Convention, where the losing party was not given proper notice or was unable to present its case.[429]

Law of Int'l Comm. Arb § 1.1 cmt. l. Both non-domestic awards and foreign awards, on the other hand, have a foreign element. Non-domestic awards refer to awards rendered in the United States that have a foreign character as they were decided under foreign law, or those decided under the laws of the U.S. where there is some pertinent connection with one or more foreign states. Non-domestic awards are distinct from (1) foreign awards, which are subject only to the terms of the Convention, and; (2) domestic awards, which are subject only to Chapter One of the FAA 9 U.S.C.A. § 202. As such, non-domestic awards are both subject to the Convention and the FAA. The courts in the United States have primary jurisdiction over domestic awards and non-domestic awards, so that they are empowered to vacate an award. *CBF Industria*, 850 F.3d at 71. Foreign awards, on the other hand, are only subject to confirmation. 9 U.S.C.A. § 207. That is to say, courts in the United States have secondary jurisdiction over foreign awards and they are only empowered to refuse the enforcement of the award in the United States. *CBF Industria*, 850 F.3d at 71. Finally, it is to be noted that international arbitral awards encompass both non-domestic awards and foreign awards, whereas domestic awards is an opposite, standalone category. Restatement (Third) U.S. Law of Int'l Comm. Arb § 1.1 cmt. p.

428 *Compare* Yusuf Ahmed Alghanim & Sons, W.L.L. v. Toys "R" Us, Inc., 126 F.3d 15, 20 (2nd Cir. 1997) (holding that the New York Convention and the FAA "have 'overlapping coverage' to the extent that they do not conflict") *with* Indus. Risk Insurers v. M.A.N. Gutehoffnungshutte GmbH, 141 F.3d 1434, 1445 (11th Cir. 1998) (considering the grounds for non-enforcement stipulated in Art. V of the Convention as grounds for vacatur where the award is non-domestic). *See also* Victoria Orlowski, *FAA Section 10 Applications to Vacate an Award (Including "Manifest Disregard")*, *in* International Arbitration in the United States 503, 504 (Laurence Shore et al. eds., 2017); Kenneth R. Davis, *Unconventional Wisdom: A New Look at Articles V and VII of the Convention on the Recognition and Enforcement of Foreign Arbitral Awards*, 37 Tex. Int'l L.J. 43, 73 n.211 (2002).

429 Orlowski, *supra* note 428, at 512.

Nonetheless, as the book discussed before, it has been also raised under the public policy exception.[430] The case history reveals that the party seeking to vacate the award has often alleged fraud—alone or together with other grounds—rather than alleging corruption or undue means alone. U.S. courts generally impose a three-pronged test to determine whether an award may be vacated for fraud.[431] This test requires the moving party to establish: (1) by "clear and convincing evidence" that there was a fraud; (2) that the fraud was not discoverable through the exercise of due diligence prior to or during the arbitration; and (3) that the fraud was materially related to an issue in the arbitration.[432] In *Biotronik*, where the plaintiff moved to confirm the ICC award made in Switzerland, the defendant alleged that the plaintiff's failure to disclose the evidence to the arbitral panel meant the award had been "procured by... fraud" and also argued as an alternative defense that the fraud constituted a public policy exception to enforcement under Article V(2)(b) of the Convention.[433] The Court found the public policy defense to be "*a fortiori* inapplicable" because Medford was unable to establish fraud under FAA s.10(a)(1).[434] The Court found itself "distinctly incapable" of holding that the award violated U.S. public policy, where the Court did not find fraud under FAA s.10(a)(1).[435] Likewise, in *Floridians* the Court "declined the defendants" invitation to vacate the award on public policy grounds' where the Court found that the defendants had failed to establish fraud under the three-prong test laid out above.[436] Both *Biotronik* and *Floridians* signal that a claimant must meet the requirements provided under FAA s.10(a)(1) in order to raise a public policy challenge for the Court's consideration. This, once again, demonstrates the appeal of a robust pro-arbitration policy.

---

430 *E.g.* Biotronik Mess-Und Therapiegeraete GmbH & Co. v. Medford Med. Instrument Co., 415 F. Supp. 133 (D.N.J. 1976) (rejecting the alternative public policy defense under the Convention where the Court did not find fraud under FAA § 10(a)(1))

431 Orlowski, *supra* note 428, at 513–14.

432 *E.g.* Bonar v. Dean Witter Reynolds, Inc., 835 F.2d 1378, 1383 (11th Cir. 1988); Domnarski v. UBS Fin. Servs., 919 F. Supp. 2d 183, 188 (D. Mass. 2013); Odeon Capital Grp. LLC v. Ackerman, 864 F.3d 191, 197 (2nd Cir. 2017); Int'l Bhd. of Teamsters, Local 701 v. CBF Trucking, Inc., 440 F. App'x 76, 78 (3rd Cir. 2011); *Karaha Bodas*, 364 F.3d at 306.

433 *Biotronik*, 415 F. Supp. at 137.

434 *Id.* at 140.

435 *Id.*

436 Floridians for Solar Choice v. PCI Consultants, Inc., 314 F. Supp. 3d 1346, 1355 n.4 (S.D. Fla. 2018)

3.2.2.2 FAA Section 10(a)(2): Where There Was Evident Partiality or Corruption By The Arbitrators

This ground is akin to Articles V(1)(b) and V(1)(d) of the Convention, whereby a party was "otherwise unable to present his case" and where the "composition of the arbitral authority ... was not in accordance with the agreement of the parties, or ... with the law of the country where the arbitration took place."[437] It has also been raised under the public policy exception.

As the book has indicated, a lack of impartiality is one of the few grounds for refusing the enforcement of arbitral awards. Therefore, it is arguably one of the grounds where the award can be found contrary to public policy within the meaning of the Convention. In *Commonwealth Coatings v. Continental Cas. Co*, the neutral member of the arbitral panel had an undisclosed, "sporadic" yet "repeated and significant" business relationship with one of the parties.[438] Justice Black, writing for the plurality of the Court, adopted the rule that the arbitrators' failure to disclose his interest created an appearance of bias sufficient to vacate the arbitral award.[439] Justice White, on the other hand, in his concurring opinion, noted the difference between arbitral and Court proceedings and cautioned against over-regulation of the former, as the parties to an arbitration are generally sophisticated merchants.[440] He nevertheless reiterated the transparency principle by emphasizing that all non-trivial prior business relations between a party and an arbitrator must be disclosed.[441] As such, he sought a balance or necessary "trade-off" between expertise and the needs of arbitrations and impartiality.

As a plurality decision, *Commonwealth Coatings* has led courts to draw on numerous factors in their analyses of "evident partiality," thus producing a split among the circuits. Initially, the minority of circuits adopted the "appearance of bias" standard articulated by Justice Black.[442] Over time—in parallel to the

---

437 Orlowski, *supra* note 428, at 516.

438 Commonwealth Coatings Corp. v. Cont'l Cas. Co., 393 U.S. 145, 145 (1968).

439 *Id.* at 150 (White, J., concurring).

440 *Id.*

441 Stephen K. Huber, *State Regulation of Arbitration Proceedings: Judicial Review of Arbitration Awards by State Courts*, 10 Cardozo J. Conflict Resol. 509, 550 (2009).

442 *See e.g.* PaineWebber Grp., Inc. v. Zinsmeyer Trs. P'ship, 187 F.3d 988, 995 (8th Cir. 1999); Tamari v. Bache Halsey Stuart, Inc., 619 F.2d 1196, 1198 n.3. (7th Cir. 1980) (holding that even if actual bias or corruption is not found, the appearance of bias will void the award).

growth and reliability of arbitration—courts have adopted more demanding standards for vacatur. As such, courts have adopted views more akin to Justice White's.[443] The recent trend in the majority of courts, however, has been to adopt the "reasonable person" standard, which asks whether a reasonable person would conclude that an arbitrator was partial to one party to the arbitration.[444]

This spectrum of analysis hints that courts will likely continue to draw on numerous factors in deciding whether "evident partiality" exists.[445] Of these standards, Justice White's concurrence providing a more stringent standard than "appearance of bias" is in more conformity with the recent practice of international arbitration. In fact, the reasonable person standard is just another facet of the standard articulated from Justice White's concurrence.[446] Regardless of which of these two standards is applied, it suffices here to say that a higher standard than the appearance of bias is more in accord with the practice of arbitration.

Unlike the diversified "evident partiality" standard and its application under domestic arbitration, the courts have required a higher burden in proving

---

443 *See e.g.* Positive Software Sols., Inc. v. New Century Mortg. Corp., 476 F.3d 278, 279 (5th Cir. 2007) (interpreting *Commonwealth* as to Justice White's view and holding that a mere appearance of bias does not suffice to establish evident partiality); Univ. Commons-Urbana, Ltd. v. Universal Constructors Inc., 304 F.3d 1331, 1339 (11th Cir. 2002) ("Arbitration award may be vacated due to the evident partiality of an arbitrator only when either (1) an actual conflict exists, or (2) the arbitrator knows of, but fails to disclose, information which would lead a reasonable person to believe that a potential conflict exists."). The Ninth Circuit, on the other hand, requires a proof of "reasonable impression of partiality" that imposes a higher burden than the mere "appearance of bias." *See e.g.* Sussex v. United States Dist. Court for the Dist. of Nev., 781 F.3d 1065, 1074 (9th Cir. 2015); Schmitz v. Zilveti, 20 F.3d 1043, 1045 (9th Cir. 1994).

444 *See e.g.*, Ploetz v. Morgan Stanley Smith Barney LLC, 894 F.3d 894, 898 (8th Cir. 2018) (*citing* Dow Corning Corp. v. Safety Nat'l Cas. Corp., 335 F.3d 742, 750 (8th Cir. 2003) (stating that whether a reasonable person could assume that the arbitrator had improper motives); Freeman v. Pittsburgh Glass Works, LLC, 709 F.3d 240, 255 (3rd Cir. 2013); Scandinavian Reinsurance Co. v. Saint Paul Fire & Marine Ins. Co., 668 F.3d 60, 73 (2nd Cir. 2012); Uhl v. Komatsu Forklift Co., 512 F.3d 294, 298 (6th Cir. 2008); JCI Communs., Inc. v. IBEW, Local 103, 324 F.3d 42, 51 (1st Cir. 2003); ANR Coal Co. v. Cogentrix of N.C., Inc., 173 F.3d 493, 500 (4th Cir. 1999) (adding a four-factor test in applying the 'reasonable person' standard).

445 See Kirill Kan, *The Importance of FINRA's Arbitrator Selection Process and Clarity in the "Evident Partiality" Standard in the Wake of Morgan Keegan*, 18 Fordham J. Corp. & Fin. L. 167, 180 (2012).

446 Braydon Robert, *An Evident Contradiction: How Some Evident Partiality Standards Do Not Facilitate Impartial Arbitration*, 43 Iowa J. Corp. L. 681, 695–96 (2018).

"evident partiality" in international arbitration cases. In the recent case of *Belize Bank Ltd. v. Gov't of Belize*, Mr. Douglas, whom LCIA appointed as an arbitrator in the Government of Belize's (the Government) stead, was a member of Matrix Chambers.[447] The opposing party's arbitrator was also a member of the same Chamber.[448] Both had done business with the Belize Bank and against the Government.[449] By citing *Commonwealth*, the Government argued that if the rules of professional conduct applicable to U.S. law firms were applied to Douglas and Matrix Chambers, the award would be tainted by a lack of impartiality "viewed through the lens of United States public policy."[450]

The Court disagreed with the Government for two reasons. Initially, the Court found that the Government had failed to prove the evident partiality as established under FAA s.10(a)(2).[451] Further, the Court opined that even if the alleged conduct did satisfy FAA s.10(a)(2), the Court would be unable to deny enforcement on the grounds of public policy because the award did not violate this country's "most basic notions of morality and justice."[452] Hence, the Court held that no matter what the standard, satisfaction of FAA s.10(a)(2) alone would not meet the threshold necessary to refuse the enforcement on public policy grounds.

Analogously, in *Matter of Andros Compania Maritima*—a case regarding enforcement of an arbitral award made in New York between Swiss and Panamanian parties—the losing party moved to vacate because there was an undisclosed relationship between a neutral arbitrator and the operator of the vessel involved in the arbitral proceeding.[453] One of the issues was whether the action fell under FAA s.10(a)(2) or the New York Convention.[454] The Court found this question

---

447 Belize Bank Ltd. v. Gov't of Belize, 852 F.3d 1107, 1111 (D.C. Cir. 2017)

448 *Id.* at 1109.

449 *Id.*

450 *Id.* at 1111.

451 *Id.* at 1113.

452 *Id.* at 1112 (quoting TermoRio S.A. E.S.P. v. Electranta S.P., 487 F.3d 928, 938 (D.C. Cir. 2007)). The Court explained that "an allegation that an arbitral tribunal member is a member of the same English chambers as another barrister who, in proceedings unrelated in fact and time, represented a conflicting interest, is insufficient to meet that burden, let alone to demonstrate that enforcement would violate the United States' most basic notions of morality and justice." *Id.* at 1108.

453 Matter of Andros Compania Maritima, S.A. (Marc Rich & Co., A.G.), 579 F.2d 691, 701 (2nd Cir. 1978).

454 *Id.* at 699 n.11.

"intriguing" but did not resolve it.[455] Nonetheless, the Court opined that "if the Convention applies... the only such ground conceivably pertinent to this case" would be Article V(2)(b) of the Convention, *i.e.*, the enforcement being contrary to the public policy of the United States. The Court further stated that the party moving for vacatur had failed to establish the evident partiality under FAA s.10(a)(2), and for this reason, resort to the Convention would not alter the result since "the Convention is no more liberal" than FAA s.10 with regard to vacating awards.[456]

The case law demonstrates that establishing evident partiality under FAA s. 10(a)(2) is extremely demanding as an arbitrator's decision is entitled to great deference. Denying the enforcement on public policy grounds, then, requires a gross violation of impartiality principles.

3.2.2.3 FAA Section 10(A)(3): Where the Arbitrators Were Guilty of Misconduct In The Hearing Process Prejudicing A Party

The FAA s.10(a)(3) states that the award may be vacated "where the arbitrators were guilty of misconduct in refusing to postpone the hearing, upon sufficient cause shown, or in refusing to hear evidence pertinent and material to the controversy; or of any other misbehavior by which the rights of any party have been prejudiced." The article encompasses a range of procedural irregularities, including an arbitrator's refusal to postpone hearings or hear evidence. The concluding catchall provision also provides that other kinds of arbitrator misbehavior may result in vacatur of the award. Hence, this ground is also akin to Article V(1)(b) of the Convention and also encompassed by the public policy exception.[457]

The Due Process Clauses under the Fifth and Fourteenth Amendments of the U.S. Constitution provide that governments (both federal and state) may not deprive a person of life, liberty, or property without due process of law.[458] When construing the required due process standard, the courts have repeatedly held that the right to due process in arbitration is not as extensive and formal as in

455 *Id.*

456 *Id.*

457 *E.g.*, Sphere Drake Ins., Ltd. v. Lincoln Nat'l Life Ins. Co., No. 05 C 6411, 2006 U.S. Dist. LEXIS 70533, at *9 (N.D. Ill. Sep. 13, 2006) (stating that Article V(1)(b) of the Convention and FAA s.10(a)(3) are "two overlapping grounds for denying enforcement of and vacating the arbitration award.")

458 *Compare* U.S. Const. amend. V *with* U.S. Const. amend. XIV, § 1.

a courtroom.[459] As such, as long as "the opportunity to be heard at a meaningful time and in a meaningful manner" is given by the arbitrators, a minimal due process threshold is met.[460] Hence, although the language in the article suggests its scope of application is quite broad, the case history presents few cases wherein a Court has, in fact, vacated an award.[461] The courts in the United States have deferred to arbitrators in choosing how arbitration proceedings should be directed, and this ground has only become applicable where the proceeding has been found "fundamentally unfair or severely prejudic[ial to] a party's basic procedural rights."[462]

Parties have often alleged that erroneous application of substantive law—which in American legal jargon mostly corresponds to manifest disregard of the law[463]—and lack of reasons suffice to vacate an award under FAA s. 10(a)(3). As

---

459 *E.g.* Forsythe Int'l, S.A. v. Gibbs Oil Co. of Texas, 915 F.2d 1017, 1022 (5th Cir. 1990) ("Parties to voluntary arbitration may not superimpose rigorous procedural limitations on the very process designed to avoid such limitations") (citation omitted); Bell Aerospace Co. Div. of Textron v. Local 516, Int'l Union, United Auto., Aerospace & Agr. Implement Workers of Am. (UAW), 500 F.2d 921, 923 (2nd Cir. 1974) ("In handling evidence an arbitrator need not follow all the niceties observed by the federal courts"); Rai v. Barclays Capital Inc., 739 F. Supp. 2d 364, 371–72 (S.D.N.Y. 2010), *aff'd*, 456 F. App'x 8 (2nd Cir. 2011) (finding that arbitrators are "... not required to hear all the evidence proffered by a party.") (citation omitted);In re Trans Chem. Ltd. & China Nat. Mach. Imp. & Exp. Corp., 978 F. Supp. 266, 310 (S.D. Tex. 1997), *aff'd sub nom.* Trans Chem. Ltd. v. China Nat. Mach. Imp. & Exp. Corp., 161 F.3d 314 (5th Cir. 1998) (stating that the right to due process does not encompass the complete set of procedural rights, and by agreeing to arbitration, the award-losing party freely subjected itself to the advantages and disadvantages of arbitration).

460 Mathews v. Eldridge, 424 U.S. 319, 333 (1976). *See also* Tempo Shain Corp. v. Bertek, Inc., 120 F.3d 16, 20 (2nd Cir. 1997) (stating that only violations of "fundamental fairness" construe arbitrator misconduct under FAA s.10(a)(3)).

461 *See e.g.*, Hoteles Condado Beach, La Concha & Convention Ctr. v. Union De Tronquistas Local 901, 763 F.2d 34, 37–38 (1st Cir. 1985) (vacating the award where the arbitrator refused to consider the trial transcript of the criminal court's findings).

462 Restatement (Third) U.S. Law of Int'l Comm. Arb § 4–19 cmt. a.

463 As briefly pointed out before, manifest disregard of law is a non-statutory ground for vacating the award in the United States, and it is often invoked with FAA s.10(a)(3) and s.10(a)(4). *E.g.* Hall St. Assocs., L.L.C. v. Mattel, Inc., 552 U.S. 576, 585 (2008) ("... manifest disregard may have been shorthand for § 10(a)(3) or § 10(a)(4)")(citations omitted). Nonetheless, the U.S. Supreme Court's unclear language from *Hall Street* has resulted in a split among the circuit courts as to whether the manifest disregard of law survived as an independent ground for vacatur. Some circuits rejected that the manifest disregard as a viable ground. Stanley A. Leasure, *Arbitration Law in Tension*

the book pointed out before, in international arbitration practice, the courts have often found that these grounds are not sufficient to refuse the enforcement on the ground that the award is contrary to public policy. Likewise, the U.S. courts have denied motions to vacate an award under FAA s.10(a)(3) on these bases.[464]

In *Agility Pub. Warehousing v. Supreme Foodservice,* certain witnesses for the winning party refused to testify by invoking privilege, and the arbitrators failed to apply the procedural law of New York—the place of arbitration—which requires that claims be dismissed when a party invokes a privilege so as not to testify.[465] Instead—rather than dismissing the winning party's claim—the arbitrators decided to draw an adverse inference from refusal to testify.[466] The losing party argued that the arbitrator's failure to apply New York procedural law amounted to a manifest disregard of law that violated "American standards of due process" under FAA s.10(a)(3) and Art. V(1)(b) of the Convention.[467] Further, the losing party contended that the enforcement of the award was also contrary to public policy under the Convention.[468] The Court emphasized that the public policy exception "must be construed very narrowly" to concern only "violations of basic,

---

After Hall Street: Accuracy or Finality?, 39 U. Ark. Little Rock L. Rev. 75, 85 (2016). The majority of the circuits, including the Second, Fourth, Seventh and Ninth Circuits, have decided that manifest disregard is a still viable ground. *Id.* at 90–102. Yet, within those circuits, there is a split as to whether manifest disregard survived as a statutory ground shorthand for § 10(a)(3) or § 10(a)(4) or as a non-statutory ground for vacatur. *See* MyLinda K. Sims & Richard A. Bales, *Much Ado About Nothing: The Future of Manifest Disregard After Hall Street*, 62 S.C. L. Rev. 407, 424 (2010). For the purposes of book, the manifest disregard of law ground can be accepted as the American counterpart of the erroneous application of law ground, though it requires a heavier burden of proof. *See e.g.* Kyocera Corp. v. Prudential-Bache T Servs., 341 F.3d 987, 989 (9th Cir. 2003) (finding that manifest disregard of law is more than merely interpreting or applying the governing law incorrectly); Merrill Lynch, Pierce, Fenner & Smith, Inc. v. Bobker, 808 F.2d 930, 931 (2nd Cir. 1986) (holding that manifest disregard "... clearly means more than error or misunderstanding with respect to the law.").

464 *E.g. Karaha Bodas*, 364 F.3d at 306. ("Erroneous legal reasoning... is generally not a violation of public policy within the meaning of the New York Convention"). *See also supra* note 255 and accompanying text.

465 Agility Pub. Warehousing Co. K.S.C. v. Supreme Foodservice GmbH, 495 F. App'x 149, 152 (2nd Cir. 2012). *See* Agility Pub. Warehousing Co. K.S.C. v. Supreme Foodservice GmbH, 840 F. Supp. 2d 703, 708 (S.D.N.Y. 2011), *aff'd sub nom.* 495 F. App'x at 149.

466 *Agility Pub. Warehousing*, 495 F. App'x at 152.

467 *Id.* at 152–54.

468 *Id.* at 150.

fundamental policies, rather than with the policies of particular states within the United States"—which was the New York public policy in the case at hand.[469]

In *In Re Trans Chemical*, the District Court denied the losing party's motion to vacate and confirmed an arbitration award over the objections that the arbitrators' irrational scheduling order and failure to render a written opinion that stipulated the rationale for the award. The losing party asserted this was a violation of due process as protected under FAA s.10(a)(3).[470] In answering the defenses invoked by the losing party, the Court considered Article V(1)(b) and Article V(2)(b) defenses together, stating that the public policy exception is a duplicative defense under Article V(1)(b).[471] In its analysis under the FAA, the Court found that the arbitrator's scheduling order did not deprive the losing party of a fair hearing and that the arbitrators were not required to disclose the reasons underlying the award.[472] More strikingly, when analyzing the losing party's defenses under Article V(1)(b) and Article V(2)(b) of the Convention, the Court did not conduct a different analysis for each separate base (*i.e.*, considering them together) and held that the losing party may not avoid enforcement based on the reasons for denying the motion to vacate under the FAA.[473]

As in *In Re Trans Chemical*, in *Kolel Beth Yechiel Mechil of Tartikov. v. YLL Irrevocable Trust,* the Second Circuit evaluated the award debtor's claims together that the award is contrary to public policy under the Convention and also violates the right to due process under FAA s.10(a)(3).[474] Confirming the District Court's refusal to vacate an award, the Second Circuit found that arbitrators are not required to hear all the evidence proffered by a party, and thus the "District court properly declined to vacate the award pursuant to s. 10(a)(3) or under the Convention."[475]

In light of *In Re Trans Chemical* and *Kolel Beth*, the author would conclude that in order to find that the enforcement of an award violates public policy, U.S. courts require that the existence of procedural irregularities rise to the level justifying vacatur under FAA s. 10(a)(3).

469 *Id.* at 151–52.

470 *In re Trans Chem.*,978 F. Supp. at 306 *aff'd sub nom. Trans Chem.*, 161 F.3d at 314.

471 *Id.* at 310.

472 *Id.* at 307.

473 *Id.* at 310.

474 Kolel Beth Yechiel Mechil of Tartikov, Inc. v. YLL Irrevocable Trust., 729 F.3d 99, 107 (2nd Cir. 2013)

475 *Id.*

3.2.2.4 FAA Section 10(a)(4): Where The Arbitrators "Exceeded Their Powers"

Under FAA s.10(a)(4), U.S. courts may vacate awards "where the arbitrators exceeded their powers, or so imperfectly executed them that a mutual, final, and definite award upon the subject matter submitted was not made."[476] This ground is analogous to Art. V(1)(c) of the Convention, which allows the enforcing Court to refuse confirmation of award when the award is rendered "on matters beyond the scope of the submission to arbitration."[477] Seeing the public policy exception as a blanket exception, losing parties have also invoked public policy when challenging the scope of the arbitral panel's authority.[478]

Parties invoking FAA s.10(a)(4) generally allege that either the arbitral tribunal had no authority to rule on certain issues or that the tribunal had some level of authority but improperly exercised its authority.[479] In this regard, courts are reluctant to find that arbitrators exceed their authority where they ordered punitive damages,[480] attorneys' fees,[481] or interest;[482] or where awards were not made in the required time;[483] or when the arbitrator ordered a remedy that it was not authorized to order.[484]

It is noteworthy that s. 10(a)(4) is the most frequently invoked ground for vacating an arbitral award, either alone or together with "manifest disregard of law."[485] Nonetheless, in parallel with the explanation above, it is not enough to show that the arbitrator committed errors of facts or misinterpretations of law.[486]

---

476 9 U.S.C.A. § 10

477 *Parsons & Whittemore*, 508 F.2d at 976 ("This provision [Article V(1)(c)] tracks in more detailed form [§ 10(a)(4)] of the Federal Arbitration Act... which authorizes vacating an award 'where the arbitrators exceeded their powers.'")

478 *E.g.* Four Seasons Hotels & Resorts v. Consorcio Barr S.A., 377 F.3d 1164, 1170 (11th Cir. 2004).

479 Orlowski, *supra* note 428, at 525–26.

480 *E.g.* South East Atlantic Shipping, Ltd. V, Garnac Grain Co. 356 F2d 189 (1966)

481 *E.g.* Marcy Lee Mfg. Co. v. Cortley Fabrics Co. 354 F2d 42 (2nd Cir. 1965)

482 *E.g.* A/S Siljestad v. Hideca Trading, Inc., 541 F. Supp. 58 (S.D.N.Y. 1981), *aff'd*, 678 F.2d 391 (2nd Cir. 1982).

483 *E.g.* Svoboda v. Negey Associates, Inc. 655 F Supp 1329 (1987); Koch Oil, S.A. v. Transocean Gulf Oil Co., 751 F.2d 551, 554 (2nd Cir. 1985)

484 E.g. id.

485 E.g. Andrew M. Campbell, *Construction and Application of § 10(a)(4) of Federal Arbitration Act (9 U.S.C.A. § 10(a)(4)) Providing for Vacating of Arbitration Awards Where Arbitrators Exceed or Imperfectly Execute Powers*, 136 A.L.R. Fed. 183 (1997).

486 *See supra* note 463 and accompanying text.

Overall, U.S. courts have been reluctant to vacate the commercial awards pursuant s.10(a)(4) where the arbitration agreement includes no express restriction on the remedies that an arbitrator is authorized to award.[487] As such, the close examination of the case law indicates that courts apply a high bar to meet the grounds of FAA s.10(a)(4) and Art.V(2)(b) of the Convention for vacating of and an award.

In *Bayer CropScience AG v. Dow AgroSciences LLC*, for example, the Federal Circuit affirmed the lower Court's confirmation of the award, with the Court noting that the disputing party must meet high standards for an award to be vacated pursuant to s.10(a)(4) or for one to be refused or confirmed as contrary to public policy.[488] Similarly, in *Banco de Seguros del Estado v. Mut. Marine Office,* Banco challenged the arbitrator's interim order, arguing that the arbitrators had exceeded their authority by awarding pre-judgment security, which also violated the public policy of the States.[489] The Second Circuit affirmed the District Court's decision, finding that "arbitrators have the discretion to order remedies they determine appropriate, so long as they do not exceed the power granted to them by the contract itself."[490] Thus, by according "the narrowest of readings" to s.10(a)(4), the Second Circuit found that the interim order did not violate FAA s.10(a)(4).[491] Subsequently, in examining Banco's argument that the arbitrators offended public policy in awarding pre-judgment security, the Second Circuit affirmed the District Court's finding that "Banco has simply recycled its contention."[492] In another District Court case, where the losing party filed a motion to vacate the award on FAA s.10(a)(4) grounds and not to enforce the award on public policy grounds, the Court found the arguments "similarly unavailing" and as such, denied the motion.[493]

---

487 *E.g.* Bamberger Rosenheim, Ltd. (Isr.) v. OA Dev., Inc. (United States), 862 F.3d 1284, 1286 (11th Cir. 2017).

488 Bayer CropScience AG v. Dow AgroSciences LLC, 680 F. App'x 985, 987 (Fed. Cir. 2017).

489 Banco de Seguros del Estado v. Mut. Marine Office, Inc., 344 F.3d 255, 258, 264 (2nd Cir. 2003)

490 *Id.* at 262.

491 *Id.* (*citing* Westerbeke Corp. v. Daihatsu Motor Co., Ltd., 304 F.3d 200, 220 (2nd Cir. 2002))

492 *Id.* at 258.

493 Gas Nat. Aprovisionamientos SDG, S.A. v. Atl. LNG Co. of Trinidad & Tobago, No. 17-CV-0110 (LAK), 2017 WL 4513564 (S.D.N.Y. Sept. 26, 2017).

Accordingly, federal courts have consistently stated that each of the four grounds for vacatur is difficult to prove. Additionally, resorting to a public policy defense has not eased this burden, regardless of the legal standard applied by the courts for each ground.

3.2.3 International Arbitral Awards Made in the United States and the Public Policy Exception

Does Chapter 1 of the Federal Arbitration Act—which governs domestic arbitrations and awards—apply to a motion to vacate a Convention award made in the United States? This was one of the issues raised in *Yusuf*,[494] where an arbitration was held in the United States but governed by the New York Convention because the award included the American corporation Toys "R" Us and a Kuwaiti licensee. A crucial question arose in this case—namely, whether the award should be governed by Chapter 1 of the FAA (since it was made in the United States), or whether it should be exclusively governed by the Convention (as it included a Kuwaiti licensee). In other words, did it fall within the Convention's scope of application?[495]

The answer to the above question has a bearing on how courts in the United States interpret the public policy defense. FAA s.10 grounds are of importance for the purposes of this book, notwithstanding the fact that public policy is not prescribed as a ground for vacatur under the FAA.[496] This is so since the United States is a common law system, and thus arbitration law derives not only from statutes or treaties but also from Court decisions interpreting them. Hence, a body of federal common law establishing non-statutory grounds for vacating arbitral awards, including violation of public policy, has emerged since the mid-1980s although there is no public policy statutory ground other than the four articulated in Section 10(a) of the FAA.[497] Moreover, violations of any or all of the four grounds seldom amount to a violation of public policy.

---

494 *Yusuf*, 126 F.3d at 23.

495 *Compare* the New York Convention *supra* note 15, Art. I(1) (providing that awards "not considered as domestic awards in the State where their recognition and enforcement are sought" are subject to domestic enforcement regime) *with* 9 U.S.C.A. § 202 (providing that arbitral proceedings held in the several U.S. states will nevertheless fall under the Convention if it involves a non-U.S. party or has "some other reasonable relationship with one or more foreign states).

496 *See supra* Sections 3.2.1 and 3.2.2.

497 Stephen L. Hayford & Scott B. Kerrigan, *Vacatur: The Non-Statutory Grounds for Judicial Review of Commercial Arbitration Awards*, DISP. RESOL. J., Oct. 1996, at 22, 22.

The public policy standard developed under common law differs from the public policy standard applicable to foreign awards.[498] Hence, the acceptance that non-domestic awards made in the United States are not only governed by the Convention but also the FAA will implicate the federal common law grounds for vacatur—including the violation of public policy as applied in domestic awards. Conversely, if it is accepted that the award is governed by the Convention exclusively, courts will most likely interpret the public policy defense without resorting to common law. Hence, revising what was stated above, the question is whether the New York Convention provides an exclusive remedy for non-domestic awards that are rendered in the United States.

The author will turn back to *Yusuf* to answer this question. In *Yusuf*, the award made in the United States was in favor of the Kuwaiti licensee, and he moved to have the award confirmed.[499] The American corporation Toys "R" Us cross-petitioned to have the award vacated on the manifest disregard of law ground (together with other grounds under Article V of the Convention), which is another non-statutory ground for vacatur of domestic awards under common law.[500]

The Second Circuit has squarely addressed the issue of whether the domestic grounds for vacatur embodied in Section 10 of the FAA applies to reviews of an arbitral award rendered in the United States and falling under the Convention—and has answered in the affirmative. The Court held that the FAA grounds for vacatur might also be applied to awards falling under the New York Convention if the award is rendered in the United States.[501] It further interpreted Art. V(1)(e) of the Convention—which refers to an award that "has been set aside or suspended *by a competent authority* of the country in which, or *under the law of which,* that award was made"—so as "to allow a Court in the country under whose law the arbitration was conducted to apply domestic arbitral law, in this case the FAA, to a motion to set aside or vacate that arbitral award."[502]

Accordingly, the Second Circuit confirmed the District Court's finding of the double standard for review—namely, that the grounds for a refusal to enforce the award under the Convention applied to the Kuwaiti licensee's petition, but that the grounds for vacatur under the FAA applied to Toys "R" Us' cross-petition.[503]

---

498 *See generally supra* Section 3.3.

499 *Yusuf*, 126 F.3d at 17.

500 *Id.* at 18.

501 *Id.* at 23.

502 *Id.* at 21.

503 Katlyn Thomas, *On Drafting An "Ideal" Arbitration Statute*, 25 Am. Rev. Int'l Arb. 117, 126 (2014).

Although the manifest disregard of the law ground was not embodied in the FAA, this acknowledgment by the Second Circuit incorporated the non-statutory grounds for vacatur into the discussion.

This position is nonetheless not taken by every circuit. The circuits are currently split on whether the FAA Section 10 grounds or the Convention grounds apply to actions to vacate Convention awards made in the United States. Most of the circuits that have addressed the issue have followed the Second Circuit and applied the FAA s.10 grounds. To that extent, the Third,[504] Fifth,[505] and Sixth[506] Circuits endorsed *Yusuf*. Four courts within the Ninth Circuit have also adopted the reasoning established in *Yusuf*.[507]

In contrast to these circuits, in *Industrial Risk Insurers*, the Eleventh Circuit held that the grounds for refusal to enforce an award enumerated in Article V

---

504 Ario v. Underwriting Members of Syndicate 53 at Lloyd's for the 1998 Year of Account, 618 F.3d 277 (3rd Cir. 2010) (following the Second Circuit in *Yusuf* and holding that the District Court correctly applied the domestic grounds of the FAA to the award even though the award was made in an international arbitration falling under the Convention).

505 *Compare Karaha Bodas*, 364 F.3d at 287 ("Only a Court in a country with primary jurisdiction over an arbitral award may annul that award. Courts in other countries have secondary jurisdiction; a Court in a country with secondary jurisdiction is limited to deciding whether the award may be enforced in that country.") (citations omitted) *with* Ved P. Nanda et al, U.S. Rendered Awards, 3 Litigation of International Disputes in U.S. Courts § 19:30 (Under Article V(1)(e) of the Convention, courts whose *lex loci arbitri* applies are said to have "primary jurisdiction" and thus jurisdiction to vacate the award whereas courts asked to enforce awards are said to have "secondary jurisdiction" and thus jurisdiction to refuse or confirm the award.). *See also* Gulf Petro Trading Co., Inc. v. Nigerian Nat. Petroleum Corp., 512 F.3d 742, 746 (5th Cir. 2008) (later adopting *Yusuf*'s dual standard for review of arbitral awards)

506 Jacada, Ltd. v. Int'l Mktg. Strategies, Inc., 401 F.3d 701, 709 (6th Cir. 2005) *overruled on other grounds by Hall Street*, 552 U.S. at 576 ("Because this award was made in the United States, we can apply domestic law, found in the FAA, to vacate the award.")

507 *E.g.* Glob. Bldg. Prods. v. Chemco, Inc., No. C12-1017 RSM, 2012 U.S. Dist. LEXIS 150317, at *12 (W.D. Wash. Oct. 18, 2012) ("In the absence of direction from the Ninth Circuit and because of the great weight of well-reasoned authority of the various circuit courts and the district courts within the Ninth Circuit, the Court adopts the reasoning provided by the Second Circuit in *Yusuf*..."); ESCO Corp. v. Bradken Res. Pty Ltd., No. 10-788-AC, 2011 U.S. Dist. LEXIS 46460, at *23 (D. Or. Jan. 31, 2011); Kaliroy Produce Co. v. Pac. Tomato Growers, Inc., 730 F. Supp. 2d 1036, 1040 (D. Ariz. 2010); LaPine v. Kyocera Corp., No. C 07-06132 MHP, 2008 U.S. Dist. LEXIS 41172, at *17 (N.D. Cal. May 22, 2008)

of the Convention are exclusive bases on which to review an award made in the United States.[508] In this case, arbitration took place in Tampa under Florida law, and all parties save one German corporation were American.[509] The Eleventh Circuit considered FAA s.202 to find that the award was non-domestic for purposes of Art. I of the Convention, as the award was not entirely between citizens of the United States.[510] The Court then turned to defining the applicable grounds for vacatur and held that the U.S. Congress, in enacting FAA s. 207, has determined that the only grounds for vacatur are those set forth in Art. V of the Convention.[511] Hence, the Court found that the Convention—and not the FAA—applies to non-domestic awards. The Eleventh Circuit has not been alone in such decisions. A District Court within the Fourth Circuit also relied on the judgment handed down in *Industrial Risk*, which was affirmed by the Fourth Circuit.[512]

Some commentators stated that unlike the Second Circuit, the Eleventh Circuit did not conduct such an in-depth analysis and failed to recognize that Article V(1)(e) of the New York Convention accepted that there could be separate legal regimes for recognition and vacatur of convention awards that are made in the state where the award was rendered.[513] The author, however, argues that the problem does not merely arise from the Eleventh Circuit's failure to consider Art. V(1)(e) of the Convention but also from the conflict between s.202 of FAA Chapter 2 and Art. I(1) of the Convention.

Section 202, which was poorly drafted and phrased in the negative, suggests that there are two types of awards: domestic awards, which are governed by FAA Chapter 1, and all others which are governed by the Convention.[514] Thus, Section

---

508 *Indus. Risk Insurers*, 141 F.3d at 1437–39.

509 *Id.* at 1445–46.

510 *Id.* at 1441.

511 *Id.* at 1446.

512 *RZS Holdings*, 598 F.Supp.2d at 762.

513 Harout Jack Samra, *Two to Tango: Domestic Grounds for Vacatur Under The New York Convention*, 20 AM. REV. INT'L ARB. 367, 390 (2009); Marc J. Goldstein, *Setting Aside N.Y. Convention Awards Made in the U.S.: The Latest Decision Errors*, 64 J. DISP. RESOL. 11, 11 (2009).

514 *Compare* 9 U.S.C.A. § 202 "An agreement or award... which is *entirely between citizens of the United States shall be deemed not to fall under the Convention* unless that relationship involves property located abroad, envisages performance or enforcement abroad, or has some other reasonable relation with one or more foreign states." (emphasis added) *with* Rau, *supra* note 425 at 230. ("The intention here was obviously to carve out, from the Convention, agreements or awards that are to remain strictly

202 fails to recognize non-domestic awards as a separate category. [515] As such, FAA s. 202 and Art. I(1) of the Convention offer different categorizations for awards, even though both apply to such a non-domestic award.[516] Accordingly, for non-domestic awards made in the United States, the decision regarding the extent to which grounds to vacate a domestic award are applicable has been left to the appellate courts. If courts apply the Convention directly to non-domestic awards as in *Yusuf*, they will rule that the award is governed by domestic arbitration law, FAA Chapter 1. On the other hand, if the courts look at FAA Chapter 2, which implements the Convention (rather than the Convention directly) as in *Industrial Risk*, then they will determine that the Convention governs the award.

The U.S. Supreme Court has not addressed these issues directly, although in *Stolt-Nielsen S.A. v. Animal Feeds Int'l Corp.* the Court relied on FAA s.10(a)(4), rather than the corresponding ground under the Convention, in concluding that the Convention award made in the United States should be vacated.[517] Yet,

---

within the 'domestic' FAA of Chapter I—insuring at a minimum that an American award, between two American parties and without some relation to a foreign state, must not fall within the treaty").

515 *See supra* note 427 for the categorizations of the awards under the Convention as applied by the Second Circuit.

516 This statement points to the question of whether the Convention is a self-executing treaty so that it supersedes Chapter 2 of the FAA under the "last in time" rule and becomes directly applicable in both federal and state courts. *E.g.*, Restatement (Third) Of Foreign Relations Law § 115 cmt. a (Am. Law Inst. 1987) ("An act of Congress and a self-executing treaty of the United States are of equal status in United States law, and in case of inconsistency the later in time prevails."); Restatement (Fourth) of Foreign Relations Law § 309 Reporters' Notes 3 (Am. Law Inst., 2018) ("Only self-executing treaty provisions can be applied by the judiciary to override a federal statute, since non-self-executing treaty provisions are not directly enforceable in courts in the United States."). *But see id.* § 309(2) ("When there is a conflict between a self-executing treaty provision and a federal statute, courts in the United States will apply whichever reflects the latest expression of the will of the U.S. political branches."). Whether the Convention is self-executing or not is a hotly-debated topic that often divides opinion. Gary B. Born, *The New York Convention: A Self-Executing Treaty*, 40 Mich. J. Int'l L. 115, 130 n.77–79 (2018) (collecting cases and secondary sources). Although most U.S. courts have held or assumed that the Convention is self-executing, some have not. *Id.* Today, there is no certain answer to this question. The author takes the position that the Convention should be treated as self-executing as the Second Circuit has done in *Yusuf* to achieve the Convention's most important objectives: uniformity and harmonization.

517 *Stolt-Nielsen*, 559 U.S. at 662.

in relying on FAA Chapter 1, the Court did consider the arguments made by the Second and the Eleventh Circuits.[518] Interestingly, in its earlier drafts, the Restatement also aligned the grounds for vacatur applicable to non-domestic awards made in the United States with the grounds for refusal to enforce a foreign award rather than with the grounds for vacating domestic arbitration awards.[519] That is to say, if the award is made in the United States, it may be vacated by the U.S. courts if one of the defenses under Article V of the Convention is satisfied. Hence, today, many commentators are in consensus that the issue may be ripe for review and clarification by the Supreme Court if another Federal Circuit follows the ruling handed down in *Industrial Risk Insurers*.[520]

What are the implications of the significant disagreements among the circuit courts for the application of the public policy defense? The Court in *Yusuf* considered a common law ground (*i.e.*, the award is in manifest disregard of the law) applicable to the award made in the U.S., although it found that the defendant did not sufficiently establish this ground to justify the vacatur of the award.[521] Nonetheless, the Second Circuit's acceptance of domestic grounds for vacatur duplicates the applicable public policy standards—one is Article V(2)(b) of the Convention, and one is the common law public policy defense. Thus, it could be deduced that the courts following *Yusuf* can consider public policy standards as applied in domestic awards and U.S.-seated non-domestic awards.

Conversely, the Eleventh Circuit's apparent rejection of domestic grounds for vacatur excludes common law public policy grounds, considering only Article V(2)(b) of the Convention.[522] In fact, in *Industrial Risk*, the Eleventh Circuit

518 *See generally* ENFORCING ARBITRATION AWARDS IN THE US, Practical Law 9-500-4550 9 (last visited Feb. 27, 2022)

519 *Compare* RESTATEMENT (THIRD) U.S. LAW OF INT'L COMM. ARB § 4.11 cmt. a (AM. LAW INST., Tentative Draft No. 2, 2012) ("Although the courts of appeals currently are divided on the grounds for vacating U.S. Convention awards, the Restatement takes the position that under FAA § 207, the exclusive vacatur grounds are those set out in Article V.") *with* RESTATEMENT (THIRD) U.S. LAW OF INT'L COMM. ARB § 4.9 cmt. a ("Although the courts of appeals currently are divided on the grounds for vacating U.S. Convention awards, the Restatement takes the position that the exclusive vacatur grounds are those set out in FAA § 10.). *See* Orlowski, *supra* note 428, at 510.

520 *E.g.* Goldstein, *supra* note 513, at 11; ABBY COHEN SMUTNY ET AL., THIRD CIRCUIT APPLIES DOMESTIC FAA TO US INTERNATIONAL ARBITRATION AWARD (Sept. 1, 2010) Practical Law 1-503-2076

521 *Yusuf*, 126 F.3d at 24.

522 *Indus. Risk Insurers*, 141 F.3d at 1445–46 (affirming the denial of the appellants' "arbitrary and capricious" defense and holding that the arbitral award made in Florida

refused to consider whether the award violated another common law ground (*i.e.*, that the award is arbitrary and capricious), holding that "the Convention's enumeration of defenses is exclusive."[523]

One implication of this would be "the specter of forum shopping" in arbitration within the United States.[524] In fact, the Eleventh Circuit has already been praised as the Court friendliest to international arbitration in the United States because it is the only Federal Circuit to eliminate domestic grounds for vacating international arbitration awards rendered in the United States.[525] Forum-shopping would pose risks to the reliability of arbitration practice as a means of alternative dispute resolution since awards rendered in some parts of the United States would have greater finality than in others.[526] The goal of uniform treatment of international awards—repeatedly asserted as a major reason behind the United States' accession to the Convention in the first place—could also be at risk.[527]

The author agrees with the Second Circuit in *Yusuf*. Accordingly, the Convention award made in the United States ought to be governed both by the FAA and the Convention. Section 208 of the FAA reads that "Chapter 1 applies to actions and proceedings brought under this Chapter to the extent that chapter is not in conflict with this chapter or the Convention as ratified by the United States." That is to say, Section 208 incorporates domestic grounds for vacatur into Chapter 2 (which itself incorporated the New York Convention into U.S. law.) The author accepts what the Second Circuit has pointed out—namely that the Convention and the FAA work together as they have "overlapping coverage."[528] The circuit split arises from the fact that the United States federal arbitration code on governing domestic arbitration has not evolved in parallel to the majority of domestic arbitration codes worldwide—which are mostly based on the Model Law. This is, arguably, the cost of having one of the first modern arbitration codes in

under Florida law falling under the Convention should be reviewed under Article V regardless of the standards set forth in Section 10 of the FAA or any grounds that are not specified in the Convention).

523 *Id.* 1446.

524 Samra, *supra* note 513, at 390.

525 *E.g.*, Shelby R. Grubbs & Glenn P. Hendrix, *International Commercial Arbitration, Southern-Style*, 48 Tenn. B.J. 20, 21 (2012).

526 Samra, *supra* note 513, at 390.

527 E.g. Richard W. Hulbert, *The Case for A Coherent Application of Chapter 2 of the Federal Arbitration Act*, 22 Am. Rev. Int'l Arb. 45, 75 (2011)

528 *Yusuf*, 126 F.3d at 19–20.

the world, although a country's grounds for non-enforcement and vacatur need not necessarily be identical.[529]

Despite the abovementioned apparent risks, the author takes the position that the disagreement among the circuit courts does not pose a significant risk to the enforceability of U.S.-seated Convention awards on the grounds of public policy, without regard to an applicable public policy standard for review under either common law or Article V(2)(b) of the Convention. In *Industrial Risk,* the losing party asserted that admission of the testimony of an expert allegedly against the party who had previously retained him violated public policy, but nevertheless grounded their claim upon a non-statutory public policy basis by citing the standard for review for the non-statutory public policy ground.[530]

The Eleventh Circuit found that non-statutory public policy standard for review is applicable for domestic awards, but not for Convention awards. However, it held that "that rule applies with equal force in the context of international arbitral awards."[531] Thus, the Eleventh Circuit used the non-statutory public policy ground and its standard for review and held that there was no violation of public policy sufficient to sustain a defense under Article V(b)(2) of the Convention.[532] This indicates that the Eleventh Circuit had already set its mind against the non-enforceability of awards on public policy grounds regardless of the standard for review. This proves yet again that the courts in the United States are reluctant to vacate an award or refuse enforcement on the grounds that they violate public policy.

To conclude, as a California District Court noted in one case, "the answer to the question presented is perhaps academic because … the outcome is the same regardless of whether the Court applies the standards set forth under Article V of the Convention or the standards set forth in Chapter I of the FAA."[533]

3.2.4 The Effect of Federalism on International Awards: State Public Policy and the Federal Arbitration Act

In the U.S. judicial system, international commercial arbitration is regulated at both federal and state levels, as is the case with virtually all areas of law in the United States. One could assert that defining a public policy exception for once

529 Davis, *supra* note 428, at 72.

530 *Indus. Risk Insurers*, 141 F.3d at 1443.

531 *Id.* at 1445.

532 *Id.* at 1443.

533 *LaPine*, 2008 U.S. Dist. LEXIS 41172, at *14–17.

at the federal level would narrow the scope of the exception, thereby enhancing uniformity in award enforcement. This would be, however, a violation of state rights pursuant to the Tenth Amendment. This amendment defines the allocation of powers between the federal and state governments, thus asserting the entitlement of the various states of the union to enforce their own public policy in principle.[534]

State courts are unlikely to want to enforce—and are likely to be in favor of vacating—any Convention award that conflicts with state public policy. This is particularly true when the losing party is a citizen of the state in which the enforcement is sought.[535] As such, an analysis of the public policy exception under the Convention as applied in the United States begs the question of whether state or federal public policy is sufficient to refuse to enforce an arbitration award. In this part, the author briefly examines federal and state courts' jurisdiction over actions for the enforcement of a Convention award. The author then analyzes the evolution of state arbitration acts in support of international arbitration by retracing the Supreme Court's case law in favor of international arbitration, thus identifying a pro-arbitration bias since the 1970s. Finally, the author examines whether the FAA preempts international state arbitration laws, and if so, to what extent.

While the federal courts have limited subject-matter jurisdiction, state courts are courts of "general" jurisdiction so that they are empowered to hear any types of cases, except for matters of which Congress has conferred exclusive jurisdiction upon federal courts such as bankruptcy matters, patent infringement claims, and the like.[536] When a Convention award is made in the United States, it can be governed by FAA Chapter 1 as well as Chapter 2, which implements the Convention. Yet, the FAA Chapter 1 standing alone does not provide for federal jurisdiction. Therefore, the action for enforcement of such awards may well proceed in state courts.[537]

---

534 George A. Bermann, *Domesticating' the New York Convention: The Impact of the Federal Arbitration Act*, 2 J Int. Disp. Settlement 317, 331 (2011).

535 Joseph C. Sharp & Joshua D. Jewkes, *A High Hurdle Should State Public Policy Concerns Trump FAA Awards?* DRI The Voice of the Defense Bar, Oct. 2008, at 35.

536 *See* Kokkonen v. Guardian Life Ins. Co. of Am., 511 U.S. 375, 377 (1994).

537 Restatement (Third) U.S. Law of Int'l Comm. Arb § 4-24(c) ("A post-award action may also be brought in a competent state court."). *But cf.* Nanda et al., *supra* note 505, § 19:30 (stating that federal jurisdiction will usually not be an issue, as it is based upon diversity in most cases, including a Convention award).

Conversely, Section 203 of FAA Chapter 2 confers subject-matter jurisdiction on federal courts over actions for the enforcement of a Convention award, regardless of whether the award was made in the United States. [538] Nonetheless, this is not an exclusive jurisdiction so that state courts have concurrent jurisdiction with federal courts over cases arising under FAA Chapter 2.[539] When a party seeks enforcement of a Convention award in a state Court, FAA Chapter 2 grants the defendant the right to remove the case to a federal court.[540] Although removal to a federal court precludes the applicability of state anti-arbitration public policy,[541] both parties may well agree to proceed in the state court. Overall, state courts may hear actions to enforce a Convention award.

---

538 9 U.S.C.A. § 203 ("An action or proceeding falling under the Convention shall be deemed to arise under the laws and treaties of the United States."); RESTATEMENT (THIRD) U.S. LAW OF INT'L COMM. ARB § 4-24 Reporters' Notes e ("Suits to confirm or vacate U.S. Convention awards under FAA Chapter 2... may nevertheless be brought in state court, since federal jurisdiction over such actions is not exclusive.")

539 *E.g.* KPMG LLP v. Cocchi, 565 U.S. 18, 19 (2011) (finding that arbitration agreements that fall within the scope the FAA must be enforced in state and federal courts).

540 9 U.S.C.A. § 205.

541 Under the Erie doctrine, federal courts sitting in diversity apply state substantive law and federal procedural law. Gasperini v. Ctr. for Humanities, 518 U.S. 415, 427 (1996). Accordingly, it could be argued that federal courts may apply state arbitration laws as substantive law and the FAA as procedural law to a non-domestic award under the Convention. *See Southland*, 465 U.S. at 25 (O'Connor, J., dissenting) ("That history establishes conclusively that the 1925 Congress viewed the FAA as a procedural statute... "). This, however, has been uncommon especially after *Southland*, where the Supreme Court interpreted the FAA as a substantive federal law that may preempt state laws regulating arbitration. *E.g., Southland*, 465 U.S. at 15; Kindred Nursing Centers Ltd. P'ship v. Clark, 137 S. Ct. 1421, 1426 (2017) ("The FAA... preempts any state rule discriminating on its face against arbitration."). In so holding, the Supreme Court greatly expanded federal control over arbitration. *See E.g.* Hirshman, *supra* note 46, at 1350 ("The preemptive effect of the FAA after *Southland* is not confined to state law based on... hostility to arbitration: it displaces all state law limiting arbitration regardless of the underlying policy."); David S. Schwartz, *Correcting Federalism Mistakes in Statutory Interpretation: The Supreme Court and the Federal Arbitration Act*, LAW & CONTEMP. PROBS., Winter/Spring 2004, at 5. ("Despite its constant, talismanic repetition, the 'national policy favoring arbitration' is illusory and is highly dubious federalism."). Hence, even though one can argue that federal courts apply international state arbitration law where relevant, a state law requiring the award to be vacated based on state public policy violation would be preempted. *Kindred Nursing*, 137 S. Ct. at 1426. On the other hand, if state international arbitration laws supplement or complement arbitration by filling the gaps in ancillary matters (challenging

State courts generally apply state law. This holds when a party seeks the enforcement of a Convention award in a state court. From the late 1980s, American states have enacted relevant statutes in an attempt to make their states attractive seats for international arbitration.[542] As one commentator nicely put it: "These state laws are largely marketing efforts proclaiming a state's willingness to 'roll out the red carpet' to foreign enterprise." [543] The enactment of state arbitration statutes, then, are no coincidence considering the United States' accession to the Convention in 1970. This is also concurrent with the strong pro-arbitration bias that was established by the U.S. Supreme Court in a trio of international arbitration decisions from 1972 to 1985.[544]

In the wake of these developments, Florida became the first state to enact international arbitration legislation in 1986, the Florida International Arbitration Act.[545] A considerable number of states followed suit.[546] Among these, the majority have legislated international arbitration laws that implement the UNCITRAL Model Law.[547] A minority of states, however, went in a different direction and addressed matters that are not expressly provided for in Chapter 1 or 2 of the

---

the arbitrators, interim relief and the like), then it is less likely to be preempted. E. Alexandra Dosman & Clara Flebus, *The Federal Arbitration Act and State Arbitration Acts: Impact of Federalism on International Arbitration* in the U.S., *in* International Arbitration in the United States, *supra* note 428, at 43.

542 Christopher R. Drahozal, *The New York Convention and the American Federal System*, 2012 J. Disp. Resol. 101, 101 (2012)

543 Thomas H. Oehmke & Joan M. Brovins, 2 Commercial Arbitration § 41:29 (database updated December 2019), Westlaw CMLARB.

544 *See generally Mitsubishi*, 473 U.S at 614; Scherk, 417 U.S. at 506; *Bremen*, 407 U.S. at 1. *See also supra* Section 1.1.4.3.

545 Fla. Stat. Ann. §§ 684.01–683.35 (repealed 2010).

546 George K. Walker, *Trends in State Legislation Governing International Arbitrations*, 17 N.C. J. Int'l L. & Com. Reg. 419, 421 (1992)

547 *Compare Status–UNCITRAL Model Law on International Commercial Arbitration (1985), with amendments as adopted in 2006,* UNCITRAL, http://www.uncitral.org/uncitral/en/uncitral_texts/arbitration/1985Model_arbitration_status.html (last visited Feb. 27, 2022) (stating that California, Connecticut, Florida, Georgia, Illinois, Louisiana, Oregon, Texas adopted the UNCITRAL Model Law) *with* Wash. Rev. Code Ann. §§ 7.05.010–7.05.470 (West) (adopting the UNCITRAL Model Law). *See also* James Harmoush, *Colorado's Second Renaissance: Adopting the UNCITRAL Model Law on International Commercial Arbitration*, 93 Denv. L. Rev. Online 111, 123 (2016) (stating that Washington had adopted the UNCITRAL Model Law in July 2015, but the UNCITRAL website has yet to add Washington to its list).

FAA.[548] These minority statutes aim at providing a supplemental set of rules that authorize state courts to render judicial assistance to administer an international arbitration.[549]

International arbitration laws that implement the UNCITRAL Model Law are of importance for our discussion, as they establish state public policy as a ground for setting aside the award. For example, Oregon state courts may set aside an award if it "is in conflict with the public policy of the State of Oregon or of the United States." [550] As such, to determine the extent to which state public policy may be a ground to vacate a Convention award or refuse its enforcement, one must examine: (i) whether the FAA preempts state arbitration laws; and (ii) whether parties may choose to have their arbitration governed by state arbitration laws so that the state public policy may become applicable to a Convention award.

Looking at the FAA first, there is no clause in the body of the Act that explicitly preempts state laws on arbitration.[551] Neither does the legislative history of the FAA indicate such intent on the part of the Congress.[552] Further, federal law does not implicitly preempt a state's right to regulate arbitration by completely controlling arbitration so that there would be no room for state regulation. Yet, if one wishes to determine the preemptive effect and scope of the FAA, considering the text of the Act alone is insufficient because the FAA is "an edifice of [the Supreme Court's] own creation."[553]

The Supreme Court's landmark rulings on domestic arbitration elucidates that: (i) in enacting the FAA, the Congress has exercised its power under the

---

548 *E.g.* Colo. Rev. Stat. Ann. §§ 13-22-501– 13-22-507 (West).

549 *See* Besson, *supra* note 69 at 217 n.40 ("Hawaii: Hawaii International Commercial Arbitration, Mediation and Conciliation Act, Haw. Rev. Stat. §§ 658D-1-658D-9,... Maryland: Maryland International Commercial Arbitration Act, Md. Code Ann., Cts. & Jud. Proc. §§ 3-2B-01–3-2B-9; Colorado: Colo. International Dispute Resolution Act, Colo. Rev. Stat. §§ 13-22-501–13-22-507"); Daniel A. Zeft, *The Applicability of State International Arbitration Statutes and the Absence of Significant Preemption Concerns*, 22 N.C.J. Int'l L. & Com. Reg. 705, 709–10 (1997).

550 Or. Rev. Stat. Ann. § 36.520

551 *Volt*, 489 U.S. at 470. *See also Ex parte* Ala. Oxygen Co., 433 So.2d 1158, 1162 (Ala. 1983) *overruled by Southland*, 465 U.S. at 25 (engaging in a detailed analysis of why the FAA does not preempt state arbitration laws).

552 *Volt*, 489 U.S. at 477.

553 *Allied-Bruce*, 513 U.S. at 283.

Commerce Clause (*i.e.*, a power that belongs to the federal government);[554] (ii) the FAA does not take precedence over all state laws concerning commercial arbitration; [555] and (iii) the FAA preempts state laws that are in conflict with the FAA or frustrate arbitration.[556] Thus far, the Supreme Court has consistently reaffirmed the FAA's preemption over conflicting state laws.[557] The precise scope of that preemption remains to be set, but state laws that single out arbitration clauses for adverse treatment are preempted by FAA s.2.[558]

On the international arbitration side, at the time of writing, the Supreme Court has not yet explicitly ruled that state public policies may be preempted to the extent that they thwart the enforceability of a Convention arbitral award. However, there are certain cases where the courts have found that the Convention preempts the conflicting state's public policy.

In *Hartford Fire Ins. Co. v. Lloyd's Syndicate 0056 Ash*, the Federal Court sitting in Connecticut held that the Convention preempted state public policy concerning the indemnification of punitive damages.[559] In this case, the panel seated in Connecticut rendered an arbitration award directing the indemnification of the punitive damages.[560] The plaintiff brought an action to confirm the award.[561] In its cross-petition to vacate the award, the defendant responded that the federal choice-of-law rules pointed to the law of Connecticut, thus determining the award directing indemnification of punitive damages unenforceable as it was against Connecticut state public policy.[562] In denying the defendant's cross-petition to vacate the award, the Court emphasized that the parties had included a clause in their contract permitting the indemnification of punitive damages

554 *Prima Paint*, 388 U.S. at 396 (holding that Congress enacted the FAA under its commerce and admiralty powers which are granted in Article I, Section 8, of the U.S. Constitution).

555 *Volt*, 489 U.S. at 477 (*citing* Hines v. Davidowitz, 312 U.S. 52, 67 (1941)) (declaring that state arbitration laws may govern matters not addressed by the FAA "... to the extent that it 'stands as an obstacle to the accomplishment and execution of the full purposes and objectives of Congress.'")

556 *Southland*, 465 U.S. at 3; Dosman & Flebus, *supra* note 541, at 33.

557 *E.g. Kindred Nursing*, 137 S. Ct. at 1428; *AT&T Mobility*, 563 U.S. at 341.

558 Dosman & Flebus, *supra* note 541, at 38.

559 Hartford Fire Ins. Co. v. Lloyd's Syndicate 0056 Ash, Civil No. 3:97CV00009 (AVC), 1997 U.S. Dist. LEXIS 10858 (D. Conn. June 30, 1997).

560 *Id.* at 2.

561 *Id.* at 1.

562 *Id.* at 11–12.

and had also agreed on an arbitration clause which "relieved [the arbitrators] of all judicial formalities and [allowed them to] abstain from following the strict rules of law."[563] Honoring the parties' agreement to arbitrate and deferring the award, the Court found that "the Convention preempts individual state law or state public policy that might hold to the contrary."[564]

The Supreme Court's decisions on domestic arbitration offer good insight into how the Court might possibly rule on international arbitration cases.[565] There is a robust body of case law in which the Supreme Court has strongly deferred to parties' decisions to arbitrate, and that has favored the enforcement of awards. The *Hartford* Court also found that the Convention preempts state public policy in light of this federal policy favoring arbitration. Moreover, the Restatement supports the preemption of state public policy by restricting state public policy to occupy a place in the analysis under very limited circumstances.[566] Reading all this together, one can see that parochial public policies will yield to federal law so that a Convention arbitral award will be enforced in state courts.

Finally, any analysis of the applicability of state public policy must address whether parties may choose to have their arbitration governed by state arbitration laws through a general choice-of-law clause in their contract. The Supreme Court has addressed this issue in two seminal cases, *Volt* and *Mastrobuono v. Shearson Lehman Hutton*. In *Volt*, the Supreme Court upheld a California state Court's decision to apply a provision of California's arbitration law to a contract with a choice-of-law clause referencing California law.[567] The Court held that the FAA governed the arbitration but required it to be carried out as the parties agreed, namely under California rules.[568] Six years later, in *Mastrobuono*—where the parties had also incorporated a generic choice-of-law clause in their contract—the Supreme Court found that the parties only intended for state substantive rules to apply—and not state arbitration rules, which the FAA would otherwise preempt.[569] As such, the Court upheld the arbitral award of punitive damages under an arbitration clause that conflicted with New York statutory law. Further, *Mastrobuono* implies that state arbitration law that is in conflict with the

563 *Id.* at 15.
564 *Id.*
565 *Supra* Section 1.1.4.
566 Restatement (Third) U.S. Law of Int'l Comm. Arb § 1–9.
567 *Volt*, 489 U.S. at 475.
568 *Id.* at 475.
569 *Mastrobuono*, 514 U.S. at 53.

FAA may only apply to an arbitration if the parties expressly select state arbitration law over federal law via a choice-of-law clause in the contract.[570]

To construe the implication of *Volt* and *Mastrobuono* in a cogent manner is challenging. The overwhelming consensus in the scholarly literature submits that the Supreme Court has limited some of the harsher aspects of *Volt* by holding that a generic choice-of-law provision is not sufficient to indicate the parties' intent to apply state arbitration law. *Mastrobuono* establishes that a properly drafted choice-of-law clause expressly intending to invoke state public policy is sufficient to override any inconsistencies with the FAA. In fact, in *Hartford Fire*, the Court reached the same result, finding that "the Convention clearly preempts any state law or state public policy defenses unless the parties have contracted otherwise."[571]

3.3 The Common Law on Public Policy

3.3.1 Roots of The Public Policy Exception In Common Law

Over the years, U.S. federal courts have recognized judge-created, non-statutory grounds—including violation of public policy—to vacate an arbitral award. Moreover, the violation of public policy has been recognized by every circuit, whereas other non-statutory grounds have not.[572] Strikingly, these grounds are all born of labor arbitration and are thus designed with the central features of labor law in mind.[573] Overall, the public policy ground for vacating a domestic arbitral award in the United States has its roots in labor arbitration.

Labor arbitration refers to arbitration in unionized workplaces and is primarily governed by Section 301 of the Labor-Management Relations Act.[574] In a

---

570 Zeft, *supra* note 549, at 785.

571 *Hartford Fire*, 1997 U.S. Dist. LEXIS 10858, at *15 (citing *Mastrobuono*, 514 U.S. at 52).

572 Sharp & Jewkes, *supra* note 535, at 36.

573 Thomas E. Carbonneau, Cases and Materials on Arbitration Law and Practice 680 (7th ed., 2014) [hereinafter Carbonneau, Cases and Materials]

574 Labor-Management Relations Act, 29 U.S.C.A. § 185 (West) [hereinafter the LMRA] (providing that "suits for violation of contracts" between unions and employers may be brought in a federal district court, thereby establishing federal jurisdiction over disputes that arise out of collective-bargaining agreements). Interestingly enough, Section 301 makes no reference to arbitration or how to enforce arbitration agreements or awards on its face. The U.S. Supreme Court, however, found that Section 301 of the LMRA gave it the authority to develop a federal common law of collective-bargaining agreements. Textile Workers Union v. Lincoln Mills, 353 U.S. 448, 455 (1957). The Supreme Court's holding in *Textile Workers* and the lack of a governing statutory regime

collective-bargaining process, an employer and its employees (usually through a union) negotiate over the terms and conditions of employment and the resulting collective-bargaining agreement usually includes an arbitration clause.[575] As such, labor arbitration is not a mere substitute for litigation, but rather a *special kind of arbitration* designed and utilized as an alternative to strike or lockout action for resolving disputes between employers and employees.[576]

When a dispute arises between a union member and employer, arbitrators must—while adjudicating the dispute—look to and apply the terms of the collective-bargaining agreement. In cases where arbitrators have been found to have significantly amended or deviated from the parties' contract, federal courts have usually found under federal common law

i. that the award is against public policy;
ii. that the arbitrators acted in "manifest disregard of the law;"
iii. that the award is "arbitrary and capricious;"
iv. that the arbitrator issued a "completely irrational" award;
v. that the award is "fundamentally unfair," or;
vi. that the award failed to "draw its essence" from the parties' agreements.[577]

---

led the federal courts to develop non-statutory decisional grounds for reviewing labor awards. *See e.g.* CARBONNEAU, CASES AND MATERIALS *supra* note 573, at 679.

575 *Compare* Stephen L. Hayford, *Unification of the Law of Labor Arbitration and Commercial Arbitration: An Idea Whose Time Has Come*, 52 BAYLOR L. REV. 781, 786 (2000) (stating that binding arbitration provisions were part of 90–95 percent of collective-bargaining agreements in the United States as early as the 1950s) *with* PREPARING FOR LABOR ARBITRATION CHECKLIST, Practical Law 7-522-0994 (last visited Feb. 27, 2022) (illustrating that arbitration is still the primary mechanism for resolving disputes about collective-bargaining agreement as of writing this book)

576 Allison Anderson, *Labor and Commercial Arbitration: The Court's Misguided Merger*, 36 B.C. INT'L & COMP. L. REV. 1237, 1241 (2013). In *the Steelworkers Trilogy*, the Supreme Court laid down the criteria governing labor arbitration and enunciated the doctrine of judicial deference to an arbitrator's interpretation of a collective-bargaining agreement. *See* United Steelworkers of Am. v. Am. Mfg. Co., 363 U.S. 564 (1960); United Steelworkers of Am. v. Warrior Gulf Navigation Co., 363 U.S. 574 (1960); United Steelworkers of Am. v. Enter. Wheel & Car Corp., 363 U.S. 593 (1960).

577 *Compare* CARBONNEAU, *supra* note 67 at 526 (stating that the common law grounds for vacatur was elaborated in the context of labor arbitration) *with* Peter B. Rutledge, *On the Importance of Institutions: Review of Arbitral Awards for Legal Errors*, 19 J. INT'L ARB. 81, 110 n.126 (2002) (stating that the common law grounds for vacatur vary widely and thus are not uniform across the Federal Circuits and illustrating cases) *and* Hayford & Kerrigan, *supra* note 497, at 23 (collecting cases).

Three cases dubbed the Public Policy Trilogy commenced in W.R. Grace & Co. v. Rubber Workers, continued in United Paperworkers and International Union v. Misco, Inc. and reaffirmed by the Supreme Court in Eastern Associated Coal v. United Mine Workers Dist. 17. [578] In W.R. Grace, the Supreme Court confined the public policy exception in the labor arbitration context to "explicit," "well-defined," and "dominant" policies by "reference to the laws and legal precedents and not from general considerations of supposed public interests."[579] W.R. Grace's teachings were acknowledged in Misco and Eastern Associated, where both the employers asserted that arbitration awards reinstating employees discharged for using illegal substances violated public policy.

In *Misco*, an operator of dangerous equipment was found sitting alone in a vehicle in the company parking lot with a marijuana cigarette burning in the ashtray and thus discharged by the company.[580] The Supreme Court granted certiorari to determine whether a Court could vacate an arbitral award reinstating the employee based on public policy grounds. However, it left the issue on which certiorari had been granted unresolved—namely, "whether a Court may refuse to enforce an arbitration award rendered under a collective-bargaining agreement on public policy grounds only when the award itself violates positive law or requires unlawful conduct by the employer."[581]

In *Eastern Associated*, the Supreme Court again rejected public policy based challenges to the arbitral award that reinstated a truck driver who was tested positive for drugs.[582] In this case, the Court had a second chance to resolve the issue of which public policy standard to apply, but the Court's ruling stopped short of holding that the public policy exception is limited "solely to instances where the arbitration award itself violates positive law."[583]

---

578 E. Associated Coal Corp. v. United Mine Workers of Am., Dist. 17, 531 U.S. 57 (2000); United Paperworkers Int'l Union v. Misco, Inc., 484 U.S. 29 (1987); W.R. Grace & Co. v. Local Union 759, Int'l Union of United Rubber, 461 U.S. 757 (1983). *See also* Carbonneau, Cases and Material *supra* note 573 at 820 (discussing the three cases of the Public Policy Trilogy and indicating the nexus between them); Henry Drummonds, *The Public Policy Exception to Arbitration Award Enforcement: A Path Through the Bramble Bush*, 49 Willamette L. Rev. 105, 120 (2012) (coining the term "Public Policy Trilogy")

579 *E. Associated*, 531 U.S. at 62; *Misco*, 484 U.S. at 30; *W.R. Grace*, 461 U.S. at 766.

580 *Misco*, 484 U.S.. at 33.

581 *Id.* at 46 (Blackmun, J., concurring).

582 *E. Associated*, 531 U.S. at 62–67.

583 *Id.* at 63.

Federal Circuits, interpreting *Misco*, have divided between a narrow public policy interpretation of the decision and a broad public policy interpretation. Courts adopting the narrow interpretation have required evidence that enforcing the arbitration award violates a positive law and conflicts with public policy.[584] Others, in contrast, focus on whether the conduct leading to termination violated public policy.[585] In other words, if an employee, say, engaged in unlawful conduct which led to her termination (such as using or possessing marijuana on company premises), under the former standard, a Court could find the award reinstating the employee did not violate public policy "unless the law explicitly prohibited employment of an individual with a record of past illegal conduct."[586] Under the latter standard, however, the Court could hold that the arbitral award violated public policy because it reinstated an employee who had herself violated a positive law against drug use by employees.[587]

In light of this lengthy discussion, readers might ask why the public policy exception as applied in labor arbitration is of interest here at all since labor arbitration is entirely distinct from commercial arbitration and thus beyond the scope of this book. Despite the distinctions, the Supreme Court in the last three decades has converged two previously separate bodies of law—*i.e.*, labor arbitration and

---

584 *E.g.* Bos. Med. Ctr. v. SEIU, Local 285, 260 F.3d 16, 23 (1st Cir. 2001) (focusing on whether Massachusetts has a public policy, ascertained by reference to positive law, that prohibits reinstating an employee in the circumstances); IBEW, Local 97 v. Niagara Mohawk Power Corp., 143 F.3d 704, 716 (2nd Cir. 1998) (finding that the Court is "... limited to determining whether the award itself, as contrasted with the reasoning that underlies the award, creates [an] explicit conflict with other laws and legal precedents and thus clearly violates an identifiable public policy."). *See also* N. Peter Lareau, *Supreme Court's Public Policy Exception to Judicial Deferral to Arbitration*, 2017 Emerging Issues 7574 (2017) (collecting cases).

585 *E.g.* Gulf Coast Indus. Workers Union v. Exxon Co., U.S.A., 991 F.2d 244, 246 (5th Cir. 1993) (finding that the award offended public policy because it ordered "... the reinstatement of a proved drug abuser to his safety-sensitive position... "); E. I. Du Pont de Nemours & Co. v. Grasselli Emps. Indep. Assoc., 790 F.2d 611, 616 (7th Cir. 1986) (stating that the courts have never construed the public policy exception so narrowly).

586 Ann C. Hodges, *Judicial Review of Arbitration Awards on Public Policy Grounds: Lessons from the Case Law*, 16 Ohio St. J. on Disp. Resol. 91, 103 (2000).

587 *Id.*

commercial arbitration. As recently as 2018, the Supreme Court in *Epic Systems v. Lewis* confirmed this unification.[588]

The penetration of the public policy exception into the zone of FAA is troubling. The broad public policy interpretation enables courts to substitute their judgment for that of the arbitrator, thereby thwarting the enforceability of the arbitrator's decision. Further, reading FAA s.10 with the strong federal policy favoring arbitration in mind reveals that the merits review of an arbitral award is excluded, as FAA s.10 does not contain any reference to a substantive basis for review.[589] The trouble continues on the Convention side. The public policy standard for review, as applied in labor arbitration, is broader than the public policy standard for review as prescribed in the Convention. The scope of the Court's application of the public policy standard may, therefore, have a decisive effect on the outcome of a case.

3.3.2 The Juxtaposition of the Public Policy Exception Under Labor and Commercial Arbitration

In recent decades, the Supreme Court's application of the FAA has continued to expand. One implication has been the possible merger of labor arbitration with commercial arbitration. Until 2009, it had been the longstanding view that the FAA does not apply to labor arbitration.[590] In 2009, the Supreme Court in *14 Penn Plaza LLC v. Pyett* resolved a labor arbitration dispute using the principles of commercial arbitration developed under the FAA, without even mentioning Section 301 of the Labor-Management Relations Act and held that an arbitration clause within a collective-bargaining agreement was enforceable under the FAA.[591] *14 Penn Plaza* alone may not be sufficient to conclude that arbitration clauses in collective-bargaining agreements fall within the ambit of the FAA. Yet, the Supreme Court continually tailors a broader role for the FAA.

In 2011, the Supreme Court held in *Concepcion* that the FAA preempts states from protecting consumers from unconscionable fine-print contract provisions that require them to waive their rights to class-action arbitration.[592] In *Epic*

588 Epic Sys. Corp. v. Lewis, 138 S. Ct. 1612, 1642 (2018) (declining to find an inherent conflict between the FAA and other federal labor statutes).

589 *E.g.* CARBONNEAU, *supra* note 67, at 110.

590 Seth Galanter & Jeremy M. McLaughlin, *Does the Supreme Court Decision in 14 Penn Plaza Augur the Unification of the FAA and Labor Arbitration Law*, DISP. RESOL. J., May–July 2009, at 56, 56.

591 *14 Penn Plaza*, 552 U.S. at 1178.

592 *AT&T Mobility*, 563 U.S. at 333.

Systems, another corporate-friendly decision, the Supreme Court held that arbitration clauses providing for individualized proceedings that prohibit class or collective action must be enforced.[593] In deciding *Epic Systems*, the Supreme Court interpreted Section 7 of the National Labor-Relations Act—which establishes the framework by which employees can organize and form a union—narrowly.[594] While the Supreme Court has supported business interests and broadened the scope of the FAA regardless of the specific characteristic of labor or consumer law, the creation of a single, unitary arbitration law risks backfiring. To take one example, the public policy ground for review in *Misco* has been generalized by the federal courts, encouraging them to apply the public policy exception to all disputes involving enforcement of arbitral awards, whether they concern labor arbitration or not.

Most of the labor arbitration awards challenged on public policy grounds involve arbitral awards ordering the reinstatement of an employee discharged for a serious act of misconduct—usually related to drug or alcohol abuse.[595] The broad public policy interpretation permits the reviewing court to evaluate the employee's behavior, which is the role of the arbitrator, a role negotiated by the parties and included in the contract by them.[596] If the court finds that the employee's conduct itself violated public policy, then vacatur of the award on public policy ground is triggered.

The public policy ground, as developed in labor arbitration, has sharply departed from its original purpose insomuch as it has been utilized by the courts to review arbitration awards in commercial, maritime, consumer and employment law.[597] While a merits review may be appropriate in the context of labor arbitration, it is unfit for regulating the enforcement of awards that fall under the statutory regime of the FAA and the Convention.[598] To begin, the Convention award made in the United States may be governed both by the FAA and the Convention.[599] The application of U.S. law will implicate the violation of public policy as

593 *Epic Systems*, 138 S. Ct. at 1616.

594 *Id.* at 1624.

595 Hayford, *supra* note 575, at 822–23. *See also* Hodges, *supra* note 586, at 92 (collecting cases).

596 *Id.* at 95.

597 *See* Sheldon v. Vermonty, 269 F.3d 1202, 1206 (10th Cir. 2001) (acknowledging violation of public policy, for vacating an arbitration is one of the "handful of judicially created reasons" in addition to the enumerated grounds in the FAA); CARBONNEAU, CASES AND MATERIAL *supra* note 573 at 804

598 *Id.* at 680.

599 *See generally supra* Section 3.2.3.

applied in labor arbitration to the very limited bases for vacatur ordinarily available under the FAA.[600] Yet, the public policy ground for vacatur in labor arbitration authorizes courts to review the merits of arbitral determinations whereas FAA s.10 does not recognize any grounds authorizing merits review.

The next problem is the clash between legal standards for public policy exceptions. Although the public policy exception is also found in the New York Convention, the standards applicable to international arbitration cases differ from those applicable to labor arbitration cases.[601] The standard for review in *Misco* requires a violation of some explicit public policy that is "well-defined and dominant, and … to be ascertained by reference to the laws,"[602] whereas enforcement may be denied on the Convention's public policy basis "only where enforcement would violate the forum state's most basic notions of morality and justice."[603] In applying the common law public policy standard to an international award, does this mean that an arbitral award may be denied enforcement on the grounds of public policy simply because it violates some statute in effect in the United States despite not violating the most basic notions of morality of the United States?

In applying the common law public policy standard to international awards, the majority of courts have found that the awards do not violate the public policy and have repeatedly emphasized the very goal of the Convention, which is to encourage the enforcement of international awards.[604] Some courts, on the other hand, have merged the two applicable standards, without choosing one standard over another.[605] For example, in *Sharp Corp. v. Hisense USA Corp.*, as pointed to above, the Court first indicated that the public policy exception is "to be applied

600 See Thomas E. Carbonneau, *Debating the Proper Rule of National Law under the New York Arbitration Convention*, 6 Tul. J. Int'l & Comp. L. 277, 287 (1998). [hereinafter Carbonneau, *the Proper Rule of National Law*]

601 S.I. Strong, International Commercial Arbitration: A Guide for U.S. Judges 69 (2012).

602 *Misco*, 484 U.S. at 43.

603 *Parsons & Whittemore*, 508 F.2d at 974.

604 *E.g.* Research & Dev. Ctr. "Teploenergetika," LLC v. EP Int'l, LLC, 182 F. Supp. 3d 556, 568 (E.D. Va. 2016); Subway Int'l B.V. v. Bletas, No. 3:10-cv-1714 (JCH), 2012 U.S. Dist. LEXIS 33341, at *10 (D. Conn. Mar. 13, 2012); NTT Docomo, Inc. v. Ultra D.O.O., 2010 U.S. Dist. LEXIS 109377, at *7 (S.D.N.Y. Oct. 12, 2010).

605 *E.g.* Sharp Corp. v. Hisense USA Corp., 292 F. Supp. 3d 157, 174–75 (D.D.C. 2017); BCB Holdings Ltd. v. Gov't of Belize, 110 F. Supp. 3d 233, 250 (D.D.C. 2015); Karaha Bodas Co., L.L.C. v. Perusahaan Pertambangan Minyak Dan Gas Bumi Negara, 190 F. Supp. 2d 936, 955 (S.D. Tex. 2001).

only where enforcement would violate the forum state's most basic notions of morality and justice."[606] The Court later added that this public policy "must be well-defined and dominant and is to be ascertained by reference to the laws and legal precedents and not from general considerations of supposed public interests."[607] In doing so, the Court set a higher threshold and required both standards to be met in order to deny the enforcement of an award.

In sum, it appears from the case law that the courts are very reluctant to deny the enforcement of a Convention award on the ground of public policy, irrespective of the legal standard chosen by the Court for application of the public policy defense. Courts have utilized public policy standards in accordance with the needs and features of international arbitration. Hence, generalization of the common law public policy exception to the international commercial arbitration context has fortunately not increased the likelihood of vacatur of awards.

3.3.3 Public Policy After *Hall Street*

Despite the uptick in arbitration cases before the Supreme Court in the last few terms, one of the issues that remains ripe for decision is whether the common law public policy ground, besides the other non-statutory grounds for vacatur, survived *Hall Street* as a valid ground for vacatur. In 2008, the *Hall Street* decision addressed whether the grounds for vacatur set forth in FAA s.10 was "open to expansion by agreement" of the parties in as much as the parties may contractually expand the grounds for vacatur.[608]

In *Hall Street*, environmental contamination led to a dispute between landlord and tenant—namely, to the dispute as to who was responsible for clean-up costs. During litigation, the parties, with the District Court's leave, decided to submit the matter to arbitration. The submission agreement included a caveat authorizing the District Court to "vacate, modify, or correct any award if the arbitrator's conclusions of law were erroneous," which introduced a ground for vacatur that is not provided in the FAA.[609] The question presented to the Supreme Court was whether the parties contractually expand the scope of judicial review and grounds for vacatur provided in the FAA.

To show that the grounds in the FAA are not exclusive, the petitioner in *Hall Street* argued that the Court had already acknowledged "expandable judicial

606 *Sharp Corp.*, 292 F. Supp. 3d at 174–75.

607 *Id.*

608 *Hall Street*, 552 U.S. at 583.

609 *Id.* at 578.

review authority" by referencing "manifest disregard of the law" language in its earlier decision, *Wilko*.[610] In the course of its analysis, the Supreme Court, *in dictum*, called into question the viability of manifest disregard of the law ground for vacating an arbitral award, though the decision stopped short of resolving the question.[611] As a result, a circuit split has developed following *Hall Street* as to whether the Supreme Court, by implication, eliminated the non-statutory grounds for vacatur entirely.

Obviously, the Supreme Court in *Hall Street* did not explicitly address public policy as a basis for vacatur, let alone reject its validity. Not surprisingly, there has been a vast amount of literature after *Hall Street* seeking to answer whether "manifest disregard of law" exception in public policy remains as a viable ground. In contrast, the viability of the public policy exception after *Hall Street* has been poorly examined.

---

610 *Id.* at 584. The manifest disregard of the law exception as a non-statutory ground for vacatur derived from the language in the Supreme Court's decision in *Wilko*. In *Wilko*, the Court stated *in dicta*: "In unrestricted submissions... the interpretations of the law by the arbitrators in contrast to *manifest disregard* are not subject... to judicial review for error in interpretation." *Wilko,* 346 U.S. at 436–37 *overruled by Rodriguez,* 490 U.S. at 477 (emphasis added). Despite being a dictum, the manifest disregard of law ground has turned out to be a widely-cited authority. *See* Kenneth R. Davis, *End of an Error: Replacing Manifest Disregard with a New Framework for Reviewing Arbitration Awards,* 60 Clev. St. L. Rev. 87, 94 n.46 (2012) [hereinafter Davis, *End of an Error*] (collecting cases). The *Hall Street* Court rejected the petitioner's argument that the *Wilko* Court established the manifest disregard standard as a ground for vacatur for several reasons: To start with, the *Hall Street* Court found that the Petitioner's interpretation of *Wilko* was "too much for *Wilko* to bear." *Hall Street*, 552 U.S. at 585. Further, the Court emphasized that, even if *Wilko* had done so, *Wilko* does not support an inference that the parties may expand the grounds of review by agreement. *Id.* at 584. Second, the *Hall Street* Court emphasized that the phrasing in *Wilko* was vague and speculated the meaning of the term manifest disregard. *Id* at 585 ("Maybe the term 'manifest disregard' was meant to name a new ground for review, but maybe it merely referred to the § 10 grounds collectively, rather than adding to them. Or, as some courts have thought, 'manifest disregard' may have been shorthand for § 10(a)(3) or § 10(a)(4), the paragraphs authorizing vacatur when the arbitrators were 'guilty of misconduct' or 'exceeded their powers.' We, when speaking as a Court, have merely taken the Wilko language as we found it, without embellishment.") (citations omitted). As Davis rightly pointed out, "the Court, however, did not decide this issue, but rather confused the bar with alternative interpretations [of manifest disregard], scrambling words like eggs in a skillet." Davis, *End of an Error, supra* note 610, at 91.

611 *Hall Street*, 552 U.S. at 578.

The *Hall Street* decision has nonetheless heightened uncertainty as to the continuing validity of the common law public policy ground.[612] The Fifth Circuit was the first Court of appeals to find that *Hall Street* "clearly and repeatedly" rejected common law grounds for vacatur.[613] Soon after, the Eighth and Eleventh Circuits adopted the Fifth Circuit's construing of *Hall Street*.[614] Although these Circuits did not specifically address its viability, we can deduce that the Fifth, Eighth, and Eleventh Circuits have rejected the common law public policy defense. In fact, District courts within the Fifth and Eleventh Circuits have explicitly held that public policy is no ground for vacatur of an arbitration award under the FAA.[615]

Unlike the abovementioned circuits, the Second and Ninth Circuits have considered the common law public policy ground for vacatur after *Hall Street*, albeit not expressly addressing its validity. In *Lagstein v. Certain Underwriters at Lloyd's, London*, the Ninth Circuit first noted that manifest disregard survives *Hall Street* and then considered the public policy defense argument without assessing its continued validity.[616] Interestingly, the Second Circuit in *Schwartz v. Merrill Lynch & Co.* followed the Ninth Circuit when first citing its previous decision. In so doing, it concluded that manifest disregard remains a valid

---

612 *Compare* Rite Aid N.J., Inc. v. United Food Commer. Workers Union, Local 1360, 449 F. App'x 126, 129 (3rd Cir. 2011) (not precedential) (assuming that after *Hall Street*, an arbitration award can be vacated when an award violates public policy) *with* Frazier v. CitiFinancial Corp., LLC, 604 F.3d 1313, 1324 (11th Cir. 2010) (holding that judicially-created bases for vacatur are no longer valid in view of *Hall Street*.) *See also* Davis, *End of An Error, supra* note 610, at 126 n.277 (discussing why the public policy exception will survive).

613 Citigroup Global Mkts., Inc. v. Bacon, 562 F.3d 349, 353 (5th Cir. 2009).

614 Med. Shoppe Int'l, Inc. v. Turner Invs., Inc., 614 F.3d 485, 489 (8th Cir. 2010) (holding that an arbitral award may be vacated only for the reasons enumerated in the FAA); *Frazier*, 604 F.3d at 1324.

615 *E.g.*, Am. Postal Workers Union, v. U.S. Postal Serv., No. CIV.A. 3:09-CV-1084B, 2010 WL 1962676, at *2 (N.D. Tex. May 14, 2010) ("... while public policy was once recognized as a common law ground for vacating an arbitration award, in light of Hall Street and its progeny, it was no longer an adequate basis for vacatur."); DCR Const., Inc. v. Delta-T Corp., No. 8:09-CV-741-T-27AEP, 2009 WL 5173520, at *6 (M.D. Fla. Dec. 30, 2009) ("Following Hall Street, public policy is no longer a viable ground for vacatur... ")

616 Lagstein v. Certain Underwriters at Lloyd's, London, 607 F.3d 634, 641 n.4 (9th Cir. 2010). *See also* Immersion Corp. v. Sony Comput. Entm't Am. LLC, 188 F. Supp. 3d 960, 969 (N.D. Cal. 2016) (analyzing the Ninth Circuit's reading of public policy).

ground for vacating arbitration awards, thereafter reckoning with the common law public policy defense argument without engaging in a discussion regarding its viability.[617] In contrast, the Seventh Circuit expressly found that "*Hall Street* Court did not overrule *Eastern Associated Coal* or *W.R. Grace*, both of which recognized a public policy exception to the general prohibition on overturning arbitrator awards."[618]

The remaining circuits have yet to reveal their readings of *Hall Street*. The Third and Tenth Circuits have expressly declined to decide whether common law grounds are still viable, perhaps awaiting guidance from the Supreme Court. There has been no discussion following *Hall Street* by the First, Fourth, Sixth, and D.C. Circuits.[619]

The case law developed post-*Hall Street* leads to several conclusions: (i) some circuits found that common law grounds for vacatur are no longer valid after *Hall Street*; (ii) some circuits considered the public policy defense with or without explicitly stating that it survives *Hall Street*, and; (iii) some circuits have yet to reveal their reading of *Hall Street* and its impact on public policy. Hence, it is plain to see that *Hall Street* has generated a split among the federal circuits regarding the viability of the common law public policy ground. Nevertheless, the question arises: To what extent does the split matter?

When a non-domestic arbitration is conducted in the United States, a party may challenge the award under both the New York Convention and the FAA standards of review. Thus, theoretically speaking, the forum Court will consider whether a common law public policy challenge is available to the party under the FAA. If the forum Court holds that common law public policy is no longer viable after *Hall Street*, public policy ground found in Art.V(2)(b) of the Convention is nevertheless available to the party, and thus, this reading of *Hall Street* will not pose a serious challenge to the parties.[620]

In the other scenario, if the forum Court holds that common law public policy is viable after *Hall Street*, then parties will have two different public policy challenges available to them—one under the Convention and one judicially-created. As discussed in the previous subchapter, the common law public policy standard

---

617 Schwartz v. Merrill Lynch & Co., 665 F.3d 444, 452 (2nd Cir. 2011).

618 Titan Tire Corp. of Freeport v. United Steel, 734 F.3d 708, 717 n.8 (7th Cir. 2013).

619 *E.g. Rite Aid*, 449 F. App'x 126, at 129 n. 3; Legacy Trading Co. v. Hoffman, 363 F. App'x 633, 635 n.2 (10th Cir. 2010) (declining to decide on judicially-created grounds for vacatur to survive in the wake of *Hall Street*).

620 Orlowski, *supra* note 428, at 538.

for review might be construed more broadly than the public policy standard for review under the New York Convention, and one might fear that the availability of different standards of review threatens the enforceability of the award. Such concern, however, is unfounded because the courts in the United States have narrowly construed the public policy exception, especially in international arbitration cases, and thus different standards for review do not pose a serious risk.[621]

To conclude, the author believes that *Hall Street* has not abolished the public policy exception for reviewing arbitral awards because nothing in the *Hall Street* decision demonstrates such an intent to eliminate it.[622] Further, one can hardly contemplate that the Court would enforce an award that endangers public health or safety.[623] This, however, does not mean that *Hall Street* has had no impact on the applicability of the common law public policy ground. The Supreme Court in *Hall Street* has again underscored the Supreme Court's historical willingness to limit freedom of contract where it is used to impede enforcement of arbitral awards.[624]As such, after *Hall Street*, the courts even become loather to apply the broad public policy interpretation that allows merits review to cases that involve a non-domestic award.[625]

---

621 *Id.*

622 E.g. Richard C. Reuben, *Personal Autonomy and Vacatur After Hall Street*, 113 PENN. ST. L. REV. 1103, 1127–28 (2009). *See also* Codie Henderson, The Hall Street Hangover: Recovering and Rediscovering Avenues for Review of Arbitration Awards; Hall Street Assocs. v. Mattel Inc., 128 S. Ct. 1396 (2008), 10 WYO. L. REV. 299, 314 (2010) ("... public policy has an established history in the law and would be difficult to supplant"). *Cf.* Jonathan A. Mercantel, *The Crumbled Difference Between Legal and Illegal Arbitration Awards: Hall Street Associates and the Waning Public Policy Exception*, 14 FORDHAM J. CORP. & FIN. L. 597, 624–25 (2009) (stating that, because the Supreme Court in Hall Street held the grounds for vacatur enumerated in the FAA are exclusive, the non-statutory public policy ground has been abolished).

623 Davis, *End of an Error, supra* note 610, at 126–27 (illustrating that courts would seem compelled to vacate an award that gave its blessing to an unlawful monopolization of the high-tech industry, or the dangerous operation of a nuclear facility).

624 Anthony Rallo, *The Veil of Acquiescence: Between the Lines of an Intuitive Appellate Decision, The Ninth Circuit Subtly Marginalizes FAA Limitations on Judicial Review*, 24 AM. REV. INT'L ARB. 681, 690 (2013).

625 Reuben, *supra* note 622,at 1143.

3.4 Public Policy in The Context of International Arbitration Under The New York Convention

3.4.1 The Legal Standard For the Application of Public Policy As An Exception To The Enforcement of Foreign Arbitral Awards

Art.V(2)(b) of the New York Convention permits a Court to refuse the enforcement of an arbitral award if it is contrary to the public policy of the enforcing country. Courts in the United States have rigorously enforced arbitration awards, and in line with this pro-arbitration trend, the scope of public policy has been strictly constrained. As we recently marked the sixtieth anniversary of the Convention in 2018, "the public policy doctrine is not moribund," but "it is in fact rarely relied upon."[626] Though rare, U.S. courts would deny the enforcement on public policy grounds when the enforcement of the award would violate "the forum state's most basic notions of morality and justice" or "some explicit public policy that is well-defined and dominant."[627]

The celebrated case defining the legal standard for application of the public policy defense in the United States is *Parsons & Whittemore*, rendered shortly after the United States acceded to the Convention in 1970.[628] In *Parsons & Whittemore*, a U.S. construction company had contracted with an Egyptian corporation to complete a construction project in Egypt but later stopped construction, citing force majeure circumstances arising from the Arab–Israeli Six Day War of 1967, which had (temporarily) severed relations between Egypt and the United States.[629] The Egyptian corporation initiated arbitration to seek damages for breach of the contract, arguing that even as the Egyptian government has decided to expel American citizens in general, special visas were available to the U.S. Company.[630] When the Egyptian corporation sought enforcement of the award rendered in its favor, the District Court concurred, rejecting the U.S. company's argument that equated U.S. foreign policy toward Egypt with public policy.[631]

---

626 Termorio S.A. E.S.P. v. Electrificadora Del Atlantico S.A. E.S.P., 421 F. Supp. 2d 87, 101 (D.D.C. 2006), *aff'd sub nom. TermoRio*, 487 F.3d at 928.

627 *Compare Parsons & Whittemore*, 508 F.2d at 974 *with Misco*, 484 U.S. at 43.

628 The New York Convention Status *supra* note 16.

629 *Parsons & Whittemore*, 508 F.2d at 972.

630 *Id.*

631 *Id.* at 974

In affirming the District Court, the Second Circuit contrasted the New York Convention with its predecessor, the Geneva Convention of 1927, from several different perspectives. It concluded that the New York Convention's main effort was to eradicate pre-existing obstacles to the enforcement of foreign arbitration awards.[632] Emphasizing the general pro-enforcement bias surrounding the Convention, the Second Circuit stated that a narrow reading of the public policy defense is required to meet the New York Convention's goals. As such, rejecting an award on the ground of Article V(2)(b) of the Convention could only occur where enforcement would violate the aforementioned basic morality standard as set out in *Parsons & Whittemore.*

Most circuits follow the approach set by the Second Circuit and often cite *Parsons & Whittemore* for its admonition that the narrow construction of this defense is required to advance the New York Convention's goals. In 2017, the Federal Circuit in *Bayer* collected cases where the other circuits have followed the Second Circuit in *Parsons & Whittemore.*[633] Combining the *Bayer* Court's finding with a further review of case law shows that the Third, Fifth, Sixth, Seventh, Ninth, and D.C. Circuits adopted the public policy standard to review arbitral awards entered under the Convention.[634]

Unlike these circuits, the Eleventh Circuit has applied the common law public policy standard to the review of arbitral awards entered under the New York Convention. As such, a Convention award is unenforceable if the enforcement violates the aforementioned explicit and well-defined public policy standard as set out in the *Public Policy Trilogy.* [635] As the reader will recall from the discussion on Section 3.3.1, this standard was developed by the Supreme Court in the context of labor arbitration. Thus, it had no place in the international arbitration realm otherwise. Further, this standard suggests that it is easier to be met as it can be interpreted by a Court that a violation of positive law may reach the required threshold to vacate the award on public policy ground, regardless of the

---

632 *Id.* at 969, 973.

633 *Bayer*, 680 F. App'x at 994.

634 *Id.* (*quoting* Ministry of Def. & Support for the Armed Forces of the Islamic Republic of Iran v. Cubic Def. Sys., Inc., 665 F.3d 1091, 1097 (9th Cir. 2011)); *TermoRio*, 487 F.3d at 938; *Karaha Bodas*, 364 F.3d at 306; Slaney v. Int'l. Amateur Athletic Fed'n, 244 F.3d 580, 593 (7th Cir. 2001); M & C Corp. v. Erwin Behr GmbH & Co., KG, 87 F.3d 844, 851 n.2 (6th Cir. 1996); Admart AG v. Stephen & Mary Birch Found., Inc., 457 F.3d 302, 308 (3rd Cir. 2006), *as amended on reh'g* (Sept. 28, 2006).

635 *Indus. Risk Insurers*, 141 F.3d at 1445.

enforcement violates "most basic notions of morality and justice" of the United States.

Luckily, without leaving room for doubt, the Eleventh Circuit stressed that the public policy defense should be construed narrowly, citing *Parsons & Whittemore*.[636] This signals that although the Eleventh Circuit has yet to announce whether the narrow or broad public policy interpretation is its accepted standard of review for public policy defense applicable to awards in the domestic context, the Eleventh Circuit is certainly more deferential to Convention awards.[637]

In conclusion, we could draw that the Second Circuit in *Parsons & Whittemore* "legislated" the meaning of the public policy defense by broadly examining the final goal of the Convention and reasoning that reading the public policy defense cautiously would best serve the stated purpose of Convention.[638] Most circuits have followed this standard, although not the Eleventh Circuit. This, however, does not mean that the Eleventh Circuit will find violations of public policy more thoroughly, as the courts largely remain unwilling to thwart enforceability in the name of public policy.

3.4.2 Challenges to Arbitral Awards Based on Public Policy Violations

3.4.2.1 Types of Allegations That Are Frequently Invoked But Do Not Violate Public Policy

3.4.2.1.1 Misapplication of Law and Lack of Reasons

Concerning the principles underlying the Convention in favor of enforcement of awards, existing case law in the United States has been more forthcoming in providing lists of what is not a violation of public policy, rather than what is.[639] Because no exhaustive list of the latter exists, recurring and debatable allegations are our concern here.

To start with, the misapplication of substantive law or an arbitrator's error of fact in deciding a case does not rise to the level of violating public policy, nor does it constitute "manifest disregard of the law."[640] As the Second Circuit has

636 *Id.* (citing *Parsons & Whittemore*, 508 F.2d at 974)

637 *E.g.* Grubbs & Hendrix, *supra* note 525 at 21.

638 NANDA ET AL., *supra* note 505 § 19:22.

639 Lahlou et al., *supra* note 425 at 169.

640 *See e.g. Agility Pub. Warehousing*, 495 F. App'x at 154 (finding that "a mere error in the application of state law, rather than knowing disregard of applicable law" does not show manifest disregard of law)

noted, allowing the Court to inquire into the credibility of the arbitrator's decision of law or fact "would render the allegedly simple and speedy remedy of arbitration a mockery."[641] Similarly, the lack of reasons in the award is not a public policy ground when the parties have agreed that arbitrators are not required to give reasons.[642]

The idea of manifest disregard of the law by an arbitrator is similar (but not identical to) a simple misinterpretation of law and fact. To draw the contrast, manifest disregard of law allegations transpire, not because the arbitrator made an error of law or fact, but rather because the arbitrator ignored law that she was bound to apply.[643] Even though manifest disregard of the law constitutes a grosser violation than errors of law and fact, neither rises to the level of violating public policy. This is because the U.S. courts have repeatedly held that an arbitrator's manifest disregard of the law a non-existent ground under the New York Convention, even though it may be a ground for vacatur under the FAA.[644] As one New York District Court nicely elaborates, "manifest disregard of law, whatever the phrase may mean, does not rise to the level of contravening public policy, as that phrase is used in Article V of the Convention. Nor, unlike proceedings under Chapter 1 of the Federal Arbitration Act, can manifest disregard of law be urged as an independent ground for vacating an award falling within the Convention."[645]

---

641 Waterside Ocean Navigation Co. v. Int'l Navigation, Ltd., 737 F.2d 150, 152–53 (2nd Cir. 1984)

642 *See e.g.*, *Scherk*, 417 U.S. at 532 ("An arbitral award can be made without explication of reasons and without development of a record... "); Robbins v. Day, 954 F.2d 679, 684 (11th Cir. 1992); *Koch Oil*, 751 F.2d at 551 (stating that the Court must accept the unreasoned award without attempting to analyze the arbitrators' purported reasoning process); Shaw Constructors, Inc. v. HPD, LLC, 749 F. Supp. 2d 474, 484 (E.D. La. 2010).

643 Stephen L. Hayford, *Law in Disarray: Judicial Standards for Vacatur of Commercial Arbitration Awards*, 30 GA. L. REV. 731, 842 (1996).

644 *E.g.* Int'l Trading & Indus. Inv. Co. v. DynCorp Aerospace Tech., 763 F. Supp. 2d 12, 30 (D.D.C. 2011) ("There is simply no support in either the text of the New York Convention or case law for the position that an arbitrator's 'manifest disregard of the law' is a valid basis upon which the Court can deny confirmation of an arbitral award."); Ocean Partners Holdings Ltd. v. Doe Run Res. Corp., No. 4:11-CV-173 CEJ, 2012 WL 830486, at *5 (E.D. Mo. Mar. 12, 2012) (finding that manifest disregard is not one of the enumerated grounds for refusal provided in the Convention).

645 Brandeis Intsel Ltd. v. Calabrian Chemicals Corp., 656 F. Supp. 160, 165 (S.D.N.Y. 1987)

3.4.2.1.2 Punitive Damages

Another concept that does not constitute a violation of public policy is enforcement of an award of punitive damages. Although U.S. law allows for the award of punitive damages, public policy has long been an impediment to enforcement of punitive damages awards by arbitrators.[646] New York law is a case in point. New York, as a major global business hub, has been frequently selected as a venue for arbitration and its law designated as the law that should govern any such dispute. Yet, punitive damages had been long deemed not available in arbitration under *Garrity v. Lyle Stuart, Inc.*, because permitting an arbitrator to award punitive damages "displaces the Court and the jury, and therefore the State, as the engine for imposing a social sanction."[647] It was further reasoned under *Garrity* that "punitive damages is a sanction reserved to the State" so that "enforcement of an award of punitive damages as a purely private remedy would violate strong public policy."[648]

In 1995, the Supreme Court in *Mastrobuono* limited *Garrity*'s applicability when it held that applying New York law as the choice-of-law does not automatically trigger *Garrity* so that the award of punitive damages is enforceable. The Supreme Court interpreted the choice-of-law clause in a way that it only meant that New York's substantive law was applicable to the dispute, and not its provisions limiting an arbitrator's award. As such, the Supreme Court in *Mastrobuono* has one more time, as it does before nearly in all circumstances, sustained the recourse to arbitration. Recently, in 2014, New York courts followed *Mastrobuono* in adopting the Supreme Court's conclusion and holding that the arbitrators are empowered to award punitive damages.[649]

As the author has pointed out above, decisional law on domestic arbitration has a significant impact upon the case law on international arbitration developed under the New York Convention. These authorities support the conclusion that punitive damages awarded by arbitrators will be enforceable in the international arbitration context. In fact, in *Gold Reserve Inc. v. Bolivarian Republic of*

---

646 *See* Fahnestock & Co., Inc. v. Waltman, 935 F.2d 512 (2nd Cir. 1991); Shaw v. Kuhnel & Assocs., 102 N.M. 607, 698 P.2d 880 (1985); Belco Petr. Corp. v. AIG Oil Rig, Inc., 164 A.D.2d 583, 565 N.Y.S.2d 776 (1991); Garrity v. Lyle Stuart, Inc., 40 N.Y.2d 354, 353 N.E.2d 793 (1976) *as cited in* Linda L. Schlueter, 1 Punitive Damages § 4.12 n. 74 (2018).

647 *Garrity*, 40 N.Y.2d at 358.

648 *Id.* at 356.

649 Flintlock Constr. Servs., LLC v. Weiss, 122 A.D.3d 51, 55 (1st Dep't 2014).

Venezuela, the District Court in D.C. held that an award that resolved a dispute between a Canadian mining company and Venezuela did not violate the public policy of the United States, refusing Venezuela's claim that the award imposed punitive damages that violated a bilateral investment treaty between Canada and Venezuela.[650] The Court emphasized that public policy should be construed narrowly and that Venezuela's claim did not violate the aforementioned basic morality standard as set out in *Parsons & Whittemore*.[651]

3.4.2.2 Types of Allegations in Which Enforcement May Be Denied on Public Policy Grounds

3.4.2.2.1 Mandatory Rules of Law

"To date, no federal Court of appeals has refused enforcement of an international arbitration award on public policy grounds."[652] This statement is from Practical Law owned by Thomson Reuters, an online legal know-how service that offers practice area overviews and is widely used by attorneys across the United States. The statement, however, is not accurate.

Although courts have almost uniformly enforced foreign arbitration awards notwithstanding claims that the enforcement would violate public policy, there are certain cases where federal courts, including courts of appeals, have refused or have come closer to refusing the enforcement of an arbitral award on public policy grounds. Having touched upon the types of allegations that do not violate public policy, my purpose in this section is to scrutinize the arguments where they were sufficient, or theoretically sufficient, to justify refusal of enforcement on public policy grounds, regardless that the losing party's challenge eventually proved unsuccessful in that particular case.

To begin, the U.S. Court will examine a violation of public policy claims thoroughly when it involves vindication of a statutory right. Statutory rights embodied in mandatory laws are somewhat at odds with arbitration owing to the private-public dichotomy. This is because mandatory laws seek to protect the

---

650 Gold Res., Inc. v. Bolivarian Republic of Venez., 146 F. Supp. 3d 112, 131–35 (D.D.C. 2015).

651 *Id.* at 132. *See also* Ludgate Ins. Co. v. Banco De Seguros Del Estado, No. 02 Civ. 3653 (DC), 2003 WL 443584, at *8 (S.D.N.Y. Jan. 6, 2003) ("[P]unitive damages are not against the public policy of the United States, which is the policy at issue here.").

652 Challenges to Arbitral Awards in the US Based on Public Policy Violations, Practical Law W-007-8103 (last visited Feb. 27, 2022).

public interest, whereas arbitration is a form of private adjudication where the state surrenders its control over the enforcement of such laws.[653]

In searching for a balance between its pro-arbitration policy and maintaining its jurisdiction over the enforcement of U.S. statutory laws, the Supreme Court, in its seminal case *Mitsubishi*, held that a public policy defense would be an applicable ground for ensuring that arbitrators gave U.S. antitrust laws due regard in an international arbitration. That is to say, the Supreme Court regards the public policy defense as a tool in ensuring that applicable statutory rights (*e.g.*, rights arising from antitrust laws, as in *Mitsubishi*) are considered and applied in an arbitral proceeding when the party is seeking to exercise her statutory right.[654] The Supreme Court thus reserved for national courts the right to take a "second look" at the award when the party is seeking to enforce it in the United States.

Even though the second-look doctrine can be interpreted as calling for the review of an award on the merits,[655] I know of no case where a U.S. Court has refused to enforce an arbitral award on public policy grounds where the claimant challenged the tribunal's application of statutory law. In fact, decisional law shows that courts have been reluctant to use public policy as a ground for refusing enforcement where the challenge is based on a refusal to consider a statutory claim by arbitrators.[656] Hence, to date, the practical implications of the second-look doctrine are uncertain, thus remaining something of a sword of Damocles hanging over arbitrators' heads, incentivizing them to apply statutory laws to produce an enforceable award.[657]

3.4.2.2.2 Awards Based on Penalty Clauses and Awards of Interest

An Article V(2)(b) exception to enforcement can also arise from awards based on penalty clauses in a contract or awards of interest that are penal in nature, although some U.S. courts have enforced such awards despite claims that doing so

---

653 *See generally supra* Section 2.6.1.2

654 *See* Vera Korzun, *Arbitrating Antitrust Claims: From Suspicion to Trust*, 48 N.Y.U. J. Int'l L. & Pol. 867, 871 (2016).

655 *See generally* Gordon Blanke, *The "Minimalist" and "Maximalist" Approach to Reviewing Competition Law Awards: A Never-Ending Saga Revisited or the Middle Way at Last*, in Post-Hearing Issues in International Arbitration 196 (Devin Bray & Heather L. Bray eds., 2013).

656 *E.g. Baxter*, 315 F.3d at 832. *See also* Cvoro v. Carnival Corp., 234 F. Supp. 3d 1220, 1226 (S.D. Fla. 2016).

657 See Eric A. Posner, *Arbitration and the Harmonization of International Commercial Law: A Defense of Mitsubishi*, 39 Va. J. Int'l L. 647, 668 (1999).

would violate the public policy.[658] The case law thus provides no clear picture of what a successful public policy challenge requires the losing to demonstrate. It does offer, however, a certain guidance.

One District Court in New York required the claimant to prove that an award related to the punishing of public wrongs in contrast to redressing of private injuries so that the arbitrators' award of interest would be contrary to public policy.[659] One might also note that where an arbitral award of interest or an award based on penalty clauses has been deemed penalizing, rather than compensatory, in nature, the courts have partially enforced the award, denying only the excessive interest portion of the award as a violation of public policy.[660]

3.4.2.2.3 Violation of Due Process

U.S. courts may deny enforcement based on public policy grounds where fundamental procedural rules are violated. This blanket term entails cases: (1) where the award was procured through fraud or corruption;[661] (2) where the awards rendered by a biased tribunal;[662] and (3) where the parties did not have the opportunity to be heard at a meaningful time and in a meaningful manner.[663] These three grounds are similar to the first three grounds of section 10(a) of the FAA.[664]

---

658 *E.g.* PDV Sweeny, Inc. v. Conocophillips Co., 670 F. App'x 23, 24 (2nd Cir. 2016) (denying the claim that an award runs afoul of public policy against penalty provisions in contracts because it is not part of "our most basic notions of morality and justice."); *Mutu*, 849 F. Supp. 2d at 1344 (enforcing the arbitral award based on a penalty clause and finding that enforcement would not violate the most basic notions of morality and justice); International Standard Elec. Corp. v. Bridas Sociedad Anonima Petrolera, Indus. Y Comercial, 745 F.Supp. 172, 180 (S.D.N.Y. 1990) (rejecting the argument that the interest component of the award should be vacated as being contrary to public policy).

659 *Brandeis*, 656 F. Supp. at 170 (*quoting Laminoirs*, 484 F. Supp. at 1069).

660 *Laminoirs,* 484 F. Supp. at 1071.

661 *E.g. Europcar Italia*, 156 F.3d at 315.

662 *E.g.* Application of York Hannover Holding A.G. v. Am. Arbitration Ass'n., No. 92 CIV. 1643 (CSH), 1993 WL 159961, at *5 n.4 (S.D.N.Y. May 11, 1993)

663 *See* National Oil Corp. v. Libyan Sun Oil Co., 733 F. Supp. 800 (D. Del. 1990)

664 The first three grounds of FAA s.10(a) contemplate vacatur of an award where the award procured by corruption, fraud or undue means; where there is evident partiality on the part of arbitrators; and where the arbitrators were guilty of misconduct in the hearing process prejudicing a party, respectively. 9 U.S.C.A. § 10(1)(a)-(c)

Therefore, cases applying these provisions offer useful guidance when assessing a challenge to a foreign award under the Convention.[665]

This, however, comes with a caveat: Decisional law demonstrates that the public policy defense applicable to Convention awards has been narrower than the public policy or the FAA defenses applicable to awards rendered in the United States.[666] As a result, when ruling on Convention cases where the claimant asserted a violation of a fundamental procedural rule, the overwhelming number of courts have found no violation of public policy that is sufficient to refuse enforcement.[667] Though the losing party's challenge ultimately proved unsuccessful in these cases, courts have deemed at least conceivably sufficient to justify a refusal to enforce an award on public policy grounds where the fundamental procedural rules are violated.[668]

3.4.2.2.4 Comity

Last but not least, U.S. courts will also likely find a violation of public policy under Article V(2)(b) where the award compels a violation of foreign law or a court order; or where the enforcement of the award would disregard the doctrine of comity, which the Supreme Court defines as "recognition which one

---

665 *See e.g. Biotronik*, 415 F. Supp. at 140 (stating that where the Court could not find fraud within the meaning of section 10(a), it could not find the award violated the "most basic notions of morality and justice" of the United States.)

666 *E.g. Belize Bank*, 852 F.3d at 1112 (noting that even if the conduct did satisfy the FAA standard of evident partiality, the Court would be unable to deny enforcement, as it is insufficient to satisfy Art.V(2)(b) of the Convention). *See* NANDA ET AL., *supra* note 505, § 19:22.

667 *E.g. Waterside Ocean*, 737 F.2d at 152 (finding that the tribunal admittance of sworn testimony that was contradictory to prior sworn testimony does not violate public policy); *Belize Bank*, 852 F.3d at 1111–13 (finding no violation of public policy where one of arbitrators in the panel was a member of an English barristers' chambers, of which another member represented interests adverse to that party); *Generica*, 1996 WL 535321 (refusing to find a public policy violation where the tribunal had limited cross-examination).

668 *E.g. Europcar Italia*, 156 F.3d at 315 (stating that a fraudulently obtained award might violate public policy and preclude enforcement); York Hannover Holding A.G. v., 1993 WL 159961, at *5 n.4("An award rendered by a panel that was tainted with bias or impartiality may conceivably be set aside under the Convention as a violation of public policy and thus within Article V(2)(b)"); *National Oil*, 733 F. Supp. at 800 (stating that misconduct by arbitrators justifies refusal when such misconduct has denied the party a fundamentally fair hearing).

nation allows within its territory to the legislative, executive or judicial acts of another nation."[669] In the international arbitration context, U.S. courts usually extend comity to foreign bankruptcy proceedings to ensure the maximum possible availability of assets for equitable distribution to all creditors.[670]

For example, in *Victrix*, when the creditor moved to enforce its foreign award in a District Court, the Court denied the motion and deferred to the Swedish courts based on comity because bankruptcy proceedings were already underway in Sweden.[671] Agreeing with the District Court's decision, the Second Circuit considered the debtor's ongoing bankruptcy proceedings in Sweden and reasoned that enforcing the foreign arbitral award would conflict with the public policy concern to ensure equitable distribution of the assets of a bankrupt.[672]

Similarly, in *Sea Dragon, Inc. & Gebr. Van Weelde Scheepvaartkantoo*r *B.V.*, the owner of a vessel sought to enforce an award ordering a charterer to make a payment to the owner despite a Dutch court's sequestration order.[673] The District Court decided that the award disregarding the Dutch order "violates public policy and warrants deviation from the general rule of confirmation of arbitration awards."[674]

Award's ordering of specific performance against a sovereign government can also potentially violate the public policy of the United States. This constitutes another dimension of international comity as the U.S. courts are loath to disregard the sovereign rights of the country against whom enforcement was sought.[675] In

---

669 Hilton v. Guyot, 159 U.S. 113, 164 (1895)

670 Remington Rand Corp. v. Business Sys. Inc., 830 F.2d 1260, 1271 (3rd Cir. 1987); Cunard S.S. Co. v. Salen Reefer Servs. AB, 773 F.2d 452, 459 (2nd Cir. 1985). *See* Christine Sandez, *The Extension of Comity to Foreign Bankruptcy Proceedings: Philadelphia Gear Corp. v. Philadelphia Gear de Mexico, S.A.*, 20 N.C.J. Int'l L. & Com. Reg. 629, 652 (1995)

671 *Victrix*, 825 F.2d at 711.

672 *Id.*

673 Sea Dragon, Inc. v. Gebr. Van Weelde Scheepvaartkantoor B.V., 574 F. Supp. 367 (S.D.N.Y. 1983)

674 *Id.*

675 Marike R. P. Paulsson, *The US Courts and Their New York Convention Public Policy Gloss Revisited: Hardy Exploration & Production (India), Inc. v. Government of India, Ministry of Petroleum & Natural Gas: Glossing with International Comity*, Kluwer Arbitration Blog (Dec. 26, 2018), http://arbitrationblog.kluwerarbitration.com/2018/12/26/the-us-courts-and-their-new-york-convention-public-policy-gloss-revisited-hardy-exploration-production-india-inc-v-government-of-india-ministry-of-petroleum-natural-gas-glossing-wi/

2018, in *Hardy Expl. & Prod. (India) v. Gov't of India*, the District Court did not enforce the award ordering specific performance (reinstating the investor as the operator of a hydrocarbons block in India) against India as being contrary to the public policy of the United States.[676] The Court reasoned that U.S. courts ought to respect "the right of other nations to control the extraction and processing of natural resources within their own sovereign territories."[677]

3.4.3 Public Policy Gloss: Confirming an Annulled Award Where the Annulment Violates Most Basic Notions of Morality and Justice

The principles of international comity have long been recognized by U.S. courts insomuch as they justify the refusal of an award on public policy grounds, as explained in the previous section. There is another interplay between comity and public policy arising from Article V(l)(e) of the Convention, which allows enforcing courts to deny the enforcement of an arbitral award provided that the award "has been set aside or suspended by a competent authority country in which, or under the law of which, that award was made."

The New York Convention authorizes the enforcing Court to exercise its discretion in enforcing awards that are vacated at the place of arbitration.[678] This provision becomes applicable, for example, when a U.S. Court in an ongoing enforcement proceeding is called to decide the effect of a Convention award rendered in France but set aside by the French courts. The question then becomes: Should the U.S. courts honor the annulment judgment given by the French courts, thus denying the enforcement in light of the principles of comity? Or should U.S. courts hold to their pro-arbitration policy and enforce the set-aside award?

Although the Supreme Court has not yet opined on the matter, courts in the United States have seldom used their discretion to enforce an annulled award.[679]

676 Hardy Expl. & Prod. (India) v. Gov't of India, 314 F. Supp. 3d 95, 114 (D.D.C. 2018)

677 *Id.* at 110.

678 The New York Convention *supra* note 15, Articles V and VII.

679 Maria Slobodchikova, *Enforcement of Annulled Arbitral Awards in the United States: Discretion to Confirm an Arbitral Award Constrain by Principles of Comity*, *in* 40 UNDER 40 INTERNATIONAL ARBITRATION 469, 470 (Carlos Gonzalez-Bueno ed., 2018). See generally Pedro J. Martinez-Fraga, *U.S. Arbitration Law and Its Dialogue with the New York Convention: The Development of Four Issues*, *in* THE AMERICAN INFLUENCES ON INTERNATIONAL COMMERCIAL ARBITRATION: DOCTRINAL DEVELOPMENTS AND DISCOVERY METHODS, supra note 84 at 151, 151.

Based on the principle of international comity, the judicial practice of U.S. courts has been to defer to the judgment of vacatur by the court in the seat of arbitration. As such, there must be a sufficient reason to not give deference to the decision of the foreign court vacating the award.[680] In this regard, in some cases, U.S. courts enforced awards that had been set aside by the court at the seat of arbitration based on V(1)(e), with using the public policy analysis of Article V(2)(b) by accepting that Article V(1)(e) has a so-called "public policy gloss."[681]

Chromalloy Aeroservices v. Arab Republic is the first case known to most to have dealt with the issue of enforcement of an award set aside by a foreign Court under the New York Convention.[682] In *Chromalloy*, a U.S. District Court enforced a Cairo award that had been set aside by the Egyptian Court on the ground that the tribunal had wrongly applied Egyptian contract law instead of applying Egyptian administrative law.[683] The Court reasoned that deferring the annulment of the award would be contrary to U.S. pro-arbitration public policy and ruled that "comity does not and may not have the preclusive effect upon U.S. law."[684] Commentators have criticized the *Chromalloy* Court as it found an arbitral award enforceable and ruled against the preclusive effect of the principle of international comity on rather unconvincing grounds.[685]

---

680 *See* Clifford Hendel & María Antonia Pérez Nogales, *Enforcement of Annulled Awards: Differences Between Jurisdictions and Recent Interpretations*, *in* 60 Years of the New York Convention: Key Issues and Future Challenges 187, 199 (Katia Fach Gomez & Ana M. Lopez-Rodriguez eds., 2019)

681 *E.g. TermoRio*, 487 F.3d at 937; Corporacion Mexicana de Mantenimiento Integral, S. de R.L. de C.V. v. Pemex-Exploracion y Produccion, 962 F. Supp. 2d 642, 656 (S.D.N.Y. 2013), *aff'd*, 832 F.3d 92 (2nd Cir. 2016).

682 *E.g.* Hendel & Pérez Nogales, *supra* note 680 at 199; Slobodchikova, *supra* note 679, at 470.

683 *Compare* Chromalloy Aeroservices v. Arab Republic, 939 F. Supp. 907, 911, 914–15 (D.D.C. 1996) *with* W. Laurence Craig, *The Arbitrator's Mission and the Application of Law in International Commercial Arbitration*, 21 Am. Rev. Int'l Arb. 243, 293 n.48 (2010).

684 *Chromalloy*, 939 F. Supp. at 913.

685 *E.g.* Carbonneau, *the Proper Rule of National Law supra* note 600, at *279* (arguing that the *Chromalloy* Court attached greater importance to the national law of the place of enforcement than national law used to set aside an international award in spite of Article VII of the Convention, which requires the maintenance of a party's domestic law rights to the enforcement of awards). *See* Marc J. Goldstein, *Annulled Awards In the U.S. Courts: How Primary Is "Primary Jurisdiction"?*, 25 Am. Rev. Int'l Arb. 19, 20 (2014); John P. Bowman, *The Panama Convention and its Implementation Under the Federal Arbitration Act*, 11 Am. Rev. Int'l Arb. 1, 66 n.169 (2000).

Other U.S. courts have not followed the approach taken in Chromalloy.[686] In the cases after *Chromalloy*, the scales have been tipped heavily in favor of international comity. For example, the Second Circuit, in *Baker Marine, Ltd. v. Chevron, Ltd.*, recognized the Nigerian courts' judgments annulling an arbitral award on the ground that "no adequate reason was shown for refusing to recognize" them.[687] Similarly, *Termorio S.A. E.S.P. v. Electranta S.P.*, the D.C. Circuit recognized that international comity principles are so supreme that when a foreign Court has set aside an arbitral award, "United States courts should not go behind that decision absent extraordinary circumstances."[688]

International comity, however, is not incontrovertible. As such, it has become subject to "public policy gloss" by the U.S. courts. Some courts have disregarded annulment awards based on V(1)(e) and enforced awards by borrowing the Article V(2)(b) analysis to reframe Article V(1)(e) as having a "public policy gloss."[689] That is to say, U.S. courts will potentially not give deference to the foreign Court judgment annulling the award if the judgment violates the U.S. public policy. Although this has been decided under the Panama Convention, the recent *Pemex* case offers a great analogy in this regard.[690]

In *Pemex*, the District Court enforced a Mexican award that had been set aside by the Mexican courts based on the retroactive application of legislation that Mexico adopted after the arbitration had commenced.[691] This later statute, therefore, made the arbitration illegal under Mexican law, leading the courts to favor Mexico's state-owned enterprise over a private party.[692] The Court first noted that "a final judgment obtained through sound procedures in a foreign country is generally conclusive unless enforcement of the judgment would offend public policy … to the extent that it is repugnant to fundamental notions of what is decent and just in the State where enforcement is sought."[693] The Court emphasized that public policy standard is "high and infrequently met" but if

---

686 E.g. TermoRio, 421 F. Supp. 2d at 937. See also Albert Jan van den Berg, *Enforcement of Arbitral Awards Annulled in Russia Case Comment on Court of Appeal of Amsterdam, April 28, 2009*, 27 J. INT'L ARB 179, 193 (2010)

687 Baker Marine, Ltd. v. Chevron, Ltd., 191 F.3d 194, 197 (2nd Cir. 1999). *See also* Spier v. Calzaturificio Tecnica, S.p.A., 71 F. Supp. 2d 279, 288 (S.D.N.Y. 1999).

688 *TermoRio*, 421 F. Supp. 2d at 938.

689 *Pemex*, 962 F. Supp. 2d at 653 *aff'd*, 832 F.3d at 92.

690 *Pemex*, 832 F.3d at 92.

691 *Id. at 99.*

692 *Id.*

693 *Id.* at 97.

the judgment "tends clearly to undermine the public interest," the Court would disregard "the goals of comity and res judicata that underlie the doctrine of recognition and enforcement of foreign judgments."[694] The Court concluded that it would exercise its discretion to enforce an annulled award where the judgment of annulment vindicates "fundamental notions of what is decent and just in the United States."[695] Therefore, the Court declined to give res judicata effect to a Mexican judgment because the losing party was denied due process in the Mexican Court because of retroactivity.[696]

In conclusion, the "public policy gloss" of Article V(1)(e) is a concept that enables U.S. courts to disregard an annulment judgment if that judgment violates the aforementioned basic morality standard prescribed in *Parsons & Whittemore*. It provides a higher threshold to be met in order for U.S. courts to deviate from the principles of comity and enforce a set aside award, notwithstanding that Article V(1)(e) does not lay this down as a condition. Because the principles of comity are so strong, it comes as no surprise that the courts borrowed the public policy standard under Article V(2)(b), as this standard has been construed narrowly by the courts and been a ground for refusal only under extraordinary circumstances.

3.5 Possible Effects of Third-Party Funding and Artificial Intelligence on the Public Policy Exception to Arbitration

3.5.1 Implications of The Use of Artificial Intelligence In The Application of The Public Policy Exception

Current legal scholarship covers the interface between arbitration and AI systems to a certain degree, but whether the use of AI in arbitration would trigger a public policy exception under the Convention has not yet been explored. [697] This is arguably because arbitration practice has yet to draw on AI to the extent

---

694 *Id.*

695 *Id.* at 107.

696 *Id.* at 106.

697 *But see* Irene Ng (Huang Ying) & Valeria Benedetti del Rio, *When the Tribunal Is an Algorithm: Complexities of Enforcing Orders Determined by a Software under the New York Convention*, in 60 Years of the New York Convention: Key Issues and Future Challenges *supra* note 680 at 123 (briefly touching upon the issue of whether an AI-rendered award would trigger the public policy exception).

that traditional practice has been disrupted. The issue of the public policy exception has thus not yet been touched. To look for the potential impact of AI on the public policy exception, there is a need to analyze the status quo and explore the opportunities and challenges of the use of technology in arbitration in order to forecast what the future might bring.

AI could be incorporated into the practice of international arbitration in several ways. These include the use of autonomous AI as an aid to human arbitrators or AI substituting for human arbitrators (*i.e.*, a machine arbitrator.)[698] In enforcing an arbitral award assisted or made by AI under the Convention in the United States, two possible issues may arise, namely: (i) whether the use of machine learning in judicial decision-making would raise several concerns that would be sufficient to trigger the public policy exception, or; (ii) whether there is a restriction against the use of machine arbitrators in the United States.

The use of AI systems for judicial decision-making raises challenging ethical concerns as well. On the one hand, an AI arbitration procedure that involves algorithms and software may seem less prone to bias and other inadvertent human errors because AI will apply the decision-making rules that it is programmed to follow.[699] For example, ROSS Intelligence conducts AI-driven research, and its systems can read and digest an enormous database of legislation, case law, and scholarly work and draw inferences based on this research.[700] Current algorithms and software, including ROSS, however, lack the fairness and justice traits attributed to humans, which (at present) cannot be mimicked or produced even by the most cutting-edge AI technology.[701] Further, where an AI algorithm lacks actual intellectual reasoning or shows bias, it is unlikely that developers will disclose an algorithm justifying a decision to the parties or the Court, as the algorithm is vital to their business.[702] As such, whether AI makes or contributes

698 *See generally supra* Section 2.6.2.6; Christine Sim, *Will Artificial Intelligence Take Over Arbitration?*, 14 Asian Int'l Arb. J. 1, 2 (2018).

699 Ayelet Sela, *Can Computers Be Fair? How Automated and Human-Powered Online Dispute Resolution Affect Procedural Justice in Mediation and Arbitration*, 33 Ohio St. J. on Disp. 91, 115 (2018)

700 *Features*, ROSS Intelligence, https://rossintelligence.com (last visited Feb. 27, 2022)

701 *See* Nick Bostrom & Eliezer Yudkowsky, *The Ethics of Artificial Intelligence*, *in* Cambridge Handbook of Artificial Intelligence 316, 321–322 (William Ramsey & Keith Frankish, eds., 2014) (stating that present-day Al systems lack moral status as they do not have the capacity to feel pain and suffering); Jan L. Jabobowitz & Justin Ortiz, *Happy Birthday Siri! Dialing in Legal Ethics for Artificial Intelligence, Smart Phones, and Real Time Lawyers*, 4 Tex. A&M J. Prop. L. 408 (2018).

702 Ng (Ying) & Benedetti del Rio, *supra* note 697, at 124; Sim, *supra* note 698, at 2.

to decisions fairly and ethically may be a possible ground for not enforcing an award, since unethical or unfair decision-making is arguably against the public policy of the United States.

We may draw on the *Pemex* case analogously here. In *Pemex*, the District Court did not respect the Mexican annulment judgment in which a Mexican Court had retroactively applied a law prohibiting the arbitrability of the dispute at stake. The District Court found the retroactive application of the law to be unfair since it was enacted with the sole purpose of favoring the Mexican state entity that was losing to the other party in the arbitration. As such, the Court found enough grounds to act against comity and enforce the award in the United States. Analogously, a U.S. court may refuse to enforce an award rendered or assisted by AI on the grounds of public policy when the award is unfair, even though the AI applied the law to the dispute in a technically correct but dry manner, based purely on the hard facts.[703] Other than these rare instances, U.S. courts are most likely to enforce awards rendered or assisted by AI, given the pro-arbitration bias. This is especially true if the parties choose AI to be used in arbitration in the light of *Volt,* where the Supreme Court held "arbitration is strictly a matter of contract" insomuch as "partied should be at liberty to choose the terms under which they will arbitrate."[704]

Lack of impartiality in the cases where AI is used for judicial decision-making in arbitration could also trigger the public policy exception so that U.S. courts may arguably refuse to enforce the award. Although AI seems less prone to bias, it is, in fact, criticized bitterly for being prejudiced. This is down to recent, highly public "fails" by AI, such as when face-recognition software mistagged human beings of African origin in online images as gorillas, and Google Ads displayed advertisements for certain lower-paying jobs only to female users.[705] AI may be driven by a form of bias as its algorithms tend to focus on the *most available* rather than *the most useful data.*[706] That is to say, unlike humans, AI cannot (yet) reflect on its own selective input and is unable to provide a rationale for its

703 *See id.* at 131; Nikolaus Pitkowitz et al., *The Vienna Innovation Propositions: Venturing into New Fields and New Ways of Arbitration–Revisiting Traditional Ways of Arbitration*, in AUSTRIAN Y.B. ON INT'L ARB. 515, 528 (Christian Klausegger et al., eds. 2019).

704 *Volt*, 489 U.S. at 472.

705 *E.g.,* Tom Simonite, *When It Comes to Gorillas, Google Photos Remains Blind*, WIRED (Nov. 1, 2018), https://www.wired.com/story/when-it-comes-to-gorillas-google-photos-remains-blind/

706 Edwin Montoya Zorrilla, *Towards a Credible Future: Uses of Technology in International Commercial Arbitration*, 16 GERMAN ARB. J. 106, 112 (2018).

decisions.[707] As such, AI biases might not be readily detected, as AI often functions as a "black box" in such a way that its operations are too intricate for any human to trace accurately.[708]

A final consideration could be whether there is a restriction in the United States against the use of machine arbitrators, machine arbitrators—that is, where an AI algorithm has wholly substituted the human arbitrator, and if so, whether this restriction could trigger public policy exception. The FAA and the Convention do not provide or imply that the arbitrators must be human, although the FAA makes reference to arbitrators using gender pronouns such as "he" or "they.[709]" Given both the FAA and the Convention were drafted before the advent of the computer age, the drafters could scarcely even have imagined the possibility of parties appointing AI as an arbitrator. Further, this sort of evolution engages with a question of semantics rather than a purposeful attempt to restrict arbitration to only human arbitrators.[710]

We can, however, at least conclude that the applicable statutes in the United States provide no outright restriction. That is to say, an arbitral award rendered by AI could technically (*i.e.*, in principle) be enforced under the FAA and the Convention. Moreover, the United States is home to many of the companies that develop AI, and American public policy has generally encouraged and facilitated AI research and development.[711] Similarly, the U.S. courts go to great lengths to enforce arbitral awards. The totality of these findings indicates that the use of AI arbitrators per se is unlikely to be deemed contrary to public policy, arguments about specific applications notwithstanding.

---

707 Ng (Ying) & Benedetti del Rio, *supra* note 697, at 130; Zorrilla, *supra* note 706, 112.

708 *Id.*

709 9 U.S.C.A. § 5

710 *E.g.* Ng (Ying) & Benedetti del Rio, *supra* note 697, at 123; Sim, *supra* note 698, at 3.

711 *See* The White House Office of Sci. and Tech. Pol'y, Summary of the 2018 White House Summit on Artificial Intelligence for American Industry (2018), https://www.whitehouse.gov/wp-content/uploads/2018/05/summary-report-of-white-house-ai-summit.pdf.; Andy Patrizio, *Top 25 Artificial Intelligence Companies*, Datamation (Apr. 10, 2018), https://www.datamation.com/applications/top-25-artificial-intelligence-companies.html

3.5.2 The Rise of Third-Party Funding and Public Policy Exception

Third-party funding of large-scale arbitral claims is relatively new in the United States because contingency attorney financing is widely available as an integral part of the U.S. legal system.[712] That being said, third-party funding has increasingly become an attractive option for commercial parties who do not have the funds to pay for arbitration or have the funds but prefer to save their capital for other uses.[713] Yet, the legal regime governing third-party funding is fraught with uncertainty concerning the applicability of maintenance and champerty doctrines as well as ethical rules.[714] Further, the FAA and the state laws on arbitration do not refer at all to third-party funding. Finally, users of third-party funding in international arbitration must look to the specific case in question to see whether their particular funding arrangement is permitted or not under its statutes and case law.

The most important legal doctrines applicable to third-party funding under U.S. state laws are maintenance and champerty, which both originated in the English common law.[715] Most U.S. states have long recognized these doctrines and deemed contracts of maintenance or champerty contrary to public policy due to a medieval suspicion of litigation and to protect access to justice and due process.[716] These doctrines, however, are only enforced in state-level courts and

---

712 See e.g. Victoria A. Shannon, *Harmonizing Third-Party Litigation Funding Regulation*, 36 Cardozo L. Rev. 861, 875–76 (2015); Jasminka Kalajdzic et al., *Justice for Profit: A Comparative Analysis of Australian, Canadian and U.S. Third Party Litigation Funding*, 61 Am. J. Comp. L. 93, 127 (2013).

713 Caroline Simson, *3rd-Party Funding Now A Top Alternative Choice for Lawyers*, Law360 (May 16, 2019), https://www.law360.com/articles/1160547/3rd-party-funding-now-a-top-alternative-choice-for-lawyers.

714 Nieuwveld & Shannon, *supra* note 399, at 129.

715 *E.g.* Ross Q. Panko, *Accrued Financial Services, Inc. v. Prime Retail, Inc.: Resurrecting Barratry Imposes Detour On Road To Modernization Of Maryland Contracts Jurisprudence*, 62 Md. L. Rev. 361, 365 (2003) (stating that in Maryland and other jurisdictions, the recognition of the doctrines of champerty and maintenance are down to the English common law prohibition against certain types of contractual arrangements); Patrick T. Morgan, *Unbundling Our Tort Rights: Assignability for Personal Injury and Wrongful Death Claims*, 66 Mo. L. Rev. 683, 691 (2001) (discussing the origin and evolution of the champerty and maintenance doctrines).

716 *See* Michele DeStefano, *A Brave New World: The Changing Face of Litigation And Law Firm Finance: Article: Claim Funders And Commercial Claim Holders: A Common Interest or A Common Problem?*, 63 DePaul L. Rev. 305, 374 (2014).

mostly in those enforcement actions where the enforcing Court decides to bring state public policy into its decision.[717] The patchwork of state laws indicates that (1) some states have abolished these doctrines or carved out exemptions for significant commercial disputes;[718] (2) some states never adopted maintenance and champerty;[719] (3) some states found that maintenance and champerty violates public policy;[720] and finally (4) some states either have not expressly addressed or have since abandoned the doctrines.[721]

Although the statute and case law constitute a patchwork, we need to go back to the basics to answer the question of whether maintenance and champerty could trigger the public policy exception under the FAA or the Convention. To state this simply, the question becomes whether state public policies could present a bar to enforcement of an international arbitral award. In the case of international arbitration, the courts have repeatedly found that state laws that conflict with or disfavor arbitration are preempted by the FAA and federal policy favoring arbitration.[722] Thus, the U.S. courts will likely enforce a funded international arbitration award, overriding any state public policy. Moreover, third-party funding of a commercial dispute would likely be favored over the funding of small-scale consumer disputes given that the bargaining power of the parties to large-scale commercial disputes is much greater than those of individuals.[723]

---

717 Nieuwveld & Shannon, *supra* note 399, at 145.

718 *See e.g.* NY CLS Jud § 489 (providing a safe harbor provision for claims over USD 500,000); Ohio Rev. Code Ann. § 1349.55 (2009); Osprey, Inc. v. Cabana Limited Partnership, 532 S.E.2d 269, 279 (S.C. 2003) (abolishing champerty finding that "it no longer is required to prevent the evils traditionally associated with the doctrine as it developed in medieval times."); Saladini v. Righellis, 687 N.E.2d 1224 (Mass. 1997) (allowing litigation funding and abolishing maintenance and champerty);

719 *See e.g.* Martin v. Morgan Drive Away, Inc., 665 F.2d 598, 605 (5th Cir. 1982) (stating that Louisiana does not apply general common law principles of champerty); Abbott Ford, Inc. v. Superior Court, 741 P.2d 124, 141–42 n.26 (Cal.1987) (finding that California has never adopted the common law doctrines of champerty and maintenance).

720 *See e.g.* Johnson v. Wright, 682 N.W.2d 671, 678 (Minn. Ct. App. 2004) ("An agreement in which a party had had no interest otherwise, and when he is in no way related to the party he aids, is champertous and void as against public policy"), *as discussed in* Ronen Perry, *Crowdfunding Civil Justice*, 59 B.C. L. Rev. 1357, 1371 (2018).

721 *See* Nieuwveld & Shannon, *supra* note 399, at 170 (stating that Puerto Rico did not expressly address the question of third-party funding).

722 *See generally supra* Section 3.2.4

723 *See e.g.* NY CLS Jud § 489.

Finally, third-party funding may also threaten the impartiality of arbitrators and lead to conflict-of-interest problems that have the potential to trigger the public policy exception. For example, if the arbitrator fails to disclose her identity in arbitration where she serves as an arbitrator in one case and an attorney in another case (where both are funded by a third-party), the failure to disclose may give rise to justifiable doubts as to her impartiality.

The American Bar Association formed a Working Group on Alternative Litigation Finance to study the effect of third-party funding on the professional responsibilities of lawyers to their clients. As a result of this study, a report issued in 2012 provided a guideline on what the professional responsibilities of attorneys are in client cases that involve "alternative litigation finance."[724] There are, however, no certain guidelines in the United States providing for arbitrator disclosure obligations where a third-party funder is involved. Moreover, the current arbitral rules on disclosure are insufficient to adequately address conflict-of-interest problems in cases of third-party funding. Several commentators have correctly argued that the arbitral institutions should develop clear rules requiring disclosure from both the arbitrators and the funded parties.[725] Ideally, such disclosure will occur before arbitrators have been appointed because conflicts discovered only after arbitration has been initiated pose the risk that the award will be denied enforcement.

It bears repeating that a lack of impartiality by the arbitrator may amount to enforcement of the award on the grounds of being contrary to the public policy of the United States. Against this background, there is an urgent need for action to develop ethics rules in third-party funding for arbitrators before the courts refuse the awards on public policy grounds, notwithstanding the fact that failure to disclose may have been inadvertent.

---

724 Am. Bar Ass'n, Commission on Ethics 20/20 Informational Report to the House of Delegates 2–3 (2012), https://www.americanbar.org/content/dam/aba/administrative/ethics_2020/20111212_ethics_20_20_alf_white_paper_final_hod_informational_report.pdf.

725 E.g. Victoria Shannon Sahani, *Judging Third-Party Funding, 63 UCLA L. Rev. 388, 429 (2016); Jennifer A. Trusz, Full Disclosure? Conflicts of Interest Arising from Third-Party Funding in International Commercial Arbitration*, 101 Geo. L.J. 1649, 1682 (2013).

4 The Public Policy Exception in Turkey in the Light of U.S. Law and Practice

Abstract: The fourth chapter turns to discuss the public policy exception as legislated and applied in Turkey. The fourth chapter pursues two principal objectives. The first is to identify Turkish public policy as a mindset, and the second is to study the public policy exception under Turkish law and practice. The general theme of this chapter is a comparison of the strengths and weaknesses of Turkish law and practice as they pertain to the public policy exception in light of U.S. law and practice. In so doing, this chapter explores the similarities and differences between the American and Turkish approaches to addressing and applying the public policy exception. The chapter then surveys what laws apply to international awards as far as the public policy exception is concerned. It must be noted that although the public policy exception, as stipulated in Turkish domestic arbitration, is not the focus of this book, several points will be examined in a comparative context to shed light on the issue. Having pinpointed the law applicable to the public policy exception, the fourth chapter identifies the legal standard for the application of public policy in Turkish practice. Like the analysis presented in the third chapter, the fourth chapter also examines the challenges to arbitral awards based on public policy violations and compares them with their counterparts in the U.S. practice. Finally, Turkey's AI experience as an emerging country and the implications of this for the public policy exception are discussed. This discussion will be followed by a treatment of another novel subject—third-party funding in Turkey—and its possible implications for the public policy exception. One aim here is to identify, in broad strokes, the principal issues that can give rise to the public policy exception. The author is aware that two limitations may arise in this part. The first is the limited reach of both state-of-the-art AI and third-party funding in Turkey. The second is the lack of in-depth analysis and case law on these subjects. These limitations are evidence of the difficulty of studying these subjects from the public policy perspective.

Keywords: UNCITRAL arbitration, Turkish arbitration, public policy exception in Turkey

4.1 Setting the Scene: From Chiquita Bananas to International Arbitration

There is an intricate relationship between the economic model a given country adopts and its legal order. As an example, the rule of law is indispensable for a functioning market economy in order to prevent, say, corporate governance-oriented controversies such as the Enron scandal—just as the law must also adjust and respond to new market conditions and changes in demand arising from novel economic or social developments.[726] At issue in this chapter is the latter—namely, how Turkish law was compelled to adjust to the demands of the neoliberal economic policies that swept the globe in the final quarter of the 20th century. Understanding the legitimacy of international arbitration in Turkey thus entails tackling Turkey's neoliberal transformation since the early 1980s, given that arbitration has often been regarded as a part of the neoliberal agenda and that undertaking neoliberal reforms requires a judicial climate that favors arbitration.[727]

When the Republic was established in 1923, the new leaders inherited from the defeated Ottoman Empire an economy in tatters. The project of modernizing the economy from its low base thereafter proceeded through five phases. The original intention—as settled at the Izmir Economy Congress of 1923—was to implement a liberal economic system in which private companies would be the driving force of economic modernization.[728] Nevertheless, this policy did not yield the desired result, given the lack of private sector capital and the dearth of heavy industry. Through the 1930s, as the Great Depression bit, Turkey turned—like many developing countries—to a model of heavy state intervention to propel

726 Curtis J. Milhaupt, *Beyond Legal Origin: Rethinking Law's Relationship to the Economy—Implications for Policy*, 57 AM. J. COMP. 831, 842 (2009). *See also* ALAN WATSON, SOCIETY AND LEGAL CHANGE 89 (2nd ed., 2001) (emphasizing the interaction between law and social changes and needs).

727 *See e.g.* A. Claire Cutler, *International Commercial Arbitration, Transnational Governance, and the New Constitutionalism, in* INTERNATIONAL ARBITRATION & GLOBAL GOVERNANCE: CONTENDING THEORIES AND EVIDENCE, *supra* note 260, at 140, 140–67 (arguing that international arbitration serves the private interests of companies that thrive under neoliberal policies, and these companies wish to exclude themselves from state legislation and prefer to design their private law according to their needs); Amr A. Shalakany, *Arbitration and the Third World: A Plea for Reassessing Bias Under the Specter of Neoliberalism*, 41 HARV. INT'L L.J. 419, 423–24 (2000) (arguing that international enterprises in developed states use arbitration at the expense of developing states' interests).

728 E.g. O. Murat Koçtürk & Meryem Gölalan, *1923–1950 Türkiye Ekonomisinin Yapısal Analizi [Structural Analysis of Turkey's Economy of 1923–1950]*, 45 ÜÇÜNCÜ SEKTÖR KOOPERATIFÇILIK 48, 57 (2010) (Turk.); Metin Toprak, *Izmir Iktisat Kongresi: Bir Gelecek Perspektifi [Izmir Economic Convention: A Future Perspective]* IKTISAT, ISLETME VE FINANS, Ocak 2004, at 115 121 (Turk.)

growth and development.[729] This model ended in 1950 when the incumbent governing party lost power for the first time since 1923.

The early 1950s saw significant economic liberalization, as the new governing party pledged to promote the private sector and reduce the state's role in the economy.[730] The new party was successful initially in fulfilling its promises with the backing of the Marshall Plan, and the development of the agricultural sector rocketed ahead, alongside large-scale road and highway construction across the country. However, this triggered a severe balance-of-payments problem from the mid-1950s, marked by the scarcity of many essential consumer goods.[731] This forced governments in the 1960s to abandon the liberalization agenda and pursue a more interventionist strategy, turning to a model of import-substitution industrialization (ISI).[732]

Severe economic turmoil at the end of the 1970s saw yet another policy shift, unveiled in January 1980—the so-called January 24 Decisions. This policy turn closed the door on Turkey's flirtation with ISI, which was replaced by an agenda of neoliberal reform. This presaged Turkey's general embrace of almost every facet of globalization, including international arbitration.[733] The implementation of the January 24 Decisions is crucial for our understanding of the timing and manner of Turkey's introduction to international arbitration and why courts used the public policy exception as a skeleton key in the early years.

The January 24 Decisions envisaged a dramatic shift from the ISI model to an export-led growth strategy. They were originally announced in 1978 in response to the severe economic crisis enveloping the country.[734] Political instability at

---

729 Şevket Pamuk, Uneven Centuries: Economic Development of Turkey Since 1820, 176 (2018) (noting that the role of the Turkish State was designated as more important than the examples across Europe, but this has never reached the level of socialism); Fikret Şenses, *Turkey's Experience with Neoliberal Policies Since 1980*, *in* The Making of Neoliberal Turkey 15, 15 (Cenk Ozbay et al. eds, 2016); Meliha Altunişik & Özlem Tür, Turkey: Challenges of Continuity and Change 69 (2005).

730 Pamuk, *supra* note 729, at 207; Şenses, *supra* note 729, at 15; Altunişik & Tür, *supra* note 729, at 69–73.

731 Pamuk, *supra* note 729, at 211; Altunişik & Tür, *supra* note 729, at 73.

732 Pamuk, *supra* note 729, at 211; Altunişik & Tür, *supra* note 729, at 73–74.

733 Pamuk, *supra* note 729, at 246; Şenses, *supra* note 729, at 15; Altunişik & Tür, *supra* note 729, at 75–77.

734 Kenan Aksu, *A Historical Background to Turkey-Europe Relations*, *in* Turkey–EU Relations: Power, Politics and the Future 8 (2012).

the time meant the government was unable to muster support for the package, nor was there any desire on the part of the public for such a fundamental transformation.[735] Just as the package looked doomed, the military intervened in a coup in September 1980 and announced its full support as part of its program to stabilize the country, which was wracked by civil strife and violence, on top of mounting economic crisis. The military government appointed Turgut Özal, a deputy minister and former senior economist at the World Bank, to oversee the implementation of the package.

The implementation of the package triggered a significant paradigm shift in the Turkish economy. Abandoning ISI for good, exports became the main driver of growth.[736] In order to boost exports, the overvalued currency was replaced with a "real value currency," which later led to a substantial devaluation of the Turkish Lira (1 USD = 70 TRY).[737] The government put an end to subsidies for state-produced goods, leading to a rise in the prices of those commodities.[738] Until the 1980s, for example, it was almost entirely forbidden for private actors to keep foreign exchange or trade in foreign products,[739] and there was a thriving black market for smuggled foreign goods like liquor and cigarettes. The situation changed almost overnight when all foreign currency transactions and obstacles to the importation of foreign products were liberalized.[740]

Chiquita bananas were the first brand of banana to be imported under the liberalization policy of the 1980s, which triggered widespread "banana debates" through the period.[741] The public complained that this import policy would undercut local banana production, putting Turkish producers out of business.[742] The "Chiquita debate" would rage well into the 1990s, but in the early 1980s,

---

735 *Compare* Pamuk, *supra* note 729, at 248 *with* Şenses, *supra* note 729, at 16.

736 Pamuk, *supra* note 729, at 246; Altunişik & Tür, *supra* note 729, at 77.

737 *Id.*

738 Pamuk, *supra* note 729, at 247.

739 Türkiye Cumhuriyeti Merkez Bankasi [Cent. Bank of the Republic of Turk.], Küreselleşmenin Türkiye Ekonomisine Etkileri [Effects of Globalization on Turkey's Economy] 82 (2002) (Turk.)

740 *E.g.* Art 17 of Act No.: 3291, Official Gazette: 3 June 1986, No.: 19126, Enacted: 28 May 1986 (Turk.) (abolishing the prohibition of imported cigarettes).

741 See e.g. *Ana.P.'li Dizdaroğlu muz ithali durdurulunca istifadan vazgeçti* [Motherland's Dizdaroglu Not Resigned When Banana Import Stopped], Milliyet, Jan 27, 1984 at 6. (Turk.); Turhan Selcuk, *Çikita Muzdan Sonra Balon da İthal Ettik [We Imported Balloons After Chiquita Bananas]*, Milliyet, May 8, 1984 at 2. (Turk.).

742 *See e.g. Muz Savaşı [The Banana War]*, Milliyet, Feb. 3, 1986 at 3. (Turk.)

it mostly served as a whipping post for a public that wished to vent its spleen against the radical transformation package being rolled out under the repressive military junta.[743]

Despite these efforts to mend the economy, continued political instability and populist policies meant no serious steps were taken to combat Turkey's rampant inflation, which continued to be a significant problem for years.[744] The income disparities it triggered were the principal drivers of the political problems of the 1980s and the 1990s.[745] Had there been a stable democracy and democratically-led financial liberalization, the entire process would have advanced at a politically tolerable pace. Instead, the speedy implementation of the package led to a sudden and harsh opening of the economy, which saw a rash of winners and losers quickly emerge, produced economic instability, and triggered deep public reactions.[746] In the end, Chiquita bananas were freely available to sell, but with almost no one able to buy them. They were out of reach for the majority of the Turkish people due to inflation and income inequality.[747]

The circumstances under which the package was enforced and the fact that the neoliberal policies were implemented by an authoritarian military regime have had profound implications for the development of democracy in Turkey but also of international arbitration.[748] With the opening of the economy to foreign investment, privatization and BOTs came into play in order for large infrastructure projects to be financed, such as electricity production and distribution. Nevertheless, like anywhere in the world, foreign investors sought the option of resorting to arbitration rather than to the domestic courts in the event of a dispute, so as to be on a level playing field.

Against this backdrop, laws opening the way for BOTs also cleared a path for international arbitration. As discussed in Chapter 2, these laws were repeatedly

---

743 See Gizem Zencirci, *Affective Politics of Structural Adjustment: "Cruel Optimism" and Turhan Selcuk's Cartoons in Turkey*, 1983–1986, 53 J. Social History 53, 67–68 (2019).

744 *E.g.* Asaf Savaş Akat, *The Political Economy of Turkish Inflation*, 54 J. Int'l Affairs 265 (2000).

745 *See* Şenses, *supra* note 729, at 19.

746 *See* Yusuf Kemal Öztürk & Zeynep Öztürk, *The Effects of Turkey's Economic Crisis on Employment, in* Economic and Management Issues in Retrospect and Prospect 137, at 139 (Eszter Wirth et al. eds., 2018).

747 *E.g.* Cüneyt Arcayürek, *Hal-i Pür Melal [A Sad Situation]*, Milliyet, Feb. 23, 1984 at 7 (Turk.)

748 *See* Şenses, *supra* note 729, at 16.

struck down by the Constitutional Court.[749] However, in fact, it was the same Constitution that guaranteed freedom of contract in Art.48 so that the Court might just as easily have found the laws not contrary to the Constitution.[750] This inherent resistance from the courts was rooted in both the top–down and non-participatory nature of the entire transformation and the fact that international arbitration was incorporated too hastily into the Turkish legal system. Professor Bakır Çağlar, very often arguing before the European Court of Human Rights as a defense lawyer for Turkey, said as much in a newspaper interview in 1999. He noted that Turkey must follow the trends in the world, but that the country had transplanted international arbitration so quickly that not only was there a gap in the law providing rules for international arbitration but also a gap in the number of lawyers with the skills and experience to practice arbitration effectively.[751]

To conclude, just as Chiquita bananas in the 1980s and 1990s became symbolic in Turkey in relation to the country's rapid neoliberal transformation, so too international arbitration—and the use of the public policy exception as a means to resist it—emerged in the legal profession as a symbol of hasty, top–down change. Though Turkish arbitration has made great strides since the 1980s and Turkey is now an arbitration-friendly jurisdiction, there are still caveats concerning the enforcement of awards, a topic to which we now turn.

4.2 Statutory Law on the Public Policy Exception

4.2.1 International Law on Arbitration and the Public Policy Exception

4.2.1.1 Foreign Awards and the Public Policy Exception

4.2.1.1.1 Law Applicable to a Foreign Award Made in a Convention Country and the Public Policy Exception

In general, laws in Turkey and the United States are poles apart due to the fundamental disparity between the civil and common law systems. The former is more a codified system of law relying on statutes, whereas in the latter legal system, the emphasis is placed on case law. Nonetheless, the laws on the enforcement of foreign arbitral awards in both countries are almost identical thanks to the

---

749 *Id.*

750 Birsel, *supra* note 142, at 24.

751 Melih Aşık, Opinion, *Conversation on Arbitration*, MILLIYET, Aug. 5, 1999, at 15. (Turk.)

Convention's achievement in harmonizing arbitration law and practice across a vast geographic and cultural scope.

Upon their respective ratifications of the Convention, both the United States (ratified in 1970) and Turkey (1992) made the reciprocity and commercial reservations.[752] Thus, both countries reserve their rights to enforce awards made only in the territory of another signatory state and arising out of legal relationships that are considered to be commercial under the domestic laws of the United States or Turkey, correspondingly.[753]

---

752 *Contracting States—List of Contracting States*, NEW YORK CONVENTION, http://www.newyorkconvention.org/list+of+contracting+states (last visited Feb. 27, 2022). *See also* 9 U.S.C. § 202 (stating that any award or agreement that is "considered as commercial" falls under the Convention.)

753 Although both countries have made reciprocity and commercial reservations, these have had little effect in practice. Concerning the reciprocity reservation, today very few countries have not signed the Convention. *See* The New York Convention Status, *supra* note 16. Thus, it is very rare for both U.S. and Turkish courts to not to enforce an award based on a lack of reciprocity. As long as the arbitral seat is in a Contracting State, the U.S. and Turkish courts enforce the award regardless of the nationalities of the parties. *See* STRONG, *supra* note 601, at 30. Similarly, the term "commercial" has been construed broadly by both jurisdictions. Under Art. 3 and Art. 19 of the Turkish Commercial Code, the following falls to the scope of commercial affairs: (i) all matters set forth under the Turkish Commercial Code; (ii) all transactions and acts interesting a commercial undertaking; (iii) any type of merchant's debts, and; (iv) contracts, which are of commercial nature for only one of the parties, are commercial for the other. Art. 3 and Art. 19 of Act No.: 6102, Türk Ticaret Kanunu [Turkish Commercial Code] Official Gazette: 14 Feb. 2011, No.: 27846, Enacted: 13 Jan. 2011 (Turk.). In line with this scope, the transactions and acts that are not involving employees and consumers and businesses will generally fall into the scope of commercial affairs. *See* Mehmet Bahtiyar & Levent Biçer, *Adi İş/ Ticari İş/Tüketici İşlemi Ayrımı ve Bu Ayrımın Önemi* [*Differentiation Between Ordinary Transactions / Commercial Transactions / Consumer Transactions and the Importance of such Differentiation*], 22 MARMARA ÜNIVERSITESI HUKUK FAKÜLTESI HUKUK ARAŞTIRMALARI DERGISI [MUHF-HAD] 395, 431–33 (2016) (Turk.). The scope of commerciality is even broader in the United States. The U.S. courts have construed the term "commercial" to include not only transactions and disputes that arise among businesses that buy and sell goods and are intended to make a profit but also disputes involving employers and employees, consumer, and even seamen's employment contracts. Louis Del Duca & Nancy A. Welsh, *Enforcement of Foreign Arbitration Agreements and Awards: Application of the New York Convention in the United States*, 62 AM. J. COMP. L SUPP 69, 72-73 (2014) (collecting cases). Even this comparison, regardless of a micro-level, goes to indicate the U.S. Courts' pro-arbitration and anti-litigation tendencies.

If an action is brought to enforce an arbitral award issued in a signatory country other than the country in which enforcement of the award is sought, it can be considered a "foreign" award in Turkey and in the United States pursuant to Art. I(l).[754] Considering this geographic criterion, a foreign award arises out of an arbitration held outside the United States or Turkey, from the perspective of a U.S. and a Turkish court, respectively. For example, an award entered in Japan, a signatory country, can be considered as a foreign award in an action to enforce the award in Turkey or the United States.

Given that the place of arbitration usually determines the law applicable to arbitration, the U.S and Turkish courts will usually not have "primary jurisdiction" to entertain actions concerning the arbitration (*e.g.*, jurisdiction to set aside the award and the like) when there is a foreign award.[755] Instead, Turkish and U.S.

---

754 *Compare* RESTATEMENT (THIRD) U.S. LAW OF INT'L COMM. ARB. § 1.1 cmt. p ("A 'foreign award' is an arbitral award made in an arbitration having its seat outside the United States.... An award made abroad is foreign, even if rendered in a dispute between two U.S. citizens") *with* The General Assembly of the Turkish Court of Cassation, Case No: 2011/13-568, Decision No: 2012/47 (finding that under Art.I of the Convention, the "territorial criterion" is applicable insomuch as an award is a foreign one if it is made outside Turkey). As rare one might expect it to be, a proceeding outside of the United States or Turkey involving nationals of those countries would still be foreign for purposes of the New York Convention. That being said, occasional problems may arise in the United States because the language of the legislation implementing the Convention, FAA s.202, is different than the language of Art. I(1) of the Convention. To that extent, FAA s.202 places further restrictions for arbitration to be regarded as foreign between citizens of the United States—namely, that it "involves property located abroad, envisages performance or enforcement abroad, or has some other reasonable relation with one or more foreign states." 9 U.S.C.A. § 202. For example, in *Wilson v. Lignotock U.S.A.*, the U.S. Court declined to enforce the arbitration agreement under the Convention, holding that incidental connections to a Convention signatory Switzerland (which was designated as an arbitration seat under the employment contract between the U.S. parties) did not satisfy the "envisaging of performance" requirement, where the employee "had made several trips to Europe for business purposes" but his "single duty under the employment contract was to build up sales and marketing organization for distribution of the products in the metropolitan Detroit area and trips Europe were incidental to the performance of his contractual duty." Wilson v. Lignotock U.S.A., Inc., 709 F. Supp. 797, 799 (E.D. Mich. 1989). *See generally* the discussion *infra* Section 4.2.1.2 at 00.

755 *See supra* note 427 and accompanying text. Similar to U.S. practice, the distinction between primary jurisdiction and secondary jurisdiction has been recognized in Turkey. For example, in one case, the losing party in an action for declaratory judgment challenged an award made in New York and asked the Turkish court to declare that the

courts have a "secondary jurisdiction" with respect to the foreign award.[756] In these cases, only the New York Convention applies, and the courts may refuse to enforce the award only on grounds explicitly provided in Art. V of the Convention, including the public policy exception.

Hence, when the Turkish or U.S. courts are presented with a motion to deny enforcement of a foreign award—say, a Japanese award—based on the public policy exception, they both will apply Art.(V)(2) of the Convention. Unlike the following one, this comparison is straightforward for the author to make, as both the U.S. and the Turkish court will apply the same law in considering the public policy exception.

4.2.1.1.2 Law Applicable to a Foreign Award Made in a Non-Convention Country and the Public Policy Exception

Freudenberg is a German-based company manufacturing non-woven fabric products, known to most of us through its popular household and cleaning products brands, O-Cedar in the U.S. and Vileda in other countries. When the firm decided to expand into East Asia, it began a search for the best country in the region in which to invest. At the time, 1987, Japan's real estate bubble had yet to burst, and prices were vastly inflated, while China was still a relatively closed economy.[757] Freudenberg, under these circumstances, considered Taiwan a safe place to allocate its capital.[758] Starting with 20 employees, by its 25th anniversary in 2013, the Taiwan plant had become the market leader in the area of spun laid non-woven products, and Freudenberg announced plans to expand the site over the next five years to meet the growing demand.[759]

---

award contrary to Turkish public policy as the arbitration agreement was null and void from the beginning. Rejecting the losing party's argument, the General Assembly stated that the losing party may only assert these arguments in an action to enforce the award and implicitly accepted the winning parties' argument that New York law is applicable on the issue of whether the award is subject to vacatur. The General Assembly of the Turkish Court of Cassation Case No: 2009/102 Decision No: 2009/208, dated 27.5.2009 (Lexpera Hukuk Bilgi Sistemi) [Lexpera Legal Information System] (Turk.).

756 *See* note 427 and accompanying text.

757 Christian Uhlig, *A market with a future—Taiwan,* DEUTSCHE WELLE (May 16, 2013), https://p.dw.com/p/18Z8O

758 *Id.*

759 *Freudenberg celebrates anniversary in Taiwan,* FREUDENBERG (Oct. 11, 2013), https://www.freudenberg.com/newsroom/press-releases/detail/freudenberg-celebrates-anniversary-in-taiwan/; *Freudenberg expands capacities in Taiwan,* FREUDENBERG

It is evident that Freudenberg was right in its decision to invest in Taiwan from the business perspective, but there remains a significant hurdle from the legal perspective: Taiwan is not a signatory to the Convention so that many foreign parties avoid arbitrating in Taiwan or under Taiwanese law.[760] Given that several countries have not ratified the Convention but actively participate in international commerce (*e.g.*, Taiwan, Liechtenstein), questions arise as to whether and how a U.S. or Turkish court would enforce awards from a non-signatory state—say, a Taiwanese award—and whether enforcement of such an award would be denied on the grounds of violation of public policy.

In the United States, it is again hardly surprising that the legal framework governing non-Convention awards is somewhat obscure, as it is not entirely clear what law is applicable to the enforcement of non-Convention awards.[761] There are four bodies of law that could arguably apply in such cases.[762] We can begin with the Restatement. Some commentators have taken the position that the FAA Ch.1—particularly FAA s.9 that governs confirmation of arbitral awards[763]—also

---

(Mar. 22, 2018), https://www.freudenberg-pm.com/Press/2018_03_22_FPM_Freudenberg_expands_capacities_in_Taiwan

760 Rong-Chwan Chen, *Interpretation and Application of the New York Convention in Taiwan, in* Recognition and Enforcement of Foreign Arbitral Awards The Interpretation and Application of the New York Convention by National Courts *supra* note 373 at 945.

761 Restatement (Third) U.S. Law of Int'l Comm. Arb. § 4.3 cmt. e. For the purposes of this book, a non-Convention foreign award is one that is not subject to the New York Convention. That being said, such an award may nonetheless be subject to the Panama Convention, or the ICSID Convention in the United States or, to the ICSID Convention in Turkey pursuant to BITs. Here, the author discusses the situations where the award is not subject to any of the Conventions to which the United States or Turkey is a signatory.

762 *Id.* § 4.3 Reporters' Notes e.

763 The text of the FAA s.9 provides on its face that awards are enforceable *only if* the arbitration clause provides for entry of judgment on the award by a U.S. court. 9 U.S.C.A. § 9 ("If the parties in their agreement have agreed that a judgment of the court shall be entered upon the award made pursuant to the arbitration, and shall specify the court,... any party to the arbitration may apply to the court so specified for an order confirming the award.... ") However, it is hardly the case in reality that an arbitration agreement providing for arbitration in a non-Convention country would specify a U.S. court as the venue for an enforcement action. Restatement (Third) U.S. Law of Int'l Comm. Arb. § 4.3 Reporters' Notes e. The Supreme Court in *Cortez Byrd Chips, Inc. v. Bill Harbert Constr. Co* held that the FAA's venue provisions are not mandatory so that a party may move to confirm an award under FAA s.9 even if the arbitration

governs awards from non-signatory countries.[764] Although FAA Ch.1 does not include any provision on the enforcement of awards rendered in another state, the reporters of the Restatement maintain that non-Convention awards nonetheless come within the plain meaning of its language.[765] Considering that FAA s.1 defining commerce covers "commerce with foreign nations," this position concludes that FAA Ch.1 as applied to non-Convention awards should be read in accordance with the "emphatic federal policy in favor of arbitral dispute resolution." [766] The reporters also propose that grounds to vacate an award under FAA s.10 should be construed as grounds to deny enforcement of a non-Convention award by analogy.[767]

Pursuant to this approach, in our hypothetical case, the Taiwanese award would be enforced under FAA s.9, and the party opposing the enforcement would have recourse to one of the grounds stipulated in FAA s.10. Hence, in this framework, the public policy exception would not be considered as a stand-alone exception by the U.S. courts as it is not one of the four grounds provided

---

clause does not provide for enforcement by a U.S. court and even if the arbitration award was rendered outside the United States. Cortez Byrd Chips, Inc. v. Bill Harbert Constr. Co., 529 U.S. 193, 195 (2000). RESTATEMENT (THIRD) OF FOREIGN RELATIONS LAW § 487 Reporters' Notes 8 ("Actions to enforce foreign arbitral awards not falling under the Convention must therefore be brought in State courts, or in federal courts in exercise of diversity of citizenship jurisdiction.")

764 RESTATEMENT (THIRD) U.S. LAW OF INT'L COMM. ARB. § 4.3. *E.g.* J. Stewart McClendon, *Enforcement of Foreign Arbitral Awards in the United States*, 4 NW J. INT'L L. & BUS. 58, 61(1982) ("If the award is made abroad, it... will undoubtedly be enforceable under Section 9.... "). *See also* Catherine A. Rogers, *Restating the U.S. Law of International Commercial Arbitration*, 113 PENN ST. L. REV. 1333, 1338 (2009). *But see* George A. Bermann, *American Exceptionalism in International Arbitration, in* CONTEMPORARY ISSUES IN INTERNATIONAL ARBITRATION AND MEDIATION: THE FORDHAM PAPERS 2011 3, 8–9 (Arthur W. Rovine ed., 2011) ("The reporters discovered that these so-called 'foreign non-Convention awards'—while few in number—were essentially homeless, in that they do not obviously fall within the scope of any of the three current chapters of the Federal Arbitration Act.")

765 2 DOMKE ON COM. ARB. § 46:2 *accord* RESTATEMENT (THIRD) U.S. LAW OF INT'L COMM. ARB. § 4.3 Reporters' Notes e.

766 RESTATEMENT (THIRD) U.S. LAW OF INT'L COMM. ARB. § 4.3 Reporters' Notes e (citing *Mitsubishi*, 473 U.S at 631).

767 9 U.S.C.A. § 10. RESTATEMENT (THIRD) U.S. LAW OF INT'L COMM. ARB. § 4.3 Reporters' Notes e; ENFORCING ARBITRATION AWARDS IN THE US, *supra* note 518 (addressing, without discussing, FAA s.10 as grounds to refuse to enforce a non-Convention award).

in the FAA s. 10. That being said, this approach begs the question of whether the common law grounds for vacatur, including the public policy exception as developed in labor law, would also be considered as grounds to deny enforcement of non-Convention awards. The Restatement and the commentators do not examine this question—perhaps the subject of the enforcement of a non-Convention award is already conjectural enough, given the far-reaching scope of the Convention.[768] The author argues that if U.S. courts adopt this approach, it is very likely that the common law grounds for vacatur would be incorporated into FAA s.10 grounds in actions to deny the enforcement of a non-Convention award, given the sweeping scope of the FAA, and U.S. courts' tendency to press the public policy exception into the zone of FAA.[769]

Overall, the strength of this approach is that it brings non-Convention awards within the scope of the FAA, thereby providing harmonization of the grounds for denying enforcement across the United States and eliminating the idiosyncratic applications of national courts. Nevertheless, as the reporters accepted, this position results in a different enforcement treatment between Convention awards and non-Convention awards.[770]

The second body of law that could be applicable to non-Convention awards is state law on arbitration together with the FAA Ch.1. As has been previously discussed, state laws may apply to the extent that the FAA does not preempt it or that it does not frustrate arbitration.[771] Parties may seek enforcement of non-Convention awards under such state statutes, or under other applicable state statutes on international arbitration or state common law provided that FAA Ch.1 does not preempt state statutory or common law.[772] This could be especially the case where state arbitration statutes are based on Model Law.[773]

---

768 *See* Alan Scott Rau, *Arbitration And National Courts: Conflict And Cooperation: Understanding (And Misunderstanding) "Primary Jurisdiction,"* 21 Am. Rev. Int'l Arb. 47, 61 (2010) (euphemistically expressing that "[s]ometimes, as every academic knows, the most trivial hypotheticals can be the most challenging—if one is really intent on taking the time to brood about them: What, for example, should be done with the "non-Convention award"—an award rendered abroad but, perhaps, made in a state like Liechtenstein that is not a party to the Convention?").

769 *See generally supra* Section 3.3.1

770 Restatement (Third) U.S. Law of Int'l Comm. Arb. § 4.3 Reporters' Notes e.

771 *See generally supra* Section 3.3.1

772 Restatement (Third) U.S. Law of Int'l Comm. Arb. § 4.3. § 4.3 cmt.e.

773 *E.g.* Fla. Stat. Ann. § 684.0002 (2010) ("This chapter applies to international commercial arbitration, subject to any agreement in force between the United States of America and *any other country or countries*.") (emphasis added); Or. Rev. Stat. Ann.

The state laws authorizing the enforcement of a non-Convention award can provide the public policy exception as a ground for denying the enforcements.[774] When this is the case, awards not falling under the Convention should not be treated less favorably than they would have been treated under the Convention in order to achieve a standardized application of arbitration law across the United States.[775] Thus, a state public policy requiring the denial of the enforcement should be preempted were the enforcement of a non-Convention award not denied under FAA s.10.[776]

Next, the reporters of the Restatement considered that federal common law, rather than FAA Ch. 1, can govern the enforcement of non-Convention awards, together with a state law not frustrating arbitration.[777] This proposition is solidly grounded upon (and comports with) the liberal policy of favoring international arbitration adopted by the Supreme Court and the U.S. courts in general.[778]

---

§ 36.522 ("An arbitral award, *irrespective of the country in which it was made...* shall be enforced.... ") (emphasis added); CONN. GEN. STAT. ANN. § 50a-101 ("This chapter applies to international commercial arbitration, subject to any agreement in force between the United States of America, including all territories and possessions, and *any other country or countries*.") (emphasis added).

774 *E.g.* FLA. STAT. ANN. § 684.0048 ("The recognition or enforcement of the award would be contrary to *the public policy of this state*.") (emphasis added); OR. REV. STAT. ANN. § 36.524 ("The recognition or enforcement of the arbitral award would be contrary to *the public policy of the State of Oregon* or of the United States.") (emphasis added); CONN. GEN. STAT. ANN. § 50a-136 ("The recognition or enforcement of the award would be contrary to *the public policy of this state*.") (emphasis added).

775 RESTATEMENT (THIRD) U.S. LAW OF INT'L COMM. ARB. § 4.3.

776 *See generally supra* Section 3.2.4.

777 RESTATEMENT (THIRD) U.S. LAW OF INT'L COMM. ARB. § 4.3 cmt.e.

778 *E.g. Mitsubishi*, 473 U.S at 615 (stating that the federal policy in favor of arbitration applies with special force in the realm of international commerce); *Moses H. Cone.*, 460 U.S. at 24; Republic of Ecuador v. ChevronTexaco Corp. (ChevronTexaco I), 376 F. Supp. 2d 334, 356 (S.D.N.Y. 2005)(promoting application of federal common law in order to unify international arbitration law citing Smith/Enron Cogeneration Ltd. P'ship v. Smith Cogeneration Int'l 198 F.3d 88, 96 (2nd Cir. 1999)). It must be noted that neither of these cases nor the Restatement cite or discuss the implications of *Erie* in this regard. Given the extreme pro-arbitration policy in the United States, it could be argued that federal courts can apply federal common law when they encounter important federal interest—such as increased enforceability of arbitral awards—that are not covered by a statute, so that there will be no *Erie* issue as federal substantive and procedural law would control. *See* Certain Underwriters at Lloyd's London v. Argonaut Ins. Co., 500 F.3d 571, 579 (7th Cir. 2007) (citing Texas Indus., Inc. v. Radcliff

"Federal common law fleshes out the bones of the FAA's skeletal structure," as one commentator puts it. [779] This is because federal common law has filled the vacuum in the FAA left by the Congress concerning certain subjects.[780] Hence, if it is accepted that the plain meaning of FAA Ch.1 does not cover non-Convention awards, this gap in the FAA may once again be filled by court decisions. [781] When this is the case, common law grounds for vacatur, including the public policy exception, can arguably be construed as grounds to deny the enforcement of a non-Convention award by analogy. Nonetheless, neither the reporters of the Restatement nor the author found any case applying federal common law to the enforcement of non-Convention awards, much less a case citing a public policy exception.[782]

Finally, the doctrine of comity might be considered as a different body of law when enforcing a non-Convention award.[783] Comity has always been an important doctrine in the U.S. legal system for the enforcement of judgments rendered by non-U.S. courts, as the United States has not ratified any treaty requiring such an award to be enforced in the States.[784] Thus, U.S. courts have afforded comity

---

Materials, Inc., 451 U.S. 630, 640 (1981)) ("We believe that this overarching federal concern with the uniformity of treatment of international arbitration agreements requires that the issue before us be resolved by a federal common law rule, rather than by a state rule of decision.")

779 Bookman, *supra* note 83, at 1139.

780 *E.g.*, First Options of Chicago, Inc. v. Kaplan 514 U.S. 938 (1995) (finding that arbitrators have jurisdiction to decide their own jurisdiction, although the FAA has no *kompetenz–kompetenz* clause).

781 *See* Restatement (Third) U.S. Law of Int'l Comm. Arb. § 4.3; Alan Scott Rau, *Federal Common Law and Arbitral Power*, 8 Nev. L.J. 169, 202 (2007).

782 *See* Restatement (Third) U.S. Law of Int'l Comm. Arb. § 4.3 Reporters' Notes e.

783 *See* Stephen Michael Sheppard, Bouvier Law Dictionary, Comity, 2012 (LexisNexis) ("In particular it refers to an act by one state or sovereign made for the convenience of another, though not under a legal obligation to do so, even though a reciprocal benefit might be implied by the doing."); Glossary, comity, Practical Law 2-201-5616 (last visited Feb. 27, 2022) ("The legal doctrine under which courts recognize and enforce each others' legal decisions as a matter of courtesy, or based on the need for reciprocity, but not necessarily as a matter of law."). *See also* Joel R. Paul, *The Transformation of International Comity*, Law & Contemp. Probs., Summer 2008, at 19, 20 (stating that courts and commentators have classified the doctrine of comity as a synonym for private international law, a moral obligation, a courtesy, or a rule of domestic law.)

784 In 2009, United States signed the Hague Convention on Choice of Court Agreements, which requires a court in one contracting state to enforce a judgment issued in a court

to the judgments made by non-U.S. courts when such judgments satisfy the essentials of due process and fair treatment.[785]

Drawing an analogy between the enforcement regimes of judgments and arbitral awards, U.S. courts can use the doctrine of comity to enforce non-Convention awards in the States. For example, in *Weizmann Institute of Science v. Neschis*, one District Court took a common law, comity-based approach, and recognized a non-Convention award made in Liechtenstein.[786] In its decision, the Court underlined that comity is a long-accepted doctrine.[787] The Court also emphasized that comity existed before the United States adopted the Convention and was in use in recognizing foreign arbitral awards.[788]

If this analogy between the enforcement of non-U.S. judgments and non-U.S. awards is accepted, a natural question arises is: "Is public policy a ground for non-enforcement, and if so, what is the standard for the purposes of a refusal to enforce?" The answer is that public policy, in this context, too, has been one of the bases for the non-enforcement of judgments.[789] As such, U.S. courts have denied a foreign court judgment when the judgment is repugnant to public policy.[790] Similar to the public policy exception as applied in arbitral awards, this standard has remained high and infrequently met.[791] Hence, it could be deduced that a non-Convention award can be subject to public policy under this body of law, as well.

As briefly touched upon, unlike U.S. law, Turkish law provides a clearer picture of the applicable law to the award from a non-signatory country.[792] In 2007,

---

of another contracting state. But the Hague Convention has not yet been ratified. *Convention of 30 June 2005 on Choice of Court Agreements*, HCCH, https://www.hcch.net/en/instruments/conventions/status-table/?cid=98 (last visited Feb. 27, 2022)

785 9 Am. Jur. Proof of Facts 3d 687, Comity § 1.5 Westlaw (database updated Feb 2020).

786 Weizmann Inst. of Sci. v. Neschis, 421 F. Supp. 2d 654, 674–75 (S.D.N.Y. 2005)

787 See *id.*

788 *Id.* at 674.

789 Oehmke & Brovins, *supra* note 543 § 41:113.

790 *E.g. Pemex*, 832 F.3d at 97; Yahoo! Inc. v. La Ligue Contre Le Racisme, 433 F.3d 1199, 1213 (9th Cir. 2006); Restatement (Third) Of Foreign Relations Law Of The United States § 482.

791 *E.g.* Sarl Louis Feraud Int'l v. Viewfinder, Inc., 489 F.3d 474, 479 (2nd Cir. 2007) ("The public policy inquiry rarely results in refusal to enforce a judgment.") (citation omitted).

792 *See generally supra* Section 1.2.3

the IPPA was enacted considering the latest developments in European private international law—particularly Swiss law, as the Turkish Civil Code and the Code of Obligations are modeled on the Swiss legal system.[793] Art.60–62 of the IPPA govern the enforcement of foreign arbitral awards that are not made in a Convention country and repeats almost verbatim what is laid down in the Convention.[794] The IPPA does not specify that it governs non-Convention awards. Nevertheless, it is one of the two bodies of law governing foreign awards. As an international treaty, the Convention takes precedence over the IPPA.[795] As such, there remains the IPPA for the enforcement of non-Convention awards.[796]

Art. 62(1)(b) of the IPPA provides that "The enforcement of a foreign arbitral award *shall* be refused by the court:... If the arbitral award is against *public morality* or public policy."[797] Two noteworthy points can be extracted from this provision. First, whereas Art. V(2)(b) of the New York Convention vests a discretionary power to courts to decide whether the enforcement of a foreign arbitral award is contrary to public policy, Art. 62(1)(b) of the IPPA mandates that Turkish courts deny enforcement when they find that the award violates public policy. Despite this difference between the languages provided in the Convention and the IPPA, as far as the author is aware, it appears that no case has been published in which a Turkish court has found a Convention award to be contrary to public policy but still enforced it, entertaining its discretionary power under the Convention. Hence, it could be deduced that the language in the IPPA per se

---

793 Zeynep Derya Tarman, *The Applicable Law to Contractual and Non-contractual Obligations under Turkish Private International Law*, NEDERLANDS INTERNATIONAAL PRIVAATRECHT [NIPR], no. 1 (2009) at 15, 15.; Gülören Tekinalp, *The 2007 Turkish Code concerning Private International Law and International Civil Procedure*, 9 Y.B. PRIVATE INT'L LAW 313, 321 (2007).

794 Articles 60–62 of Act No.: 5718, the IPPA; The General Assembly of the Turkish Court of Cassation, Case No: 2011/13-568, Decision No: 2012/47 (stating that although the IPPA's scope of application has become narrower, it applies when there is an award made in a non-signatory country).

795 Art.90(5) of Act No: 2709, The Constitution of the Republic of Turkey (providing that the provisions of international treaties shall prevail in the event of a conflict between international treaties and domestic laws due to differences in provisions on the same matter.)

796 BANU ŞIT, KURUMSAL TAHKIM VE HAKEM KARARLARININ TANINMASI VE TENFIZI [INSTITUTIONAL ARBITRATION AND RECOGNITION AND ENFORCEMENT OF ARBITRAL AWARDS] 194 (2005) [Turk.]

797 Art. 62(1)(b) of Act No.: 5718, the IPPA.

does not render a non-Convention award more susceptible to non-enforcement on public policy grounds.

Second, and more importantly, violation of public morality has been set forth as a ground to deny enforcement, as if the public policy exception was not elusive enough in case law. Like public policy, public morality is a concept that is vague and subject to manipulation. In reviewing the cases under this exception, the Court of Cassation has not found any situation when considering whether the award is contrary to public morality without mentioning public policy. That is to say, public morality, and morality more generally, have always gone hand in hand with public policy in the decisions made under the IPPA.[798]

Although one of the implications is that public morality may extend the scope of the public policy exception by making non-Convention awards less readily enforceable, so far, this has not been the case. This is because Turkish courts consider the award from the perspective of whether an award is domestic or international and decide the scope of public policy in that regard, rather than based on whether the award is made in a Convention country or not. [799] Notably, Turkish courts also considered the concept of public morality or morality in deciding cases under the Convention, even though the Convention does not refer to such grounds.[800] This proves one more time that Turkish courts regard public morality and public policy as overlapping concepts, not as separate elements. Hence, any enforcement regime for a non-Convention award under the IPPA poses no attendant risks.

---

798 *E.g.* 15th Civil Chamber of Turkish Court of Cassation, Case No.: 2016/895, Decision No.: 2016/2050, dated 31.3.2016 (Kazancı İçtihat Bilgi Bankası) [Kazanci Case Law Database] (Turk.). ("Public policy is a set of rules and institutions that protects and define the society from... *morality* perspective") (emphasis added); 11th Civil Chamber of Turkish Court of Cassation, Case No.: 2015/11441, Decision No.: 2016/8701, dated 3.12.2016 (Kazancı İçtihat Bilgi Bankası) [Kazanci Case Law Database] (Turk.). ("... violation of *public morality* and public policy may lead to denial of the enforcement.") (emphasis added)

799 *See Infra* Section 4.3.1.

800 *E.g.* The General Assembly of the Turkish Court of Cassation Case No: 2011/13-568, Decision No: 2012/47 (stating in a case where the Convention governed the dispute, a violation of morality and fundamental human rights requires a public policy exception to be invoked); 13th Civil Chamber of Turkish Court of Cassation, Case No.: 2014/27460, Decision No.: 2015/23707, dated 9.7.2015 (Kazancı İçtihat Bilgi Bankası) [Kazanci Case Law Database] (Turk.). *See Infra* Section 4.3.1.

Overall, legal frameworks for enforcing a non-Convention award are quite different in each country. In the United States, the existence of numerous bodies of law that could arguably govern such awards flies in the face of the idea of unification, opening a Pandora's Box of questions. Not surprisingly, most scholars do not cover the enforcement regime for non-Convention awards, thus avoiding the treacherous ground of that field. Nonetheless, in each situation, public policy appears to find a place to itself. This goes to show that public policy is a longstanding concept and capable of existing and mutating over time under different bodies of law. Turkish law, in contrast, provides a clear picture of the legal framework governing non-Convention awards. Unlike under U.S. law, whether a public policy exception exists for a non-Convention award does not remain a matter of guesswork under Turkish law, as has been explicitly stipulated in the statute—namely, the IPPA. To conclude, this comparison proves that the statutory law governing international arbitration in the United States is an area that would greatly benefit from clarification.[801]

4.2.1.2 Non-Domestic Awards and the Public Policy Exception

Disaggregation of Art. I(l) of the Convention implies there are three types of award: "foreign," "non-domestic," and "domestic."[802] Here in this section, our attention is on non-domestic awards, *i.e.*, awards made in signatory states but falling within the scope of the Convention.[803]

As stated earlier, the question that U.S. courts have grappled with is whether the Convention's defenses to enforcement provide exclusive grounds for vacating a U.S.-seated Convention award. [804] A petition for certiorari is, in fact, pending

---

801 George A. Bermann, *Restating the U.S. Law of International Commercial Arbitration*, 42 N.Y.U. J. Int'l L. & Pol. 175, 176 (2009) (noting that commercial arbitration is "an area of the law needing clarification").

802 The New York Convention *supra* note 15, Art. I(1). *See* Edin Karakas, *Origin of Arbitral Awards and Its Impact on Applicable Enforcement Regime*, 11 Croat. Arb. Y.B. 15 (2004)

803 The New York Convention, *supra* note 15, Art. I(1).

804 To briefly recall the split, the Eleventh Circuit in *Industrial Risk* has held that the parties may solely rely on the grounds for non-enforcement under Art. V of Convention, including a public policy exception in actions to vacate an award made in the United States. Hence, this approach excludes the grounds for vacatur provided in FAA s.10. The Court's rationale is that the Convention applies exclusively to both foreign awards and non-domestic awards under FAA s.202 as required by Art. I(1) of the Convention. The majority of the circuits, on the other hand, fall on the other side. They recognize that non-domestic awards are governed by the Convention but do not accept that the

before the Supreme Court, which could resolve the more-than-20-year-old circuit split.[805] Nonetheless, the purpose of this part is not to discuss this split—as the author has already engaged in this discussion in Section 3.3.2—but instead to underline how the Turkish approach to such awards can provide a good example for the U.S Congress and that the Turkish statutory law regime better serves the primary purpose of Convention, namely, "to unify the standards by which... arbitral awards are enforced in the signatory countries."[806]

When Turkey enacted the Convention in 1991, the Original CCP—which was applicable to Turkish domestic arbitral awards and a counterpart of FAA Ch.1—was in force. Enacted in 1927 and modified over time to meet present needs, the Original CCP was nonetheless falling behind. For example, under the Original CCP, the losing party had the right to appeal the award and when the award was appealed, the Turkish Court of Cassation was able to review its merit.[807] Hence, there was a stark difference in the enforcement regime as between domestic and foreign awards. Like the U.S. statutory law regime in arbitration today, non-domestic awards were not recognized as a different category.

Until 2001, the Turkish Court of Cassation repeatedly held that arbitral awards made in Turkey, regardless of any international features, were domestic awards and subject to the Original CCP, rather than the Convention.[808] Hence,

---

Convention provides exclusive grounds for vacatur of arbitral awards. Hence, under this approach, parties seeking to vacate an arbitral award made in the United States may rely on domestic grounds provided in FAA s.10. This approach deems FAA s.10 grounds for vacatur applicable to international arbitrations by means of the residual application provision of Chapter 2. *See* 9 U.S.C.A. §§ 10, 208. *See generally supra* Section 3.2.3.

805 Petition for a Writ of Certiorari, Inversiones y Procesadora Tropical Inprosta S.A. v. Del Monte International GMBH (No. 19–117 2019), WL 3380417, *as discussed in* Rebecca Lunceford Kolb, *The New York Convention or the FAA: Circuit Split Still Stands*, AMERICANBAR (Oct. 2, 2019), https://www.americanbar.org/groups/litigation/committees/alternative-dispute-resolution/practice/2019/the-new-york-convention-or-the-faa-circuit-split-still-stands/

806 *Scherk*, 417 U.S. at 520 n.15.

807 Art. 533 of Act No.: 1086, the Original CCP.

808 *E.g.* 15th Civil Chamber of Turkish Court of Cassation, Case No.: 1998/3507 Decision No.: 1998/4108, dated 6.11.1998, *as discussed in* Nuray Ekşi, *Yargıtay Kararları Işığında Icc Hakem Kararlarının Türkiye'de Tanınması ve Tenfizi [Recognition and Enforcement of ICC Arbitral Awards in Turkey in the light of the Court of Cassation Decisions]*, 67 ANKARA BAROSU DERGISI 54, 60 (2009) (Turk.); 15th Civil Chamber of Turkish Court of Cassation, Case No.: 1996/3249, Decision No.: 1996/5584, dated 25.10.1996 (Kazancı İçtihat Bilgi Bankası) [Kazanci Case Law Database] (Turk.).

under the statutory regime then in force, Turkish courts were constrained to decide whether an award was either domestic or foreign, as non-domestic awards were not recognized or treated differently.[809]

In line with Turkey's endeavor to align its arbitral laws to international standards, the TIAL came into force in 2001 and became a significant source of law governing non-domestic awards made in Turkey. The TIAL is largely modeled on the 1985 UNCITRAL Model Law—and somewhat on Chapter 12 of the Swiss Private International Law—and drafted considering Turkey's status as an emerging country. Accordingly, the TIAL is a law based on Model Law, "with a slight Swiss flavor and Turkish touch."[810]

Art 1. of the TIAL reveals that the TIAL provides two different criteria for it to govern the enforcement of an award. First, it applies only if arbitration is seated in Turkey.[811] Second, it applies to arbitrations that feature a "foreign element" (*i.e.*, arbitration that has an international characteristic) or where its application is agreed to by the parties or arbitrators.[812] Regarding the second criterion, the TIAL deviates from Model Law and provides additional situations as an indicator of a foreign element.

The TIAL starts with the provision that arbitration is international and has a foreign element if "the parties to the arbitration agreement have their domiciles or habitual residences or places of business in different States."[813] Further, it extends the scope of internationality in order to cover cases where the place of arbitration, the place of contract performance, or the place that has the closest connection with the dispute is situated outside the State where the parties have their domiciles or habitual residences or places of business.[814] Hence, in line with Model Law, the TIAL does not consider the citizenship of the parties in enumerating the situations where a foreign element exists. To that extent, for example, an arbitration procedure between two Turkish parties seated in Turkey may nonetheless be governed by the TIAL.

Diverting from Model Law, TIAL provides that the existence of foreign capital—or the existence of a loan and/or a security agreement that had to be

809 See Nazan Candaner Elver, *Turkish International Arbitration Law and Restrictions on Its Application*, 21 J. Int'l Arb. 453, 453 (2004).

810 Tuğrul Ansay, *Current Development: International Arbitration in Turkey*, 14 Am. Rev. Int'l Arb. 333, 335 (2003).

811 Art. 1 of Act No.: 4686, TIAL.

812 *Id.*

813 *Id.* Art. 2(1).

814 *Id.* Art. 2(2).

entered to raise such capital—satisfy the foreign element requirement and thus give the arbitration an international characteristic.[815] To that extent, if at least one of the shareholders of a Turkish corporation brings foreign capital to Turkey in accordance with the laws enacted to promote foreign investment, arbitration to which the corporation is a party—notwithstanding that it is incorporated in Turkey—becomes international for the purposes of the TIAL.[816] Finally, a foreign element is established if the underlying agreement that includes the arbitration agreement provides a transfer of capital or goods from one country to another.[817]

As revealed above, the TIAL's scope of application is extremely broad. Just as a broad-spectrum antibiotic targets a wide range of bacteria, the TIAL targets the cases that have the slightest international aspect and brings them under its scope of application. Once it is decided that there is a non-domestic award made in Turkey meeting one of the foreign elements criteria, the rest is straightforward. The grounds for setting aside an arbitral award under TIAL mirror the grounds for non-enforcement of a foreign award under the New York Convention, including the public policy exception.[818] Hence, the losing party may move to vacate the award—rather than appeal the award under the Original CCP—and assert that award is contrary to public policy.

The Turkish approach to non-domestic awards, which is parallel to Model Law and the Convention, can provide a good example for the U.S Congress in amending the FAA, which is in need of amendment, as has been repeatedly emphasized in the literature.[819] First, Turkey has a specific statute that governs non-domestic awards. The language in FAA s.202, however, does not accept such awards as a different category and posits that there are two types of awards—domestic and foreign.[820]

---

815 *Id.* Art. 2(3).

816 Ziya Akinci, Arbitration Law of Turkey: Practice and Procedure 36 (2011).

817 Art. 2(4) of Act No.: 4686, TIAL.

818 *Id.* Art. 15

819 *E.g.* THOMAS E. CARBONNEAU, TOWARD A NEW FEDERAL LAW ON ARBITRATION 99 (2014); Jack M. Graves, *Arbitration As Contract: The Need for A Fully Developed and Comprehensive Set of Statutory Default Legal Rules*, 2 WM. & MARY BUS. L. REV. 227, 288 (2011); Kristina L. Morrison, *A Misstep in U.S. Arbitral Law: A Call For Change In The Enforcement Of Nondomestic Arbitral Awards*, 46 TORT & INS. L.J. 803 (2011); Park, *supra* note 94, at 83.

820 *See* 9 U.S.C.A. § 202 ("An agreement or award... which is *entirely between citizens of the United States shall be deemed not to fall under the Convention* unless that relationship involves property located abroad, envisages performance or enforcement abroad,

The problem does not stop there. Turkey and the United States followed a different path in incorporating the Convention into their national law. The Convention was incorporated verbatim into Turkish national law, so there is no inconsistency between what is in the Convention and what is in the Turkish statutes. The U.S. Congress, however, did not merely incorporate the Convention and leave it at that but instead set forth additional and different provisions in the FAA Ch. 2 regarding the application of the Convention in U.S. courts. [821] This approach has given rise to difficulties for many U.S. courts, practitioners, and scholars who study the subject—including this author. Because of this difference in the language, the circuits have reached opposite interpretations of FAA Ch.2: Looking at one provision in the FAA, the majority of the circuits posit that FAA s.10 grounds for vacatur are available for non-domestic awards whereas looking at a different provision in the FAA, the Eleventh Circuit finds otherwise.[822]

Hence, the current statutory law on non-domestic awards in the United States is like the Turkish statutory regime before the TIAL was enacted in 2001. That era resulted in a hostile environment for Turkish non-domestic awards because they were considered domestic, thereby subject to appeal. Although the current legal framework regime in the United States does not yield such a result—quite the opposite; there is a strong bias toward arbitration—the intricacies of the enforcement process for non-domestic awards are nonetheless confusing. It is most likely that parties that are familiar with Model Law would prefer to arbitrate in the Eleventh Circuit since grounds for vacatur would be limited to those in Art. V of the Convention.[823] Inconsistent treatment of awards across the United States may hinder the arbitration mechanism, produce some costly peculiarities and impair international business.[824] Hence, in order to attract international arbitration more readily, the United States should harmonize its domestic and international arbitral laws, preferably adopting Model Law.[825]

---

or has some other reasonable relation with one or more foreign states.") (emphasis added).

821 Strong, *supra* note 601, at 24.

822 *Compare* 9 U.S.C.A. §§ 10, 208 *and Yusuf*, 126 F.3d at 23 *with* 9 U.S.C.A. § 207 *and Industrial Risk* 141 F.3d at 1434.

823 See Tiina E. Vaisanen, *Incompetent Drafting and Complex Laws: Automatically Waiving Set-Aside of Foreign Arbitration Awards in the United States*, 45 Cornell Int'l L.J. 723, 754 (2012)

824 Morrison, *supra* note 819, at 822.

825 *See e.g.*, Elena V. Helmer, *International Commercial Arbitration: Americanized, "Civilized," or Harmonized?*, 19 Ohio St. J. on Disp. Resol. 35, 43 (2003); Daniel M.

That being said, enacting a law is not necessarily the only way to solve this problem in common law systems. Therefore, if the Supreme Court grants certiorari, it would resolve a split among the circuits as to how to interpret FAA Ch.2 grounds and whether the grounds stipulated in the Convention are exclusive for non-domestic awards. It took ten years for the Turkish legislator to realize and enact a law specific for non-domestic awards. Yet, it has been 50 years and counting since the U.S Congress failed to recognize the special features of non-domestic awards and elaborated the law applicable to such awards.

4.2.2 Domestic Law on Arbitration and the Public Policy Exception

Public policy is the "scapegoat" among all grounds for challenging an award: It has long been criticized for being too vague or illusory, yet these have been the exact qualities that have allowed courts to resort to this ground, regardless of whether such a ground exists in the codes. Turkey is a case in point, being a civil law country that, to the surprise of many, once had a "common law ground of public policy." Thus, while this book limits its substantive discussion to international arbitration, a better understanding of the public policy exception (or public policy as a mindset) in a comparative context can be achieved through an examination of Turkish domestic arbitration.

At first glance, the FAA and Original CCP appear to share many common points. Original CCP was enacted in 1927, two years after the FAA, and governed domestic arbitration.[826] Both laws were part of a larger movement for procedural reform and were intended as procedural statutes.[827] Similar to the FAA, the Original CCP did not stipulate public policy as a ground to challenge an award. Delving deeper into the purpose and the provisions of laws, however, reveals that the FAA and the Original CCP rest on very different foundations.

While FAA aimed to make arbitration agreements valid and enforceable, thereby eliminating the old judicial hostility to arbitration, the Original CCP did

---

Kolkey, *Reflections on the U.S. Statutory Framework for International Commercial Arbitrations: Its Scope, Its Shortcomings, and the Advantages of U.S. Adoption of the UNCITRAL Model Law*, 1 Am. Rev. Int'l Arb. 491, 492 (1990).

826 Act No.: 1086, the Original CCP.

827 *Compare* Szalai, *supra* note 100, at 119 *with* Minutes of Grand National Assembly of Turkey Period 2, Vol. 33, Session 75 at 6 (1927), available at https://www.tbmm.gov.tr/develop/owa/td_v2.sayfa_getir?sayfa=6:58&v_meclis=1&v_donem=2&v_yasama_yili=&v_cilt=33&v_birlesim=075 (Turk.).

not arise from such a necessity.[828] More strikingly, whereas FAA s.10 provided grounds for vacatur, the Original CCP allowed a merits review by providing grounds for appellate review of arbitration awards.[829] Although the Original CCP contained an exhaustive enumeration of grounds for appellate review of awards, the Turkish Court of Cassation had long held that violation of public policy was a ground for appeal.[830] Once the floodgates opened, the Turkish Court of Cassation often reversed trial court decisions on the grounds of public policy, for example, where a consumer was a party to the arbitration agreement,[831] where the award was not made within the time required,[832] or where the dispute concerned rights in rem over real properties.[833] As such, public policy at that time yielded an ever-present peril that awards would be reversed, as if Big Brother in the arbitration world was keeping a watchful eye over the awards. As a result,

---

828 *See* Nursel Atar, *The Impossibility of a Grand Transplant Theory*, 4 ANKARA L. REV. 177, 184 (2007) (stating that reception of a civil law system in Turkey in the 1920s aimed to reconstruct a new form of society through radical legal reforms).

829 *Compare* 9 U.S.C.A. § 10 ("In any of the following cases the United States court... may make an order *vacating the award*... ") (emphasis added) *and* Art. 533 of Act No.: 1086, the Original CCP ("An award entered by arbitrators is subject to *appeal* if... ")(emphasis added)

830 *Compare id.* ("An award entered by arbitrators is subject to appeal (i)where the award was made after the prescribed time; (ii) where the arbitrators entered an award upon the subject matter that was not submitted; (iii) where the arbitrators exceeded their powers; or (iv) arbitrators failed to rule on each claim asserted by the parties. ") *and* 15th Civil Chamber of Turkish Court of Cassation, Case No.: 1991/4163, Decision No.: 1991/5339, dated 7.11.1991 (Kazancı İçtihat Bilgi Bankası) [Kazanci Case Law Database] (Turk.) (finding that grounds for appellate review of awards are limited with those in the Original CCP, but an award may nonetheless be reversed if it is contrary to public policy).

831 *E.g.* 13th Civil Chamber of Turkish Court of Cassation, Case No.: 2008/3492, Decision No.: 2008/11120, dated 25.9.2008 (Kazancı İçtihat Bilgi Bankası) [Kazanci Case Law Database] (Turk.) (finding that consumers must be protected from forced arbitration agreements as dictated by the principles of Turkish law).

832 *E.g.* 15th Civil Chamber of Turkish Court of Cassation, Case No.: 1997/2567, Decision No.: 1997/3420, dated 2.7.1997 (Kazancı İçtihat Bilgi Bankası) [Kazanci Case Law Database] (Turk.) (finding that arbitrators lost the jurisdiction to rule on the dispute once they failed to enter the award within the time required, and thus the award violated the public policy).

833 *E.g.* 15th Civil Chamber of Turkish Court of Cassation, Case No.: 2003/3780, Decision No.: 2003/4370, dated 29.9.2003 (Kazancı İçtihat Bilgi Bankası) [Kazanci Case Law Database] (Turk.).

public policy became a judge-made ground for the appeal of awards, though the creation of such grounds is not a usual practice under Turkish law, where the emphasis is on codified statutes rather than judicial decisions. The judge-made ground of public policy was applied in domestic arbitration in Turkey for decades, after which it yielded to the statutory ground of public policy in 2011.

When international arbitration reached Turkey in the 1990s in line with Turkey's effort to open the economy, domestic arbitration in Turkey was profoundly affected. To briefly recall the major steps, the Turkish parliament first amended the Constitution and paved the way for a more liberal international arbitration regime, then enacted a law governing international arbitration.[834] Amendment of the domestic arbitration law can thus be perceived as an ultimate step toward solid incorporation of arbitration into Turkish law. As such, the new Civil Procedural Act entered into force in 2011, abrogating the Original CCP.[835]

The articles governing arbitration in the current Civil Procedural Act are now also based on the Model Law. That is to say, rules governing domestic arbitration in Turkey track the provisions of the TIAL and Model Law in a way that is symmetrical to the New York Convention. In this framework, public policy is now a ground to set aside an award, rather than to appeal. Hence, the Turkish Court of Cassation is no longer able to review the merits of an award, as the only recourse in domestic arbitration is now to set an award aside.

4.3 The Public Policy Exception in Relation to The New York Convention

4.3.1

The Legal Standard for the Application of Public Policy as an Exception to the Enforcement of Foreign Arbitral Awards

The reach of public policy in the United States has been limited narrowly in accordance with the pro-arbitration trend. When compared with the United States, the scope of public policy is more sweeping in Turkey, though international arbitration has been rapidly developing since the 1990s.

There are several differences between the U.S. and the Turkish judiciaries in terms of the legal standards set by the respective courts. To begin, unlike under U.S. law, there is a more precise delineation between domestic public policy and

---

834 *See generally supra* Section 1.2.2

835 *Id.*

international public policy under Turkish law. This, however, is not explicitly provided in statutes. Instead, it has been emphasized in the trial courts and the decisions of the Court of Cassation as well as the literature that public policy bears different meanings in the contexts of domestic arbitration and international arbitration.[836] Turkish courts explicitly underlined that international public policy should be interpreted more narrowly than domestic public policy insomuch as a violation of domestic public policy does not necessarily produce a violation in international arbitration.[837] This view and distinction have long found support in commentary.[838]

With this distinction in mind, the next step is to pinpoint the applicable standard for a public policy defense in international arbitration. In that regard, each jurisdiction's approach is worthy of note in developing these standards. It appears that the approaches taken by the Turkish courts and U.S. courts differ. Turkish courts have reviewed and cited a wide scope of literature, including from France and Switzerland, and cases decided by the Constitutional Court and the

---

836 *E.g.* Grand Plenary Assembly on the Unification of Judgments, Case No: 2010/1, Decision No: 2012/1, dated 10.2.2012, s.2/3, Official Gazette No:28417, dated 20.09.2012 (Turk.); 15th Civil Chamber of Turkish Court of Cassation, Case No.: 2019/1234 Decision No.: 2019/3335, dated 11.7.2019 at 6 (Turk.) (on file with author); 13th Civil Chamber of Turkish Court of Cassation, Case No.: 2015/16140, Decision No.: 2017/3322 dated 16.3.2017 at 3 (Turk.) (on file with author); 13th Civil Chamber of Turkish Court of Cassation, Case No.: 2011/19737, Decision No.: 2012/25406, dated 13.11.2012 (Kazancı İçtihat Bilgi Bankası) [Kazanci Case Law Database] (Turk.); 25th Civil Court of First Instance of Ankara, Case No.: 2014/47 Decision No.: 2015/55, dated 27.01.2015 at 4 *rev'd on other grounds*, 13th Civil Chamber of Turkish Court of Cassation, Case No.: 2015/40156, Decision No.: 2019/5664 dated 02.05.2019 at 3 (Turk.) (on file with author); Kemal Dayındarlı, MILLI-MILLETLERARASI KAMU DÜZENI VE TAHKIME ETKISI [DOMESTIC-INTERNATIONAL PUBLIC POLICY AND EFFECTS ON ARBITRATION], 68–69 (1994) (Turk.); Bilgehan Yeşilova, *Milletlerarasi Tahkimin Hukuki Niteliği Üzerine Düşünceler and Güncel Gelişmeler [Thoughts on Legal Characteristic of International Arbitration and Current Developments]*, 76 TÜRKIYE BAROLAR BIRLIĞI DERGISI [TBB DERGISI] 83, 113 (2008) (Turk.)

837 *E.g.* 13th Civil Chamber of Turkish Court of Cassation, Case No.: 2015/16140, Decision No.: 2017/3322 at 4; 13th Civil Chamber of Turkish Court of Cassation, Case No.: 2011/19737, Decision No.: 2012/25406.

838 *E.g.* Yılmaz Altuğ & Mustafa Yasan, *Milletlerarasi Özel Hukukta Kamu Düzeni* [*Public Policy in International Private Law*] *in* PROF. DR. ERGÜN ÖNEN'E ARMAĞAN 139, 141 (2003) (Turk.).; Turgut Kalpsüz, *Execution of Arbitral Awards*, 25 BANKA HUK. DERGISI 5, 15 (2009).

Grand Plenary Assembly, and the General Assembly of Civil Chambers.[839] This approach bears the characteristics of civil law, where the law is regarded as a science. This carries the attendant assumption that only one correct answer to any legal issue—*e.g.*, whether or not the award is contrary to public policy—can be extracted from a careful study of positive legislation and the advanced literature

---

839 *E.g.* 15th Civil Chamber of Turkish Court of Cassation, Case No.: 2019/1234, Decision No.: 2019/3335 at 5–6; 15th Civil Chamber of Turkish Court of Cassation, Case No.: 2016/895, Decision No.: 2016/2050. Before delving into the deeper analysis of the decisions of the Turkish courts, it helps to understand the structure of the Turkish judicial system and to what extent lower courts are bound by the decisions of higher courts. Unlike the United States, Turkey is a unitary state so that the courts are not structured as state and federal courts. Instead, Turkey has more than one supreme court, each being the final decision-making authority in its respective field. Ismail Aksel, Turkish Judicial System Bodies, Duties And Officials 31 (2013). In the previous chapters, the decisions of the Constitutional Court and the Council of State, which are two of the supreme courts, have been discussed to elicit the concept of public policy as a mindset *against* arbitration. *See generally supra* Section 1.2.2. Here in this chapter, our focus shifts to the Court of Cassation. The Court of Cassation consists of Civil Chambers, which hear appeals of some trial courts and regional court decisions. Articles 13–14 of Act No.: 2797 Yargıtay Kanunu [The Law of Court of Cassation] Official Gazette: 8 Feb. 1983, No.: 17953, enacted: 4 Feb. 1983 (Turk.). The Assembly of Civil Chambers is the superior body that finalizes the chamber decisions if first- or second-instance court judges insist on prior decisions that had been reversed by the chambers in the first place. *Id.* Art. 15. The Grand Plenary Assembly is another interior and superior body. This is also not a separate appellate body but instead an assembly of the Court of Cassation which takes cases to resolve circuit splits when it decides that there is a conflict between decisions of different chambers or assemblies. *Id.* Art. 16. As such, the Grand Plenary Assembly functions similarly to the U.S. Supreme Court when it grants a writ of certiorari to resolve a circuit split. What is different is that a Unification Judgment handed down by the Grand Plenary Assembly does not include a review of facts. It presents the issue and continues with the opinion and ruling. Only the decisions of the Grand Plenary Assembly on the Unification of Judgments are binding on civil chambers and lower courts. *Id.* That is to say, lower courts are not bound to observe the rule of *stare decisis*. Nonetheless, it is a common practice for lower courts to observe higher courts, as such a practice is regarded as one of the necessary criteria for lower court judges to be promoted to higher courts. Decision No.: 675/2, Birinci Sınıfa Ayrılan ve Birinci Sınıf Olan Hâkim ve Savcıların Çalışmalarının Değerlendirilmesi Esaslarına İlişkin Hâkimler ve Savcılar Yüksek Kurulu İlke Kararı [Rules on the Principles of Evaluation of the Work of Judges and Prosecutors who are First Class or Become First Class] Official Gazette: 25 April 2017, No:30048, dated: 05.04. 2017 (Turk.).

so that judicial discretion or interpretation has not been as essential in Turkish practice as it has been in U.S. practice.[840]

The next step is to discuss the substance of the standard as applied in international arbitration. Turkish courts have usually commenced their discussion by accepting that "the basic principles that states cannot forsake are regarded as the rules concerning public policy" [841] or defined public policy as "a set of rules protecting the basic structure and interests of society."[842] Aiming to be more specific, most courts have further elaborated that "violation of morality and fundamental rights and freedoms and violation of mandatory laws aiming to protect the public interest" have been recognized as circumstances that require the intervention of courts based on public policy.[843] By looking at the plain meaning of the language, this test is akin to the one applied in *Parsons & Whittemore*, as both consider the violations of morality and justice being contrary to public policy and emphasize that such alleged public policy should somehow represent the essential ideas of morality and justice as opposed to any other local policies that courts might require in domestic arbitration.[844]

Despite this difference, what is notable and different in the construction of this standard is that, unlike the U.S. courts, Turkish courts have often put a heavy emphasis on mandatory national laws. In order to obviate Turkish courts' intervention, for example, arbitrators should accord deference to Turkish customs laws, tax legislation, laws on paternity, inheritance, and real property, among others.[845] That alone, however, does not suffice for an award to stand. Even if

840 *See* JAMES APPLE & ROBERT DEYLING, PRIMER ON THE CIVIL-LAW SYSTEM 30 (1995); Horacio Spector, *The Future of Legal Science in Civil Law Systems*, 65 LA. L. REV. 255, 258 (2004).

841 *E.g.* 15th Civil Chamber of Turkish Court of Cassation, Case No.: 2016/895, Decision No.: 2016/2050; 13th Civil Chamber of Turkish Court of Cassation, Case No.: 2014/27460, Decision No.: 2015/23707.

842 Grand Plenary Assembly on the Unification of Judgments, Case No: 2010/1, Decision No: 2012/1, s.2/2-1.

843 *E.g.* 13th Civil Chamber of Turkish Court of Cassation, Case No.: 2014/27460, Decision No.: 2015/23707; 13th Civil Chamber of Turkish Court of Cassation, Case No.: 2012/8425, Decision No.: 2012/10348 dated 17.4.2012 at 3–4 (Turk.) (on file with author). *See* 15th Civil Chamber of Turkish Court of Cassation, Case No.: 2016/895, Decision No.: 2016/2050.

844 *See Parsons & Whittemore*, 508 F.2d at 974.

845 *E.g.* 13th Civil Chamber of Turkish Court of Cassation, Case No.: 2015/16140, Decision No.: 2017/3322 at 3–4; 15th Civil Chamber of Turkish Court of Cassation, Case

the arbitrators observe such mandatory rules and apply them correctly, Turkish courts may nonetheless find an award contrary to public policy if the issues are not at the free disposal of the parties, *i.e.*, are inarbitrable. For example, arbitrators may not rule upon a dispute concerning an issue of value-added tax (VAT), as such a dispute is not subject to the will of the parties under Turkish law—which is to say it is inarbitrable. That being so, an award resolving such claims will be contrary to public policy.[846] As this book will discuss further below, this blurs the lines between the concepts of arbitrability and public policy and enlarges the scope of the public policy exception.[847]Hence, the heavy emphasis on mandatory laws and the close connection between mandatory laws and inarbitrability culminates in a broader scope of public policy under Turkish law, which has not been the case under U.S. law.

Although the test set by Turkish courts is tantamount to the one set out in *Parsons & Whittemore*, it differs from the explicit and well-defined public policy standard postulated in the Public Policy Trilogy. As developed in labor arbitration and later disseminated into the FAA, U.S. courts applying this standard may establish such public policy "by reference to the laws and legal precedents, and not from general consideration of supposed public interests."[848] Turkish courts, however, do not necessarily require the existence of a sufficiently well-defined and dominant public policy or limit themselves with a violation of a positive law to justify refusing the enforcement of an award on public policy grounds. Hence, although Turkish practice saw the "common law ground of public policy," this did not lead to a divergence of the standards as in the U.S. practice where this led to the formation of two main camps of public policy standards: (i) one developed in labor arbitration, and (ii) one under the Convention.[849] Instead, there has been one public policy standard in Turkish courts, but its scope has varied and become narrow as the practice of arbitration progresses in Turkey and as to whether the case concerns domestic or international arbitration.

Though not common, in construing the legal standard for public policy defense, Turkish courts have reckoned with the standards of public policy as

---

No.: 2014/2183, Decision No.: 2014/3226, dated 12.05.2014 (Legalbank Elektronik Hukuk Bankası) [Legalbank Electonic Case Law Database] (Turk.).

846 The General Assembly of the Turkish Court of Cassation, Case No: 2011/13-568, Decision No: 2012/47.

847 *See generally infra* Section 4.3.2.2.3.

848 *W.R. Grace*, 461 U.S. at 766.

849 *See generally supra* Section 3.3.2.

applied in other areas of law. For example, in one case, the Constitutional Court defined public policy as the totality of the rules that aim to ensure the peace of society, the preservation of the state, and the state organization. In other words, all the rules that form the basis of the order of society in every field.[850] Though this decision was related to a criminal case—and, arguably, overly broad for international arbitration—it has been cited by the Turkish courts in defining public policy in the context of commercial arbitration.[851] This is similar to dispersing the public policy exception as applied in labor arbitration into commercial arbitration in the United States.

Another notable difference from the U.S. public policy standard is that Turkish courts have explicitly highlighted the principle of non-review of arbitral awards on the merits, with a big caveat—it may be necessary to examine the merits of an award in order to assess the challenges and to decide whether the award is contrary to public policy. Finding support in commentary, Turkish courts have further stated that this does not constitute a merit review as a matter of fact but rather a reviewing of the facts of the dispute in order to dismiss the challenges made against the award. Though this rule set by the courts is, in a sense, convincing, the application of the rule, in fact, does not reflect the stated ideology. Hence, as will be discussed in the next section, there have been many instances where Turkish courts have reviewed an award on its merits, reconsidered its reasoning, and engaged in an independent re-evaluation of the facts that allegedly gave rise to the public policy violation. This is, in fact, similar to a CEO referring to the business as being "like a family"—with the concomitant expectation that employees will offer the requisite commitment and loyalty—at one point, only to then undertake mass layoffs at another.

4.3.2 Challenges to Arbitral Awards Based on Public Policy Violations

4.3.2.1 Types of Allegations that are Frequently Invoked but Do Not Violate Public Policy Lack of Reasons

In a recent Unification Judgment, the Court of Cassation held that a foreign court decision without reasons per se does not interfere with enforcement in Turkey

850 The Constitutional Court of The Republic of Turkey, Case No.: 1963/128 Decision No.: 1964/8 dated 28.1.1964, Official Gazette No: 11685, dated 17.04.1964 (Turk.)

851 *E.g.* 15th Civil Chamber of Turkish Court of Cassation, Case No.: 2016/895, Decision No.: 2016/2050.

and is not considered to be a violation of Turkish public policy. [852] Though this decision did not explicitly indicate that it is applicable to arbitral awards, there is overwhelming evidence in support of this conclusion.

First, credit must be given to the Grand Plenary Assembly for deciding such a progressive judgment. The Court, in its majority decision, started by laying down the rules and recognized that both the Constitution and the Code of Civil Procedure require court decisions to include reasons. Having recognized this, the Court added that the need for reasons in foreign court decisions is not the same as for civil procedure law, emphasizing that the result may need to differ in the context of private international law.[853] Rejecting any possible counterarguments concerning violation of due-process rights from the beginning, the Court indicated that the violation of due process and decisions handed down without reasons are different issues, and the fact that due process is not given would contravene public policy in *domestic law*, but that the mere absence of reasons in a *foreign decision* would constitute a violation neither of due process nor public policy.[854] Further, the Court noted that the correct approach is to focus on the orders in the decision rather than to review the opinion of the foreign court and to assess whether the implications of foreign court orders when enforced would violate Turkish public policy.[855]

Nonetheless, this decision did not remain unopposed. Five justices of the 13th Circuit dissented that the court order section in a decision merely specifies the outcome of whether the plaintiff's claim is granted, but nothing more.[856] To elaborate further, the dissent exemplified that "the clause in the foreign court decision on the collection of TRY 50,000.00 from the defendant Turkish

852 Grand Plenary Assembly on the Unification of Judgments, Case No:2010/1, Decision No:2012/1 dated 10.2.2012, s.2/3.

853 *Id.*

854 *Id.*

855 *Id.* ("It is not possible for the enforcement court to review whether the foreign court [correctly] applied the law on the merits and... to examine the components of the foreign decision. It will be necessary to accept that a violation of public policy will only arise in the foreign decision's orders, not in its reasons. In examining whether the foreign court decision is contrary to the Turkish public policy, the prohibition of judicial review of arbitration awards on the merits comes into effect and it is clear that this ban cannot be disregarded by a judge at his discretion. Hence, the enforcement judge, cannot examine the foreign court decision on the merits and its compliance with the law.")

856 *Id.* at 8–9

Undersecretariat of the Treasury to plaintiff A does not apparently contradict public policy. However, if this dispute arises from tax law, such a dispute between A and the Treasury comes under the exclusive jurisdiction of the Turkish courts. Hence, this will result in the enforcement of the foreign decision being contrary to Turkish public policy."[857]

Ergo, the dissent contended that whether the foreign court decision to be enforced is contrary to public policy could only be determined by the evaluation of the order section together with the opinion.[858] The commentary has also endorsed this view. [859] As the subsequent sections further reveal, such a position taken by the dissent and commentary is threatening to the finality of the awards in many respects and constitutes a forewarning for the parties who arbitrate in Turkey, especially where the 13th Civil Chamber is "in the saddle."[860]

Nevertheless, this Unification Decision is a strong indicator that if a circuit split arises over whether a Convention award without reasons is contrary to Turkish public policy, the Grand Plenary Assembly of the Court of Cassation is most likely to rule that it is not.[861] Therefore, it can be deduced that awards

---

857 *Id.* at 9.

858 Grand Plenary Assembly on the Unification of Judgments, Case No:2010/1, Decision No:2012/1 dated 10.2.2012 (Karşı Oy) [Dissent].

859 E.g. Adnan Deynekli, In Memoriam, *Yabancı Hakem Kararlarının Türkiye'de Tanınması ve Tenfizinde Karşılaşılan Sorunlar [Problems in the Recognition and Enforcement of Foreign Arbitral Awards in Turkey]*, 16 Dokuz Eylul Universitesi Hukuk Fakultesi Dergisi 105,121 (2014) (Turk.).

860 Pelin Baysal & Bilge K. Cevik, *Could a Reduction in a State's Income Violate Public Policy– A View on Turkey?*, Kluwer Arbitration Blog (Feb. 10 2019), http://arbitrationblog.kluwerarbitration.com/2019/02/10/could-a-reduction-in-a-states-incomeviolate-public-policy-a-view-on-turkey/ (stating that the "unruly horse is not fully bridled in Turkey, especially when the 13th Civil Division of the Turkish Court of Cassation is in the saddle" by being inspired by the famous case of Richardson v. Mellish [1824] 2Bing229, 252, which describes public policy as "a very unruly horse, [and] when once you get astride it you never know where it will carry you"); *See infra* Section 4.3.2.

861 There is less evidence supporting that a non-domestic award without reasons will be enforced. *Compare* Art. 14A of Act No.: 4686, TIAL, *translated in* Akinci, *supra* note 816 at 298 ("The arbitration award shall state... legal grounds for the award and its reasoning....) (emphasis added) *with id.* Art. 15(A)(1) ("Awards may be set aside... [i] f the applicant party furnishes proof that... the said arbitration agreement is not valid under the governing law or, failing any indication thereon, *under Turkish law*") (emphasis added). Nevertheless, to this date, there is no case known to the author where the Turkish Court of Cassation sets aside an award due to a failure to state the reasons upon which the award was based.

without reasons do not violate public policy in Turkey, which is similar to the U.S. practice.[862]

4.3.2.2 Untimely Award

One of the recurring fact situations involves an award that the arbitrator has failed to render on a timely basis. Turkey carries special importance in this respect. It is one of few jurisdictions where its statute explicitly provides recourse in the event of an untimely award.[863] TIAL, unlike the Convention, Model Law and the FAA, stipulates that arbitrators must render the award within the terms of arbitration, and failure to do so may trigger setting aside of the award.[864] Entering the award within the required time was once a very significant requisite—in a similar provision of the Original CCP, it was even treated as part of the Turkish public policy—thereby resulting in setting aside the award under Turkish domestic arbitration practice.[865]

Despite this former practice, the Turkish Court of Cassation, in its recent decisions, has held that rendering of foreign awards after the date the awards were required to be entered does not rise to the level of a violation of public policy.

---

862 *See supra* Section 3.2.2.3.

863 *See* Stephan Wilske, *Legal Challenges to Delayed Arbitral Awards*, 6 CONTEMP. ASIA ARB. J. 153, 158 (2013).

864 *Compare* Art. 10(B) of Act No.: 4686, TIAL, *translated* AKINCI, *supra* note 816 at 294 ("Unless otherwise agreed by the parties, where there is a sole arbitrator, within one year of his appointment, and where there is more than one arbitrator, within one year of the issuance of the first minutes of the first hearing of the tribunal, a determination must be made by the arbitrator or arbitration tribunal on the merit of the case.") *with id.* Art. 15 A(1)(c) ("Awards may be set aside... if the applicant party furnishes proof that [t]he award was not rendered within the period of the arbitration").

865 *E.g.* 15th Civil Chamber of Turkish Court of Cassation, Case No.: 1997/2567, Decision No.: 1997/3420 (holding that the term of arbitration is considered as a part of the public policy because if the case is not limited to any period, the right holders cannot obtain the opportunity to apply to the judge while the arbitrators still have jurisdiction). One may ask what the current practice under Turkish domestic arbitration is today. The current Code of Civil Procedure has an identical provision with that of TIAL. Art. 427 and Art. 439 of Act No. 6100, New CCP. Hence, an award should be made within the required time, and failure to do so may result in annulment of the award. *Id.* Nonetheless, a search conducted in the Kazancı and LexPera databases—which are similar Turkish equivalents to LexisNexis and Westlaw—reveals that this old practice has been abandoned under Turkish domestic arbitration and that an award that is not made within the required time does not violate public policy.

In this sense, it is similar to the U.S. practice, as delay in issuing an award does not constitute misconduct under FAA s.10(a)(4), and thus, it is not a ground to vacate an award.[866] For example, in *Voset Alpine Undustrienanlagenbau Gmbh v. Ozmak Makine ve Elektrik San. A.S.*, where the winning party filed a motion to enforce a foreign award in Turkey against the losing Turkish party, the Court cited its previous rulings and held that delay in rendering an award does not cross the level of a public policy violation. [867] Therefore, today it is settled that not having entered a foreign award on time does not contravene Turkish public policy.

What is less is clear is whether non-domestic awards that are issued in an untimely manner will trigger the public policy exception. Although thus far there is no decision indicating so, in one decision, the Court of Cassation, *in dicta*, stated that an arbitrator's failure to decide on a dispute within the requested period results in the arbitrators having no jurisdiction upon the dispute according to the agreement between the parties and the TIAL.[868] The Court went on to say that jurisdiction to rule on the dispute had passed to the court, such that an arbitrator ruling on the dispute would constitute an excess of authority.[869] Nevertheless, even though an untimely award may be set aside on this ground, it does not seem to be a violation of public policy.

4.3.2.3 Awards Based on Penalty Clauses and Awards of Interest

The principles of contracts in civil law countries and those in countries with the common law system differ at certain points. An example of this would be the implications of penalty clauses in Turkey and the United States. Unlike under

866 *Supra* Section 3.2.2.4.

867 15th Civil Chamber of Turkish Court of Cassation, Case No.: 2003/181 Decision No.: 2003/1589, dated 27.3.2003 (Kazancı İçtihat Bilgi Bankası) [Kazanci Case Law Database] (Turk.) (citing 11th Civil Chamber of Turkish Court of Cassation, Case No.: 2000/3992, Decision No.: 2000/4704, dated 26.5.2000 and 19th Civil Chamber of Turkish Court of Cassation, Case No.: 2000/7171 Decision No.: 2000/7602 dated 9.11.2000). *See also* 11th Civil Chamber of Turkish Court of Cassation, Case No.: 2013/10684, Decision No.: 2014/15287, dated 9.10.2014 (Legalbank Elektronik Hukuk Bankası) [Legalbank Electonic Case Law Database] (Turk.) (upholding the untimely award).

868 15th Civil Chamber of Turkish Court of Cassation, Case No.: 2015/375 Decision No.: 2015/1233, dated 16.3.2015 (Legalbank Elektronik Hukuk Bankası) [Legalbank Electonic Case Law Database] (Turk.).

869 *Id.*

U.S. law, under Turkish law, parties can freely agree to penalty clauses in their contract—even if it is for punitive purposes.[870] The limit of its applicability, however, can be drawn by the judge who may find the agreed amount exorbitant and thus decide to mitigate.[871] Thus, though Turkey and the United States have different implications for penalty clauses, awards based on penalty clauses are enforceable in both jurisdictions.

In one case before the Turkish Court of Cassation, the parties submitted their dispute to ICC arbitration pursuant to an arbitration clause in their independent contractor agreement, and yet later settled during proceedings.[872] After the losing party failed to fulfill the debt arising from the settlement, the winning party commenced arbitration and obtained an award in his favor.[873] He then began the enforcement procedure in Turkey in order to collect the amount owed.[874] Granting the losing party's motion for non-enforcement on the grounds that an award based on an excessive penalty violates Turkish public policy and applying the above-referred mitigation principles under the Turkish Code of Obligations (contracts law), the trial court held that awards based on a penalty "would destroy or severely restrict the economic freedom and endanger the economic future of the defendant" such that "it should be considered of public policy."[875]

The 15th Civil Chamber of the Court of Cassation reversed the ruling, consistent with its pro-arbitration approach. Following its precedents in denying the public policy defenses, the Court first underlined that public policy bears different meanings in domestic law versus international law.[876] Further, the Court articulated the applicable test, which is "whether the foreign award is not contrary to the provisions of one or more codes under Turkish Law [such as the Turkish Code of Obligations] but rather to the basic values of Turkish Law, the understanding of Turkish public morality and customs, the basic understanding of justice on which Turkish laws are based, *jus cogens*, internationally accepted principles of law, bilateral agreements, morality and justice concepts adopted by developed societies, and the civilizational level, and political and economic

870 Akkayan-Yıldırım, *supra* note 300, at 357–58.
871 *Id.*
872 15th Civil Chamber of Turkish Court of Cassation, Case No.: 2014/2183, Decision No.: 2014/3226.
873 *Id.*
874 *Id.*
875 *Id.*
876 *Id.*

regimes, of such societies."[877] As verbose as this articulation of the standard is, it follows the modern approach and is akin to the basic morality standard established in *Parsons & Whittemore*, with a hint of transnational public policy.[878] What is more, the Court estopped the public policy defense on the ground that the amount imposed in the award is equal to the amount agreed by the parties in the settlement, and thus the losing party is estopped from raising a public policy exception even if it is accepted that the penalty clause is exorbitant.[879]

Similarly, in one trial court case, the court first underlined that the party challenging the award must file a well-pleaded claim of a public policy violation and bear the burden of showing that the award is contrary to public policy.[880] The Court then stated that there should be "conclusive and convincing evidence" and information and documents that were submitted to prove that the award based on a penalty clause is contrary to public policy.[881]

Awards of interest are also enforceable under Turkish law. Turkey is distinct as a constitutionally secular but Muslim-majority country (of 80 million people), like Albania, Azerbaijan, and Bosnia-Herzegovina.[882] Though Sharia forbids the payment and receipt of interest, the traditional Muslim law inherited from the Ottomans was officially repealed and replaced by secular laws almost one hundred years ago. Hence, the inclusion of interest in arbitral awards per se is not a basis for an award to be found contrary to public policy under Turkish law.

For example, in one case, the parties included an arbitration clause requiring them to arbitrate the disputes arising from the sale of goods.[883] It is understood

---

877 *Id.*

878 *See generally supra* Section 3.4.1.

879 15th Civil Chamber of Turkish Court of Cassation, Case No.: 2014/2183, Decision No.: 2014/3226.

880 *Id.*

881 25th Civil Court of First Instance of Ankara, Case No.: 2014/47, Decision No.: 2015/55 at 4 *rev'd, on other grounds*, 13th Civil Chamber of Turkish Court of Cassation, Case No.: 2015/40156, Decision No.: 2019/5664.

882 See Dominic McGoldrick, *Sharia Law in Europe? Legacies of the Ottoman Empire and the European Convention on Human Rights*, 8 Ox. J L. Religion 517, 518 (2019); Turkey–Population: Demographic Situation, Languages and Religions, European Commission (Nov. 4, 2019), https://eacea.ec.europa.eu/national-policies/eurydice/content/population-demographic-situation-languages-and-religions-103_en

883 19th Civil Chamber of Turkish Court of Cassation, Case No.: 2012/2969, Decision No.: 2012/8688, dated 23.5.2012 (Legalbank Elektronik Hukuk Bankası) [Legalbank Electonic Case Law Database] (Turk.).

from the case that upon buyer's failure to pay, the parties submitted their dispute to ICC arbitration, and the tribunal entered an award for the seller.[884] Once the seller moved to enforce the award, the buyer claimed that an arbitration award that includes the principal, as well as interest at 8 per cent, is contrary to public policy.[885] In its brief discussion, the Court of Cassation affirmed the judgment of the trial court on the ground that the trial court did not err in finding that the conditions for enforcement of foreign arbitral awards were sufficient.[886]

4.3.2.4 Scope of Choice-of-Law Clauses

In determining which set of procedural rules arbitrators may adhere to, the choice of a specific arbitration seat is a decisive factor.[887] This is particularly true if the parties have not agreed to an explicit choice of procedural law to govern their arbitration.[888] It is therefore generally accepted that the choice-of-law provision only specifies the substantive rule to be applied and does not include the procedural law to be followed by arbitrators.[889]

Despite this overwhelming acceptance in international arbitration, Turkish courts have formerly construed a contractual choice-of-Turkish-law in a way that refers to Turkish substantive and procedural laws—even if the seat of arbitration is not Turkey—and that arbitrators' failure to observe the Turkish procedural law is a ground for non-enforcement and can even be considered a matter of public policy. In *Osuuskunta METEX Andelslag V.S. (METEX) v. Turkish Electricity Authority (TEK)*, the Finnish party, METEX, and the Turkish state agency, TEK, entered into a contract for construction of a power plant in Turkey.[890] The contract between the parties had a clause for arbitration, which would be held in Zurich, Switzerland, including the following phrase: "The Board of Arbitration

884 *Id.*

885 *Id.*

886 *Id.*

887 *E.g.*, Tiffany Ng, *Choice of Procedural Law in International Commercial Arbitration: Providing "Proper Notice" to a Foreign Party to Ensure That the Arbitral Award Can Be Enforced*, 10 Hastings Bus. L.J. 491, 501 (2014); Eric Ordway, *The Importance of the Seat of Arbitration*, 25 The Advoc. (Texas) 16, 17 (2003); Jessica Thrope, *A Question of Intent: Choice of Law and the International Arbitration Agreement*, 54 Disp. Resolution J. 16 (1999).

888 Tiffany Ng, *supra* note 887, at 501.

889 *See* Born, *supra* note 14, at 574.

890 15th Civil Chamber of the Turkish Court of Cassation, No.: 1996/627, dated 1 Feb. 1996, *translated in* 22 YB Comm. Arb 807, 807 (1997).

shall take as the basis of decision the provisions of this Contract and Turkish laws in force."[891] Once the dispute arose between the parties, METEX commenced arbitration in Zurich, Switzerland.[892] During the proceedings, a dispute arose as to the procedural law applicable to the arbitration, later resolved by the tribunal in favor of Swiss procedural law.[893] The tribunal rendered a final award for METEX, who later sought enforcement before the Turkish courts.[894]

In denying the enforcement and entering judgment for the Turkish state agency, the trial court found that the award violates Art. V(1)(d) of the Convention and Turkish public policy on the grounds that the tribunal did not observe the parties' choice of law when they applied Swiss procedural law to the proceedings.[895] The 15th Civil Chamber upheld the trial court's decision, stating that "Turkish laws in force" in the contract referred not only to the *substantive* law but also to the *procedural* law.[896] The Court, however, did not decide whether the award was contrary to public policy.[897] Soon after, another decision was handed down by the General Assembly of the Turkish Court of Cassation that reached the same conclusion, thereby eliminating the possibility that this would be an isolated case.[898]

Turkish courts' misapplication of the public policy exception and non-enforcement of a legitimate award to protect (in this case) state interests, have not escaped commentators' attention and have been harshly criticized in both the foreign and Turkish literature.[899] This decision also embodies the general

891 *Id.* at 811.
892 *Id.* at 807.
893 *Id.*
894 *Id.* at 808.
895 *Id.* at 808–9.
896 *Id.* at 809.
897 *Id.*
898 The General Assembly of the Turkish Court of Cassation Case No: 1999/15-235, Decision No: 1999/273, dated 5.5.1999, *as discussed in* Ekşi, *supra* note 808, at 63.
899 *E.g. id.* at 68; Moses, *supra* note 207, at 218–19 ("Although a number of countries construe the public policy defense narrowly, there is room for it to be used parochially to protect national political interests. To the extent that a country does this, it undermines the utility of the Convention. For example, the Turkish Court of Cassation in 1995 refused to enforce an ICC award where the tribunal in Zurich had applied Turkish substantive law, but the procedural law of the canton of Zurich.... Here, the Turkish Court used public policy as a basis for refusing enforcement on a point of law, and one that did not matter to the ultimate decision. This appears to be an unfortunate use of the public policy defense as a basis to reach a decision more favored by the Turkish court"); Albert Jan Van den Berg, *Why Are Some Award Not*

hostility Turkish courts' had to arbitration during the 1990s. Just as the "Chiquita bananas debate" came to represent broad-based societal antipathy toward the neoliberal economic reform agenda of the 1980s and 1990s, the *METEX* decision reflects a more general "protest" by Turkish courts to the "imposition" of a new legal approach—arbitration—against the grain of the established way of doing things. Therefore, the response by courts is significant.

Another decision on the same subject, but reaching an opposite conclusion, was handed down by the 11th Civil Chamber in 2000. In this particular case, a dispute arising from an options contract between the German company and two Turkish firms resulted in an arbitral award for the German party.[900] The parties had selected Turkish law to govern their contract together with a clause indicating that ICC rules of arbitration would be applied as procedural law.[901] Once the trial court granted the German party's motion for enforcement, the Turkish parties appealed the case on the grounds that arbitrators' purported failure to apply Turkish procedural law violates the Turkish public policy.[902] Upholding the trial court's decision, the 11th Civil Chamber held that choosing Turkish law means choosing Turkish substantive law but not Turkish procedural laws and did not find any violation of public policy.[903]

Today, there is considerable evidence to suggest that the parties' choice of law only refers to substantive law but not procedural law, and even if the court were to find otherwise, this is not a violation of Turkish public policy. This argument

---

Enforceable?, *in* NEW HORIZONS IN INTERNATIONAL COMMERCIAL ARBITRATION AND BEYOND 291, 304 (Albert Jan Van den Berg ed., 2004) (finding the decision surprising); Michael Kerr, *Concord and Conflict in International Arbitration*, 13 ARB. INT'L 121, 140 (1997) ("With all due respect, this decision provides an example of a triple error. As in other cases already referred to, it fails to distinguish between the applicability of the procedural law of the place of arbitration and the substantive law; it assumes a right to review the award...; and it interprets the public policy exception to enforcement inordinately widely.")

900 *E.g.*, 11th Civil Chamber of Turkish Court of Cassation, Case No.: 2015/11441, Decision No.: 2016/8701 (enforcing the ICC award conducted under the ICC Rules of arbitration, arising from a contract including a choice-of-Turkish-law clause); 11th Civil Chamber of Turkish Court of Cassation, Case No.: 2000/3992, Decision No.: 2000/4704.

901 *Id.* Such an explicit choice-of-procedural-law clause did not exist in *Metex*. 15th Civil Chamber of the Turkish Court of Cassation, No.: 1996/627 at 809 *supra* note 890.

902 11th Civil Chamber of Turkish Court of Cassation, Case No.: 2000/3992, Decision No.: 2000/4704.

903 *Id.*

is supported by a more recent decision handed by the Court of Cassation.[904] This argument must be considered together with the evolving pro-arbitration view of the Court that began to form in the 2000s. In fact, since the 1990s, no available decision handed by the Court has reached the result that an arbitrator's failure to apply Turkish procedural law violates public policy. There is also growing understanding in the literature that such an application does not trigger grounds for vacatur, much less the public policy exception.[905]

It is unfortunate that, due to its notoriety, *METEX* is still cited in the foreign literature despite its negative history.[906] As the old adage suggests, "give a dog a bad name and hang him." And yet, there is a truth in these criticisms. Some circuits in the Court of Cassation, namely the 13th Civil Chamber, have evinced a perennial animosity and mistrust of international arbitration and, thus, protects the State's interest whenever an award is against it.[907] Nonetheless, this particular ground no longer rises to the level of non-enforcement and violation of public policy.

In summary, the issue of the proper interpretation of a contract containing both a general choice-of-law clause and an arbitration clause resulted in different decisions in Turkey and the United States. The Turkish courts initially tended to protect their jurisdiction, as in *METEX*, favoring a general choice-of-Turkish-law clause at the expense of an arbitration clause. In the United States, a similar issue yielded a different result in *Mastrobuono*, where the Supreme Court favored an arbitration clause over a choice-of-law clause.[908] The Supreme Court made punitive damages available in arbitration—even though the law chosen by the parties did not allow for this—and "prevent[ed] choice-of-law clauses from transforming into an anti-arbitration 'device'."[909]

Whereas in Turkey there was a suspicion of arbitration in the beginning—one that, it must be said, to some extent lingers—the U.S. Courts have consistently insisted on a pro-arbitration policy, at the expense, arguably, of parties with unequal bargaining power, *e.g.*, employees and consumers. *METEX* and *Mastrubono*,

904 *Id.*

905 *See* Asli Bayata Canyas, *Enforcement of Foreign Arbitral Awards in Turkey: Further Steps Towards a More Arbitration Friendly Approach*, 31 ASA Bulletin 537, 544 (2013).

906 E.g. Moses O. Dickson, *Party autonomy and justice in international commercial arbitration*, 60 Int'l J. L. Mgmt 114, 123 (2018).

907 *Infra* Section 4.3.2.2.2.

908 *Mastrobuono*, 514 U.S. at 53. *Supra* Section 3.2.4.

909 Petition for Writ of Certiorari, Applied Underwriters Captive Risk Assurance Co. v. Citizens of Humanity, LLC, 139 S. Ct. 274 (No. 18–174).

therefore, provide great insight into the Turkish and U.S. courts' respective axia on arbitration.

4.3.2.5 *Types of Allegations in Which Enforcement May Be Denied on Public Policy Grounds*

4.3.2.5.1 *Misapplication of Law*

In modern arbitration and U.S. practice, any arbitrator error in applying the law or in interpreting a contract does not, by itself, trigger grounds for vacatur or non-enforcement, much less public policy.[910] One may counterargue that a common law ground of manifest disregard of the law permits vacatur of arbitral awards, though the FAA does not explicitly provide for the judicial review of awards over legal errors.[911] Nevertheless, manifest disregard of the law is a frequently invoked ground, albeit one that is rarely a successful, given the pro-arbitration bias of the U.S. courts. [912] In the eyes of some Turkish courts, however, awards can be reviewable for errors of law, especially where the parties agreed that Turkish law governs the contract, and the losing party is a Turkish state agency.[913] Hence, although Turkey has enacted modern legislation on arbitration, proper enforcement and application of these laws remain problematic.

The TIAL, similar to Model Law, stipulates that arbitrators must decide the dispute based on the rules of the law chosen by the parties.[914] However, mere misapplication of substantive law is not a ground to set aside or not enforce under either the TIAL, the Model Law, or the Convention. In order to circumvent this "obstacle" in the way of merit review, Turkish courts, especially the 13th Civil Chamber, cites an old Unification Judgment—which was rendered in 1994 before the modern Turkish arbitration codes that are based on the Model

---

910 *Supra* Section 3.2.2.3. *Karaha Bodas*, 364 F.3d at 306 ("... misapplication of law is generally not a violation of public policy within the meaning of the New York Convention."); Jean-Paul Beraudo, *Egregious Error of Law as Grounds for Setting Aside an Arbitral Award*, 23 J. INT'L ARB. 351 (2006); Steven Walt, *Decision by Division: The Contractarian Structure of Commercial Arbitration*, 51 RUTGERS L. REV. 369, 384 (1999).

911 Beraudo, *supra* note 910, at 365–66.

912 *E.g.* N.Y. City Bar Comm. on Int'l Commercial Disp., The "Manifest Disregard of Law" Doctrine and International Arbitration in New York 7–12 (2012). *See* Born, *supra* note 14, at 1103.

913 *Infra* Section 4.3.2.2.2

914 Art. 4(3) of Act No.: 4686, TIAL.

Law and the Convention were enacted[915]—and reasons that "if the parties agreed to a substantive law applicable to the contract, then this law should govern the dispute" such that "arbitrators should decide on the dispute in accordance with these rules and public policy as construed under these rule[s...]."[916] From there, the Circuit moves to enumerate the grounds for non-enforcement with the emphasis on public policy and goes on to say that a violation of the public policy of the law applicable to the dispute (which is usually Turkish law, and as a result, Turkish public policy) justifies the vacatur of the award.

Following this pattern, the 13th Civil Chamber analyzed the factual and legal findings in the award, relying on the exception of public policy, and reversed the awards made by the trial court with the order of conducting an independent reexamination of the facts and the arbitrators' ruling that allegedly gave rise to the violation of public policy.[917] Hence, the 13th Civil Chamber's expansive intervention hampers the binding and final nature of international awards made in Turkey and renders the occasional misapplication of law subject to the court's intervention under a public policy exception, broadening the scope of the exception. What is worse is that the 13th Civil Chamber can sometimes protect state agencies at the expense of private companies, undermining the rule of law.[918] As the following section will discuss in more detail, this not only violates the principle of *pacta sunt servanda* and the rule of law but makes awards extensively reviewable, reducing the degree of deference to arbitrators' legal rulings.

915 Grand Plenary Assembly on the Unification of Judgments, Case No: 1993/4, Decision No: 1994/1, dated 28.1.1994 (Kazancı İçtihat Bilgi Bankası) [Kazanci Case Law Database] (Turk.); (deciding in the context of domestic arbitration that choice-of-law clauses also encompass the public policy of the applicable law, so the courts should consider the both in an appellate review of an arbitral award).

916 *See e.g.* 13th Civil Chamber of Turkish Court of Cassation, Case No.: 2015/16140, Decision No.: 2017/3322 at 6. ("If the parties have chosen the law in the arbitration agreement under which the disputes will be governed, then the arbitrators are obliged to accept that the parties have also chosen the public policy of the law applied. In other words, public policy needs to be evaluated in accordance with the chosen law."); 13th Civil Chamber of Turkish Court of Cassation, Case No.: 2014/8201, Decision No.: 2016/5293 dated 23.02.2016 (Lexpera Hukuk Bilgi Sistemi) [Lexpera Legal Information System] (Turk.).

917 *Infra* Section 4.3.2.2.2.

918 *Id.*

4.3.2.5.2 *Reduction in the Turkish State's Revenue*

The old Turkish arbitration practice was distinguished by the use of the public policy exception by the national courts to protect their jurisdiction as covered throughout this book. First, in the 1980s and 1990s the Constitutional Court and the Council of the State struck down the laws allowing international arbitration in BOTs and concessions agreements based on, among other things, public policy.[919] This was subsequently followed by the Court of Cassation when the parties approaching the Court to enforce foreign awards against Turkish state entities encountered strong resistance based on public policy and public interest grounds. Finally, the 2000s saw a change in direction for the better with the enactment of legislation based on modern practice and with the transformation in the Turkish courts' view of arbitration.[920] This continuing trend was foreshadowed by the 13th Civil Chamber starting from the 2010s.

Though only two of the relevant cases are detailed here, a total of five different decisions were handed down by the 13th Civil Chamber at various points between 2012 and 2017, which all revolve around the same facts. The contractual issues arose from concession agreements between Turkish GSM operators and the Information and Communication Technologies Authority of Turkey ("Communication Authority"), which grants GSM operators the right to establish and/or operate telecommunication services in Turkey. In all cases, the contractual issues arose from the question of which items are to be included in gross sales figures when calculating the Treasury share and the contribution share.[921] In all cases, the parties submitted their dispute to ICC arbitration due to the arbitration

919 *Supra* Section 1.2.2

920 *Id.*

921 *E.g.* 13th Civil Chamber of Turkish Court of Cassation, Case No.: 2015/16140, Decision No.: 2017/3322 (award on whether a facility usage fee is included in gross sales); 13th Civil Chamber of Turkish Court of Cassation, Case No.: 2014/8201, Decision No.: 2016/5293 (award on whether reimbursements resulting from retroactive application of interconnection tariffs are included in calculating the Treasury share base); 13th Civil Chamber of Turkish Court of Cassation, Case No.: 2013/16287, Decision No.: 2016/5292 dated 23.2.2016 (Turk.) (on file with author) (award on whether the reimbursements are included in calculating the base); 13th Civil Chamber of Turkish Court of Cassation, Case No.: 2012/8425, Decision No.: 2012/10348. (award on whether the discounts applied to distributors for wholesale sales are included in gross sales); 13th Civil Chamber of Turkish Court of Cassation, Case No.: 2011/19737 Decision No.: 2012/25406 (award on whether the discounts applied to subscribers and third-parties prior to sale are included in gross sales).

clauses in their contracts, and the tribunals rendered awards in favor of the GSM operators, resulting in a reduction in the total value of the amount owed to the Communication Authority and another state agency that are in the position of being third-party beneficiaries under the agreements. All the relevant awards were set aside by the 13th Civil Chamber on the ground that the enforcement of such awards would lead to a reduction in public income, being thus contrary to public policy.

The most recent example is the aforementioned case of *Information and Communication Technologies Authority of Turkey v. Turkcell,* where the parties entered into a concession agreement concerning GSM operation services.[922] Pursuant to the contract, Turkcell, the GSM operator, agreed to pay a certain percentage of its monthly gross sales to another state agency, the Turkish Undersecretariat of the Treasury, as the "Treasury share" and to the Communication Authority as the "contribution share."[923] The dispute arose from whether the facility usage fee needs to be included in the calculation of gross sales and, therefore, in the allocations of the Treasury share and the contribution share.[924] The tribunal entered the award for Turkcell, finding that the facility usage fee could be deducted from gross sales in computing the base, thereby resulting in a reduced value of the payments to the respective state agencies.[925]

The Communication Authority brought an action to set aside the award in Turkey, claiming the award was repugnant to public policy because (i) the Council of State, not the arbitrators, had the jurisdiction to rule on the dispute; (ii) the tribunal exceeded its authority by issuing an award against non-signatories, *i.e.*, the Treasury; (iii) arbitrators misapplied Turkish law to the contract, and finally; (iv) the decision of the arbitrator, which resulted in a reduction in public revenues, adversely affected the public interest.[926] As such, the state agency regarded public policy as a ground that would allow the award to be set aside on any legal ground,

922 13th Civil Chamber of Turkish Court of Cassation, Case No.: 2015/16140 Decision No.: 2017/3322 at 1.

923 *Id* at 5.

924 *Id.*

925 6th Civil Court of First Instance of Ankara, Case No.: 2013/273, Decision No.: 2014/382, dated 1.6.2014 at 3 *rev'd,* 13th Civil Chamber of Turkish Court of Cassation, Case No.: 2015/16140 Decision No.: 2017/3322

926 Id. at 1–3.

recasting any violation of the law as a violation of public policy.[927] Rejecting the state agency's desperate attempts under the disguise of public policy, the trial court found that "the reduction of public income cannot, by itself, be considered as a violation of public policy, as the purpose of concession agreements is to facilitate provision of a public service by private persons and not to generate revenue from such contracts in the name of the state or the public."[928]

These arguments, rather than the trial court's reasoning, "spoke to" the protectionist side of the 13th Civil Chamber. In this case, the 13th Civil Chamber first emphasized that Turkish law governs the contract between the parties so that the award must be in conformity with Turkish law, including Turkish public policy. Before moving to examine the public policy challenge, the Court defined the concession agreement[929] and underlined that an examination on the merits of the dispute might be necessary in order to rule on the challenges as to the violation of public policy, justifying that it would not be possible to conduct an evaluation of the challenges otherwise.[930] Acknowledging the principle of no-merit-review in arbitral awards, the Court noted that such examinations of the issues "do not necessarily purport to be a review of the case on the merits but is rather a review in a technical sense."[931]

Doing the exact opposite of what it just established, the Court reversed the decision of the trial court, finding that "reducing the state's income would obviously

---

927 *See* Stephen Murphy, *Judicial Review Of Arbitration Awards Under State Law*, 96 Va. L. Rev. 887, 919 2010 (*citing* Brief of Appellee at 2, BBF, Inc. v. Alstom Power, 645 S.E.2d 467 (Va. 2007) (No. 061317), 2006 WL 4701769))

928 6th Civil Court of First Instance of Ankara, Case No.: 2013/273 Decision No.: 2014/382 at 7 *rev'd,* 13th Civil Chamber of Turkish Court of Cassation, Case No.: 2015/16140 Decision No.: 2017/3322.

929 13th Civil Chamber of Turkish Court of Cassation, Case No.: 2015/16140, Decision No.: 2017/3322 at 4. ("Public concession agreements pertains to the operation of the public service for a certain period by a private person who is determined and supervised by the state. *The main purpose of these contracts is the public interest*. Concession agreements... are mainly determined by the unilateral will of the administration. The Concessionaire has the opportunity to fully accept or reject the terms and conditions prepared by the Contracting Entity. The state entity has a number of superior rights and powers than the Concessionaire [such as]... to enforce audit and sanction, the unilateral amendment to the contract and the revocation of the concession... The reason for granting such... right[s] to the concessionaire is *the public interest* in the continuation of the public service carried out by the concessionaire.") (emphasis added)

930 *Id.* at 6.

931 *Id.*

violate public policy, and yet the trial court erred in granting the enforcement without determining whether the enforcement of the award would reduce public revenues." The Court remanded the case to the trial court and directed the court to consider "how the contract between the parties provides for the procedure on payment," "the accounting application of the GSM company before and after the contract," "the amount of facility usage fees received from pre-paid cardholders, together with how these purchases were made, their share, and contribution," and "how the Treasury share will differ under the arbitral award when it is compared with what the court will find based on the expert witness report that will be prepared by the accounting experts."[932] In fact, the court directed that the trial court must obtain and compare the expert witnesses' report with the arbitral award and then decide whether the enforcement of an award would result in a reduction in public revenue contrary to the Turkish public policy. These, of course, are a perfect example of the manner of questioning the findings and conclusions of the tribunal in rendering the award, *i.e.*, merit review.

Also interesting in this decision is that the Court of Cassation did not examine the first three challenges the Communication Authority raised. Doing so would have required a meticulous examination of the issues, such as whether a non-signatory—which, in this case, enjoys the status of a third-party beneficiary—is bound by the arbitration clause.[933] Instead, the Court examined the most controversial—and arguably the weakest—challenge, which is that the reduction in the state's income violates public policy. Moreover, such a ruling clearly denies the evaluation of the public policy challenge under modern practice. The national courts cannot conclude that an award is contrary to public policy only because the judges could have decided the case differently from the arbitrators, whether it be an action to set aside or to enforce the award.[934]

In another decision dated 2012, the Court, in fact, reached the same conclusion with a twist, when it added a touch of "violation of mandatory laws" such as those concerning taxes. In this particular case, the dispute between Turkcell and the Communication Authority arose from the question of whether the discounts

---

932 *Id.*

933 *See* Gizem Halis Kasap, *Etching the Borders of Arbitration Agreement: The Group of Companies Doctrine in International Commercial Arbitration under the U.S. and Turkish Law*, 2 U. Bologna L. Rev. 89, 105 (2017) (discussing whether a third-party beneficiary in a contract can be bound by the arbitration clause in the contract under Turkish law).

934 Beraudo, *supra* note 910 at 360.

applied to distributors on wholesale sales are to be included in gross sales, and thus, in the calculation of the Treasury share.[935]

The 13th Civil Chamber interpreted Art. 8 and 9 of the concession agreement that gave rise to the dispute and identified that these provisions in the contract are precisely transplanted from Supplemental Art. 36 of the Law no. 5398, which amended the Telephone and Telegraph Law.[936] Considering this, the Court considered that the provisions in the concession contract should not be construed independently from Supplemental Art.36 and the reasons that necessitated the enactment of such a law in the first place.[937] Looking at the legislative history, the Court stated that the legislator had acted with the intent of eliminating the disputes and hesitations that had previously stemmed from the application of the Telephone and Telegraph Law, and thus shifted from "gross income" to "gross sales," and exhaustively set out the items that are not to be included in the base of gross sales.[938]

Next, the Court turned to justify why Supplemental Art. 36 is so essential for the State that the violation of this provision would constitute a violation of public policy. First, the Court stated that the court would deny enforcement of an award on public policy grounds if it were rendered in contradiction of (i) the fundamental principles that States cannot abandon; (ii) mandatory legal provisions that have the purpose of protecting public interest, and; (iii) legislation concerning the economic structure of the society.[939] Turning back to the evaluation of the case at hand, the Court posed that even though they do not constitute taxation, the Treasury share and the contribution share which were to be paid pursuant to the concession agreement are substantial and constant elements of state income, which emerges from the transfer of the public service by the State.[940] The subtext can be readily observed in this part of the opinion—namely, that is, the Treasury and the contribution shares are as important and indispensable as taxes for the State.

Applying the rule that is just established to the dispute, the Court ruled that the exclusion of the discounts from the basis for the calculation of the gross sales

---

935 13th Civil Chamber of Turkish Court of Cassation, Case No.: 2012/8425, Decision No.: 2012/10348 at 4.

936 *Id* at. 8–9.

937 *Id.*

938 *Id.*

939 *Id.*

940 *Id.*

on which the payment of the Treasury share is based is contrary to the purpose of the Supplemental Art. and thus Art.8 and 9 of the concession agreement because "it is apparent that the Treasury share from which the State intends to procure a continuous income will decrease; the balance of the budget balances will be affected; and accordingly, the economic balances and public policy will be undermined."[941]

As these decisions reveal, the 13th Civil Chamber tends to interpret the public policy defense in very broad terms. The Court repeatedly employed the public policy exception as an escape valve, in effect encouraging the State parties to employ this exception to avoid responsibility for their actions arising from a contract that they agreed to.[942] Although Turkey is an arbitration-friendly jurisdiction, the 13th Civil Chamber sends a message to the practitioners that there is a difference between enforcing an award *in* Turkey and enforcing an award *against* Turkey (or, in this case, Turkish state agencies).

Interestingly enough, the winning party does not have the possibility of shopping a forum and filing a motion to enforce the award in a city that is under a circuit other than the 13th Civil Chamber. Unlike the United States, where each circuit covers a different geographical region, the "division of work" between the circuits of the Turkish Court of Cassation is based on the nature of the dispute.[943] The 13th Circuit, in general, has jurisdiction over the contracts that do not fall under any of the other circuits' jurisdictions, *e.g.*, concession agreements. [944] On the other hand, the 15th Circuit, which is a pro-arbitration circuit, has jurisdiction over construction agreements, among others. Hence, whereas an award arising from a construction agreement is more likely to be enforced, the same is not true for an award arising from concession agreements.

For example, in one case regarding the enforcement of a foreign ICC award heard by the 15th Civil Chamber, the parties entered into a government contract for the construction of a light rail system.[945] The defendant filed a motion to deny enforcement of the award claiming to be a state agency so that the award

941 *Id.*

942 E.g. Ersin Erdoğan & Belkis Vural Çelenk, *The Culture Of Dispute Resolution In Turkey And The Istanbul Arbitration Centre*, L. & Justice R., June 2016, at 157, 168; Baysal & Cevik, supra note 860

943 Art. 14 of Act No.: 2797, The Law of Court of Cassation.

944 The General Assembly of The Court of Cassation, Decision No:1, dated 30.01.2019 (Turk.).

945 15th Civil Chamber of Turkish Court of Cassation, Case No.: 2016/895, Decision No.: 2016/2050.

entered against the defendant requiring compensation for the damages of the winning party is contrary to public policy.[946] What is immediately striking is that this argument is one of the remnants of the old judicial hostility toward arbitration and evolves from the notion that the state courts are paternal and protective toward state agencies.

Luckily, neither the trial court nor the 15th Civil Chamber was deterred by this argument. In affirming the trial court, the 15th Civil Chamber stated that the enforcement of a foreign award cannot be denied merely because the law applied on the merits is different from the Turkish law or violates some mandatory rules of Turkish law.[947] Instead, the Court emphasized that enforcement may be denied only when the outcomes of an enforced award would themselves be contrary to public policy.[948] In this sense, this approach focuses on the end result instead of reviewing the merits of the case and is similar to the narrow interpretation of public policy as applied in the United States in questions of labor arbitration.[949]

Overall, this decision ruled by the 15th Civil Chamber entails that the national courts cannot substitute their rulings for that of the arbitrators and use public policy as a means to investigate whether or not the courts properly applied Turkish legislation. The 13th Civil Chamber, however, has directed trial courts to conduct merits reviews of awards. At this juncture, then, whether or not an award resulting from a contract to which a state agency is a party will be enforced remains unsettled.

4.3.2.5.3 Mandatory Laws and Subject-Matter Arbitrability

Arbitrability is one of the critical requirements for an arbitration agreement and award to be legitimate under Turkish law. Parties may only consent to arbitrate if they can exercise their contractual independence in respect of a dispute or, as the TIAL sets out if the dispute is "within the parties' disposal."[950] Failure to do so will result in setting aside the award.[951] Not surprisingly, there is no explicit provision that exhaustively enumerates what is and what is not arbitrable, other

946 *Id.*
947 *Id.*
948 *Id.*
949 *See supra* Section 3.3.1.
950 Art. I(4) of Act No.: 4686, TIAL.; Akinci, *supra* note 816, at 153.
951 Art. 15(2)(a) of Act No.: 4686, TIAL.

than the outright restriction provided in the TIAL that disputes concerning in rem rights over real properties are not arbitrable.[952]

As discussed in the previous chapters, one of the considerations under the discussion of arbitrability is whether the disputes concerning mandatory laws are inarbitrable by their very nature, given that such rules are so fundamental for the state that they can only be invoked before a national court, thereby ousting any possible jurisdiction of arbitral tribunals.[953] Though this was once the widespread construal of the relationship between arbitrability and mandatory laws, the current practice advocates for a wider scope of arbitrable matters and allowing the offsetting of any negative result with the application of the public policy exception. The Supreme Court's seminal case *Mitsubishi*—together with its legacy, the second-look doctrine—is a leading example of this sort of application.[954]

Turkish courts have participated in this trend and allowed the widening of the range of arbitrable matters. In fact, only two years after, the Supreme Court delivered *Mitsubishi*, the General Assembly reached an analogous result in a case regarding the arbitrability of the retainer fee in a domestic arbitration case. In this case, the Court first noted that the retainer agreement concerns public policy and laid out the rule that parties cannot submit disputes to arbitration if the dispute concerns public policy.[955] But instead of stopping there and finding the contract unenforceable due to the inarbitrability of retainer fees, the General Assembly continued its analysis and compared the rules regarding the payment of the retainer fee that the parties determined would be applied by the arbitrators in their contract and the rules provided under the Turkish Attorneyship Law.[956] The Court then noted that insofar as the rules agreed by the parties do not contradict the rules on retainer fees under the Attorneyship Law, the arbitration agreement can stand.[957] The Court, however, forewarned the arbitrators, stating that arbitrators must observe the mandatory rules of the Attorneyship Law, or otherwise the award will not be enforced based on the public policy violations.[958]

---

952 *Id.* Art. I; Akinci, *supra* note 816, at 41.

953 *See* Bermann, *supra* note 260, at 335.

954 *Mitsubishi*, 473 U.S at 638, n.19.

955 The General Assembly of the Turkish Court of Cassation Case No: 1986/3413, Decision No: 1986/325, dated 15.4.1987 (Legalbank Elektronik Hukuk Bankası) [Legalbank Electonic Case Law Database] (Turk.).

956 *Id.*

957 *Id.*

958 *Id.*

This decision of the General Assembly bears a striking resemblance to *Mitsubishi*. First, similar to the Supreme Court in *Mitsubishi,* the General Assembly employed arbitrability and public policy concepts interchangeably and mainly addressed the arbitrability issue from the public policy perspective. Moreover, the General Assembly refrained from judicial intervention in the arbitration process and postponed it to the enforcement stage in the event that the mandatory rules are not observed, which is the second-look doctrine as a substitute to inarbitrability as was laid down in *Mitsubishi*.[959]

Despite the resemblance between *Mitsubishi* and the decision handed by the General Assembly in 1976, Turkish courts have more rigorously applied the doctrine. As the *Baxter* Court identified in interpreting *Mitsubishi*, the second-look doctrine does not require courts to "throw the result in the waste basket and litigate the... issues anew," as this "would just be another way of saying that... [such] matters are not arbitrable."[960] Yet, such a review was exactly what the 13th Civil Circuit and the General Assembly conducted in *Dorsch Consult-Ants Joint Venture v. Housing Development Administration of Turkey (TOKI)*.

This case has a long and complex procedural history—spanning a period of more than eight years—running against the idea that foreign awards are readily enforceable under the Convention in signatory countries. In this particular case, the parties concluded a consultancy agreement for the purposes of the Marmara Earthquake Emergency Reconstruction Project, in which TOKI was receiving advisory services for the supervision of the reconstruction of earthquake-damaged housing units.[961] The dispute arose between the parties as to who bears the burden of paying the taxes.[962] To that end, in 2007, the ICC tribunal entered an award for the Joint Venture, requiring TOKI to return the amount paid by the Joint Venture to the Turkish Revenue Administration.[963]

In the same year and in an action to enforce the award, the trial court considered the expert witnesses' report and held that contracts with tax elements are valid only in the internal relationship between the parties and are not binding in terms of tax administration in the taxation process and that challenges as to

959 See Hilmi Bolatoğlu, *Rekabet Uyuşmazlıklarının Tahkime Elverişliliğine İlişkin Hukuki Çerçeve [Legal Framework Concerning Arbitrability of Competition Disputes]*, 7 Hacettepe HFD 305, 323 (2017) (Turk.)

960 *Baxter*, 315 F.3d at 832.

961 13th Civil Chamber of Turkish Court of Cassation, Case No.: 2009/4018, Decision No.: 2009/15528, dated 29.12.2009 at 1(on file with author) (Turk.).

962 *Id.* at 2.

963 *Id.* at 7.

the issuance of fraudulent invoices (also known as "nylon invoices") and tax evasion are baseless.[964] Thus, the Court found that the award does not violate any Turkish tax laws and public policy.[965]

Upon the appeal of TOKI, in 2009 the 13th Civil Chamber—which is notorious for its expansive review—handed down a 3-to-2 decision and reversed the trial courts' decision on the ground that the trial court had erred in conducting a thorough review of the case. The Chamber directed the Court to obtain a new expert witness's report and ascertain "who is liable for the taxes that the arbitrators decided TOKI to return the Joint Venture" and "whether there is any violation of tax legislation, tax evasion, fraudulent and collusive transactions or a situation for disguised remuneration."[966] As such, it directed the trial court to just about review the merits of the case, ordering certain findings.

Likely considering the 3-to–2 nature of the 13th Civil Chamber's decision, the trial court was ready to insist its decision be upheld, so the case moved to the General Assembly. Yet, the General Assembly agreed with the 13th Civil Chamber's findings and remanded the case to the trial court in 2012, ordering it to reconsider its decision.[967] It must be noted that this was also a majority decision, though the dissents in both of the decisions did not offer a detailed analysis.[968]

In 2013, following the General Assembly's order, the trial court obtained another expert witness's report, which reported that the dispute arose from the contract and as to who bears the burden of paying taxes.[969] As such, there are no unpaid taxes—or otherwise, the Revenue Administration would have taken action.[970] Given that the Revenue Administration already received the taxes, the contractual issue between the parties does not concern public policy, so the award is enforceable.[971] Upon the objection of TOKI to the report, the trial court

964 *Id.*

965 *Id.* at 6.

966 *Id.* at 7–8.

967 The General Assembly of the Turkish Court of Cassation, Case No: 2011/13-568, Decision No: 2012/47.

968 In both cases, the dissent contended that the trial court did not err in its finding so much so that the award should be enforceable. *Compare* 13th Civil Chamber of Turkish Court of Cassation, Case No.: 2009/4018 Decision No.: 2009/15528 at 8 *with* The General Assembly of the Turkish Court of Cassation, Case No: 2011/13-568, Decision No: 2012/47.

969 13th Civil Chamber of Turkish Court of Cassation, Case No.: 2014/27460, Decision No.: 2015/23707.

970 *Id.*

971 *Id.*

obtained a supplemental report in the same year, which reached the same exact result.[972] After obtaining two reports, the trial court declared that the award is not contrary to public policy and that it must be enforced.[973] Finally, in 2015, the 13th Civil Chamber again remanded the case to the trial court based on inadequate examination of the case and ordered the court to again examine any possible tax legislation violations, tax evasion, fraudulent and collusive transactions or a situation of disguised remuneration.[974]

Similar to its decisions regarding the reduction in the Turkish State's income, the 13th Civil Chamber employed the same method in its examinations. First, it laid down that merit review is not allowed in arbitration. But it then raised an exception to this rule when considering the public policy challenges. At this point, the Court emphasized that an award that constitutes fraud and collusion against the customs and tax legislation of Turkey does violate Turkish public policy. In order to identify any possible fraud and collusion, the court stated that the examination of the dispute on the merits might be necessary. Then again, the Court noted that such an examination of the issues would "not necessarily purport to be a review of the case on the merits but rather [would be] a review in a technical sense."[975]

It must be noted that such an application is not limited to the 13th Civil Chamber. When the tax is at issue, there is a tendency in the Court of Cassation to review the contents of awards for their conformity with Turkish public policy. For example, in a case from 2007, the 11th Civil Chamber held that a foreign ICC award violated Turkish public policy and that the tribunal had exceeded its power in granting that the losing party should reimburse the VAT to the winning party. [976] The Court ruled that tax matters, such as VAT, are dealt with solely by Turkish courts.

Though this kind of proposition is readily understandable, the VAT had, in fact, already been paid to the Revenue Administration, and the tribunal had not ruled on whether the VAT was owed to or should be collected from the Turkish Revenue Administration. As the dissent pointed out, the issue was a contractual

972 *Id.*

973 *Id.*

974 *Id.*

975 *Id.*

976 11th Civil Chamber of Turkish Court of Cassation, Case No.: 2007/10205, Decision No.: 2007/13081, dated 19.10.2007 (Lexpera Hukuk Bilgi Sistemi) [Lexpera Legal Information System] (Turk.).

one—more specifically, ascertaining who bears responsibility for paying the taxes owed, as in *Dorsch Consult-Ants*—and was thus by no means concerned with Turkish public policy.

Once the Supreme Court delivered *Mitsubishi,* there was much debate as to the finality of foreign awards that might entail enforcement in the States.[977] And yet, to date, the U.S. courts have not taken a "second look" to refuse to enforce a foreign award. [978] As revealed in *Dorsch Consult-Ants* and other decisions, this has not been the case in Turkey. Thus, although Turkish courts have a policy similar to the second-look doctrine when disputes concerning mandatory laws—and especially taxes and customs—arise, there is, in fact, a high possibility that the award will not be enforced based on public policy violations.

Another point of discussion has been whether *Mitsubishi* required a thorough examination of whether the tribunal correctly applied the law, or merely required a technical examination of whether the tribunal had taken the American statutes into account.[979] Neither of these possibilities applies in Turkish law, given that in disputes concerning Turkish tax and customs laws, the courts have acted almost like appellate bodies and reviewed cases de novo. As proven in *Dorsch Consult-Ants* and the 11th Civil Chamber's decision from 2007, even if the tribunal gives due regard to Turkish tax and customs laws, national courts deem these areas so essential for the Turkish State that they are not willing to share their jurisdiction with the tribunals. Such a stand, however, is disillusioning for the parties, who validly submit their disputes to arbitration, obtain a result but are unable to enforce and end up in long-running litigation—or as the *Baxter* Court stated, litigation that "throw[s] the [arbitration] result in the waste basket."[980]

Interestingly, such a stringent review is not the usual practice if the case does not concern tax, customs, or foreign trade law. For example, in one case, the dispute stemmed from the license agreement between the parties regarding the

977 See e.g. Thomas E. Carbonneau, *Mitsubishi: the folly of quixotic internationalism*, 2 Arb. Int'l 116 (1986); Jill A. Pietrowski, *Enforcing International Commercial Arbitration Agreements–Post-Mitsubishi Motors Corp. v. Soler Chrysler-Plymouth, Inc.*, 36 Am. U.L. Rev. 57 (1986).

978 *Supra* note 288 and accompanying text. *See supra* Sections 2.6.1.2 and 3.4.2.2.1.

979 William W. Park, *The Internationalization of Law and Legal Practice: National Law and Commercial Justice: Safeguarding Procedural Integrity in International Arbitration*, 63 Tul. L. Rev. 647, 669 (1989).

980 *Baxter*, 315 F.3d at 832.

payment of license fees and the transfer of know-how rights.[981] During ICC arbitration proceedings, the defendant's request for a technical examination was rejected.[982] In action brought by the plaintiff in Turkey, the defendant challenged the enforcement on the grounds that the decision of the tribunal is unlawful without a technical examination, as the subject matter of such an examination is of great importance in terms of product safety and human health.[983] Moreover, the defendant contended that mandatory provisions of competition law are violated, as the claim arising from the contract was invalid in terms of competition legislation due to exclusivity, and argued that this was a matter concerning public policy and requested the rejection of the case.[984]

The trial court's analysis, upheld by the 2nd Civil Chamber, showcases how such challenges should be treated in modern arbitration practice. First, the Court stated that an allegation that arbitral award violates the mandatory provisions of Turkish competition law cannot be considered during enforcement, implying such objections can only be made during arbitral proceedings or shall be deemed waived otherwise.[985] Noting that the applicable law to the agreement is Italian law, the Court deferred the tribunal's finding as to whether the license agreement is valid under Italian law.[986] The Court also estopped the defendant from raising the challenge that the health and safety of the product—which the defendant had been marketing for years—runs contrary to the good faith principle under Turkish law. [987] The Court equitably estopped the losing party arguing from the mandatory provisions of the Turkish competition law, and in so doing, this case went one step beyond the second-look doctrine as laid down in *Mitsubishi* and construed by the *Baxter* Court. This is because the 2nd Civil Chamber did not act sua sponte or even mechanically oversee whether the tribunal had actually observed the mandatory requirements of Turkish competition law.

---

981 11th Civil Chamber of Turkish Court of Cassation, Case No.: 2016/725, Decision No.: 2016/7777, dated 6.10.2016 (Lexpera Hukuk Bilgi Sistemi) [Lexpera Legal Information System] (Turk.).

982 *Id.*

983 *Id.*

984 *Id*; H. Ercüment Erdem, *Turkey*, *in* The International Arbitration Review 490 (James H Carter ed., 8th ed, 2017).

985 11th Civil Chamber of Turkish Court of Cassation, Case No.: 2016/725, Decision No.: 2016/7777. *See* Erdem, *supra* note 985, at 490.

986 11th Civil Chamber of Turkish Court of Cassation, Case No.: 2016/725, Decision No.: 2016/7777.

987 *Id.*

To a large extent, it would be unfair to postulate that Turkish courts are unfavorably disposed to arbitration if there is an award based on statutory claims. This is because awards of statutory claims justify a greater need for a judicial review by the national courts, as such an award does not merely concern the arbitrating parties, but the public. Nonetheless, the Court of Cassation's general approach to awards concerning mandatory laws can be questioned, especially if the award concerns Turkish tax matters in any way. The awards referred to above do not relate directly to tax matters but, instead, to a right to reclaim taxes already paid by one party. This is one of the issues on which the parties can exercise their freedom of contract and does not have any bearing on public policy.

4.3.2.5.4 Violation of Due Process

The decisions handed down by the Turkish Court of Cassation on the subject of due process of rights range from one end of the spectrum to the other. In 1976, for example, the Court held that judicial supervision of arbitration proceedings by the ICC Court of Arbitration interferes with the tribunal's impartiality to the extent that it violates due-process rights as well as Turkish public policy.[988] The Court back then closely scrutinized the award, despite it being a foreign one, and found "eccentric" reasons to not enforce in this particular case. Long after, in 2019, the Court of Cassation in a different case went on to say that violation of due-process rights does not constitute a violation of Turkish public policy so that the courts need not consider such violations ex officio in a domestic arbitration case—even where the scope of public policy is deemed to be broader.[989]

To start from the principles, parties must be treated fairly and given due process to present their claims and defenses in an arbitration proceeding pursuant to the mandatory provisions of Turkish laws on domestic and international arbitration and as guaranteed by the Turkish Constitution.[990] As construed in the

988 15th Civil Chamber of Turkish Court of Cassation, Case No.: 1617, Decision No.:1052 dated 10 Mar. 1976, *reported in* Mauro Rubino-Sammartoano, *The Keban Arbitration*, 45 J. Chartered Inst. Arbitrators 211, 241 (1980).

989 15th Civil Chamber of Turkish Court of Cassation, Case No.: 2019/1062, Decision No.: 2019/2725, dated 12.06.2019 at 2 (on file with the author) (Turk.) ("... the right of equal treatment by arbitrators and the right to be heard should continue in the arbitral proceedings. Since these matters are not related to public policy, it is not possible for the Court to set aside the award sua sponte unless the challenging party raises and proves such violations.") (emphasis added)

990 Art. 36 of Act No: 2709, The Constitution of the Republic of Turkey ("Everyone has the right of litigation either as plaintiff or defendant and the right to a fair trial... ")

precedents, under the principle of equal treatment, arbitrators are required to treat the parties impartially, by giving them equal opportunity and time to present their claims and defenses, and maintain the impartiality and avoid behaviors that may raise suspicion of impartiality during the proceedings.[991]

The *Keban Dam Arbitration* is one of the most notorious decisions from the old era of judicial hostility in Turkish arbitration. It was handed down by the 15th Civil Chamber in 1976 before the Convention entered into force in Turkey.[992] In this decision, the dispute arose from the agreement regarding the construction of the Keban Dam on the Euphrates River between a French enterprise and a Turkish state agency, the General Directorate of State Hydraulic Works.[993] Pursuant to the contract, the parties submitted their dispute to ICC Arbitration in Lausanne, agreeing its procedural rules.[994]

The 15th Civil Chamber, representing the general stance of the Turkish Court of Cassation toward arbitration at that time, did not enforce the ICC award for the French party. The Court first identified that Turkish courts do not have jurisdiction to review an award on the merits under the Original CCP, as this was rendered outside their jurisdiction.[995] Accepting that the award, in this case, was a foreign one, the Court then moved on to the issue of whether the award could be enforced.[996] The Court found the award contrary to Turkish public policy because the arbitrators did not observe Turkish procedural rules.[997] More specifically, "the fact that in the arbitration agreement the appointment and the procedure to be followed by the arbitrators were subject to the ICC regulations, the submission of the request to arbitrate to the Secretary of the ICC Court of

Art. 27 of Act No. 6100, New CCP ("The parties to the case, intervenors, other persons involved in the proceedings have the right to be heard in connection with their rights."); Art. 8(B) of Act No.: 4686, TIAL, *translated in* Akinci, *supra* note 816, at 293 ("The parties shall have the same rights and competencies in the arbitration proceedings. The parties shall be given an opportunity to present their respective claims and defenses.")

991 15th Civil Chamber of Turkish Court of Cassation, Case No.: 2019/1062, Decision No.: 2019/2725, at 2.

992 15th Civil Chamber of Turkish Court of Cassation, Case No.: 1617, Decision No.:1052, *reported in* Rubino-Sammartoano, *supra* note 989, at 241.

993 *Id.*

994 *Id.* at 242.

995 *Id.*

996 *Id.*

997 *Id.*

Arbitration, the fact that the file had to be transferred to the arbitrators by the Secretary of the Court, and the requirement of the approval of the award by said Court of Arbitration, all show that Turkish procedural rules were not applied in their proper sense, since our procedural rules do not foresee a Court of Arbitration or Secretary."[998]

This decision can be questioned for several reasons.[999] First, there is no reason for arbitrators to follow Turkish procedural laws, as this was not the applicable procedural law agreed by the parties. By submitting to the ICC, the parties recognized the ICC Court's role in the award-making and cannot regard its position as vitiating the legitimacy of the award.[1000] As a matter of fact, the ICC Court of Arbitration's aim does not review the merits of the arbitrator's decision but, in fact, makes the award "sound in form and substance" so the parties can voluntarily accept it without challenging the award.[1001] Moreover, simply because the procedure of reviewing an award by the ICC Court was unfamiliar to the Court of Cassation's understanding, the Court regarded such procedure as interfering with the arbitrators' independence. The Court not only failed to properly question whether there was concrete evidence to that effect but also applied a very low bar for meeting the public policy ground.[1002]

Surprisingly, the *Keban Dam Arbitration* became a rare instance in which the Court overruled itself. Some 25 years later, when the same issue was presented to the 15th Civil Chamber, the Court changed its view and found that the ICC Court's review of the award did not violate the Turkish public policy, though the Court's reasons to overrule itself is not clear.[1003] Since then, the Court has

---

998 *Id.*

999 MAURO RUBINO-SAMMARTOANO, INTERNATIONAL ARBITRATION: LAW AND PRACTICE 809 (2001); Bezen, *supra* note 132, at 164; Jan Paulsson, *Vicarious Hypochondria and Institutional Arbitration*, 6 ARBITRATION INT'L, no.3, 1990, at 232.

1000 15th Civil Chamber of Turkish Court of Cassation, Case No.: 1617, Decision No.:1052, dated 10 Mar. 1976, *reported in* Rubino-Sammartoano, *supra* note 989, at 241; Jacques El-Hakim, *Should the Key Terms Award, Commercial and Binding be Defined in the New York Convention?*, 6 J. INT'L ARB. 161, 163–64 (1989).

1001 Int'l Chamber of Commerce, *Final Report on Interim and Partial Awards*, 1 ICC INT'L COURT ARB. BULL. 26, 28 (1990).

1002 Bayata Canyas, supra note 905, at 552. *See* Günseli Öztekin, Yargıtay 15. Hukuk Dairesi'nin 22.9.1989 Tarihli Kararının Eleştirisi [A Critique of 15th Civil Chamber's Decision Dated 22.9.1989], 13 MILLETLERARASI HUKUK VE MILLETLERARASI OZEL HUKUK BULTENI (MHB) 33, 40 (2011) (Turk.).

1003 *See* 15th Civil Chamber of Turkish Court of Cassation, Case No.: 2383, Decision No.:3667 dated 10 July 1991, *as discussed in* Ekşi, *supra* note 808, at 62 n.33.

repeatedly reaffirmed its position.[1004] From the perspective of current events, the Court's decision to overrule itself can be seen as heralding a new era in Turkish arbitration. Modern-day decisions also support the proposition that the Court has made significant strides in the direction of buttressing arbitration.

For example, in 1999, the General Assembly was presented with the question of whether a provision of a contract that gives the claimant the right to select an arbitration institute can be regarded as contrary to Turkish public policy.[1005] In this particular case, the buyer and the seller agreed in their original agreement to submit any dispute arising from the contract to the Arbitration Institute of the Stockholm Chamber of Commerce (SCC).[1006] Seven months later, in an addendum, the parties agreed that any dispute arising from the contract could also be resolved by the Moscow Chamber of Commerce in addition to SCC.[1007]

In an action to enforce a foreign award, the trial court refused to enforce the award for the seller, finding that, since just one of the parties, *i.e.*, the claimant, retained the right to select the site or center for the arbitration, that party was superior to or held leverage at the expense of the other party; thus, such an award would violate due-process rights and Turkish public policy.[1008] In reversing the trial court's decision and concurring with the 19th Civil Chamber, the General Assembly held that the right to choose the arbitration institution is recognized *for both parties* and thus the seller who happened to be a claimant was not in a superior position, and thus the award cannot be considered contrary to Turkish public policy.[1009] It is also notable that the Court of Cassation did not act with nationalistic motives to favor the Turkish buyer (the losing party) over the Russian seller (the winning party).

The Court of Cassation has maintained a neutral position in other cases, as well. For example, in one case, a dispute between the Turkish party and the

---

1004 *E.g.* 19th Circuit of the Turkish Court of Cassation, Case No.: 2003/2061, Decision No.: 2003/7606 dated 10.07.2003 (Legalbank Elektronik Hukuk Bankası) [Legalbank Electonic Case Law Database] (Turk.); 15th Circuit of the Turkish Court of Cassation, Case No.: 1996/3249, Decision No.:1996/5584; 15th Circuit of the Turkish Court of Cassation, Case No.: 1992/1736, Decision No.: 1992/4425 dated 1.10.1992, *reported by* Öztekin, *supra* note 1003, at 33–35.

1005 The General Assembly of the Turkish Court of Cassation Case No: 1999/19-467, Decision No: 1999/489, dated 9.6.1999, *reported by* Birsel, *supra* note 142, at 35.

1006 *Id.*

1007 *Id.*

1008 *Id.*

1009 *See Id.* at 36–37.

German party arbitrated in ICC Switzerland by a single arbitrator who is from a German-speaking canton of Switzerland.[1010] The Turkish party opposed the enforcement in Turkey, stating that the arbitrator was not impartial.[1011] In rejecting the Turkish party's motion, the Court of Cassation emphasized many important points. First, the Court found that just because arbitration includes a German party and a single arbitrator who speaks German, this is not sufficient to prove that the arbitrator did not maintain his independence and impartiality, thus holding that the Turkish party could not prove the bias.[1012] Moreover, the Court refused to review the impartiality issue on the merits and deferred to the arbitrator's decision, stating that the issue had already been raised by the Turkish party in arbitration but denied by the arbitrator.[1013]

This case can be placed in juxtaposition to the Supreme Court's *Commonwealth Coatings* judgment, though the Court there applied the "appearance of bias" standard to vacate the award based on evident partiality. Nevertheless, the Court of Cassation's ruling requiring evidence of actual partiality is on a par with the majority of U.S courts, which have adopted higher standards for vacatur, and with Justice White's concurring opinion in *Commonwealth Coatings*, in which he articulated a higher standard than "appearance of bias."[1014]

Finally, the Court of Cassation's construing of due process in arbitration very much resembles the U.S. courts' understanding, which requires only a minimal due process threshold to be met. This is exemplified in one specific case in which the parties entered into a contract for the sale of cotton and agreed on arbitration at the International Cotton Association ("ICA").[1015] When the buyer failed to pay the agreed amount, the seller commenced arbitration at the ICA, and the tribunal entered an award for the seller.[1016] In an action to enforce the award in Turkey, the buyer opposed the enforcement alleging that the tribunal failed

---

1010 11th Civil Chamber of Turkish Court of Cassation, Case No.: 2015/11441 Decision No.: 2016/8701.

1011 *Id.*

1012 *Id.*

1013 *Id.*

1014 *See supra* Sections 2.6.2.4 and 3.2.2.2.

1015 19th Civil Chamber of Turkish Court of Cassation, Case No.: 2014/360, Decision No.: 2014/4182, dated 3.3.2014 (Lexpera Hukuk Bilgi Sistemi) [Lexpera Legal Information System] (Turk.).

1016 *Id.*

to serve notice of its proceedings and the award to him, and thus enforcement would violate Turkish public policy.[1017]

The Court held that delivery receipts provided by the shipping or email services can be evidence that the due process requirements have been met and that these means were appropriate to apprise the buyer of the proceedings and thereby afforded him an opportunity to present his objections.[1018] As such, the Court enforced the award, noting that the right to due process in arbitration need not be as robust and structured as in a courtroom when establishing the required due process requirement.[1019] In its brief analysis, the Turkish Court of Cassation upheld the decision, noting that the buyer's public policy defense, among others, was not viable.

As explored above, the Court of Cassation has not refused to enforce any award on due process and public policy grounds in any of these recent cases. However, the Court has deemed it possible that denying enforcement on public policy grounds is justified where the award is contrary to due-process rights. This is identical to U.S. practice, where the courts have emphasized that violation of fundamental procedural rules may constitute a public policy violation, even as most of the claims have not risen to the level of such a violation.[1020]

However, what is different between the U.S. and Turkish practices is the existence, where relevant, of applicable tests to determine whether an award may be vacated for, say, fraud or evident partiality or any other due process violation. Such tests are abundant in U.S. practice, whereas there has been no elaboration of such a test on the part of Turkish courts. This difference arguably stems from the civil law versus common law court distinction in the two cases, wherein the latter brings case law, rather than statutes, to the fore. Overall, analysis of the decisions of the Court of Cassation on the right to due process offers a colorful picture of current and past practice and indicates how the Court's stance on arbitration has gradually developed—and become friendlier—over time.

1017 *Id.*
1018 *Id.*
1019 *Id.*
1020 *See supra* note 459.

4.4 Third-Party Funding and Artificial Intelligence on The Public Policy Exception to Arbitration

4.4.1 Turkey's AI Experience as an Emerging Country: Implications for the Public Policy Exception

Rome, as the saying goes, was not built in a day, nor are AI technologies likely to be. AI's efficacy relies on data—the more data the AI has, the more accurate the AI becomes.[1021] In that sense, the United States and China are in the most advantaged positions, because they are not only two of the world's most populous countries but also the two largest economies, giving them access to the largest pools of country data.[1022] As an emerging economy, Turkey is falling behind the United States or China in Artificial Intelligence research or investment. Thus, any analysis of the use of AI in arbitration and its implications on the public policy exception in Turkish practice entail a preliminary discussion of AI's current stance in Turkey.

Turkey's investment in AI technologies has outpaced that of all other countries in the region in the past ten years, as a 2018 report prepared by Microsoft and Ernst & Young entitled "Artificial Intelligence in the Middle East and Africa" has revealed.[1023] Both the public and the government appear to have grasped that AI will likely be disruptive to traditional practices and have thought a lot about how AI might be deployed in many areas. For example, Turkey's Ministry of Science, Industry, and Technology published a "Digital Turkey Road Map" in 2018 under the rubric of "Turkey's Industrial Revolution." The report, which was initiated with the support of relevant stakeholders from the public and private sectors, establishes the steps for the digital transformation of Turkey's manufacturing industry.[1024] In the same year, reckoning with the public demand and other digital

---

1021 Pedro Domingos, *A Few Useful Things to Know About Machine Learning*, 55 Communications of the ACM 78, 78 (2012).

1022 *See World Economic Outlook–GDP, current prices Billions of U.S. dollars*, International Monetary Fund (Oct. 2019), https://www.imf.org/external/datamapper/NGDPD@WEO/OEMDC/ADVEC/WEOWORLD/CHN/USA; Population (Total), *The World Bank*, https://data.worldbank.org/indicator/SP.POP.TOTL?name_desc=-false (last visited Feb. 27, 2022).

1023 Microsoft. & EY Consulting, Artificial Intelligence in Middle East and Africa: Outlook for 2019 and Beyond 20 (2018).

1024 T.C. Bilim, Sanayi ve Teknoloji Bakanliği [Ministry Sci., Industry & Tech. Turkish Republic], Turkiye'nin Sanayi Devrimi "Dijital Turkiye Yol Haritasi"[Turkey's Industrial Revolution "Digital Turkey Road Map"] (2018) (Turk.).

reformist movements in the public sector, the Presidential Digital Transformation Office was founded in order to collate research on cyber security, national technologies, big data, and AI.[1025] On the legal side, the most notable move has been made by Turkey's largest bar associations—those of Istanbul, Ankara, and Izmir—working collaboratively to establish a Task Force on Law in the Era of Artificial Intelligence. The Task Force released its report in December 2019.[1026] As a rather preliminary treatment of recent developments in the field, the report declined to cover most subjects in any depth and most notably, shied away from analyzing the potential of machine arbitrators and the wider implications of AI in the arbitration realm. Nevertheless, we can glean several important points from the report for the purposes of our discussion here.

If an arbitral proceeding involves the use of AI as an aid in judicial decision-making, the first question that arises is whether such usage might result in non-enforcement on public policy grounds, and if so, in precisely what way. In Turkish practice, digital systems—such as the National Judiciary Informatics System (UYAP) and e-Government—are already well established, but predictive justice is different from the digitization of the judicial system.[1027]

Adalet Hanım [Lady Justice] is Turkish AI-based software that functions as a legal assistant, conducts legal analyses, edits legal texts, and offers virtual office management capabilities. [1028] Such AI-based services are up-and-coming in Turkey, and use of them is encouraged by the Task Force.[1029] However, the reliability of these services is hindered by data scarcity, *i.e.*, the lacune in the court decisions that are fully available to the public. Given that data is critical for the

---

1025 Cumhurbaşkanlığı Teşkilatı Hakkında Cumhurbaşkanlığı Kararnamesi (Kararname Numarası: 1) [Presidential Decree on Presidential Organization (Decree Number: 1)] Official Gazette: 10.07.2018, No.: 30474, Enacted: 30474 (Turk.).

1026 ISTANBUL, ANKARA, VE IZMIR BAROLARI [ISTANBUL, ANKARA AND IZMIR BAR ASSOCIATIONS], YAPAY ZEKA ÇAĞINDA HUKUK [LAW IN THE ERA OF ARTIFICIAL INTELLIGENCE] (2019) (Turk.). [hereinafter LAW IN THE ERA OF ARTIFICIAL INTELLIGENCE]

1027 *See* Başak Buluz, *Türkiye'de Avukatlık ve Teknoloji [Lawyering and Technology in Turkey], in* LAW IN THE ERA OF ARTIFICIAL INTELLIGENCE *supra* note 1027, at 30, 31. (Turk.).

1028 ADALET HANIM, https://adalethanim.com (last visited Feb. 27, 2022). This is quite a clever play on words. Since Adalet is also a common Turkish female given name, analogous to the Anglo-American name "Sue," and hanım translates roughly as the honorific "Ms.," "Adalet Hanım" can also be translated as "Ms. Sue." Here, the nod to the English verb "to sue"—to embark on a lawsuit—completes the pun.

1029 Buluz, *supra* note 1028, at 31.

success of Artificial Intelligence and that AI works best if it is trained by large quantities of rich data, high courts but also trial courts should grant free comprehensive access to their records.[1030]

Even if court decisions become fully available, the problems continue. In order for natural language processing (NLP) to put these data to good use and render them valuable for arbitrators as an aid in proceedings, the algorithms need to excel in the Turkish language.[1031] Nevertheless, as has been noted by the Task Force, NLP in Turkish is not as developed as in English since the structure of the Turkish language differs from English.[1032]

Considering the current stage of AI in Turkey, arbitrators' use of something like *Adalet Hanım* to aid in the more effective execution of arbitration is unlikely to trigger a public policy exception. The high bar of such an exception and the difficulty of proving causation between such algorithms and the violation underscore this point. Moreover, in discussing AI's implications for arbitration in the United States, one of the issues was whether AI biases could result in non-enforcement due to lack of impartiality to the extent that it becomes a public policy violation.[1033] Such topics, however, have not ripened to the point of being

1030 *See e.g.* M. Ayyüce Kızrak, *Hukuk ve Teknoloji Ilişkişi [Relationships between Law and Technology]*, *in* LAW IN THE ERA OF ARTIFICIAL INTELLIGENCE, *supra* note 1027, at 14, 15 (Turk.); Servet Yetim, *Yargı Kararlarına Erişim Hakkı [Right to Access to Court Decisions]*, UYUŞMAZLIK MAHKEMESI DERGISI no.4, 2014 at 47. (Turk.).

1031 *See* Kızrak, *supra* note 1031, at 14; Benjamin Alarie et al., *How Artificial Intelligence Will & Affect the Practice of Law*, 68 UNIV. OF TORONTO L.J. 106, 115–16 (2018) ("Natural language processing... [is] specific subfield of artificial intelligence. Natural language processing examines the use of words and phrases to draw connections within and across written or spoken language. [It] enables machines to adapt when evaluating text. A keyword search is literal in its approach, looking for exact words or phrases. By contrast, natural language processing allows the user to identify materials that are likely relevant to her search, even if the materials do not contain words or phrases expressly within her list of keywords.").

1032 Kızrak, *supra* note 1031, at 14. Unlike English, Turkish is an agglutinative language. That is to say, in Turkish, words and suffixes would be added one after another to the root in order to form a word with a pursued meaning. For example, "*they were once opticians*" would be expressed as "*gözlükçüymüşler*" in Turkish as a single word with "*gözlükçü (optician)*" as the root. Tarık Kışla & Bahar Karaoğlan, *A Hybrid Statistical Approach to Stemming in Turkish: An Agglutinative Language*, 17 ANADOLU U. J. SCI. & TECH. A–APPLIED SCI. & ENG'N 401, 401–2 (2016).

1033 *Supra* Section 3.5.1

an issue in Turkey, as the penetration of AI in the country is still quite limited when compared with the United States.

A far more salient issue at present is the possibility that AI will, in fact, replace arbitrators —this has clear implications for the public policy exception in Turkish practice. The Task Force's report regards AI as a tool that can *complement* the work of the lawyer rather than *substitute* for it.[1034] This is not surprising given that the availability of such algorithms is limited and their credibility a matter of controversy, at least currently.[1035] The question that emerges is hypothetical: Assuming that a machine arbitrator renders an international award, can the public policy exception prevent the enforcement of such an award in Turkey?

The TIAL, similar to the FAA and the Convention, does not provide that arbitrators must be human. Though one of the questions in the context of the FAA and the Convention was whether such laws make reference to human arbitrators by using gender pronouns such as "he" or "she," this sort of inquiry is in vain when it comes to the TIAL, as the Turkish language has no gender-specific pronouns. That being said, Art.10 of the TIAL, which concerns the terms of reference, refers to an arbitrator as *someone with a first and last name*. This semantic analysis provides a significant indication that the Turkish legislator perceived the arbitrator as a human being, which is in line with the conventional understanding. Nonetheless, it must be noted that unlike the FAA and the Convention, the TIAL was enacted rather recently, in 2011. One could certainly presume that Turkish legislators at least considered the possibility of parties retaining AI as an arbitrator yet deliberately omitted such a possibility in the legislation. The legislative history, however, does not suggest the legislators explicitly considered AI's implications for arbitration, and so it makes sense to dismiss the likelihood as quite small. Overall, the semantic inquiry reveals that Turkish law provides no outright restriction in this regard.

Even though Turkey has modern arbitration law and is a party to the Convention, there are a considerable number of decisions in Turkish case law on arbitration that run against the principles of modern arbitration practice, *e.g.*,

---

1034 Nagihan Özdemir, *Yapay Zeka Işığında Avukatlık Mesleğinin Dönüşümü: Üniversiteler ve Baroların Rolü [Transformation of Lawyering in the Light of Artificial Intelligence: The Role of Universities and Bar Associations*], *in* LAW IN THE ERA OF ARTIFICIAL INTELLIGENCE supra note 1027, at 34, 34. (Turk.).

1035 *See e.g.* Maxi Scherer, *Artificial Intelligence and Legal Decision-Making: The Wide Open?*, 36 J. INT'L ARB. 539 (2019); Ugo Pagallo & Massimo Durante, *The Pros and Cons of Legal Automation and its Governance*, 7 EUROPEAN J. RISK REGULATION 323, 326 (2016).

finding a public policy violation in the event of a reduction in the State's income. As such, one could opine that even if it can be accepted that Turkish law does not restrict the use of machine arbitrators, the courts can apply the law in a way that would prevent such use. The aforementioned *Keban Dam Arbitration* could be considered exemplary here. Even though Turkey was not a party to the Convention when the Court of Cassation rendered this decision, there was nothing in the then-Turkish law that suggested the procedure of reviewing an award by the ICC Court violated Turkish public policy. And yet, the Court found that submission of the award to the ICC Court for scrutiny violated Turkish public policy since—as cited above—the Turkish "procedural rules did not foresee a Court of Arbitration or Secretary."[1036]

With the *Keban Dam Arbitration* in mind, some might argue that Turkish courts have an occasional hostility to unfamiliar concepts, despite the pro-arbitration bias encouraged by the setting aside of decisions or the refusal to enforce rules. In reality, the Court of Cassation overruled its decision in the *Keban Dam Arbitration*, and the judiciary's stance toward arbitration is much more supportive. Moreover, it has been repeatedly emphasized in the Turkish court decisions that the concept of public policy differs by time and location so that it is most fitting to vest judges with the discretion in this regard to review whether the arbitral award complies with the public policy.[1037] Considering the latest practice of the Court, the use of machine arbitrators per se is unlikely to be deemed contrary to public policy—despite the Court of Cassation's possible fear of the unknown as in the *Keban Dam Arbitration* and more rigorous approach to awards where the Turkish state agency is a party.

4.4.2 Third-Party Funding in Turkey and the Public Policy Exception

The legitimacy of litigation or arbitration funding is one of the areas where U.S and Turkish laws differ owing to the civil law/common law dichotomy. Any discussion on third-party funding in the United States needs to cover the extent

---

1036 15th Civil Chamber of Turkish Court of Cassation, Case No.: 1617, Decision No.:1052, dated 10 Mar. 1976, *reported in* Rubino-Sammartoano, *supra* note 989, at 242.

1037 25th Civil Court of First Instance of Ankara, Case No.: 2014/47 Decision No.: 2015/55 at 4 *rev'd on other grounds*, 13th Civil Chamber of Turkish Court of Cassation, Case No.: 2015/40156, Decision No.: 2019/5664. *See also* Grand Plenary Assembly on the Unification of Judgments, Case No: 2010/1, Decision No: 2012/1, s.2/2-1.

to which the maintenance and champerty doctrines are applicable. Identical doctrines, however, do not exist under Turkish law, although judges have the authority to sanction parties and lawyers who file frivolous lawsuits.[1038] In fact, third-party funding is neither prohibited nor explicitly permitted by any statute in Turkey. The current situation is only to be expected, seeing that neither third-party litigation nor arbitration funding has been common in Turkey until recently. As such, to date, there is no decision on third-party funding by the Court of Cassation.

As third-party funding has become more widespread in the world, its popularity in Turkey has also grown. More concretely, legal practitioners have observed that a need for third-party funding in arbitration has arisen out of recent economic difficulties triggered by volatility in the Turkish currency and the high rate of inflation.[1039] This raises the question of what the legal regime of third-party funding is and whether it has any implications for the enforcement of an award and the public policy exception in Turkey.

The Turkish Code of Obligations recognizes freedom of contract and provides that parties are free to choose to contract with whomever they wish, as well as to decide the subject matter of the contract unless otherwise provided by the law. [1040] Though the maintenance and champerty doctrines are unknown, one of the applicable contract defenses to the third-party funding arrangement would be unconscionability.

Under the Turkish Code of Obligations, if there is an evident discrepancy in performances passing between the parties under a contract concluded as a result of "one party's exploitation of the other's straitened circumstances," the prejudiced party may rescind the contract and demand restitution of any performance already made or may honor the contract demanding to meet the disproportion between the performances adhering to the contract.[1041] Considering the high possibility that a party that is facing bankruptcy or insolvency (*i.e.*, "in straitened circumstances") is more likely to seek funding to pursue her claims in arbitration, the question then becomes whether the contract terms that envisages an

---

1038 Art.329 of Act No. 6100, New CCP.

1039 Serdar Paksoy et al., *Third party funding in litigation or arbitration: a look at Turkey's approach*, Lexology (Dec.3, 2019), https://www.lexology.com/library/document.ashx?g=029426a1-0756-45a6-b5a4-ff0b6f645502

1040 Art. 26–27 of Act No: 6098 Türk Borçlar Kanunu [Turkish Law of Obligations] Official Gazette: 4.2.2011, No.: 27836, Enacted: 11.1.2011 (Turk.)

1041 *Id.* Art. 28.

excessively high expected return to the funder or gives the funder excessive control over the proceedings or power to interfere with the funded party's strategy decision in arbitration create an unconscionability problem in the third-party agreement to the extent that it make the arbitral award unenforceable due to public policy violations.[1042]

For a finding of unconscionability, the Court of Cassation requires that not only the prejudiced party should be in straitened circumstances but also that the other party should know and benefit from this situation, or in other words, exploit the situation of the prejudiced party.[1043] Hence, it is not enough for the funder to know, for example, that the bankrupt party has made this unbalanced third-party funding agreement because of her particular circumstances. Instead, the funder must derive a benefit from this situation.[1044]

Even if these demanding conditions are met, and unconscionability is proven, the doctrine of unconscionability—unlike those of maintenance and champerty—is not found to be a part of Turkish public policy either by statutes or by court decisions. Hence, it can be concluded that unconscionability challenges do not have a bearing on the issue of enforceability of the award and the merits of the underlying claim, and instead relates to the internal relationship between the funder and the funded party.[1045] Ultimately, given that Turkey has neither explicit statutes nor a public policy against third-party funding, this mechanism can be viewed as permitted prima facie.

Another matter of concern pertains to procedural public policy. As explained before, third-party funding may compromise the impartiality of arbitrators and create conflict-of-interest problems to the extent that it constitutes a public policy exception. The Turkish Attorneyship Law that sets out professional conduct rules for lawyers in the event of conflicts of interest does not beget arbitrator or party-disclosure duties in the event of a third-party funding arrangement. Although the American Bar Association released a report regarding alternative

---

1042 *E.g.* 7th Civil Chamber of Turkish Court of Cassation, Case No.: 2015/31804, Decision No.: 2015/17391, dated 1.10.2015 (Kazancı İçtihat Bilgi Bankası) [Kazanci Case Law Database] (Turk.).

1043 *E.g.* The General Assembly of the Turkish Court of Cassation Case No:2007/19–63, Decision No:2007/52, dated 07.2.2007 (Legalbank Elektronik Hukuk Bankası) [Legalbank Electonic Case Law Database] (Turk.); The General Assembly of the Turkish Court of Cassation Case No: 2004/19-346 Decision No: 2004/374, dated 23.6.2004 (Kazancı İçtihat Bilgi Bankası) [Kazanci Case Law Database] (Turk.).

1044 *See id.*

1045 *See* Nieuwveld & Shannon, *supra* note 399, at 102–3.

litigation finance, no study regarding litigation or arbitration financing has been conducted by any bar associations in Turkey. This reflects the fact that these concepts are truly novel and have never previously been regarded as a distinct area that needs to be stipulated.[1046]

Turkey's most prominent arbitration establishment, the Istanbul Arbitration Center ("ISTAC"), recently entered into a cooperation agreement with the Istanbul Arbitration Association ("ISTA"), and one of the goals of this cooperation agreement is to establish ethical conduct for arbitrators.[1047] Though ISTA published the Arbitrator Codes of Ethics in 2018, these rules do not envisage any provision that requires disclosure of a third-party funding relationship. Although the ISTA might well have addressed arbitration funding in its 2018 code, it, in fact, shied away from doing so. It appears that there is no other study or action committee in Turkey that discusses ethical conduct concerning a third-party funding arrangement.

In the absence of any requirements, one can assume that undisclosed conflicts of interest might already have occurred in private or will happen in the future. Thus, in the absence of legislative or judicial guidance, the bar associations in Turkey need to recognize the increasing use of third-party funding in arbitration and thus establish a task force to provide guidance for counsel in this area. A lack of impartiality by the arbitrator may amount to non-enforcement of the award on the grounds of being contrary to public policy in Turkey, as in the United States. The establishment of ethical rules in the field of third-party financing is urgently needed before the courts reject the award on public policy grounds

1046 *See* Sarah Steven, *GAR Live Lookback: Istanbul—How to 'do' third-party funding*, GAR (Jan. 19, 2018), https://globalarbitrationreview.com/print_article/gar/article/1151952/gar-live-lookback-istanbul-how-to-do-third-party-funding?print=true (reporting Noyan Goksu's speech in which he indicated that the funding of cases has recently emerged as a standalone profession).

1047 *ISTA ve ISTAC Arasında İşbirliği Protokolü İmzalandı [ISTA and ISTAC Entered into Cooperation Agreement]*, Istanbul Arb. Ass'n https://ista.org.tr/tr/blog/ista-ve-istac-arasinda-isbirligi-protokolu-imzalandi (last visited Feb. 27, 2022).

5 Concluding Remarks on the Comparison

Abstract: The book concludes by summarizing the key findings and works offering several proposals that can serve as pivotal points for change and further research. The final chapter elaborates on the public policy exception as well as public policy mindsets both *against* and *in favor of* arbitration, where public policy as a mindset *in favor of* arbitration is described as the third facet of public policy. Using this typology, the ultimate goal is to lay out the key findings of the book in an accessible summary form.

Keywords: public policy mindsets, public policy exception

This book has set out to consider and debate the public policy exception under the New York Convention as stipulated and applied in the United States and Turkey and how the two jurisdictions are juxtaposed within this field. A secondary focus of this book has been to answer whether public policy *as a mindset*—and its different stages of development across each jurisdiction—have a bearing on the issues and challenges that each jurisdiction is facing today concerning arbitration, and if so, what the wider implications for international arbitration are. To this end, the book adopts two different meanings of public policy:

i. Public policy as a mindset *against* arbitration
ii. The public policy exception to the enforcement of arbitral awards under The New York Convention

   This book has demonstrated that there is, in fact, one more facet of public policy that could be counted as a third meaning of the concept, namely:
iii. Public policy as a mindset *in favor of* arbitration.

The following hypothetical table could be used to express the subsequent analyses specified in numbers. On a scale of 0 to 10—where 0 is the most anti-arbitration, and 10 is the most favorable toward arbitration—a jurisdiction's approach to arbitration can be described figuratively as follows (Tab. 1):

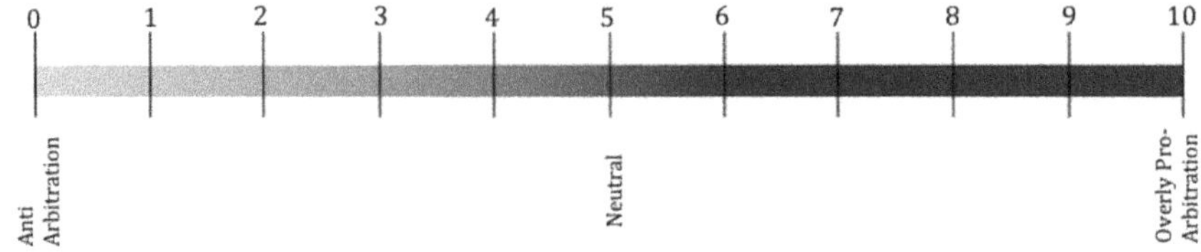

Fig. 1: Hypothesized Numerical Rating of a Jurisdiction's Approach to Arbitration

0	=	Arbitration is not allowed as a legal dispute resolution method
1–4	=	Arbitration is allowed in the legal arena, but there is a hostility to the enforcement of arbitration agreements and awards
5	=	Arbitration is not favored over litigation or vice versa
6–9	=	Arbitration applies with special force
10	=	Arbitration is the only allowed legal dispute resolution method

Tab. 1: Hypothesized Scale of a Jurisdiction's Approach to Arbitration

With this typology in mind, the key findings, issues, and challenges in each jurisdiction can be summarized as follows:

- *Judicial hostility toward arbitration has existed in both the United States and Turkey*. In former practice, when the use of arbitration was still in its infancy, the judiciary in both the United States and Turkey (then the Ottoman Empire) was wary of arbitration. This represents the first facet of public policy where the courts in both jurisdictions perceived it as a suspicious form of private justice and readily used the notion of public policy to curtail arbitrators' jurisdiction:
  - o In this era, at most until 1925, the U.S. common law saw arbitration as a threat to judicial authority so much so that the parties could not oust the courts and replace them with arbitrators as a substitution for court litigation. Despite a cautious trust by the courts and the revocability of arbitration agreements, arbitration remained in use in U.S. dependent territories and by merchants.
  - o During the Ottoman era, arbitration was also employed, but there were restrictions stemming from Sharia law, from which the Ottoman legal code drew heavily. Like the United States, arbitration was mainly employed by

merchants, whether they were Muslim or non-Muslim, even as the form practiced was quite primitive when compared to the United States.

- o The author posits that the Ottoman agnosticism toward arbitration was not remarkably different than the old judicial hostility in the United States. The wariness toward arbitration emanated from the common law in the United States whereas the culprit was the Islamic restrictions embedded in Ottoman law in the case of Turkish practice. As such, both jurisdictions experienced public policy as a mindset *against* arbitration. In this sense, each jurisdictions' stance toward arbitration in this era fell between the numbers 1 and 4 on the scale in figure 4. That is to say, arbitration was allowed, but the courts were hostile and resistant to arbitration agreements and awards.

•Both the United States and Turkey enacted their first comprehensive arbitration laws at relatively similar times a part of the reform movements, and these laws brought an end to the first facet of the public policy, *i.e.*, public policy as a mindset *against* arbitration.

- o Enacted in 1925, the FAA was not only envisioned as a statute covering commercial arbitration of contract disputes between merchants. It was also part of a larger movement of procedural reform during the early twentieth century to expand access to justice by unburdening the existing complex court system. Congress did not intend the scope of the FAA to become as extensive it has today, and in fact, reserved a role for states to hold arbitration agreement to the standards of generally applicable state contract law. In this sense, it can be said that the language of the FAA was rather neutral to arbitration (equal to 5 on the scale in figure 4), or at most slightly favorable toward it (6 on the scale in figure 4).
- o In Turkey, the Original CPA was enacted based on the procedural code of the Swiss Canton of Neuchatel in 1927, and the eighth book of this code governed arbitration. This law was more deferential to arbitration than Ottoman law both in terms of arbitration agreements and awards. Like the FAA, the Original CPA was part of a reform movement; indeed, a broad range of sweeping reforms in the legal but also the political, social, economic, and cultural spheres carried out with the intent to transform the new Republic of Turkey into a secular and modern nation-state. The language of the Original CPA does not indicate that arbitration is favored over litigation, and as such, it could be rated as 5 on the scale in figure 4.
- o Overall, in the beginning of the twentieth century, both countries had then-contemporary laws on arbitration compared to what they had had before, despite the differences between these laws. Arbitration gained

greater deference and accountability by contrast with the old era in each jurisdiction. It follows that public policy as used in its first meaning (public policy as a mindset *against* arbitration) ended in the United States and Turkey with the enactment of these laws.

- Parting of the ways has started with the level of participation in the neoliberalism and the differing roles taken in the course. Despite the roughly similar historical developments of arbitration for the purposes of public policy in the United States and Turkey, the similarity of the routes ended with the rise of neoliberalism. As such, there is a strong correlation between levels of economic development in the U.S. and Turkey and international commercial arbitration in each jurisdiction.
  - The U.S. economy has been referred to as "the biggest and by most measures the most successful in the world's history."[1048] It follows that such an economy, among others, needed to form a feasible adjudicatory process for transnational commercial activity.[1049] The late twentieth century witnessed the policy favoring arbitration with the emergence of neoliberal economic discourse. In line with that, the United States became a party to the Convention in 1970, and between 1972 and 1985, the U.S. Supreme Court handed down decisions that established the hegemony of arbitration for resolving international commercial disputes. Starting from this era, the U.S. Courts regularly avowed this policy. Thus, the second and third facets of public policy (the public policy exception and public policy as a mindset arbitration *in favor of* arbitration, respectively) have come into play in terms of U.S. international arbitration.
  - Severe economic turmoil at the end of the 1970s, *inter alia*, fomented the opening of the Turkish economy to foreign capital and trade starting from the 1980s. The opening of markets and liberalization of the Turkish economy were contingent upon implementing a bundle of economic policies and legal mechanisms that complement neoliberal discourse. With this intent, Turkey acceded to the New York Convention in 1992, among other treaties. The 1990s saw the resurgence of the first facet of public policy—namely, resistance by Turkish courts to the international arbitration system (public policy as a mindset *against* arbitration). The idea of the free market being geared toward economic development went against

1048 McCraw, *supra* note 60, at 301.

1049 Carbonneau, *Arbitral Law-Making supra* note 37, at 1195.

the idea of Turkish courts' sovereignty over foreign investment and the courts' ability to oversee all economic activity. Hence, from the 1980s to the early 2000s, the first and second facets of public policy had an impact on Turkish international arbitration.

- o In essence, the fact that each country has experienced neoliberal policies differently has had a direct bearing on the subsequent development of international arbitration in each jurisdiction. When it is elaborated numerically, after the 1970s, U.S. international commercial arbitration has fallen between 6 and 9 on the scale in figure 4, with an increasing trend approaching 9. On the Turkish side, however, from the 1980s to the early 2000s, international commercial arbitration has mainly been practiced between 1 and 4 on the scale in figure 4.

•When it comes to how the public policy exception is stipulated in each country, Turkish laws are more modern and clearer to follow for the litigants from abroad, whereas U.S. laws are complex, multifaceted, and very nuanced.

- o Since 2001, Turkey has had contemporary international arbitration laws based on the Model Law. Unlike Turkey, the United States has not enacted the Model Law, and almost a century-long FAA provides the legal framework for arbitration. While it is true that the FAA operates fairly well at the domestic level, the same is not true at the international level. One of the most notable differences between the FAA and the Model Law is with respect to the basis for setting aside an award, and this concerns the issue of whether the public policy exception is applicable to non-domestic awards that are made in the United States. That is to say, a non-domestic award is subject to simultaneous motions to vacate (by the losing party) as well as to enforce (by the winning party). Turkish laws, on the other hand, provide a clearer answer regarding the grounds to set aside a non-domestic award.
- o Another issue that the Turkish law does tackle (although need not do) is preemption. There is a certain level of uncertainty as to whether the FAA can preempt state public policy. Although a positive answer can arguably be provided to this question with existing case law in the United States, there remains uncertainty over the issue, as the Supreme Court has not yet explicitly ruled on that question.
- o Because the Turkish law on international arbitration is based on the Model Law, whose language the Convention parallels, parties can easily familiarize themselves in terms of the public policy exception. In the United States, however, the parties must take into account both the FAA and state

law of the jurisdiction in which the arbitration is held and how the public policy exception is treated under each body of arbitration law.

- On the international arbitration front, U.S. courts' judicial deference to international arbitral awards facilitates efficient dispute resolution between sophisticated commercial parties in an international setting, whereas Turkish courts, in certain subject areas, have a tendency to second-guess the arbitrators on the merits of a dispute.
  - Since the late-twentieth century, U.S. courts have eagerly enforced international arbitral awards and seldom resort to the public policy exception either under the Convention or common law. This sort of deference is desirable if arbitration is made between two sophisticated parties who are on a relatively level playing field in terms of negotiating the methods to resolve their dispute.
  - Although not the majority, some Turkish courts tend to second-guess the arbitrators on the merits of a dispute, especially when the award has a reducing impact on the Turkish State's revenue or concerning mandatory national laws—*e.g.*, taxes or foreign trade. Some courts have repeatedly used the public policy exception as an escape valve, promoting the State parties to employ this exception to avoid accountability for their actions stemming from a contract that they have freely negotiated.
  - In comparison with the U.S. international arbitration practice, the scope of public policy is more extensive in Turkey. Nonetheless, these shortcomings are not meant to downplay the advanced state of international commercial arbitration practice in Turkey. Rather, they are reminders that some serious non-enforcement issues, emerging under the disguise of public policy, still exist and that these must be resolved. To illustrate numerically, it could be said that the international commercial arbitration is being practiced at the level of 9 today in the United States with a rare resort to the public policy exception. In contrast, in Turkey, the current level is nearer to 7 or 8, with an incidental decrease below level 5.
- The U.S. Supreme Court is *overly pro-arbitration* when it gives free rein to adhesive arbitration, ignoring the imperative distinctions between international commercial arbitration and adhesive arbitration. Under Turkish law, in contrast, the distinction between the two is not blurred.
  - Although it has not been the focus of the book, it has been pointed out, when necessary, that the U.S. Supreme Court has utilized the FAA as a "Swiss army knife" by applying it to virtually all types of non-criminal disputes in defiance of the differences in the level of judicial supervision

appropriate to each type of dispute. While the laissez-faire court review may be appropriate in the context of commercial arbitration between sophisticated actors, mandating to resolve the disputes between businesses and employees or consumers through arbitration is problematic and unfair. In this sense, mandatory arbitration in the United States is arguably *overly pro-arbitration*, leaving no alternative way to resort litigation, thereby being at the level of 10.

- Unlike the U.S. practice, under Turkish law, the businesses cannot mandate that their and employees or consumer resolve their disputes using mandatory arbitration. This is based on the premise that consumers and employees do not agree to arbitration voluntarily.
- The U.S. Supreme Court's *overly pro-arbitration approach* is threatening to international commercial arbitration, as it can tarnish the practice's reputation and eviscerate its real meaning, thus undermining the importance of arbitration as a dispute resolution method.

The analysis conducted in this book leads to several proposals that can serve as pivotal points for change and further research:

i. To bring clarification to the public policy exception, the FAA needs to be revised. Specifically, one might propose a clarification of its terms to fill the gaps and bring certainty to the relationship between federal and state law, *i.e.*, its preemptive power over state laws, and how the domestic chapter of the FAA works with the New York Convention.

ii. The fact that the U.S. Supreme Court regards arbitration as a mechanism that could outsource the U.S. Courts' duty to distribute justice in every field of law harbors the idea that arbitration is unfair in every field. Although it is not the subject of this book, on the domestic front, the FAA should be amended to protect consumers and parties who are historically presumed to have less bargaining power historically by prohibiting pre-dispute arbitration, thereby defining the lines between commercial and adhesive arbitration. In this way, when some public interest is involved, like an antitrust issue as in *Mitsubishi*, the litigants and the public can have more trust in international arbitration and be assured that publicly promulgated laws that concern not only the parties to arbitration but also the public will be enforced.

iii. The fact that a reduction in the Turkish State's revenue can be a ground for non-enforcement of an international award creates a major red flag for foreign parties arbitrating under Turkish legal jurisdiction. The most important way to make Turkish arbitration attractive to foreign parties is to ensure that Turkish courts do not reconsider a case on the merits at the enforcement stage.

iv. Finally, future research is needed to examine whether the use of AI in arbitration would trigger a public policy exception under the Convention, once the state of the art becomes sufficiently ripe to answer the question in-depth.

References

Primary Sources

Constitutions

U.S. Const.

Act No: 2709, The Constitution of the Republic of Turkey, Official Gazette: 9 Nov. 1982, No: 17863,

Enacted: 7 Nov. 1982 (Turk.).

Treaties and other international agreements

United Nations Convention on Contracts for the International Sale of Goods, Apr. 11, 1980, 1489 U.N.T.S. 3.

The Convention on the Recognition and Enforcement of Arbitral Awards 21 U.S.T. 2617, 330 U.N.T.S. 3 9 codified in 9 U.S.C.A. §§201–208 [1970] [the New York Convention].

Statutes

9 U.S.C.A. §§ 1–16; 201–208; 301–301.

22 U.S.C. § 1650a.

Labor-Management Relations Act, 29 U.S.C.A. § 185 [the LMRA].

31 L.P.R.A. § 3372.

Colo. Rev. Stat. Ann. §§ 13-22-501–13-22-507.

Conn. Gen. Stat. Ann. §§ 50a-100–50a-139.

Fla. Stat. Ann. §§ 684.0001–684. 0049 (2010).

La. Civ. Code Ann. Art.2030.

New York Arbitration Law, 1920. N.Y. Sess. Laws 1920, c. 275 (current version at N.Y. C.P.L.R. Law §§ 7501–7515 (Consol., Lexis Advance through 2020 released Chapters 1–22)).

NY CLS Jud § 489.

Ohio Rev. Code Ann. § 1349.55 (2009).

Or. Rev. Stat. Ann. §§ 36.450–36.558.

Wash. Rev. Code Ann. §§ 7.05.010–7.05.470 (West).

Fla. Stat. Ann. §§ 684.01– 683.35 (repealed 2010).

Law No. 131 of 1948 (Civil Code), *al-Waqā'i' al-Miṣrīyah*, vol. 108 bis (a), 29 July 1948 (Egypt).

English Arbitration Act 1996 c. 23 Art.24-29 (Eng.), http://www.legislation.gov.uk/ukpga/1996/23/data.pdf.

Décret n°2011-48 du 13 janvier 2011—Art. 1520, Code de procédure civile, *translated in* The French Code Of Civil Procedure in English (2019).

Bürgerliches Gesetzbuch [BGB] [Civil Code], *translation at* https://www.gesetze-im-internet.de/englisch_bgb/englisch_bgb.html#p1244 (Ger.).

Arbitration and Mediation Legislation (Third Party Funding) (Amendment) Ordinance, No. 6 (2017) A137 O.H.K. (H.K.).

Iraqi Civil Code No. 40 of 1951 (Iraq).

Civil Law (Third-Party Funding) Regulations 2017 (No. S 68) (Sing.).

Act No.: 6102, Türk Ticaret Kanunu [Turkish Commercial Code] Official Gazette: 14 Feb. 2011, No.: 27846, Enacted: 13 Jan. 2011 (Turk.).

Act No.: 6100, Hukuk Muhakemeleri Kanunu [Code of Civil Procedure] Official Gazette: 12 Jan. 2011, No.: 27836, Enacted 4 Feb. 2011 (Turk.). [New CCP]

Act No: 6098 Türk Borçlar Kanunu [Turkish Law of Obligations] Official Gazette: 4.2.2011, No.: 27836, Enacted: 11.1.2011 (Turk.).

Act No.: 5718, Milletlerarası Özel Hukuk ve Usul Hukuku Hakkında Kanun [The Turkish International Private and Procedural Law], Official Gazette: 27 Nov. 2007, No.: 26728, Enacted 12 Dec. 2007 [the IPPA].

Act No.: 4686, Milletlerarası Tahkim Kanunu [Turkish International Arbitration Law], Official Gazette: 21 Jun. 2001 No.: 24453, Enacted 5 July 2001 (Turk.) [TIAL].

Act No: 3731, Yabancı Hakem Kararlarının Tanınması ve Icrası Hakkındaki New York Sözleşmesinin Onaylanmasının Uygun Bulunduğuna Dair Kanun [Law on the Ratification of the New York Convention], Official Gazette: 21 May 1991, No.: 20011, Enacted: 8 May 1991 (Turk.).

Act No.: 3465, Karayolları Genel Müdürlüğü Dışındaki Kuruluşlarla Erişme Kontrollü Karayolu (Otoyol) Yapımı, Bakımı ve İşletilmesi ile Görevlendirilmesi Hakkında Kanun [Act on Granting Authorization of Construction, Maintenance, and Operation of Highways to Enterprises other than the General Directorate of Highways] Official Gazette, 2 Jun. 1988 No.: 19830, Enacted 28 May 1988 (Turk.).

Act No: 3460, Devletler ve Diğer Devletlerin Vatandaşları Arasındaki Yatırım Uyuşmazlıklarının Çözümlenmesi Hakkında Sözleşmenin Onaylanmasının Uygun Bulunduğuna Dair Kanun [Law on the Ratification of the ICSID Convention], Official Gazette: 2 June 1988, No.: 20011, Enacted: 6 Dec. 1988 (Turk.).

Act No.: 3291, Official Gazette: 3 June 1986, No.: 19126, Enacted: 28 May 1986 (Turk.).

Act No.: 3096, Türkiye Elektrik Kurumu Dışındaki Kuruluşların Elektrik Üretimi, İletimi, Dağıtımı ve Ticareti ile Görevlendirilmesi Hakkında Kanun [Act on Granting Authorization of Generation, Transmission, Distribution, and Trade of Electricity to Enterprises other than the Turkish Electricity Institution] Official Gazette, 19 Dec. 1984, No.: 18610, Enacted 4 Dec. 1984 (Turk.).

Act No.: 2797 Yargıtay Kanunu [The Law of Court of Cassation] Official Gazette: 8 Feb. 1983, No.: 17953, enacted: 4 Feb. 1983 (Turk.).

Act No.: 1086, Hukuk Usulü Muhakemeleri Kanunu [Code of Civil Procedure] Official Gazette: 18 June 1927, No.: 622-624, enacted: 2–4 July 1927 (Turk.) [the Original CCP].

Act No.: 576, Menafii Umumiyeye Müteallik İmtiyazat Hakkında Kanun [Act on Concessions Relating to Public Service] Official Gazette: 24 June 1910, No: 576, Enacted 10 June 1910 (Turk.).

Cases

Epic Sys. Corp. v. Lewis, 138 S. Ct. 1612 (2018).

Kindred Nursing Centers Ltd. P'ship v. Clark, 137 S. Ct. 1421 (2017).

KPMG LLP v. Cocchi, 565 U.S. 18 (2011).

AT&T Mobility LLC v. Concepcion, 563 U.S. 333 (2011).

Stolt-Nielsen S. A. v. AnimalFeeds Int'l Corp., 559 U.S. 662 (2010).

14 Penn Plaza, LLC v. Pyett, 556 U.S 247 (2009).

Hall St. Assocs., L.L.C. v. Mattel, Inc., 552 U.S. 576 (2008).

EEOC v. Waffle House, Inc., 534 U.S. 279 (2002).

Circuit City Stores v. Adams, 532 U.S. 105 (2001).

Green Tree Fin. Corp.-Ala. v. Randolph, 531 U.S. 79 (2000).

E. Associated Coal Corp. v. United Mine Workers of Am., Dist. 17, 531 U.S. 57 (2000).

Cortez Byrd Chips, Inc. v. Bill Harbert Constr. Co., 529 U.S. 193 (2000).

O'Gilvie v. United States, 519 U.S. 79 (1996).

Gasperini v. Ctr. for Humanities, 518 U.S. 415 (1996).

Vimar Seguros Y Reaseguros v. M/V Sky Reefer, 515 U.S. 528)1995).

First Options of Chicago, Inc. v. Kaplan 514 U.S. 938 (1995).

Allied-Bruce Terminix Cos. v. Dobson, 513 U.S. 265 (1995).

Honda Motor Co. v. Oberg, 512 U.S. 415 (1994).

Kokkonen v. Guardian Life Ins. Co. of Am., 511 U.S. 375 (1994).

Gilmer v. Interstate/Johnson Lane Corp., 500 U.S. 20 (1991).

Rodriguez de Quijas v. Shearson/American Express, Inc., 490 U.S. 477 (1989).

Volt Info. Scis., Inc. v. Bd. of Trustees of Leland Stanford Junior Univ., 489 U.S. 468 (1989).

United Paperworkers Int'l Union v. Misco, Inc., 484 U.S. 29 (1987).

Shearson/Am. Express v. McMahon, 482 U.S. 220 (1987).

Mitsubishi Motors Corp. v. Soler Chrysler-Plymouth, 473 U.S. 614 (1985).

Southland Corp. v. Keating, 465 U.S. 1 (1984).

W.R. Grace & Co. v. Local Union 759, Int'l Union of United Rubber, 461 U.S. 757 (1983).

Moses H. Cone Memorial Hosp. v. Mercury Const. Corp., 460 U.S. 1 (1983).

Mathews v. Eldridge, 424 U.S. 319 (1976).

Scherk v. Alberto-Culver Co., 417 U.S. 506 (1974).

M/S Bremen v. Zapata Off-Shore Co., 407 U.S. 1 (1972).

Commonwealth Coatings Corp. v. Cont'l Cas. Co., 393 U.S. 145 (1968).

Prima Paint Corp. v. Flood & Conklin Mfg. Co., 388 U.S. 395 (1967).

South East Atlantic Shipping, Ltd. V, Garnac Grain Co. 356 F2d 189 (1966).

United Steelworkers of Am. v. Enter. Wheel & Car Corp., 363 U.S. 593 (1960).

United Steelworkers of Am. v. Warrior Gulf Navigation Co., 363 U.S. 574 (1960).

United Steelworkers of Am. v. Am. Mfg. Co., 363 U.S. 564 (1960).

Wilko v. Swan, 346 U.S. 427 (1953), *overruled by* Rodriguez de Quijas v. Shearson/Am. Exp., Inc.,, 490 U.S. 477 (1989).

Swift v. Tyson, 41 U.S. 1 (1842) *overruled by* Erie R.R. v. Tompkins, 304 U.S. 64 (1938).

Textile Workers Union v. Lincoln Mills, 353 U.S. 448, 455 (1957).

Hilton v. Guyot, 159 U.S. 113 (1895).

Hamilton v. Home Ins. Co., 137 U.S. 370 (1890).

Hamilton v. Liverpool, London & Globe Ins. Co., 136 U.S. 242 (1890).

Doyle v. Cont'l Ins. Co., 94 U.S. 535 (1876).

Home Ins. Co. of N.Y. v. Morse, 87 U.S. 445 (1874).

Maybin v. Coulon, 4 U.S. 298 (1804).

Watson v. Ins. Co. of N. Am., 4 U.S. 283 (1803).

Ploetz v. Morgan Stanley Smith Barney LLC, 894 F.3d 894 (8th Cir. 2018).

Odeon Capital Grp. LLC v. Ackerman, 864 F.3d 191 (2nd Cir. 2017).

CBF Industria de Gusa v. AMCI Holdings, Inc., 850 F.3d 58 (2nd Cir. 2017).

Bamberger Rosenheim, Ltd. (Isr.) v. OA Dev., Inc. (United States), 862 F.3d 1284 (11th Cir. 2017).

Bayer CropScience AG v. Dow AgroSciences LLC, 680 F. App'x 985 (Fed. Cir. 2017).

PDV Sweeny, Inc. v. Conocophillips Co., 670 F. App'x 23 (2nd Cir. 2016).

Sussex v. United States Dist. Court for the Dist. of Nev., 781 F.3d 1065 (9th Cir. 2015).

Kolel Beth Yechiel Mechil of Tartikov, Inc. v. YLL Irrevocable Trust., 729 F.3d 99 (2nd Cir. 2013).

Freeman v. Pittsburgh Glass Works, LLC, 709 F.3d 240 (3rd Cir. 2013).

Titan Tire Corp. of Freeport v. United Steel, 734 F.3d 708 (7th Cir. 2013).

F.D.I.C. v. IIG Capital LLC, 525 F. App'x 904 (11th Cir. 2013).

Scandinavian Reinsurance Co. v. Saint Paul Fire & Marine Ins. Co., 668 F.3d 60 (2nd Cir. 2012).

Agility Pub. Warehousing Co. K.S.C. v. Supreme Foodservice GmbH, 495 F. App'x 149 (2nd Cir. 2012).

Schwartz v. Merrill Lynch & Co., 665 F.3d 444 (2nd Cir. 2011).

Doe v. Princess Cruise Lines, Ltd., 657 F.3d 1204 (11th Cir. 2011).

Rite Aid N.J., Inc. v. United Food Commer. Workers Union, Local 1360, 449 F. App'x 126 (3rd Cir. 2011).

Int'l Bhd. of Teamsters, Local 701 v. CBF Trucking, Inc., 440 F. App'x 76 (3rd Cir. 2011).

Ario v. Underwriting Members of Syndicate 53 at Lloyd's for the 1998 Year of Account, 618 F.3d 277 (3rd Cir. 2010).

Med. Shoppe Int'l, Inc. v. Turner Invs., Inc., 614 F.3d 485 (8th Cir. 2010).

Lagstein v. Certain Underwriters at Lloyd's, London, 607 F.3d 634 (9th Cir. 2010).

Legacy Trading Co. v. Hoffman, 363 F. App'x 633 (10th Cir. 2010).

Frazier v. CitiFinancial Corp., LLC, 604 F.3d 1313 (11th Cir. 2010).

Gulf Petro Trading Co., Inc. v. Nigerian Nat. Petroleum Corp., 512 F.3d 742 (5th Cir. 2008).

Citigroup Global Mkts., Inc. v. Bacon, 562 F.3d 349 (5th Cir. 2009).

Uhl v. Komatsu Forklift Co., 512 F.3d 294 (6th Cir. 2008).

Sarl Louis Feraud Int'l v. Viewfinder, Inc., 489 F.3d 474 (2nd Cir. 2007).

Positive Software Sols., Inc. v. New Century Mortg. Corp., 476 F.3d 278 (5th Cir. 2007).

Certain Underwriters at Lloyd's London v. Argonaut Ins. Co., 500 F.3d 571 (7th Cir. 2007).

Admart AG v. Stephen & Mary Birch Found., Inc., 457 F.3d 302 (3rd Cir. 2006), *as amended on reh'g* (Sept. 28, 2006).

Yahoo! Inc. v. La Ligue Contre Le Racisme, 433 F.3d 1199 (9th Cir. 2006).

Electrolux Home Prods. v. United Auto. Aero. & Agric. Implement Workers of Am., 416 F.3d 848 (8th Cir. 2005).

Jacada, Ltd. v. Int'l Mktg. Strategies, Inc., 401 F.3d 701 (6th Cir. 2005) *overruled on other grounds by* Hall St. Assocs., L.L.C. v. Mattel, Inc., 552 U.S. 576 (2008).

Four Seasons Hotels & Resorts v. Consorcio Barr S.A., 377 F.3d 1164 (11th Cir. 2004).

JCI Communs., Inc. v. IBEW, Local 103, 324 F.3d 42 (1st Cir. 2003).

Banco de Seguros del Estado v. Mut. Marine Office, Inc., 344 F.3d 255 (2nd Cir. 2003).

Baxter Int'l, Inc. v. Abbott Labs., 315 F.3d 829 (7th Cir. 2003).

Kyocera Corp. v. Prudential-Bache T Servs., 341 F.3d 987 (9th Cir. 2003).

Univ. Commons-Urbana, Ltd. v. Universal Constructors Inc., 304 F.3d 1331 (11th Cir. 2002).

Bos. Med. Ctr. v. SEIU, Local 285, 260 F.3d 16 (1st Cir. 2001).

Slaney v. Int'l. Amateur Athletic Fed'n, 244 F.3d 580 (7th Cir. 2001).

Sheldon v. Vermonty, 269 F.3d 1202 (10th Cir. 2001).

Baker Marine, Ltd. v. Chevron, Ltd., 191 F.3d 194 (2nd Cir. 1999).

ANR Coal Co. v. Cogentrix of N.C., Inc., 173 F.3d 493 (4th Cir. 1999).

PaineWebber Grp., Inc. v. Zinsmeyer Trs. P'ship, 187 F.3d 988 (8th Cir. 1999).

Europcar Italia, S.P.A. v. Maiellano Tours, 156 F.3d 310 (2nd Cir. 1998).

IBEW, Local 97 v. Niagara Mohawk Power Corp., 143 F.3d 704 (2nd Cir. 1998).

Indus. Risk Insurers v. M.A.N. Gutehoffnungshutte GmbH, 141 F.3d 1434 (11th Cir. 1998).

Yusuf Ahmed Alghanim & Sons, W.L.L. v. Toys "R" Us, Inc., 126 F.3d 15 (2nd Cir. 1997).

Tempo Shain Corp. v. Bertek, Inc., 120 F.3d 16 (2nd Cir. 1997).

M & C Corp. v. Erwin Behr GmbH & Co., KG, 87 F.3d 844 (6th Cir. 1996).

Productos Mercantiles E. Industriales, S.A. v. Faberge USA, 23 F.3d 41 (2nd Cir. 1994).

Schmitz v. Zilveti, 20 F.3d 1043 (9th Cir. 1994).

Gulf Coast Indus. Workers Union v. Exxon Co., U.S.A., 991 F.2d 244 (5th Cir. 1993).

Robbins v. Day, 954 F.2d 679 (11th Cir. 1992).

Fahnestock & Co., Inc. v. Waltman, 935 F.2d 512 (2nd Cir. 1991).

Forsythe Int'l, S.A. v. Gibbs Oil Co. of Texas, 915 F.2d 1017 (5th Cir. 1990).

Stone v. E.F. Hutton & Co., Inc., 898 F.2d 1542 (11th Cir. 1990).

Bonar v. Dean Witter Reynolds, Inc., 835 F.2d 1378 (11th Cir. 1988).

Victrix S.S. Co. v. Salen Dry Cargo AB, 825 F.2d 709 (2nd Cir. 1987).

Remington Rand Corp. v. Business Sys. Inc., 830 F.2d 1260 (3rd Cir. 1987).

Merrill Lynch, Pierce, Fenner & Smith, Inc. v. Bobker, 808 F.2d 930, 931 (2nd Cir. 1986).

E. I. Du Pont de Nemours & Co. v. Grasselli Emps. Indep. Assoc., 790 F.2d 611 (7th Cir. 1986).

Hoteles Condado Beach, La Concha & Convention Ctr. v. Union De Tronquistas Local 901, 763 F.2d 34 (1st Cir. 1985).

Cunard S.S. Co. v. Salen Reefer Servs. AB, 773 F.2d 452 (2nd Cir. 1985).

Koch Oil, S.A. v. Transocean Gulf Oil Co., 751 F.2d 551 (2nd Cir. 1985).

Waterside Ocean Navigation Co. v. Int'l Navigation, Ltd., 737 F.2d 150 (2nd Cir. 1984).

Martin v. Morgan Drive Away, Inc., 665 F.2d 598 (5th Cir. 1982).

Tamari v. Bache Halsey Stuart, Inc., 619 F.2d 1196 (7th Cir. 1980).

Matter of Andros Compania Maritima, S.A. (Marc Rich & Co., A.G.), 579 F.2d 691 (2nd Cir. 1978).

Fotochrome, Inc. v. Copal Co., 517 F.2d 512 (2nd Cir. 1975).

Parsons & Whittemore Overseas Co. v. Societe Generale De L'Industrie Du Papier (RAKTA), 508 F.2d 969 (2nd Cir. 1974).

Bell Aerospace Co. Div. of Textron v. Local 516, Int'l Union, United Auto., Aerospace & Agr. Implement Workers of Am. (UAW), 500 F.2d 921 (2nd Cir. 1974).

Alberto-Culver Co. v. Scherk, 484 F.2d 611 (7th Cir. 1973), *rev'd*, 417 U.S. 506.

American Safety Equipment Corp. v. J.P. Maguire & Co. 391 F.2d 821 (2nd Cir. 1968).

Marcy Lee Mfg. Co. v. Cortley Fabrics Co. 354 F2d 42 (2nd Cir. 1965).

Genesco, Inc. v. United Shoe Workers, 341 F.2d 482 (2nd Cir. 1965).

Robert Lawrence Co. v. Devonshire Fabrics, Inc., 271 F.2d 402 (2nd Cir. 1959).

Karppinen v. Karl Kiefer Mach. Co., 187 F.2d 32 (2nd Cir. 1951).

Am. Sugar Ref. Co. v. Anaconda, 138 F.2d 765 (5th Cir. 1943).

Kulukundis Shipping Co. v. Amtorg Trading Corp., 126 F.2d 978 (2nd Cir. 1942).

Floridians for Solar Choice v. PCI Consultants, Inc., 314 F. Supp. 3d 1346 (S.D. Fla. 2018).

Hardy Expl. & Prod. (India) v. Gov't of India, 314 F. Supp. 3d 95 (D.D.C. 2018).

Belize Bank Ltd. v. Gov't of Belize, 852 F.3d 1107 (D.C. Cir. 2017).

Sharp Corp. v. Hisense USA Corp., 292 F. Supp. 3d 157 (D.D.C. 2017).

Gas Nat. Aprovisionamientos SDG, S.A. v. Atl. LNG Co. of Trinidad & Tobago, No. 17-CV-0110 (LAK), 2017 WL 4513564 (S.D.N.Y. Sept. 26, 2017).

Cvoro v. Carnival Corp., 234 F. Supp. 3d 1220 (S.D. Fla. 2016).

Immersion Corp. v. Sony Comput. Entm't Am. LLC, 188 F. Supp. 3d 960 (N.D. Cal. 2016).

Research & Dev. Ctr. "Teploenergetika," LLC v. EP Int'l, LLC, 182 F. Supp. 3d 556 (E.D. Va. 2016).

Gold Res., Inc. v. Bolivarian Republic of Venez., 146 F. Supp. 3d 112 (D.D.C. 2015).

BCB Holdings Ltd. v. Gov't of Belize, 110 F. Supp. 3d 233 (D.D.C. 2015).

In re Oil Spill by the Oil Rig "Deepwater Horizon" in the Gulf of Mex., 77 F. Supp. 3d 500 (E.D. La. 2015).

Corporacion Mexicana de Mantenimiento Integral, S. de R.L. de C.V. v. Pemex-Exploracion y Produccion, 962 F. Supp. 2d 642 (S.D.N.Y. 2013), *aff'd*, 832 F.3d 92 (2nd Cir. 2016).

Domnarski v. UBS Fin. Servs., 919 F. Supp. 2d 183 (D. Mass. 2013).

Subway Int'l B.V. v. Bletas, No. 3:10-cv-1714 (JCH), 2012 U.S. Dist. LEXIS 33341, at *10 (D. Conn. Mar. 13, 2012).

Ocean Partners Holdings Ltd. v. Doe Run Res. Corp., No. 4:11-CV-173 CEJ, 2012 WL 830486, at *5 (E.D. Mo. Mar. 12, 2012).

Glob. Bldg. Prods. v. Chemco, Inc., No. C12-1017 RSM, 2012 U.S. Dist. LEXIS 150317, at *12 (W.D. Wash. Oct. 18, 2012).

Chelsea Football Club Ltd v. Mutu, 849 F.Supp.2d 1341 (S.D. Fla. 2012).

Int'l Trading & Indus. Inv. Co. v. DynCorp Aerospace Tech., 763 F. Supp. 2d 12 (D.D.C. 2011).

ESCO Corp. v. Bradken Res. Pty Ltd., No. 10-788-AC, 2011 U.S. Dist. LEXIS 46460, at *23 (D. Or. Jan. 31, 2011).

Agility Pub. Warehousing Co. K.S.C. v. Supreme Foodservice GmbH, 840 F. Supp. 2d 703, 708 (S.D.N.Y. 2011), *aff'd sub nom.* 495 F. App'x at 149.

Shaw Constructors, Inc. v. HPD, LLC, 749 F. Supp. 2d 474 (E.D. La. 2010).

NTT Docomo, Inc. v. Ultra D.O.O., 2010 U.S. Dist. LEXIS 109377, at *7 (S.D.N.Y. Oct. 12, 2010).

Rai v. Barclays Capital Inc., 739 F. Supp. 2d 364 (S.D.N.Y. 2010), *aff'd*, 456 F. App'x 8 (2nd Cir. 2011)

Kaliroy Produce Co. v. Pac. Tomato Growers, Inc., 730 F. Supp. 2d 1036 (D. Ariz. 2010).

Am. Postal Workers Union, v. U.S. Postal Serv., No. CIV.A. 3:09-CV-1084B, 2010 WL 1962676, at *2 (N.D. Tex. May 14, 2010).

DCR Const., Inc. v. Delta-T Corp., No. 8:09-CV-741-T-27AEP, 2009 WL 5173520, at *6 (M.D. Fla. Dec. 30, 2009).

RZS Holdings AVV v. PDVSA Petroleos S.A., 598 F. Supp. 2d 762 (E.D. Va. 2009).

LaPine v. Kyocera Corp., No. C 07-06132 MHP, 2008 U.S. Dist. LEXIS 41172 (N.D. Cal. May 22, 2008).

Termorio S.A. E.S.P. v. Electrificadora Del Atlantico S.A. E.S.P., 421 F. Supp. 2d 87 (D.D.C. 2006), *aff'd sub nom. TermoRio*, 487 F.3d at 928.

Sphere Drake Ins., Ltd. v. Lincoln Nat'l Life Ins. Co., No. 05 C 6411, 2006 U.S. Dist. LEXIS 70533, at *9 (N.D. Ill. Sept. 13, 2006).

Weizmann Inst. of Sci. v. Neschis, 421 F. Supp. 2d 654 (S.D.N.Y. 2005).

Republic of Ecuador v. ChevronTexaco Corp. (ChevronTexaco I), 376 F. Supp. 2d 334 (S.D.N.Y. 2005).

Ludgate Ins. Co. v. Banco De Seguros Del Estado, No. 02 Civ. 3653 (DC), 2003 WL 443584, at *8 (S.D.N.Y. Jan. 6, 2003).

Osprey, Inc. v. Cabana Limited Partnership, 532 S.E.2d 269 (S.C. 2003).

Dandong Shuguang Axel Corp. v. Brilliance Mach. Co., No. C 00-4480 SC, 2001 WL 637446 (N.D. Cal. June 1, 2001).

Karaha Bodas Co., L.L.C. v. Perusahaan Pertambangan Minyak Dan Gas Bumi Negara, 190 F. Supp. 2d 936 (S.D. Tex. 2001).

Spier v. Calzaturificio Tecnica, S.p.A., 71 F. Supp. 2d 279 (S.D.N.Y. 1999).

Hartford Fire Ins. Co. v. Lloyd's Syndicate 0056 Ash, Civil No. 3:97CV00009 (AVC), 1997 U.S. Dist. LEXIS 10858 (D. Conn. June 30, 1997).

In re Trans Chem. Ltd. & China Nat. Mach. Imp. & Exp. Corp., 978 F. Supp. 266 (S.D. Tex. 1997), *aff'd sub nom.* Trans Chem. Ltd. v. China Nat. Mach. Imp. & Exp. Corp., 161 F.3d 314 (5th Cir. 1998)

Skandia Am. Reinsurance Corp. v. Seguros Law Republica, No. 96-CIV-2289 SS, 1996 WL 622559 (S.D.N.Y. Sept. 20, 1996).

Generica Ltd. v. Pharm. Basics, Inc., 1996 WL 535321 (N.D. Ill. Sept. 18, 1996) *aff'd*, 125 F.3d 1123 (7th Cir. 1997).

Chromalloy Aeroservices v. Arab Republic, 939 F. Supp. 907 (D.D.C. 1996).

Application of York Hannover Holding A.G. v. Am. Arbitration Ass'n., No. 92 CIV. 1643 (CSH), 1993 WL 159961 (S.D.N.Y. May 11, 1993).

International Standard Elec. Corp. v. Bridas Sociedad Anonima Petrolera, Indus. Y Comercial, 745 F.Supp. 172 (S.D.N.Y. 1990).

National Oil Corp. v. Libyan Sun Oil Co., 733 F. Supp. 800 (D. Del. 1990).

Wilson v. Lignotock U.S.A., Inc., 709 F. Supp. 797 (E.D. Mich. 1989).

Societe Nationale Algerienne Pour La Recherche, etc. v. Distrigas Corp., 80 B.R. 606 (D. Mass. 1987).

Brandeis Intsel Ltd. v. Calabrian Chemicals Corp., 656 F. Supp. 160 (S.D.N.Y. 1987).

Svoboda v Negey Associates, Inc. 655 F Supp 1329 (1987).

Sea Dragon, Inc. v. Gebr. Van Weelde Scheepvaartkantoor B.V., 574 F. Supp. 367 (S.D.N.Y. 1983).

A/S Siljestad v. Hideca Trading, Inc., 541 F. Supp. 58 (S.D.N.Y. 1981), *aff'd*, 678 F.2d 391 (2nd Cir. 1982).

Laminoirs-Trefileries-Cableries de Lens, S. A. v. Southwire Co., 484 F. Supp. 1063 (N.D. Ga. 1980).

Biotronik Mess-Und Therapiegeraete GmbH & Co. v. Medford Med. Instrument Co., 415 F. Supp. 133 (D.N.J. 1976).

In re Fotochrome Inc., 377 F. Supp. 26 (E.D.N.Y. 1974) *affd sub. nom.* Fotochrome, Inc. v. Copal Co., 517 F.2d 512 (2nd Cir. 1975).

Prince Steam-Shipping Co. v. Lehman, 39 F. 704 (S.D.N.Y. 1889).

Oregon & W. Mortg. Sav. Bank v. American Mortg. Co., 35 F. 22 (C.C.D. Or. 1888).

Tobey v. County of Bristol, 23 F. Cas. 1313 (C.C.D. Mass. 1845).

Ex parte Ala. Oxygen Co., 433 So. 2d 1158 (Ala. 1983) *overruled by* Southland Corp. v. Keating, 465 U.S. 1 (1984).

Knepp v. Credit Acceptance Corp. (In re Knepp), 229 B.R. 821 (Bankr. N.D. Ala. 1999).

Glaser, Weil, Fink, Jacobs & Shapiro, LLP v. Goff, 194 Cal. App. 4th 423 (2011).

Minkowitz v. Israeli, 433 N.J. Super. 111 (Super. Ct. App. Div. 2013).

Abbott Ford, Inc. v. Superior Court, 741 P.2d 124 (Cal.1987).

Shaw v. Kuhnel & Assocs., 102 N.M. 607, 698 P.2d 880 (1985).

Garrity v. Lyle Stuart, Inc., 40 N.Y.2d 354, 353 N.E.2d 793 (1976).

Flintlock Constr. Servs., LLC v. Weiss, 122 A.D.3d 51 (1st Dep't 2014).

Belco Petr. Corp. v. AIG Oil Rig, Inc., 164 A.D.2d 583, 565 N.Y.S.2d 776 (1991).

Hurst v. Litchfield, 39 N.Y. 377 (N.Y. 1868).

Saladini v. Righellis, 687 N.E.2d 1224 (Mass. 1997).

Mansfield v. Doughty, 3 Mass. 398 (1807).

Johnson v. Wright, 682 N.W.2d 671 (Minn. Ct. App. 2004).

Schaefer v. Allstate Ins. Co., 63 Ohio St. 3d 708, 718 (1992).

Oberster Gerichtshof [OGH] [Supreme Court], Jan. 26, 2005, 30 Y.B. COMM. ARB 421 (2005) (Austria).

Traxys Europe S.A. v. Balaji Coke Industry Pvt Ltd., [2012] FCA 276 (Austl.).

Campbell's Cash and Carry Pty Ltd v Fostif Pty Ltd [2006] 229 ALR 58 (Austl.).

Quarella SpA v. Scelta Marble Australia Pty Ltd, [2012] SGHC 166 (Austl.).

S.T.J. No.5.692/US, Relator: Ministro Ari Pargendler 20.08.2014, Superior Tribunal de Justiça Jurisprudência [S.T.J.J.], 01.09.2014, 1 (Braz.).

Smart Systems Technologies Inc. v. Domotique Secant Inc., [2008] QCCA 444 (Can.), *reported in* 33 Y.B. COMM. ARB. 464 (2008).

Schreter v. Gasmac Inc., [1992] 7 O.R. (3d) 608.

HTM LLC v. Fomento de Catalizadores—FOCA S.A.S., Corte Suprema de Justicia, SC8453-2016, Junio 24, 2016 (Colom.).

Petrotesting Colombia S.A. & Southeast Investment Corporation v. Ross Energy S.A., Corte Suprema de Justicia [C.S.J.] [Supreme Court], julio 27, 2011, 11001-0203-000-2007-01956-00 (Colom.).

Maḥkamat al-Naqḍ [Court of Cassation], case no. 810/71, 25 January 2008 (Egypt), *reported in* 1 INT'L J. ARAB ARB. 148 (2009).

Maḥkamat al-Isti'nāf [Court of Appeal], session of 23 May 2001, case no. 25/116 (Egypt).

Cavendish Square Holding BV v Talal El Makdessi [2015] UKSC 67.

Giles v. Thompson [1993] UKHL 2 (Eng.).

Ruxley Electronics and Construction Ltd v Forsyth [1996] AC 344 (HL) 365 (Eng.).

Rookes v Barnard [1964] AC 1129 (Eng.).

Addis v Gramophone Co Ltd [1909] UKHL 1 (Eng.).

Arkin v. Borchard Lines Ltd and others [2005] EWCA Civ 655(Eng.).

Eco Swiss China Time Ltd. v. Benetton International, NV [1999] 2 All ER (Comm) (Eng.).

Tenke Fungurume Mining SA v Katanga Contracting Services SAS [2021] EWHC 3301 (Comm) (Eng.).

Westacre Investments Inc. v. Judoimport-SDPR Holdings Co. [1999] 3 All ER 864 (Eng.).

Ali Shipping Corporation v. Shipyard Trogir [1997] APP.L.R. 12/19 (Eng.).

Re Trepca Mines (No. 2) [1962] 3 All E.R. 351 (Eng.).

Nikolay Viktorovich Maximov v. Open Joint Stock Company "Novolipetsky Metallurgichesky Kombinat", [2017] EWHC 1911 (Eng.), *reported* in 42 Y.B. Comm. Arb., 558 (2017).

Pencil Hill Limited v US Citta Di Palermo S.p.A, [2016] EWHC (QB) 71 (Eng.), *as discussed in* 42 Y.B. Comm. Arb. 535, 535 (2017).

A & Ors v B & Anor [2011] EWHC 2345 (Comm) (Eng.).

Tame Shipping Ltd v. Easy Nav. Ltd [2004] EWHC (Comm.) 1862 (Eng.).

Westacre Investment, Inc. v. Jugoimport-SP-DR Holdings, [2000] Q.B. 288 (Eng.).

Soleimany v Soleimany [1999] QB 785 (CA) (Eng.).

Lemenda Trading Co. v. African Middle East Petroleum Co., [1988] QB 448 (High Court, England).

Wellington v. Mackintosh, 2 Atk. 569 (1743) (Eng.).

Kill v. Hollister, 95 Eng. Rep. 532 (K.B. 1746) (Eng.).

Vynior's Case 77 Eng. Rep. 597 (K.B. 1609) (Eng.).

Cour de cassation [Cass.] [supreme court for judicial matters] 1e civ., May 6, 2009, n°08-10.281, JCP Ed. Gen. 2009, n°20, May 13, 2009, act. 135 (Fr.).

Cour d'appel [CA] [regional court of appeal] (1Ch. C), civ., Sept. 30, 1993.

[Cour d'appel of Reims] Denis Coakley Ltd. v. Sté Michel Reverdy, 23 July 1981, *translated in* 9 Y.B. Comm. Arb.400 (1984).

Intrafor Cofor v Gagnant, [1985] 299 Rev Arb, 212/n98 (Fr.).

Bundesgerichtshof [BGH] [Federal Court of Justice] Dec. 20, 2012, III ZB 8/12 (Ger.), *as reported in* 38 Y.B. Comm. Arb. 379 (2013).

Oberlandesgericht [OLG] Düsseldorf Germany, VI Sch (Kart) 1/02, 21 July 2004.

Oberlandesgericht [OLG], Sept. 2, 1999, 8 Sch 01/99, *reported in* 29 Y.B. Comm. Arb. 697 (2004).

Stuttgart Oberstes Landesgericht [OLG Stuttgart] [Stuttgart Higher Regional Court] Jul. 30, 2010, 1 Sch 3/10, SchiedsVZ 2011 49 (Ger.).

Rechtsprechung der Oberlandesgerichte in Zivilsachen [OLGZ] [Higher Regional Court in Civil Matters] Jan. 4, 2012, No. 9 Sch 2/09 (Ger.).

Bayerusches Oberstes Landesgericht [BayObLG] [Bavarian Higher Regional Court], 4Z Sch 50/99, Mar. 16, 2000 (Ger.), *translated in* 27 Y.B. Comm. Arb. 445 (2002).

Areios Pagos [A.P.] [Supreme Court] 1665/2009 (Greece), *reported in* 36 Y.B. Comm. Arb., 284 (2011.)

A. v. R. [2009] 3 H.K.L.R.D. 389 (H.C.).

Karaha Bodas Co. LLC v. Perusahaan Pertambangan Minyak Dan Gas Bumi Negara, [2007] 4 H.K.L.R.D. 1002 (H.K.).

Hebei Import & Export Corp. v. Polytek Engineering Co. Ltd., [1999] 2 H.K.C. 205 (H.K.).

Ssangyong Engineering v. National Highways Authority of India (2019) 3 ARBLR 152(SC).

Renusagar v General Electric, (1994) AIR SC 860 (India), *translated in* 20 Y.B. Comm. Arb. 681, 692 (1995).

COSID Inc v Steel Authority of India Ltd, (1985) XI Y.C.A. 502 (HC India).

Corte Cost., Cass., 8 febbraio 1982, n.722, Foro it., 1982, I, 2285 (It.).

Corte d'Appello di Venezia, 15 ottobre 2001, n. 1359, Giur. it. 2002, II (It.).

Allsop Automatic Inc. v. Tecnoski snc, Corte d'Apello di Milano, 4 December 1992 (It.), *translated in* 22 Y.B. Com. Arb. 725.

Saikō Saibansho [Sup.. Ct.] July 11, 1997, 51 no 6 Minshu 2573 (Japan).

K.M. v. UAB A. Sabonio Žalgirio krepšinio centras, 3K-3-411/2011 (Lith.).

Hof's-Gravenhage 24 maart 2005, NJF 2005, 239 (Marketing Displays International Inc. (MDI)/VR) (Neth.), *translated in* 31 Y.B. Comm. Arb. 808 (2006).

(Hof) Amsterdam 16 juli 1992 NJ 1994, 181 HKB (G.W.L. Kersten & Co. B.V. / Société Commerciale Raoul-Duval et Cie (Neth.), *translated in* 19 Y.B. Comm. Arb. 708 (1994).

Attorney General of New Zealand v. Mobil Oil New Zealand Ltd. [1989] 2 NZLR 668.

[Federal Arbitrazh Court], KG-A40/8723-05-P, 22 September 2005, *reported in* 33 Y.B. Comm. Arb. 678 (2008).

[United World Ltd., v. Krasny Yakor] Fed. Com. Ct. of Volga-Vyatka Cir., Case No. A43-10716/02-27-10isp (2003) (Russ.).

Ciments Français v. OAO Holding Company Siberian Cement, Highest Arbitrazh Court, Russian Federation, No. VAS-17458/11, 27 August 2012.

Brostrom Tankers AB (Sweden) v. Factorias Vulcano SA (Spain), [2004] IEHC 198 2003 44 SP, *reported in* 30 Y.B. Comm. Arb. 591 (2005) (Ir.).

Liao Eng Kiat v. Burswood Nominees Ltd. [2004] SGCA 45 (Sing.).

S.T.S., Nov. 13, 2001 (Exequátur, No. 2039/1999) (Spain).

Bundesgericht [BGer] [Federal Supreme Court] Mar. 2, 2017 4A_405/2016 (Switz.).

Bundesgericht [BGer] [Federal Supreme Court] Feb. 7, 2017 4A_478/2016 (Switz.), *reported in* 30 ASA Bull. 591 (2012).

Bundesgericht [BGer] [Federal Supreme Court] Mar. 8, 2006, 4P.278/2005 (Switz.), X. S.p.A. v. Y. S.r.l, *translated in* 24 ASA Bulletin 554 (2006).

Tribunal fédéral [TF] [Federal Tribunal] Feb. 26, 2015 4A_374/2014 (Switz.), *reported in* 41 Y.B. Comm. Arb. 567 (2016).

Tribunal fédéral [TF] [Federal Tribunal] Oct. 18, 2004 4P. 104/2004 (Switz.), *reported in* 23 ASA Bul. 164 (2005).

The Constitutional Court of The Republic of Turkey, Case No.: 1963/128 Decision No.: 1964/8 dated 28.1.1964, Official Gazette No: 11685, dated 17.04.1964 (Turk.).

Grand Plenary Assembly on the Unification of Judgments, Case No: 1993/4, Decision No: 1994/1, dated 28.1.1994 (Kazancı İçtihat Bilgi Bankası) [Kazanci Case Law Database] (Turk.).

The General Assembly of The Court of Cassation, Decision No:1, dated 30.01.2019 (Turk.).

Grand Plenary Assembly on the Unification of Judgments, Case No: 2010/1, Decision No: 2012/1, dated 10.02.2012, s.2/3, Official Gazette No:28417, dated 20.9.2012 (Turk.).

The General Assembly of the Turkish Court of Cassation, Case No: 2011/13-568, Decision No: 2012/47, dated 8.2.2012 (Kazancı İçtihat Bilgi Bankası) [Kazanci Case Law Database] (Turk.).

The General Assembly of the Turkish Court of Cassation Case No: 2009/102 Decision No: 2009/208, dated 27.5.2009 (Lexpera Hukuk Bilgi Sistemi) [Lexpera Legal Information System] (Turk.).

The General Assembly of the Turkish Court of Cassation Case No: 2004/19-346 Decision No: 2004/374, dated 23.6.2004(Kazancı İçtihat Bilgi Bankası) [Kazanci Case Law Database] (Turk.).

The General Assembly of the Turkish Court of Cassation Case No: 1999/19-467, Decision No: 1999/489, dated 9.6.1999 (Turk.).

The General Assembly of the Turkish Court of Cassation Case No: 1986/3413, Decision No: 1986/325, dated 15.4.1987 (Legalbank Elektronik Hukuk Bankası) [Legalbank Electonic Case Law Database] (Turk.).

The General Assembly of the Turkish Council of State Case No: 1973/12 Decision No:1975/8 dated 28.2.1975 (Lexpera Hukuk Bilgi Sistemi) [Lexpera Legal Information System] (Turk.).

15th Civil Chamber of Turkish Court of Cassation, Case No.: 2019/1234 Decision No.: 2019/3335, dated 11.7.2019 (Turk.) (on file with author).

15th Civil Chamber of Turkish Court of Cassation, Case No.: 2019/1062, Decision No.: 2019/2725, dated 12.6.2019 (on file with the author) (Turk.).

Decision No.: 675/2, Birinci Sınıfa Ayrılan ve Birinci Sınıf Olan Hâkim ve Savcıların Çalışmalarının Değerlendirilmesi Esaslarına İlişkin Hâkimler ve Savcılar Yüksek Kurulu İlke Kararı [Rules on the Principles of Evaluation of the Work of Judges and Prosecutors who are First Class or Become First Class] Official Gazette: 25 April 2017, No:30048, dated: 05.04. 2017 (Turk.).

13th Civil Chamber of Turkish Court of Cassation, Case No.: 2015/16140, Decision No.: 2017/3322 dated 16.3.2017 (Turk.) (on file with author).

11th Civil Chamber of Turkish Court of Cassation, Case No.: 2015/11441, Decision No.: 2016/8701, dated 3.12.2016 (Kazancı İçtihat Bilgi Bankası) [Kazanci Case Law Database] (Turk.).

11th Civil Chamber of Turkish Court of Cassation, Case No.: 2016/725, Decision No.: 2016/7777, dated 6.10.2016 (Lexpera Hukuk Bilgi Sistemi) [Lexpera Legal Information System] (Turk.).

15th Civil Chamber of Turkish Court of Cassation, Case No.: 2016/895, Decision No.: 2016/2050, dated 31.3.2016 (Kazancı İçtihat Bilgi Bankası) [Kazanci Case Law Database] (Turk.).

13th Civil Chamber of Turkish Court of Cassation, Case No.: 2014/8201, Decision No.: 2016/5293 dated 23.2.2016 (Lexpera Hukuk Bilgi Sistemi) [Lexpera Legal Information System] (Turk.).

13th Civil Chamber of Turkish Court of Cassation, Case No.: 2013/16287, Decision No.: 2016/5292 dated 23.2.2016 (Turk.) (on file with author).

7th Civil Chamber of Turkish Court of Cassation, Case No.: 2015/31804, Decision No.: 2015/17391, dated 1.10.2015 (Kazancı İçtihat Bilgi Bankası) [Kazanci Case Law Database] (Turk.).

13th Civil Chamber of Turkish Court of Cassation, Case No.: 2014/27460, Decision No.: 2015/23707, dated 9.7.2015 (Kazancı İçtihat Bilgi Bankası) [Kazanci Case Law Database] (Turk.).

15th Civil Chamber of Turkish Court of Cassation, Case No.: 2015/375 Decision No.: 2015/1233, dated 16.3.2015 (Legalbank Elektronik Hukuk Bankası) [Legalbank Electonic Case Law Database] (Turk.).

11th Civil Chamber of Turkish Court of Cassation, Case No.: 2013/10684, Decision No.: 2014/15287, dated 9.10.2014 (Legalbank Elektronik Hukuk Bankası) [Legalbank Electonic Case Law Database] (Turk.).

15th Civil Chamber of Turkish Court of Cassation, Case No.: 2014/2183, Decision No.: 2014/3226, dated 12.5.2014 (Legalbank Elektronik Hukuk Bankası) [Legalbank Electonic Case Law Database] (Turk.).

19th Civil Chamber of Turkish Court of Cassation, Case No.: 2014/360, Decision No.: 2014/4182, dated 3.3.2014 (Lexpera Hukuk Bilgi Sistemi) [Lexpera Legal Information System] (Turk.).

9th Civil Chamber of Turkish Court of Cassation, Case No.: 2013/1773, Decision No.: 2013/6664, dated 25.2.2013 (Kazancı İçtihat Bilgi Bankası) [Kazanci Case Law Database] (Turk.)

13th Civil Chamber of Turkish Court of Cassation, Case No.: 2011/19737, Decision No.: 2012/25406, dated 13.11.2012 (Kazancı İçtihat Bilgi Bankası) [Kazanci Case Law Database] (Turk.).

19th Civil Chamber of Turkish Court of Cassation, Case No.: 2012/2969, Decision No.: 2012/8688, dated 23.5.2012 (Legalbank Elektronik Hukuk Bankası) [Legalbank Electonic Case Law Database] (Turk.).

13th Civil Chamber of Turkish Court of Cassation, Case No.: 2012/8425, Decision No.: 2012/10348 dated 17.4.2012 at 3-4 (Turk.) (on file with author).

13th Civil Chamber of Turkish Court of Cassation, Case No.: 2009/4018, Decision No.: 2009/15528, dated 29.12.2009 (on file with author) (Turk.).

13th Civil Chamber of Turkish Court of Cassation, Case No.: 2008/6195, Decision No.: 2008/12026, dated 20.10.2008 (Kazancı İçtihat Bilgi Bankası) [Kazanci Case Law Database] (Turk.).

13th Civil Chamber of Turkish Court of Cassation, Case No.: 2008/3492, Decision No.: 2008/11120, dated 25.9.2008 (Kazancı İçtihat Bilgi Bankası) [Kazanci Case Law Database] (Turk.).

11th Civil Chamber of Turkish Court of Cassation, Case No.: 2007/10205, Decision No.: 2007/13081, dated 19.10.2007 (Lexpera Hukuk Bilgi Sistemi) [Lexpera Legal Information System] (Turk.).

The General Assembly of the Turkish Court of Cassation Case No:2007/19-63, Decision No:2007/52, dated 07.2.2007 (Legalbank Elektronik Hukuk Bankası) [Legalbank Electonic Case Law Database] (Turk.).

15th Civil Chamber of Turkish Court of Cassation, Case No.: 2003/3780, Decision No.: 2003/4370, dated 29.9.2003 (Kazancı İçtihat Bilgi Bankası) [Kazanci Case Law Database] (Turk.).

19th Circuit of the Turkish Court of Cassation, Case No.: 2003/2061, Decision No.: 2003/7606, dated 10.7.2003 (Legalbank Elektronik Hukuk Bankası) [Legalbank Electonic Case Law Database] (Turk.).

15th Civil Chamber of Turkish Court of Cassation, Case No.: 2003/181 Decision No.: 2003/1589, dated 27.3.2003 (Kazancı İçtihat Bilgi Bankası) [Kazanci Case Law Database] (Turk.).

15th Civil Chamber of Turkish Court of Cassation, Case No.: 1998/3507 Decision No.: 1998/4108, dated 6.11.1998.

Board of Administrative Affairs of the Turkish Council of State Case No: 1998/85, Decision No: 1998/81, dated 11.06.1998 (Lexpera Hukuk Bilgi Sistemi) [Lexpera Legal Information System].

15th Civil Chamber of Turkish Court of Cassation, Case No.: 1997/2567, Decision No.: 1997/3420, dated 2.7.1997 (Kazancı İçtihat Bilgi Bankası) [Kazanci Case Law Database] (Turk.).

15th Civil Chamber of Turkish Court of Cassation, Case No.: 1996/3249, Decision No.: 1996/5584, dated 25.10.1996 (Kazancı İçtihat Bilgi Bankası) [Kazanci Case Law Database] (Turk.).

15th Civil Chamber of the Turkish Court of Cassation, No.: 1996/627, dated 1 Feb. 1996, *as translated in* 22 YB COMM. ARB 807(1997).

15th Circuit of the Turkish Court of Cassation, Case No.: 1992/1736, Decision No.: 1992/4425 dated 1.10.1992.

15th Civil Chamber of Turkish Court of Cassation, Case No.: 1991/4163, Decision No.: 1991/5339, dated 7.11.1991 (Kazancı İçtihat Bilgi Bankası) [Kazanci Case Law Database] (Turk.).

15th Civil Chamber of Turkish Court of Cassation, Case No.: 2383, Decision No.:3667 dated 10.7.1991.

15th Civil Chamber of Turkish Court of Cassation, Case No.: 1617, Decision No.:1052, dated 10.3.1976.

25th Civil Court of First Instance of Ankara, Case No.: 2014/47 Decision No.: 2015/55, dated 27.1.2015 at 4 *rev'd on other grounds*, 13th Civil Chamber of Turkish Court of Cassation, Case No.: 2015/40156, Decision No.: 2019/5664 dated 02.5.2019 (Turk.) (on file with author).

Arbitral Awards

World Duty Free Co. Ltd v Kenya (Respondent) (ICSID Case No. ARB/00/7).

Oxus Gold v. Republic of Uzbekistan, UNCITRAL, Final Award (Dec. 17, 2015).

X v. Y and Z, 2 Le Cahiers de l'Arbitrage 399 (ICC Arb., 2013).

Metal-Tech v Republic of Uzbekistan (ICSID Case No. ARB/10/3).

Legislative Materials

Nat'l Comm'n on the BP Deepwater Horizon Oil Spill and Offshore Drilling, Deep Water: The Gulf Oil Disaster and the Future of Offshore Drilling (2011).

H. R. REP. No. 96, 68th Cong., 1st Sess., 1–2 (1924).

Turkiye Buyuk Millet Meclisi [Grand Nat'l Assemb. of Turk], Hukuk Muhakemeleri Kanunu Tasarısı ve Adalet Komisyonu Raporu [Draft Act of No. 6100 and its Preamble] 4 (2008) (Turk.) available at http://www.kgm.adalet.gov.tr/Tasariasamalari/Kanunlasan/2011Yili/kanmetni/6100ss.pdf.

Turkiye Buyuk Millet Meclisi [Grand Nat'l Assemb. of Turk], Milletlerarası Tahkim Kanunu Tasarisi [Draft Act of TIAL] 1 (2001).

Minutes of Grand National Assembly of Turkey Period 2, Vol. 33, Session 75 at 6 (1927), available at https://www.tbmm.gov.tr/develop/owa/td_v2.sayfa_getir?sayfa=6:58&v_meclis=1&v_donem=2&v_yasama_yili=&v_cilt=33&v_birlesim=075 (Turk.).

Administrative and Executive Materials

Cumhurbaşkanlığı Teşkilatı Hakkında Cumhurbaşkanlığı Kararnamesi (Kararname Numarası: 1) [Presidential Decree on Presidential Organization (Decree Number: 1)] Official Gazette: 10.07.2018, No.: 30474, Enacted: 30474 (Turk.).

Records, Briefs, and Petitions

Petition for a Writ of Certiorari, Inversiones y Procesadora Tropical Inprosta S.A. v. Del Monte International GMBH, (No. 19-117 2019), WL 3380417.

Petition for Writ of Certiorari, Applied Underwriters Captive Risk Assurance Co. v. Citizens of Humanity, LLC, 139 S. Ct. 274 (No. 18-174).

Secondary Sources

Uniform Codes, Model Codes, And Restatements.

Restatement (Third) U.S. Law of Int'l Comm. Arb. (Am. Law Inst., Proposed Final Draft No. 4, 2019).

Restatement (Fourth) of Foreign Relations Law (Am. Law Inst., 2018).

Guidelines on Conflicts of Interest in International Arbitration (Int'l Bar Assoc, 2014) [IBA Guidelines].

Restatement (Third) U.S. Law of Int'l Comm. Arb (Am. Law Inst., Tentative Draft No. 2, 2012).

Restatement (Third) Of Foreign Relations Law (Am. Law Inst. 1987)

U.N. Comm'n on Int'l Trade Law (UNCITRAL), Report of the United Nations Commission on International Trade Law on the Work of Its Eighteenth Session, Annex I, U.N. Doc. A/40/17 (June 21, 1985) [UNCITRAL Model Law].

Restatement (Second) on Contract (1981).

Books

2 Domke on Com. Arb.

Akdağ, Mustafa, Türk Halkının Dirlik ve Düzenlik Kavgası & "Celaliler İsyanları [Turkish People's Fight for Peace and Harmony: The Celali Rebellions] 48 (1974) (Turk.).

Akinci, Ziya, Arbitration Law of Turkey: Practice and Procedure (2011).

Aksel, Ismail, Turkish Judicial System Bodies, Duties And Officials (2013).

Altunişik, Meliha & Tür, Özlem, Turkey: Challenges of Continuity and Change (2005).

Aminn, S.H., Islamic Banking and Finance: The Experience of Iran (1986).

Apple, James & Deyling, Robert, Primer on the Civil-Law System (1995).

Bagheri, Mahmood, International Contracts And National Economic Regulation: Dispute Resolution Through International Commercial Arbitration (2000).

Baker & McKenzie, Baker and McKenzie International Arbitration Yearbook 2014-2015 (2015).

Balcı, Muharrem, Ihtilafların Çözüm Yolları ve Tahkim [Methods of Dispute Resolution and Arbitration] (1999) (Turk.).

Born, Gary B., International Arbitration: Cases and Materials (2011).

Çalışkan, Yusuf, The Development of International Investment Law: Lessons from the OECD MAI Negotiations and Their Application to a Possible Multilateral Agreement on Investment (2008).

Carbonneau, Thomas E. & Butler, William E., International Litigation and Arbitration (2nd ed., 2013).

Carbonneau, Thomas E., Cases and Materials on Arbitration Law and Practice (7th ed., 2014) [Carbonneau, Cases and Materials].

Carbonneau, Thomas E., The Law and Practice of Arbitration (5th ed., 2014).

Carbonneau, Thomas E., Toward a New Federal Law on Arbitration (2014).

Chen, Helena Hsi-Chia, Predictability of "Public Policy" in Article V of the New York Convention under Mainland China's Judicial Practice (2017).

Çizakça, Murat, A Comparative Evolution of Business Partnerships: The Islamic World and Europe, With Specific Reference to the Ottoman Archives (1996).

Cole, Tony & Ortolani, Pietro, Understanding International Arbitration (2019).

Faroqhi, Suraiya, Osmanlı'da kentler ve kentliler: kent mekânında ticaret zanaat ve gıda üretimi [Towns and Townsmen of Anatolia: Trade, Crafts and Food Production in an Urban Setting] (Neyyir Kalaycıoğlu trans., 2000) (Turk.).

Fellmeth, Aaron X. & Horwitz, Maurice, Guide to Latin in International Law (2011).

Fitzmaurice, Gerald, The Law and Procedure of the International Court of Justice (1986).

Fouchard, Gaillard, Goldman on International Commercial Arbitration (Emmanuel Gaillard & John Savage eds., 1999).

Gary Born, International Commercial Arbitration: Commentary And Materials (2001).

Genç, Mehmet, Osmanlı Imparatorlugunda Devlet ve Ekonomi [State and Economy in the Ottoman Empire] (2000) (Turk.).

Girsberger, Daniel & Voser, Nathalie, International Arbitration: Comparative and Swiss Perspectives (3rd ed., 2016).

Gocek, Fatma Muge, East Encounters West: France and the Ottoman Empire in the Eighteenth Century (1987).

González, Santiago Alvarez, Liber amicorum Bernardo Cremades (M.A. Fernández Ballesteros & D. Arias eds. 2011).

Gozler, Kemal, Idare Hukuku II [Administrative Law] (2003) (Turk.).

Hale, William, Turkish Foreign Policy 1774-2000 (2002).

Harari, Yuval Noah, Sapiens: A Brief History of Humankind (2015).

Istanbul, Ankara, vc Izmir Baroları [istanbul, Ankara and Izmir Bar Associations], Yapay Zeka Çağında Hukuk [Law in the Era of Artificial Intelligence] (2019) (Turk.).

Kellor, Frances, Arbitration and The Legal Profession: A Report Prepared for The Survey of The Legal Profession (1952).

Letterman, G. Gregory, Letterman's Law of Private International Business (1990).

Maurer, Anton G., Public Policy Exception Under The New York Convention: History, Interpretation, and Application (rev. ed. 2013).

McCraw, Thomas K., Creating Modern Capitalism: How Entrepreneurs, Companies, and Countries Triumphed in Three Industrial Revolutions (2003).

Microsoft. & EY Consulting, Artificial Intelligence in Middle East and Africa: Outlook for 2019 and Beyond (2018).

Miller, Russell A. & Bratspies, Rebecca M., Progress in International Law (2008).

Moses, Margaret L., The Principles and Practice of International Commercial Arbitration (2008).

N.Y. City Bar Comm. on Int'l Commercial Disp., The "Manifest Disregard of Law" Doctrine and International Arbitration in New York (2012).

Nanda et al., Ved P., U.S. Rendered Awards, 3 Litigation of International Disputes in U.S. Courts § 19:30.

Nieuwveld, Lisa Bench & Shannon, Victoria, Third-Party Funding in International Arbitration (2nd ed., 2017).

Pamuk, Şevket, Uneven Centuries: Economic Development of Turkey Since 1820 (2018).

Rubino-Sammartoano, Mauro, International Arbitration: Law and Practice (2001).

Saleh, Nabil A., Unlawful Gain And Legitimate Profit In Islamic Law (2nd ed., 1992).

Sayed, Abdulhay, Corruption in International Trade and Commercial Arbitration (2004).

Schlueter, Linda L., Punitive Damages (2018).

Schultz, Thomas, Information Technology and Arbitration: A Practitioner's Guide (2006).

Schwarzenberger, George, International Law and Order (1971).

Seyadi, Reyadh Mohamed, The Effect of the 1958 New York Convention on Foreign Arbitral Awards in the Arab Gulf States (2017).

Şit, Banu, Kurumsal Tahkım ve Hakem Kararlarının Tanınması ve Tenfizi [Institutional Arbitration and Recognition and Enforcement of Arbitral Awards] (2005) [Turk.].

Strong, S.I., International Commercial Arbitration: A Guide for U.S. Judges (2012).

Symeonides, Symeon C., Choice of Law 84 (2016).

Szalai, Imre, Outsourcing Justice: The Rise Of Modern Arbitration Laws In America (2013).

T.C. Bilim, Sanayi ve Teknoloji Bakanlığі [Ministry Sci., Industry & Tech. Turkish Republic], Turkiye'nin Sanayi Devrimi "Dijital Turkiye Yol Haritasi"[Turkey's Industrial Revolution "Digital Turkey Road Map"] (2018) (Turk.).

The Quran

Toprak, Zafer, Milli Iktisat—Milli Burjuvazi [National Economics—National Bourgeoisie] (1995).

Türkiye Barolar Birliği [the Union of Turkish Bar Associations] Idari Sözleşmeler ve Uluslararası Tahkim [Administrative Contracts and International Arbitration] (1999) (Turk.).

Türkiye Cumhuriyeti Merkez Bankası [Cent. Bank of the Republic of Turk.], Küreselleşmenin Türkiye Ekonomisine Etkileri [Effects of Globalization on Turkey's Economy] (2002) (Turk.).

van den Berg, Albert Jan The New York Arbitration Convention of 1958—Towards a Uniform Judicial Interpretation (1981).

Van Den Boogert, Maurits H., Capitulations and the Ottoman Legal System: Qadis, Consuls and Beratlis in the eighteenth Century (2005).

Watson, Alan, Legal Transplants: An Approach to Comparative Law (2nd ed., 1993).

Watson, Alan, Society And Legal Change (2nd ed., 2001)

Webster, Thomas H. & Buhler, Michael, Handbook of ICC Arbitration: Commentary, Precedents, Materials (2014).

Works in Journals

Ahmad, Feroz, Ottoman Perceptions of The Capitulations: 1800–1914, 11 J. Islamic Stud. 1 (2000).

Ahmed, Dawood I. & Gouda, Moamen, *Measuring Constitutional Islamization: The Islamic Constitutions Index*, 38 Hastings Int'l & Comp. L. Rev. 1 (2015).

Akat, Asaf Savaş, *The Political Economy of Turkish Inflation*, 54 J. Int'l Affairs 265 (2000).

Akkayan-Yıldırım, Ayça, Cezai Şartin İşlevi Türk ve Amerikan Hukukları Açısından Karşılaştırmalı Bir Değerlendirme, [A Comparative Study on Functions of Penalty Clause under Turkish and American Laws], 61 Istanbul Hukuk Mecmuasi [IUHFM] 357 (2003) (Turk.).

Aksu, Kenan, *A Historical Background to Turkey-Europe Relations*, *in* Turkey–EU Relations: Power, Politics and the Future (2012).

Alarie et al., Benjamin, *How Artificial Intelligence Will & Affect the Practice of Law*, 68 Univ. of Toronto L.J. 106 (2018).

Altuğ, Yılmaz & Yasan, Mustafa, *Milletlerarasi Özel Hukukta Kamu Düzeni* [*Public Policy in International Private Law*] *in* Prof. Dr. Ergün Önen'e Armağan 139 (2003) (Turk.).

Anderson, Allison, *Labor and Commercial Arbitration: The Court's Misguided Merger*, 36 B.C. Int'l & Comp. L. Rev. 1237 (2013).

Ansay, Tuğrul, Current Development: International Arbitration in Turkey, 14 Am. Rev. Int'l Arb. 333 (2003).

Atar, Nursel, The Impossibility of a Grand Transplant Theory, 4 Ankara L. Rev. 177 (2007).

Bahtiyar, Mehmet & Biçer, Levent, Adi İş/ Ticari İş/Tüketici İşlemi Ayrımı ve Bu Ayrımın Önemi [Differentiation Between Ordinary Transactions / Commercial Transactions / Consumer Transactions and the Importance of such Differentiation], 22 Marmara Üniversitesi Hukuk Fakültesi Hukuk Araştirmalari Dergisi [MUHF-HAD] 395 (2016) (Turk.).

Barraclough, Andrew & Waincymer, Jeff, *Mandatory Rules of Law in International Commercial Arbitration*, 6 Melb. J. Int'l L. 205 (2005).

Barry, Robert A.J., Application of the Public Policy Exception to the Enforcement of Foreign Arbitral Awards under the New York Convention: A Modest Proposal, 51 TEMPLE L.Q. 832 (1978).

Behr, Volker, Punitive Damages in American and German Law—Tendencies Towards Approximation of Apparently Irreconcilable Concepts, 78 CHI. KENT L. REV. 105 (2003).

Benson, Bruce, An Exploration of the Impact of Modern Arbitration Statutes on the Development of Arbitration in the United States, 11 J. L. ECON. ORGAN. 479 (1995).

Bentwich, Norman, *The Abrogation of the Turkish Capitulations,* 5 J. COMP. LEGISLATION & INT'L L. no.4 (1923), at 182.

Beraudo, Jean-Paul, Egregious Error of Law as Grounds for Setting Aside an Arbitral Award, 23 J. INT'L ARB. 351 (2006).

Bermann et al., George A., *Restating the U.S. Law of International Commercial Arbitration,* 113 PENN ST. L. REV. 1333 (2009).

Bermann, George A., *American Exceptionalism in International Arbitration, in* CONTEMPORARY ISSUES IN INTERNATIONAL ARBITRATION AND MEDIATION: THE FORDHAM PAPERS 2011 (Arthur W. Rovine ed., 2011).

Bermann, George A., Domesticating the New York Convention: The Impact of the Federal Arbitration Act, 2 J INT. DISP. SETTLEMENT 317 (2011).

Bermann, George A., *Interpretation and Application of the New York Convention by National Courts, in* GENERAL REPORTS OF THE XIXTH CONGRESS OF THE INTERNATIONAL ACADEMY OF COMPARATIVE LAW 29 (Martin Schauer & Bea Verschraegen eds., 2017).

Bermann, George A., *Mandatory Rules of Law in International Arbitration, in* CONFLICT OF LAWS IN INTERNATIONAL ARBITRATION (2010).

Bermann, George A., *Restating the U.S. Law of International Commercial Arbitration,* 42 N.Y.U. J. INT'L L. & POL. 175 (2009).

Besson, Sebastien, The Utility of State Laws Regulating International Commercial Arbitration and Their Compatibility with the FAA, 11 AM. REV. INT'L ARB. 211 (2000).

Bezen, Serdar, *Recent Developments in International Commercial Arbitration* in Turkey, 67 CHARTERED INST. OF ARB. J., no.2, May 2001.

Birsel, Mahmut Tevfik, Türkiye'de Yabancı Hakem Kararlarının Tenfizinin Anayasal ve Küresel Boyutları [*Constitutional and Global Dimensions of Enforcement of Foreign Arbitral Awards in Turkey*], 7 DOKUZ EYLUL UNIVERSITESI HUKUK FAKULTESI DERGISI 1 (2005) (Turk.).

Biukovic, Ljiljana, International Commercial Arbitration in Cyberspace: Recent Developments, 22 NW. J. INT'L L. & BUS. 319 (2002).

Blanke, Gordon, The "Minimalist" and "Maximalist" Approach to Reviewing Competition Law Awards: A Never-Ending Saga Revisited or the Middle Way at Last, in POST-HEARING ISSUES IN INTERNATIONAL ARBITRATION 196 (Devin Bray & Heather L. Bray eds., 2013).

Bolatoğlu, Hilmi, Rekabet Uyuşmazlıklarının Tahkime Elverişliliğine İlişkin Hukuki Çerçeve [Legal Framework Concerning Arbitrability of Competition Disputes], 7 HACETTEPE HFD 305 (2017) (Turk.).

Bookman, Pamela K., *The Arbitration-Litigation Paradox*, 72 VAND. L. REV. 1119 (2019).

Born, Gary B., *The New York Convention: A Self-Executing Treaty*, 40 MICH. J. INT'L L. 115 (2018).

Bostrom, Nick & Yudkowsky, Eliezer, *The Ethics of Artificial Intelligence*, *in* CAMBRIDGE HANDBOOK OF ARTIFICIAL INTELLIGENCE 316 (William Ramsey & Keith Frankish, eds., 2014).

Bowman, John P., The Panama Convention and its Implementation Under the Federal Arbitration Act, 11 AM. REV. INT'L ARB. 1 (2000).

Bozkurt, Gülnihal, *Türk Hukuk Tarihinde Azınlıklar [Minorities in History of Turkish Law]*, 64 ANKARA UNIVERSITESI HUKUK FAKULTESI DERGISI [AUHFD] 49 (1993) (Turk.).

Brekoulakis, Stavros L., International Arbitration Scholarship and The Concept of Arbitration Law, 36 FORDHAM INT'L L.J. 745 (2013).

Brekoulakis, Stavros, The Historical Treatment of Arbitration under English Law and the Development of the Policy Favouring Arbitration, 39 OXFORD J. LEGAL STUD. 124 (2019).

Buchanan, Mark A., Public Policy and International Commercial Arbitration, 6 AM. BUS. L.J. 511 (1988).

Buluz, Başak *Türkiye'de Avukatlık ve Teknoloji [Lawyering and Technology in Turkey]*, *in* Istanbul, Ankara, ve Izmir Baroları [Istanbul, Ankara and Izmir Bar Associations], Yapay Zeka Çağında Hukuk [Law in the Era of Artificial Intelligence] 30 (2019) (Turk.).

Burton, Steven, New Judicial Hostility to Arbitration: Federal Preemption, Contract Unconscionability, and Agreements to Arbitrate, 2006 J. DISPUTE RESOL. 469 (2007).

Calleros, Charles R., Punitive Damages, Liquidated Damages, and Clauses Penales in Contract Actions: A Comparative Analysis of the American Common Law and the French Code Civil, 32 BROOKLYN J. INT' L. 67 (2006).

Campbell, Andrew M., Construction and Application of § 10(a)(4) of Federal Arbitration Act (9 U.S.C.A. § 10(a)(4)) Providing for Vacating of Arbitration Awards Where Arbitrators Exceed or Imperfectly Execute Powers, 136 A.L.R. FED. 183 (1997).

Candaner Elver, Nazan, Turkish International Arbitration Law and Restrictions on Its Application, 21 J. INT'L ARB. 453 (2004).

Canyas, Asli Bayata, Enforcement of Foreign Arbitral Awards in Turkey: Further Steps Towards a More Arbitration Friendly Approach, 31 ASA BULLETIN 537 (2013).

Carbonneau, Thomas E., *Arbitral Law-Making*, 25 MICH. J. INT'L L. 1183 (2004) [Carbonneau, *Arbitral Law-Making*].

Carbonneau, Thomas E., Arbitration and the U.S. Supreme Court: A Plea for Statutory Reform, 5 OHIO ST. J. DISP. RESOL. 231 (1990).

Carbonneau, Thomas E., *Debating the Proper Rule of National Law under the New York Arbitration Convention*, 6 TUL. J. INT'L & COMP. L. 277 (1998). [Carbonneau, the Proper Rule of National Law].

Carbonneau, Thomas E., *Judicial Approbation in Building the Civilization of Arbitration*, 113 PENN STATE REV. 1343 (2009) [Carbonneau, Judicial Approbation].

Carbonneau, Thomas E., Mitsubishi: the folly of quixotic internationalism, 2 ARB. INT'L 116 (1986).

Carbonneau, Thomas E., The Exercise of Contract Freedom in the Making of Arbitration Agreements, 36 VAND. J. TRANSNAT'L L. 1189 (2003).

Carbonneau, Thomas E., *The Reception of Arbitration in United States Law*, 40 ME. L. REV. 263 (1988).

Carbonneau, Thomas E., *The Revolution in Law Through Arbitration*, 56 CLEV. ST. L. REV. 233 (2008) [Carbonneau, *The Revolution in Law*].

Chung, John J., In Re Qimonda Ag: The Conflict Between Comity and The Public Policy Exception in Chapter 15 of the Bankruptcy Code, 32 B.U. INT'L L.J. 89 (2014).

Cohen, Julius & Dayton, Kenneth, *The New Federal Arbitration Law*, 12 VA. L. REV. 265 (1926).

Cohen, Paul & Nappert, Sophie, *Case Study: The Practitioner's Perspective, in* The Brave New World of Arbitration: The Role of Technology and the Internet in International Arbitration—The Practitioner's Perspective 126 (2018).

Cole, Richard A., The Public Policy Exception to the New York Convention on the Recognition and Enforcement of Arbitral Awards, 1 OHIO ST. J. ON DISP. RES. 365 (1986).

Craig, W. Laurence, The Arbitrator's Mission and the Application of Law in International Commercial Arbitration, 21 AM. REV. INT'L ARB. 243 (2010).

Cremades, Bernardo M. & Cairns, David J. A., *Trans-national Public Policy in International Arbitral Decisionmaking: The Cases of Bribery, Money Laundering and Fraud, in* ARBITRATION: MONEY LAUNDERING, CORRUPTION AND FRAUD, DOSSIERS OF THE ICC INSTITUTE OF WORLD BUSINESS LAW 65 (Kristine Karsten & Andrew Berkeley eds., 2003).

Curtin, Kenneth-Michael, Redefining Public Policy in International Arbitration of Mandatory National Laws, 64 DEF. COUNSEL J. 271 (1997).

Cutler, A. Claire, *International Commercial Arbitration, Transnational Governance, and the New Constitutionalism, in* INTERNATIONAL ARBITRATION & GLOBAL GOVERNANCE: CONTENDING THEORIES AND EVIDENCE at 140 (Walter Mattli & Thomas Dietz eds., 2014).

Dasser, Felix, International Arbitration and Setting Aside Proceedings in Switzerland: A Statistical Analysis, 25 ASA BUL. 444 (2007).

Davis, Kenneth R., End of an Error: Replacing Manifest Disregard with a New Framework for Reviewing Arbitration Awards, 60 CLEV. ST. L. REV. 87 (2012) [Davis, End of an Error].

Davis, Kenneth R., Unconventional Wisdom: A New Look at Articles V and VII of the Convention on the Recognition and Enforcement of Foreign Arbitral Awards, 37 TEX. INT'L L.J. 43 (2002).

Dayındarlı, Kemal, Milli-Milletlerarası Kamu Düzeni ve Tahkime Etkisi [*Domestic-International Public Policy and Effects on Arbitration*] (1994) (Turk.).

de Enterria, Javier Garcia, *The Role of Public Policy in International Commercial Arbitration*, 21 LAW POLICY INT. BUS. 389 (1989).

de Morpurgo, Marco, A Comparative Legal and Economic Approach to Third-Party Litigation Funding, 9 CARDOZO J. INT'L & COMP. L. 360 (2011).

Del Duca, Louis & A. Welsh, Nancy, Enforcement of Foreign Arbitration Agreements and Awards: Application of the New York Convention in the United States, 62 AM. J. COMP. L 72 (2014).

Delaume, Georges R., Arbitration with Governments: "Domestic" v. "International" Awards, 17 INT. LAWYER 687 (1983).

Derains, Yves, Specific Issues Arising in the Enforcement of EC Antitrust Rules by Arbitration Courts, 2001 EUR. COMPETITION. L. ANN. 323 (2001).

DeStefano, Michele, A Brave New World: The Changing Face of Litigation And Law Firm Finance: Claim Funders And Commercial Claim Holders: A Common Interest or A Common Problem?, 63 DEPAUL L. REV. 305 (2014).

Deynekli, Adnan, In Memoriam, Yabancı Hakem Kararlarının Türkiye'de Tanınması ve Tenfizinde Karşılaşılan Sorunlar [*Problems in the Recognition and Enforcement of Foreign Arbitral Awards in Turkey*], 16 DOKUZ EYLUL UNIVERSITESI HUKUK FAKULTESI DERGISI 105,121 (2014) (Turk.).

Di Brozolo, Luca G. Radicati, Antitrust: A Paradigm of the Relations Between Mandatory Rules and Arbitration—A Fresh Look at the "Second Look", 7 INT'L ARB. L. REV. 23 (2004).

Dickson, Moses O., Party Autonomy and Justice in International Commercial Arbitration, 60 INT'L J. L. MGMT 114 (2018).

Dillenz, Oliver, *Drafting International Commercial Arbitration Clauses*, 21 SUFFOLK TRANSNAT'L L. REV. 221 (1998).

Dohaney, M. Scott, *The Independence and Neutrality of Arbitrators*, 9 J. INT'L ARB. 31 (1992).

Domingos, Pedro, *A Few Useful Things to Know About Machine Learning*, 55 COMMUNICATIONS OF THE ACM 78 (2012).

Donegan, Susan L., ADR in Colonial America: A Covenant for Survival, ARB. J., June 1993 at 14.

Dore, Laurie Kratky, Public Courts Versus Private Justice: It's Time To Let Some Sun Shine In On Alternative Dispute Resolution, 81 CHI.-KENT L. REV. 463 (2006).

Dosman, E. Alexandra & Flebus, Clara, The Federal Arbitration Act and State Arbitration Acts: Impact of Federalism on International Arbitration in the U.S., in INTERNATIONAL ARBITRATION IN THE UNITED STATES.

Drahozal, Christopher R., *The New York Convention and the American Federal System*, 2012 J. DISP. RESOL. 101 (2012).

Drummonds, Henry, The Public Policy Exception to Arbitration Award Enforcement: A Path Through the Bramble Bush, 49 WILLAMETTE L. REV. 105 (2012).

Edwards, Harry T., *Advantages of Arbitration Over Litigation: Reflections of a Judge*, *in* ARBITRATION1982 CONDUCT OF THE HEARING PROCEEDINGS OF THE THIRTY-FIFTH ANNUAL MEETING NATIONAL ACADEMY OF ARBITRATORS 16 (James L. Stern et al. eds., 1983).

Ekşi, Nuray, Yargıtay Kararları Işığında Icc Hakem Kararlarının Türkiye'de Tanınması ve Tenfizi [*Recognition and Enforcement of ICC Arbitral Awards in Turkey in the light of the Court of Cassation Decisions*], 67 ANKARA BAROSU DERGISI 54 (2009) (Turk.).

El-Hakim, Jacques, Should the Key Terms Award, Commercial and Binding be Defined in the New York Convention?, 6 J. INT'L ARB. 161 (1989).

Erdem, H. Ercüment, *Turkey*, *in* The International Arbitration Review (James H Carter ed., 8th ed., 2017).

Erdoğan, Ersin & Vural Çelenk, Belkis, The Culture of Dispute Resolution in Turkey and the Istanbul Arbitration Centre, L. & Justice R., June 2016, at 157.

Erickson et al., Helena Tavares, *Looking Back, and Ahead: The Panama Convention After 30 Years*, Alternatives to High Cost Litig. Dec. 2005, at 184.

Frankel, Richard, *The Arbitration Clause As Super Contract*, 91 Wash. U.L. Rev. 531 (2014).

Frignani, Aldo, *Interpretation and Application of the New York Convention in Italy, in* Recognition and Enforcement of Foreign Arbitral Awards: The Interpretation and Application of the New York Convention by National Courts 561(George A. Bermann ed., 2017).

Gaillard, Emmanuel, *The Representations of International Arbitration*, 1 J. Int'l Dispute Sett. 271 (2010).

Galanter, Seth & McLaughlin, Jeremy M., Does the Supreme Court Decision in 14 Penn Plaza Augur the Unification of the FAA and Labor Arbitration Law, Disp. Resol. J., May-July 2009, at 56.

Gibson, Christopher S., Arbitration, Civilization and Public Policy: Seeking Counterpoise between Arbitral Autonomy and the Public Policy Defense in View of Foreign Mandatory Public Law, 113 Penn State Law Rev. 1227 (2008).

Goldstein, Marc J., Annulled Awards In the U.S. Courts: How Primary Is "Primary Jurisdiction"?, 25 Am. Rev. Int'l Arb. 19 (2014).

Goldstein, Marc J., Setting Aside N.Y. Convention Awards Made in the U.S.: The Latest Decision Errors, 64 J. Disp. Resol. 11 (2009).

Goodman, Bryce & Flaxman, Seth, European Union Regulations on Algorithmic Decision-Making and A "Right to Explanation", 38 AI Mag. 50, 56 (2017).

Gotanda, J.Y., Charting Developments Concerning Punitive Damages: Is the Tide Changing?, 45 Columbia J. Trans'l L., 515 (2007).

Graves, Jack M., Arbitration As Contract: The Need for A Fully Developed and Comprehensive Set of Statutory Default Legal Rules, 2 Wm. & Mary Bus. L. Rev. 227 (2011).

Grossi, Simona, Rethinking the Harmonization of Jurisdictional Rules, 86 Tul. L. Rev. 623 (2012).

Grubbs, Shelby R. & Hendrix, Glenn P., *International Commercial Arbitration, Southern-Style*, 48 Tenn. B.J. 20 (2012).

Guriz, Adnan, *Sources of Turkish Law, in* Introduction to Turkish Law (Don Wallace, Jr. & Tugrul Ansay eds., 5th ed. 2004).

Halis Kasap, Gizem Etching the Borders of Arbitration Agreement: The Group of Companies Doctrine in International Commercial Arbitration under the U.S. and Turkish Law, 2 U. Bologna L. Rev. 89 (2017).

Hanotiau, Bernard, *The Law Applicable to Arbitrability*, *in* Improving The Efficiency Of Arbitration Agreements And Awards: 40 Years Of Application Of The New York Convention 146 (1998).

Harlow, Harry F., *The Nature of Love*, 13 Am. Psychologist 673 (1958).

Harmoush, James, Colorado's Second Renaissance: Adopting the UNCITRAL Model Law on International Commercial Arbitration, 93 Denv. L. Rev. Online 111 (2016).

Hayford, Stephen L., & Kerrigan, Scott B., Vacatur: The Non-Statutory Grounds for Judicial Review of Commercial Arbitration Awards, Disp. Resol. J., Oct. 1996, at 22.

Hayford, Stephen L., Law in Disarray: Judicial Standards for Vacatur of Commercial Arbitration Awards, 30 Ga. L. Rev. 731 (1996).

Hayford, Stephen L., Unification of the Law of Labor Arbitration and Commercial Arbitration: An Idea Whose Time Has Come, 52 Baylor L. Rev. 781 (2000).

Helmer, Elena V., International Commercial Arbitration: Americanized, "Civilized," or Harmonized?, 19 Ohio St. J. on Disp. Resol. 35 (2003).

Hendel, Clifford & Pérez Nogales, María Antonia, *Enforcement of Annulled Awards: Differences Between Jurisdictions and Recent Interpretations*, *in* 60 Years of the New York Convention: Key Issues and Future Challenges 187 (Katia Fach Gomez & Ana M. Lopez-Rodriguez eds., 2019).

Henderson, Codie, The Hall Street Hangover: Recovering and Rediscovering Avenues for Review of Arbitration Awards; Hall Street Assocs. v. Mattel Inc., 128 S. Ct. 1396 (2008), 10 Wyo. L. Rev. 299 (2010).

Hirshman, Linda R., The Second Arbitration Trilogy: The Federalization of Arbitration Law, 71 Va. L. Rev. 1305, 1309 (1985).

Hodges, Ann C., Judicial Review of Arbitration Awards on Public Policy Grounds: Lessons from the Case Law, 16 Ohio St. J. on Disp. Resol. 91 (2000).

Holtzmann, Howard M., Arbitration: An Indispensible Aid to Multinational Enterprise, 10 J. Int'l L. & Econ. 337 (1975).

Huber, Stephen K., State Regulation of Arbitration Proceedings: Judicial Review of Arbitration Awards by State Courts, 10 Cardozo J. Conflict Resol. 509 (2009).

Hulbert, Richard W., The Case for A Coherent Application of Chapter 2 of the Federal Arbitration Act, 22 Am. Rev. Int'l Arb. 45 (2011).

Int'l Chamber of Commerce, *Final Report on Interim and Partial Awards*, 1 ICC Int'l Court Arb. Bull. 26 (1990).

Jablonski, Scott R., Translation and Comment: Enforcing U.S. Punitive Damages Awards in Foreign Courts—A Recent Case in the Supreme Court of Spain, 24 J.L. & Com. 225 (2005).

Jabobowitz, Jan L. & Ortiz, Justin, Happy Birthday Siri! Dialing in Legal Ethics for Artificial Intelligence, Smart Phones, and Real Time Lawyers, 4 Tex. A&M J. Prop. L. 408 (2018).

Jime⊠nez-Figueres et al., Dyala⊠, *Report on the VIII Congress on International Commercial Arbitration—ICC Costa Rica 2017*, *in* Revista Brasileira de Arbitragem 182 (Joa⊠o Bosco Lee & Daniel de Andrade Levy eds., 2017).

Jones, William Catron, Three Centuries of Commercial Arbitration in New York: A Brief Survey, 1956 Wash. Univ. L. Q. 193 (1956).

Kalajdzic et al., Jasminka, Justice for Profit: A Comparative Analysis of Australian, Canadian and U.S. Third Party Litigation Funding, 61 Am. J. Comp. L. 93 (2013).

Kalpsüz, Turgut, *Execution of Arbitral Awards*, 25 Banka Huk. Dergisi 5 (2009).

Kan, Kirill, The Importance of FINRA's Arbitrator Selection Process and Clarity in the "Evident Partiality" Standard in the Wake of Morgan Keegan, 18 Fordham J. Corp. & Fin. L. 167 (2012).

Karakas, Edin, Origin of Arbitral Awards and Its Impact on Applicable Enforcement Regime, 11 Croat. Arb. Y.B. 15 (2004).

Karamanian, Susan L., The Road to the Tribunal and Beyond: International Commercial Arbitration and United States Courts, 34 Geo. Wash. Int'l L. Rev. 17 (2002).

Karsten, Ingo, *Islam and Financial Intermediation,* 29 Staff Pap. Int. Monet. Fund 108 (1982).

Kerr, Michael, Concord and Conflict in International Arbitration, 13 Arb. Int'l 121 (1997).

Khayat, Dany, *Bankruptcy and Arbitration Laws in France, in* Mayer Brown, International Arbitration Perspectives on Insolvency 15 (2010).

Khoukaz, George, Sharia Law and International Commercial Arbitration: The Need for an Intra-Islamic Arbitral Institution, 2017 J. Disp. Resol. 181 (2017).

Kirby, Jennifer, Efficiency in International Arbitration: Whose Duty Is It?, 32 J. Int'l Arb. 689 (2015).

Kışla, Tarık & Karaoğlan, Bahar, *A Hybrid Statistical Approach to Stemming in Turkish: An Agglutinative Language*, 17 ANADOLU U. J. SCI. & TECH. A- APPLIED SCI. & ENG'N 401, 401-2 (2016).

Kızrak, M. Ayyüce, *Hukuk ve Teknoloji Ilişkişi [Relationships between Law and Technology]*, *in* YAPAY ZEKA ÇAĞINDA HUKUK [LAW IN THE ERA OF ARTIFICIAL INTELLIGENCE] 14 (2019) (Turk.).

Knight, *Public Policy in English Law*, 38 L.Q. REV. 207 (1922).

Koçtürk, O. Murat & Gölalan, Meryem, 1923- 1950 Türkiye Ekonomisinin Yapısal Analizi [*Structural Analysis of Turkey's Economy of 1923-1950*], 45 ÜÇÜNCÜ SEKTÖR KOOPERATIFÇILIK 48, 57 (2010) (Turk.)

Kolkey, Daniel M., Reflections on the U.S. Statutory Framework for International Commercial Arbitrations: Its Scope, Its Shortcomings, and the Advantages of U.S. Adoption of the UNCITRAL Model Law, 1 AM. REV. INT'L ARB. 491 (1990).

Komninos, Assimakis, Dutch Court Refuses to Enforce US Arbitral Awards on Public Policy Grounds for Violation of EU Competition Law, 19 INT'L DISPUTE RESOL. 5 (2006).

Korzun, Vera *Arbitrating Antitrust Claims: From Suspicion to Trust*, 48 N.Y.U. J. INT'L L. & POL. 867 (2016).

Kröll, Stefan Michael, *Commentary on the German Arbitration Law (10th Book of the German Code of Civil Procedure)*, *in* ARBITRATION IN GERMANY: THE MODEL LAW IN PRACTICE 443 (2nd ed., 2015).

Kuck, Lea H. & Kalantirsky, Amanda R., Vacating an International Arbitration Award Rendered in the United States: Does the New York Convention, the Federal Arbitration Act or State Law Apply?, 3 Y.B. ARB. & MEDIATION 1 (2011).

Kuran, Timur, The Economic Ascent of the Middle East's Religious Minorities:The Role of Islamic Legal Pluralism, 33 J. LEGAL STUD. 475 (2004).

Lahlou et al., Yasmine, Substantive Barriers to Recognition and Enforcement of Foreign Awards under Article V(2) of New York and Panama Conventions, in ENFORCEMENT OF FOREIGN ARBITRAL AWARDS AND JUDGMENTS IN NEW YORK 153 (Andreas A. Frischknecht et al. eds., 2018).

Lalive, Pierre, *Transnational (or Truly International) Public Policy and International Arbitration*, *in* COMPARATIVE ARBITRATION PRACTICE AND PUBLIC POLICY IN ARBITRATION (Pieter Sanders ed., 2005).

Lamm, et al., Carolyn B. *Fraud and Corruption in International Arbitration, in* LIBER AMICORUM: BERNARDO CREMADES 699 (Miguel Angel Fernandez-Ballester & David Arias eds., 2010).

Lareau, N. Peter, Supreme Court's Public Policy Exception to Judicial Deferral to Arbitration, 2017 EMERGING ISSUES 7574 (2017).

Leasure, Stanley A., Arbitration Law in Tension After Hall Street: Accuracy or Finality?, 39 U. ARK. LITTLE ROCK L. REV. 75 (2016).

Lefèvre, et al., Françoise, *Legality of Third-party Funding Mechanisms Under Belgian Law*, 2017 BELGIAN REV. OF ARB 35 (2017).

Lorenzen, Ernest G., *The French Rules of the Conflict of Laws*, 36 YALE L. J. 731 (1927).

Mackaay, Ejan, *Good Faith in Civil Law Systems. A Legal-Economic Analysis*, 18 REVISTA CHILENA DE DERECHO PRIVADO 149 (2012).

Mann, Bruce H., The Formalization of Informal Law: Arbitration Before the American Revolution, 59 N.Y.U. L. REV. 443 (1984).

Martinez-Fraga, Pedro J., *U.S. Arbitration Law and Its Dialogue with the New York Convention: The Development of Four Issues*, *in* THE AMERICAN INFLUENCES ON INTERNATIONAL COMMERCIAL ARBITRATION: DOCTRINAL DEVELOPMENTS AND DISCOVERY METHODS 151 (2009).

Martinez-Fraga, Pedro J., *Wilko v. Swan, Scherk v. Alberto-Culver, and Mitsubishi v. Soler: Crafting a Level Playing Field*, *in* THE AMERICAN INFLUENCES ON INTERNATIONAL COMMERCIAL ARBITRATION: DOCTRINAL DEVELOPMENTS AND DISCOVERY METHODS 15 (2009).

Matray, Didier & van Rompaey, Sigrid, *An Introduction to Third-Party Funding*, 2017 BELGIAN REV. OF ARB 175 (2017).

Mattli, Walter & Dietz, Thomas, *Mapping and Assessing the Rise of International Commercial Arbitration in the Globalization Era: An Introduction*, *in* INTERNATIONAL ARBITRATION AND GLOBAL GOVERNANCE: CONTENDING THEORIES AND EVIDENCE 1 (Walter Mattli & Thomas Dietz eds., 2014).

Mayer, Pierre & Sheppard, Audley, Final ILA Report on Public Policy as a Bar to Enforcement of International Arbitral Awards, 19 ARBITR. INT. 249 (2003) [ILA's Final Report].

Mayer, Pierre, *Effect of International Public Policy in International Arbitration*, *in* PERVASIVE PROBLEMS IN INTERNATIONAL ARBITRATION, INTERNATIONAL ARBITRATION 61 (Loukas A. Mistelis et al. eds., 2006).

Mayer, Pierre, Mandatory Rules of Law in International Arbitration, 2 ARB. INT'L 274 (1986).

McClendon, J. Stewart, *Enforcement of Foreign Arbitral Awards in the United States*, 4 NW J. INT'L L. & BUS. 58 (1982).

McGoldrick, Dominic, Sharia Law in Europe? Legacies of the Ottoman Empire and the European Convention on Human Rights, 8 OX. J L. RELIGION 517 (2019).

McManus, Michael & Silverstein, Brianna, Brief History of Alternative Dispute Resolution in the United States, CADMUS J., Oct. 2016.

Mercantel, Jonathan A., The Crumbled Difference Between Legal and Illegal Arbitration Awards: Hall Street Associates and the Waning Public Policy Exception, 14 FORDHAM J. CORP. & FIN. L. 597 (2009).

Milhaupt, Curtis J., Beyond Legal Origin: Rethinking Law's Relationship to the Economy—Implications for Policy, 57 AM. J. COMP. 831 (2009).

Moglen, Eben, Commercial Arbitration in the Eighteenth Century: Searching for the Transformation of American Law, 93 YALE LAW J. 135 (1983).

Morgan, Patrick T., Unbundling Our Tort Rights: Assignability for Personal Injury and Wrongful Death Claims, 66 MO. L. REV. 683 (2001).

Morrison, Kristina L., A Misstep in U.S. Arbitral Law: A Call For Change in the Enforcement Of Nondomestic Arbitral Awards, 46 TORT & INS. L.J. 803 (2011).

Moses, Margaret L., *Arbitration Law: Who's in Charge?*, 40 SETON HALL L. REV. 147 (2010).

Murphy, Kent, The Traditional View of Public Policy and Ordre Public in Private International Law, 11 GA. J. INT. COMP. L. 591 (2015).

Murphy, Stephen, Judicial Review Of Arbitration Awards Under State Law, 96 VA. L. REV. 887, 919 (2010).

Nater-Bass, Gabrielle & Mosimann, Olivier, *The Award and Courts—Effects of Foreign Bankruptcy on International Arbitration in* 2011 AUSTRIAN Y.B. ON INT'L ARB. 163 (Nikolaus Pitkowitz et al. eds, 2011).

Newport, Travis, *Tortious Interference with International Contracts*, 9 CURRENTS INT'L TRADE L.J. 80 (2000).

Ng, (Huang Ying) Irene & Benedetti del Rio, Valeria, *When the Tribunal Is an Algorithm: Complexities of Enforcing Orders Determined by a Software under the New York Convention, in* 60 YEARS OF THE NEW YORK CONVENTION: KEY ISSUES AND FUTURE CHALLENGES 123 (Katia Fach Gomez & Ana M. Lopez-Rodriguez eds., 2019).

Ng, Tiffany, Choice of Procedural Law in International Commercial Arbitration: Providing "Proper Notice" to a Foreign Party to Ensure That the Arbitral Award Can Be Enforced, 10 HASTINGS BUS. L.J. 491 (2014).

Noyes, Henry S., If You (Re)Build It, They Will Come: Contracts To Remake The Rules Of Litigation In Arbitration's Image, 30 HARV. J.L. & PUB. POL'Y 579 (2007).

Oldham, James & Kim, Su Jin, Arbitration in America: The Early History, 31 L. HIST. REV. 241 (2013)..

Öniş, Ziya, Turgut Özal and His Economic Legacy: Turkish Neo-Liberalism in Critical Perspective, 40 MIDDLE EASTERN STUDIES 113 (2004).

Ordway, Eric, *The Importance of the Seat of Arbitration*, 25 THE ADVOC. (TEXAS) 16 (2003).

Orlowski, Victoria, *FAA Section 10 Applications to Vacate an Award (Including "Manifest Disregard"), in* INTERNATIONAL ARBITRATION IN THE UNITED STATES 503 (Laurence Shore et al. eds., 2017).

Örücü, Esin, Conseil d'Etat: *The French Layer of Turkish Administrative Law*, 49 INT. COMP. LAW Q. 679 (2000).

Ostoni, Lucia, Italian Rejection of Punitive Damages in a U.S. Judgement, 24 J. L. & COM. 245 (2005).

Otto, Dirk & Elwan, Omaia, *Article V(2), in* Recognition and Enforcement of Foreign Arbitral Awards: A Global Commentary on the New York Convention 346 (Herbert Kronke et al. eds, 2010).

Özdemir, Nagihan, Yapay Zeka Işığında Avukatlık Mesleğinin Dönüşümü: Üniversiteler ve Baroların Rolü [Transformation of Lawyering in the Light of Artificial Intelligence: The Role of Universities and Bar Associations], in ISTANBUL, ANKARA, VE IZMIR BAROLARI [ISTANBUL, ANKARA AND IZMIR BAR ASSOCIATIONS], YAPAY ZEKA ÇAĞINDA HUKUK [LAW IN THE ERA OF ARTIFICIAL INTELLIGENCE] 34 (2019) (Turk.).

Öztekin, Günseli, Yargıtay 15. Hukuk Dairesi'nin 22.9.1989 Tarihli Kararının Eleştirisi [A Critique of 15th Civil Chamber's Decision Dated 22.9.1989], 13 MILLETLERARASI HUKUK VE MILLETLERARASI OZEL HUKUK BULTENI (MHB) 33 (2011) (Turk.).

Öztürk, Yusuf Kemal & Öztürk, Zeynep, *The Effects of Turkey's Economic Crisis on Employment, in* ECONOMIC AND MANAGEMENT ISSUES IN RETROSPECT AND PROSPECT 137 (Eszter Wirth et al. eds., 2018).

Pagallo, Ugo & Durante, Massimo, *The Pros and Cons of Legal Automation and its Governance*, 7 EUROPEAN J. RISK REGULATION 323 (2016).

Panko, Ross Q., Accrued Financial Services, Inc. v. Prime Retail, Inc.: Resurrecting Barratry Imposes Detour On Road To Modernization Of Maryland Contracts Jurisprudence, 62 MD. L. REV. 361 (2003).

Park, William W., *Amending the Federal Arbitration Act*, 13 AM. REV. INT'L ARB. 75 (2002).

Park, William W., The Internationalization of Law and Legal Practice: National Law and Commercial Justice: Safeguarding Procedural Integrity in International Arbitration, 63 TUL. L. REV. 647 (1989).

Parker, Matthew, Changing Tides: The Introduction of Punitive Damages into The French Legal System, 41 GA. J. INT'L & COMP. L. 389 (2013).

Paul, Joel R., *The Transformation of International Comity*, LAW & CONTEMP. PROBS., Summer 2008, at 19.

Paulsson, Jan, *Vicarious Hypochondria and Institutional Arbitration*, 6 ARBITRATION INT'L, no.3, 1990, at 232.

Petsche, Markus A., Punitive Damages in International Commercial Arbitration: Much Ado about Nothing?, 29 ARBITR. INT. 89 (2013).

Petti, Angelina M., Judicial Enforcement of Arbitration Agreements: The Stay-Dismissal Dichotomy of FAA Section 3, 34 HOFSTRA L. REV. 565 (2005).

Phillips, F. Peter, Ancient and Comely Order: The Use and Disuse of Arbitration By New York Quakers, 2016 J. DISP. RESOL. 81 (2016).

Piers, Maud & de Meulemeester, Dirk, *The New Arbitration Law—Belgium Adopted the UNCITRAL Model Law*, 9 ASIAN INT'L ARB. J. 147 (2013).

Pietrowski, Jill A., Enforcing International Commercial Arbitration Agreements—Post-Mitsubishi Motors Corp. v. Soler Chrysler-Plymouth, Inc., 36 AM. U.L. REV. 57 (1986).

Pitkowitz et al., Nikolaus, The Vienna Innovation Propositions: Venturing into New Fields and New Ways of Arbitration–Revisiting Traditional Ways of Arbitration, in AUSTRIAN Y.B. ON INT'L ARB. 515 (Christian Klausegger et al., eds. 2019).

Platt, Rowan, The Appeal of Appeal Mechanisms in International Arbitration: Fairness over Finality?, 30 J. INT'L ARB 531 (2013).

Poncet, Charles, The Decision of the Swiss Supreme Court ("Federal Tribunal") of March 8, 2006, 24 ASA Bulletin, 550 (2006).

Pope, Herbert, *The English Common Law in the United States*, 24 HARV. L. REV. 6 (1910).

Posner, Eric A., Arbitration and the Harmonization of International Commercial Law: A Defense of Mitsubishi, 39 VA. J. INT'L L. 647 (1999).

Puig, Sergio, *Social Capital in the Arbitration Market*, 25 EUR J INT LAW 387 (2014).

Rallo, Anthony, The Veil of Acquiescence: Between the Lines of an Intuitive Appellate Decision, The Ninth Circuit Subtly Marginalizes FAA Limitations on Judicial Review, 24 AM. REV. INT'L ARB. 681 (2013).

Rau, Alan Scott, Arbitration And National Courts: Conflict And Cooperation: Understanding (And Misunderstanding) "Primary Jurisdiction", 21 Am. Rev. Int'l Arb. 47 (2010).

Rau, Alan Scott, *Federal Common Law and Arbitral Power*, 8 Nev. L.J. 169 (2007).

Rau, Alan Scott, *The New York Convention in American Courts*, 7 Am. Rev. Int'l Arb. 213 (1996).

Renner, Moritz, *Towards a Hierarchy of Norms in Transnational Law?*, 26 J. Int'l Arbitration 533 (2009).

Reuben, Richard C., *Personal Autonomy and Vacatur After Hall Street*, 113 Penn. St. L. Rev. 1103 (2009).

Robert, Braydon, An Evident Contradiction: How Some Evident Partiality Standards Do Not Facilitate Impartial Arbitration, 43 Iowa J. Corp. L. 681 (2018).

Roberts, Niall Mackay, Definitional Avoidance: Arbitration's Common-Law Meaning and the Federal Arbitration Act Note, 49 UC Davis L. Rev. 1570 (2015).

Rogers, Catherine A., Restating the U.S. Law of International Commercial Arbitration, 113 Penn St. L. Rev. 1333 (2009).

Rogers, Catherine A., The Arrival of the "Have-Nots" in International Arbitration, 8 Nev. L.J. 341 (2007).

Rowan, Solène, Reflections on the Introduction of Punitive Damages for Breach of Contract, 30 Oxf. J. Leg. Stud. 495, 498 (2010).

Rubino-Sammartoano, Mauro, *The Keban Arbitration*, 45 J. Chartered Inst. Arbitrators 211 (1980).

Rutledge, Peter B., On the Importance of Institutions: Review of Arbitral Awards for Legal Errors, 19 J. Int'l Arb. 81 (2002).

Saleh, Samir, *The Recognition and Enforcement of Foreign Arbitral Awards in the States of the Arab Middle East*, *in* Contemporary Problems in International Arbitration 340 (Julian D. M. Lew ed., 1987).

Samra, Harout Jack, Two to Tango: Domestic Grounds for Vacatur Under The New York Convention, 20 Am. Rev. Int'l Arb. 367 (2009).

Sandez, Christine, The Extension of Comity to Foreign Bankruptcy Proceedings: Philadelphia Gear Corp. v. Philadelphia Gear de Mexico, S.A., 20 N.C.J. Int'l L. & Com. Reg. 629 (1995).

Scherer et al., Maxi, Third Party Funding in International Arbitration in Europe: 1—Funders' Perspectives, 2 Int'l Bus. L. J. 207 (2012).

Scherer, Matthew U., Regulating Artificial Intelligence Systems: Risks, Challenges, Competencies, and Strategies, 29 Harv. J.L. & Tech 353 (2015).

Scherer, Maxi, Artificial Intelligence and Legal Decision-Making: The Wide Open?, 36 J. Int'l Arb. 539 (2019).

Schwartz, David S., Correcting Federalism Mistakes in Statutory Interpretation: The Supreme Court and the Federal Arbitration Act, Law & Contemp. Probs., Winter/Spring 2004, at 5.

Sela, Ayelet, Can Computers Be Fair? How Automated and Human-Powered Online Dispute Resolution Affect Procedural Justice in Mediation and Arbitration, 33 Ohio St. J. on Disp. 91 (2018).

Şenses, Fikret, *Turkey's Experience with Neoliberal Policies Since 1980*, *in* The Making of Neoliberal Turkey 15 (Cenk Ozbay et al. eds, 2016).

Shalakany, Amr A., Arbitration and the Third World: A Plea for Reassessing Bias Under the Specter of Neoliberalism, 41 Harv. Int'l L.J. 419 (2000).

Shannon Sahani, Victoria, *Judging Third-Party Funding*, 63 UCLA L. Rev. 388 (2016).

Shannon, Victoria A., *Harmonizing Third-Party Litigation Funding Regulation*, 36 Cardozo L. Rev. 861 (2015).

Sharp, Joseph C. & Jewkes, Joshua D., *A High Hurdle Should State Public Policy Concerns Trump FAA Awards?* DRI The Voice of the Defense Bar, Oct. 2008, at 35.

Shaw, Gary J., Third-party Funding in Investment Arbitration: How Non-disclosure Can Cause Harm for the Sake of Profit, 33 Arb. Int'l. 109 (2017).

Sheppard, Audley, Interim ILA Report on Public Policy as a Bar to Enforcement of International Arbitral Awards, 19 Arbitr. Int. 217 (2003) [ILA's Interim Report].

Sheppard, Audley, Public Policy and the Enforcement of Arbitral Awards: Should there be a Global Standard?, 1 Transnat'l Disp. Mgmt. 1 (2004).

Sim, Christine, Will Artificial Intelligence Take Over Arbitration?, 14 Asian Int'l Arb. J. 1 (2018).

Simões, Fernando Dias, Powered by Expertise: Selecting Arbitrators in Energy Disputes, 8 J World Energy L. & Bus 501 (2015).

Sims, MyLinda K. & Bales, Richard A., Much Ado About Nothing: The Future of Manifest Disregard After Hall Street, 62 S.C. L. Rev. 407 (2010).

Slobodchikova, Maria, Enforcement of Annulled Arbitral Awards in the United States: Discretion to Confirm an Arbitral Award Constrain by Principles of Comity, in 40 under 40 International Arbitration 469 (Carlos Gonzalez-Bueno ed., 2018).

Snyder, David V., Comparative Law in Action: Promissory Estoppel, the Civil Law, and the Mixed Jurisdiction, 15 Ariz. J. Int'l & Comp. L. 695 (1998).

Solas, Gian Marco, Alternative Litigation Funding and the Italian Perspective, 2 Eur. Rev. Private L. 253 (2016).

Spector, Horacio, The Future of Legal Science in Civil Law Systems, 65 La. L. Rev. 255 (2004).

Stramignoni, Igor, The King's One Too Many Eyes: Language, Thought, and Comparative Law, 2 Utah L. Rev. 739 (2002).

Strong, S. I., Writing Reasoned Decisions and Opinions: A Guide for Novice, Experienced, and Foreign Judges, 2015 J. Disp. Resol. 93 (2015).

Strong, S.I., *Limits of Procedural Choice of Law*, 39 Brooklyn J. Int'l L. 1027, 1082 (2014)

Sutcliffe, Jonathan & Rogers, James, Effect of Party Insolvency on Arbitration Proceedings: Pause for Thought in Testing Times, 76 Arb. 277 (2010).

Szalai, Imre Stephen, Exploring the Federal Arbitration Act through the Lens of History Symposium, 2016 J. Disp. Resol. 115 (2016).

Tarman, Zeynep Derya, The Applicable Law to Contractual and Non-contractual Obligations under Turkish Private International Law, Nederlands Internationaal Privaatrecht [NIPR], no. 1 (2009) at 15.

Tekinalp, Gülören, The 2007 Turkish Code concerning Private International Law and International Civil Procedure, 9 Y.B. Private Int'l Law 313 (2007).

Tettenborn, Andrew, Punitive Damages—A View from England Symposium: Remedies Discussion Forum, 41 San Diego Law Rev. 1551 (2004).

Thomas, Katlyn, *On Drafting An "Ideal" Arbitration Statute*, 25 Am. Rev. Int'l Arb. 117 (2014).

Thrope, Jessica, A Question of Intent: Choice of Law and the International Arbitration Agreement, 54 Disp. Resolution J. 16 (1999).

Tolani, Madeleine, U.S. Punitive Damages Before German Courts: A Comparative Analysis with Respect to the Ordre Public, 17 Annual Survey of Int'l & Comp. Law 185 (2011).

Toprak, Metin, Izmir Iktisat Kongresi: Bir Gelecek Perspektifi [Izmir Economic Convention: A Future Perspective] Iktisat, Isletme ve Finans, Ocak 2004, at 115 (Turk.).

Townsend, John M., Drafting Arbitration Clauses: Avoiding the Seven Deadly Sins, 58 Disp. Resol. J. 28 (2003).

Trakman, Leon, Domestic Courts Declining to Recognize and Enforce Foreign Arbitral Awards: A Comparative Reflection, 6 Chinese J. Comp. L., 174 (2018).

Trusz, Jennifer A., Full Disclosure? Conflicts of Interest Arising from Third-Party Funding in International Commercial Arbitration, 101 Geo. L.J. 1649 (2013).

Ulusoy, Ali & Oğuz, Fuat, The Privatization of Electricity Distribution in Turkey: A Legal and Economic Analysis, 35 ENERGY POL'Y 5021 (2007).

Unal, Birsen, *Education Policies during Ataturk Period*, 174 PROCEDIA SOCIAL AND BEHAVIORAL SCIENCES 1717 (2015).

Vaisanen, Tiina E., Incompetent Drafting and Complex Laws: Automatically Waiving Set-Aside of Foreign Arbitration Awards in the United States, 45 CORNELL INT'L L.J. 723 (2012).

van den Berg, Albert Jan, Enforcement of Arbitral Awards Annulled in Russia Case Comment on Court of Appeal of Amsterdam, April 28, 2009, 27 J. INT'L ARB 179 (2010).

Van den Berg, Albert Jan, *Why Are Some Award Not Enforceable?, in* NEW HORIZONS IN INTERNATIONAL COMMERCIAL ARBITRATION AND BEYOND 291 (Albert Jan Van den Berg ed., 2004).

van den Berg, Albert Jan, *Why Are Some Awards Not Enforceable?, in* NEW HORIZONS IN INTERNATIONAL COMMERCIAL ARBITRATION AND BEYOND 291 (2005).

Vannieuwenhuyse, Gauthier, *Arbitration and New Technologies: Mutual Benefits*, 35 J. INT'L ARB. 119 (2018).

Wahab, Mohamed S. Abdel & Katsh, Ethan, Revolutionizing Technologies and the Use of Technology in International Arbitration: Innovation, Legitimacy, Prospects and Challenges, in ARBITRATION IN THE DIGITAL AGE: THE BRAVE NEW WORLD OF ARBITRATION 27 (Maud Piers&Christian Aschauer et al., 2018).

Wakim, Mark, Public Policy Concerns regarding Enforcement of Foreign International Arbitral Awards in the Middle East, 21 NY INT'L L REV 1 (2008).

Walker, George K., Trends in State Legislation Governing International Arbitrations, 17 N.C. J. INT'L L. & COM. REG. 419 (1992).

Walt, Steven, Decision by Division: The Contractarian Structure of Commercial Arbitration, 51 RUTGERS L. REV. 369 (1999).

Wang, Margaret, Are Alternative Dispute Resolution Methods Superior to Litigation in Resolving Disputes in International Commerce?, 16 ARB. INT'L. 189 (2000).

Westbrook, Jay L., Theory and Pragmatism in Global Insolvencies: Choice of Law and Choice of Forum, 65 AM. BANKR. L.J. 457, 482 (1991).

Wilske, Stephan, *Legal Challenges to Delayed Arbitral Awards*, 6 CONTEMP. ASIA ARB. J. 153 (2013).

Wilson, Jodi, How the Supreme Court Thwarted the Purpose of the Federal Arbitration Act, 63 CASE W. RES. L. REV. 91 (2012).

Yamamoto, Takashi B., *Japanese Court Jurisdiction Over International Cases*, 30 COMP. L. Y.B INT'L BUS. 1 (2008)

Yang, Inae, Procedural Public Policy Cases in International Commercial Arbitration, 69 DISP. RESOLUTION J. 61 (2014).

Yeşilova, Bilgehan, Milletlerarasi Tahkimin Hukuki Niteliği Üzerine Düşünceler and Güncel Gelişmeler [Thoughts on Legal Characteristic of International Arbitration and Current Developments], 76 TÜRKIYE BAROLAR BIRLIĞI DERGISI [TBB DERGISI] 83 (2008) (Turk.).

Yetim, Servet, Yargı Kararlarına Erişim Hakkı [Right to Access to Court Decisions], UYUŞMAZLIK MAHKEMESI DERGISI no.4, 2014 (Turk.).

Yetkin, Aydın, Development Process of the Rule of Law in the Ottoman Empire, 6 J. INT'L SOC. RES. 380 (2013).

Youssef, Karim, The Death of Inarbitrability, *in* ARBITRABILITY: INTERNATIONAL AND COMPARATIVE PERSPECTIVES 47 (Loukas A. Mistelis & Stavros L. Brekoulakis eds., 2009).

Zeft, Daniel A., The Applicability of State International Arbitration Statutes and the Absence of Significant Preemption Concerns, 22 N.C.J. INT'L L. & COM. REG. 705 (1997).

Zencirci, Gizem, Affective Politics of Structural Adjustment: "Cruel Optimism" and Turhan Selcuk's Cartoons in Turkey, 1983–1986, 53 J. SOCIAL HISTORY 53 (2019).

Zhou, Jian, Judicial Intervention in International Arbitration: A Comparative Study of the Scope of the New York Convention in U.S. And Chinese Courts, 15 PAC. RIM L. & POL'Y J. 403 (2006).

Zorrilla, Edwin Montoya, Towards a Credible Future: Uses of Technology in International Commercial Arbitration, 16 GERMAN ARB. J. 106 (2018).

Zürcher, Erik Jan, *Atatürk as a Young Turk*, 41 NEW PERSPECTIVES ON TURKEY 211 (2009).

Magazine and Newspaper Articles.

Ana.P.'li Dizdaroğlu muz ithali durdurulunca istifadan vazgeçti [*Motherland's Dizdaroglu Not Resigned When Banana Import Stopped*], MILLIYET, Jan 27, 1984. (Turk.).

Arcayürek, Cüneyt, *Hal-i Pür Melal [A Sad Situation]*, MILLIYET, Feb. 23, 1984 (Turk.).

Aşık, Melih, Opinion, *Conversation on Arbitration*, MILLIYET, Aug. 5, 1999, at 15. (Turk.).

Daley to Support Turkish Energy Projects, HURRIYET DAILY NEWS, Jan. 24, 1998.

Ecevit Sol'ladi [Ecevit Overtook on the Left], SABAH, Aug. 5, 1999, (Turk.).

Howe, Marvine, Man In The News: Turgut Özal; Turkish Ally Of Capitalism, N.Y. Times, Nov. 9, 1983, at A11.

Muz Savaşı [The Banana War], Milliyet, Feb. 3, 1986 at 3. (Turk.).

Selcuk, Turhan, Çikita Muzdan Sonra Balon da İthal Ettik [We Imported Balloons After Chiquita Bananas], Milliyet, May 8, 1984. (Turk.).

Working Papers

Landi, Niccolo & A. Rogers, Catherine, *Arbitration of Antitrust Claims in the United States and Europe* (Bocconi Legal Studies Research, Paper No. 07-01, 2007) available at https://ssrn.com/abstract=962334.

Electronic Sources.

2015 International Arbitration Survey: Improvements and Innovations in International Arbitration, Queen Mary University of London (2015), available at http://www.arbitration.qmul.ac.uk/docs/164761.pdf [2015 International Arbitration Survey].

2018 HKIAC Administered Arbitration Rules, https://www.hkiac.org/sites/default/files/ck_filebrowser/PDF/arbitration/2018_hkiac_rules.pdf

9 Am. Jur. Proof of Facts 3d 687 Westlaw (database updated Feb. 2020).

Adalet Hanim, https://adalethanim.com (last visited Feb. 27, 2022).

Am. Bar Ass'n, Commission on Ethics 20/20 Informational Report to the House of Delegates (2012), https://www.americanbar.org/content/dam/aba/administrative/ethics_2020/20111212_ethics_20_20_alf_white_paper_final_hod_informational_report.pdf.

Angwin et al., Julia, *Machine Bias*, ProPublica, (May 23, 2016), https://www.propublica.org/article/machine-bias-risk-assessments-in-criminal-sentencing report

Appellate Arbitration Procedure, CPR, https://www.cpradr.org/resource-center/rules/arbitration/appellate-arbitration-procedure (last visited Feb. 27, 2022).

Baysal, Pelin & Cevik, Bilge K., *Could a Reduction in a State's Income Violate Public Policy—A View on Turkey?*, Kluwer Arbitration Blog, (Feb. 10 2019), http://arbitrationblog.kluwerarbitration.com/2019/02/10/could-a-reduction-in-a-states-incomeviolate-public-policy-a-view-on-turkey/

Brodsky, Stephen L., *Cross-Border Arbitration: A Beneficial Alternative to Resolving International Commercial Disputes*, A.B.A. (July 03, 2019), https://www.americanbar.org/groups/litigation/committees/commercial-business/articles/2019/spring2019-cross-border-arbitration-international-commercial-disputes/.

Case Crunch, http://www.case-crunch.com (last visited Feb. 27, 2022).

Challenges to Arbitral Awards in the US Based on Public Policy Violations, Practical Law W-007-8103 (last visited Feb. 27, 2022).

Chen, Rong-Chwan, *Interpretation and Application of the New York Convention in Taiwan, in* Recognition and Enforcement of Foreign Arbitral Awards The Interpretation and Application of the New York Convention by National Courts 945 (George A. Bermann ed., 2017).

Cohen, Paul & Nappert, Sophie, *The March of The Robots*, Global Arb. Review (Feb. 15, 2017), https://globalarbitrationreview.com/article/1080951/the-march-of-the-robots.

Contracting States—List of Contracting States, New York Convention, http://www.newyorkconvention.org/list+of+contracting+states (last visited Feb. 27, 2022).

Convention of 30 June 2005 on Choice of Court Agreements, HCCH, https://www.hcch.net/en/instruments/conventions/status-table/?cid=98 (last visited Feb. 27, 2022).

de la Jara et al., José María, *Machine Arbitrator: Are We Ready?*, Kluwer Arb. Blog (May. 4, 2017).

eBrevia, https://ebrevia.com/ (last visited Feb. 27, 2022).

Enforcing Arbitration Awards in the US, Practical Law 9-500-4550 9 (last visited Feb. 27, 2022).

Freudenberg celebrates anniversary in Taiwan, Freudenberg (Oct. 11, 2013), https://www.freudenberg.com/newsroom/press-releases/detail/freudenberg-celebrates-anniversary-in-taiwan/

Freudenberg expands capacities in Taiwan, Freudenberg (Mar. 22, 2018), https://www.freudenberg-pm.com/Press/2018_03_22_FPM_Freudenberg_expands_capacities_in_Taiwan.

Ghibradze, Nata, *Georgia—Positive Changes in the Caucasus Region?!*, Kluwer Arb. Blog (Dec. 1, 2015), http://arbitrationblog.kluwerarbitration.com/2015/12/01/georgia-positive-changes-in-the-caucasus-region/

Glossary, comity, Practical Law 2-201-5616 (last visited Feb. 27, 2022).

ISTA ve ISTAC Arasında İşbirliği Protokolü İmzalandı [ISTA and ISTAC Entered into Cooperation Agreement], Istanbul Arb. Ass'n https://ista.org.tr/tr/blog/ista-ve-istac-arasinda-isbirligi-protokolu-imzalandi (last visited Feb. 27, 2022).

Kalicki, Jean E., *Third-Party Funding in Arbitration: Innovations and Limits in Self-Regulation (Part 2 of 2)*, Kluwer Arb. Blog (Mar. 14, 2012), http://kluwerarbitrationblog.com/blog/2012/03/14/third- party-funding-in-arbitration-innovations-and-limits-in-self-regulation-part-2-of-2.

Keach, Sean, Google Fixed "Racist" Photos App by Banning Gorillas from Auto-tagging Feature, After Black Developer Was Incorrectly Marked as an Ape, THE SUN, (Jan. 15, 2018), https://www.thesun.co.uk/tech/5341606/google-photos-racist-gorillas/

Koçak, Cemil, *Parliament Membership during the Single-Party System in Turkey (1925-1945)*, EUROPEAN J. TURKISH STUD. vol.3, 2005, available at https://journals.openedition.org/ejts/497?lang=tr

Lunceford Kolb, Rebecca, *The New York Convention or the FAA: Circuit Split Still Stands,* AMERICANBAR (Oct. 2, 2019), https://www.americanbar.org/groups/litigation/committees/alternative-dispute-resolution/practice/2019/the-new-york-convention-or-the-faa-circuit-split-still-stands/

Michael Sheppard, Stephen, Bouvier Law Dictionary, 2012 (LexisNexis).

NEW YORK CONVENTION GUIDE, *Article V(2)(b),* http://newyorkconvention1958.org/index.php?lvl=cmspage&pageid=10&menu=626&opac_view=-1 (last visited Feb. 27, 2022).

Oehmke, Thomas H. & Brovins, Joan M., 2 Commercial Arbitration (database updated December 2019), Westlaw CMLARB.

Paksoy et al., Serdar, *Third party funding in litigation or arbitration: a look at Turkey's approach*, LEXOLOGY (Dec. 3, 2019), https://www.lexology.com/library/document.ashx?g=029426a1-0756-45a6-b5a4-ff0b6f645502

Patrizio, Andy, *Top 25 Artificial Intelligence Companies*, Datamation (Apr. 10, 2018), https://www.datamation.com/applications/top-25-artificial-intelligence-companies.html

Paulsson, Marike R. P., The US Courts and Their New York Convention Public Policy Gloss Revisited: Hardy Exploration & Production (India), Inc. v. Government of India, Ministry of Petroleum & Natural Gas: Glossing with International Comity, KLUWER ARBITRATION BLOG (Dec. 26, 2018), http://arbitrationblog.kluwerarbitration.com/2018/12/26/the-us-courts-and-their-new-york-convention-public-policy-gloss-revisited-hardy-exploration-production-india-inc-v-government-of-india-ministry-of-petroleum-natural-gas-glossing-wi/

Perry, Sebastian, *The cost of Yukos*, GLOBAL ARB. REV. (Aug. 15, 2014), http://globalarbitrationreview.com/article/1033686/the-cost-of-yukos.

Population (Total), *The World Bank*, https://data.worldbank.org/indicator/SP.POP.TOTL?name_desc=false (last visited Feb. 27, 2022).

PREPARING FOR LABOR ARBITRATION CHECKLIST, Practical Law 7-522-0994 (last visited Feb. 27, 2022).

ROSS INTELLIGENCE, https://rossintelligence.com (last visited Feb. 27, 2022).

S&T Oil Equipment and Machinery Ltd. v. Romania, ICSID Case No. ARB/07/13, Order of Discontinuance of the Proceeding (July 16, 2010), https://www.italaw.com/sites/default/files/case-documents/ita0743.pdf.

Simonite, Tom, *When It Comes to Gorillas, Google Photos Remains Blind*, WIRED (Nov. 1, 2018), https://www.wired.com/story/when-it-comes-to-gorillas-google-photos-remains-blind/

Simson, Caroline, *3rd-Party Funding Now A Top Alternative Choice for Lawyers*, LAW360 (May 16, 2019), https://www.law360.com/articles/1160547/3rd-party-funding-now-a-top-alternative-choice-for-lawyers.

Smutny et al., Abby Cohen, Third Circuit Applies Domestic FAA to US International Arbitration Award (Sept. 1, 2010) Practical Law 1-503-2076

Status–UNCITRAL Model Law on International Commercial Arbitration (1985), with amendments as adopted in 2006, UNCITRAL, http://www.uncitral.org/uncitral/en/uncitral_texts/arbitration/1985Model_arbitration_status.html (last visited Feb. 27, 2022)

Status: Convention on the Recognition and Enforcement of Foreign Arbitral Awards, UNCITRAL, http://www.uncitral.org/uncitral/en/uncitral_texts/arbitration/NYConvention_status.html (last visited Feb. 27, 2022). [the New York Convention Status].

Steven, Sarah, *GAR Live Lookback: Istanbul—How to "do" third-party funding*, GAR (Jan. 19, 2018), https://globalarbitrationreview.com/print_article/gar/article/1151952/gar-live-lookback-istanbul-how-to-do-third-party-funding?print=true

Tapson, Jonathan, *Google's Go Victory Shows AI Thinking Can be Unpredictable, and That's a Concern,* THE CONVERSATION, (Mar. 18, 2016), https://theconversation.com/googles-go-victory-shows-ai-thinking-can-be-unpredictable-and-thats-a-concern-56209

The Supreme Arbitrazh Court Clarifies Russian Public Policy, LEXOLOGY (May 24, 2013), https://www.lexology.com/library/detail.aspx?g=bf8077ed-8ab0-4fed-9f9d-4b18cf643309

The White House Office of Sci. and Tech. Pol'y, Summary of the 2018 White House Summit on Artificial Intelligence for American Industry (2018), https://www.whitehouse.gov/wp-content/uploads/2018/05/summary-report-of-white-house-ai-summit.pdf.

Turkey—Population: Demographic Situation, Languages and Religions, EUROPEAN COMMISSION (Nov. 4, 2019), https://eacea.ec.europa.eu/national-policies/eurydice/content/population-demographic-situation-languages-and-religions-103_en

Uhlig, Christian, *A market with a future—Taiwan,* DEUTSCHE WELLE (May 16, 2013), https://p.dw.com/p/18Z8O

Understanding US Arbitration Law, Practice Note Overview WestLaw https://www.westlaw.com/4-500-4468?transitionType=Default&contextData=(sc.Default)&VR=3.0&RS=cblt1.0 (last visited Feb. 27, 2022).

van der Haegen, Olivier, *Belgium in the Spotlight*, Kluwer Arb. Blog (Apr. 30, 2014), http://arbitrationblog.kluwerarbitration.com/2014/04/30/belgium-in-the-spotlight/

World Economic Outlook—GDP, current prices Billions of U.S. dollars, International Monetary Fund (Oct. 2019), https://www.imf.org/external/datamapper/NGDPD@WEO/OEMDC/ADVEC/WEOWORLD/CHN/USA

Yasseri, Taha, *Forget killer robots—Wikipedia Bot Study Warns Even "Good" AI can be "Scarily Unpredictable"*, DailyMail (Aug. 25, 2017), http://www.dailymail.co.uk/sciencetech/article-4823684/Even-good-robots-scarily-unpredictable.html#ixzz56oo1I6hd

Index

www.ingramcontent.com/pod-product-compliance
Ingram Content Group UK Ltd.
Pitfield, Milton Keynes, MK11 3LW, UK
UKHW020834290926
15470UKWH00004B/1349

9 783631 868249